WE, THE ROBOTS?

Should we regulate artificial intelligence (AI)? Can we? From self-driving cars and high-speed trading to algorithmic decision-making, the way we live, work, and play is increasingly dependent on AI systems that operate with diminishing human intervention. These fast, autonomous, and opaque machines offer great benefits – and pose significant risks. This book examines how our laws are dealing with AI, as well as what additional rules and institutions are needed – including the role that AI might play in regulating itself. Drawing on diverse technologies and examples from around the world, the book offers lessons on how to manage risk, draw red lines, and preserve the legitimacy of public authority. Though the prospect of AI pushing beyond the limits of the law may seem remote, these measures are useful now – and will be essential if it ever does.

Simon Chesterman is Dean and Provost's Chair Professor of the National University of Singapore Faculty of Law and Senior Director of AI Governance at AI Singapore. His work has opened up new areas of research on public authority – including the rules and institutions of global governance, the changing functions of national security agencies, and the emerging role of AI and big data.

T0370955

WE, THE ROBOTS?

Regulating Artificial Intelligence and the Limits of the Law

SIMON CHESTERMAN

National University of Singapore

CAMBRIDGE
UNIVERSITY PRESS

Shaftesbury Road, Cambridge CB2 8EA, United Kingdom

One Liberty Plaza, 20th Floor, New York, NY 10006, USA

477 Williamstown Road, Port Melbourne, VIC 3207, Australia

314–321, 3rd Floor, Plot 3, Splendor Forum, Jasola District Centre, New Delhi – 110025, India

103 Penang Road, #05–06/07, Visioncrest Commercial, Singapore 238467

Cambridge University Press is part of Cambridge University Press & Assessment, a department of the University of Cambridge.

We share the University's mission to contribute to society through the pursuit of education, learning and research at the highest international levels of excellence.

www.cambridge.org
Information on this title: www.cambridge.org/9781009332071

DOI: 10.1017/9781009047081

First published 2021
First paperback edition 2022

A catalogue record for this publication is available from the British Library

Library of Congress Cataloging-in-Publication data
Names: Chesterman, Simon, author.
Title: We, the robots? : regulating artificial intelligence and the limits of the law / Simon Chesterman, National University of Singapore.
Description: Cambridge, United Kingdom ; New York, NY, USA : Cambridge University Press, 2021. | Includes bibliographical references and index.
Identifiers: LCCN 2021010083 (print) | LCCN 2021010084 (ebook) | ISBN 9781316517680 (hardcover) | ISBN 9781009048316 (paperback) | ISBN 9781009047081 (ebook)
Subjects: LCSH: Artificial intelligence – Law and legislation.
Classification: LCC K564.C6 C44 2021 (print) | LCC K564.C6 (ebook) | DDC 343.09/99–dc23
LC record available at https://lccn.loc.gov/2021010083
LC ebook record available at https://lccn.loc.gov/2021010084

ISBN   978-1-316-51768-0   Hardback
ISBN   978-1-009-33207-1   Paperback

Nic není člověku cizejšího než jeho obraz.
Nothing is more alien to a man than his own image.
       Karel Čapek, R.U.R. (Rossum's Universal Robots) *(1921)*

SUMMARY CONTENTS

Preface   *page* xv
Acknowledgements   xvii
List of Abbreviations   xix

Introduction   1

PART I   **Challenges**   13

1 Speed   15

2 Autonomy   31

3 Opacity   63

PART II   **Tools**   83

4 Responsibility   85

5 Personality   114

6 Transparency   144

PART III   **Possibilities**   171

7 New Rules   173

8 New Institutions   195

9 Regulation *by* AI?   224

Conclusion: We, the Robots?   243

Bibliography   247
Index   280

CONTENTS

Preface   xv
Acknowledgements   xvii
List of Abbreviations   xix

Introduction   1

Outline of the Book   6

Precaution vs Innovation   10

PART I **Challenges**   13

1 Speed   15

1.1 The Globalization of Information   18

1.2 High-Frequency Trading   21

1.3 Competition Law   25

1.4 The Problem with Speed   28

2 Autonomy   31

2.1 Driverless Cars and the Management of
   Risk   33
   2.1.1 Civil Liability   36
   2.1.2 Criminal Law   38
   2.1.3 Ethics   41

2.2 Killer Robots and the Morality of
   Outsourcing   44
   2.2.1 International Humanitarian Law   46
   2.2.2 Human-out-of-the-Loop?   48
   2.2.3 Lessons from Mercenaries   51

2.3 Algorithmic Decision-Making and
      Legitimacy   53
      2.3.1 Contracts and Knowledge   55
      2.3.2 Automated Processing   57

2.4 The Problem with Autonomy   60

3 Opacity   63

3.1 Inferior Decisions   67

3.2 Impermissible Decisions   69
      3.2.1 How Bias Is Learned   70
      3.2.2 Unlearning Bias   74

3.3 Illegitimate Decisions   75
      3.3.1 Public Decisions   76
      3.3.2 Courts   79

3.4 The Problem with Opacity   81

PART II   **Tools**   83

4 Responsibility   85

4.1 Managing Risk   87
      4.1.1 Negligence   88
      4.1.2 Strict Liability   91
      4.1.3 Product Liability   93
      4.1.4 Insurance   97

4.2 Non-delegable Duties   101
      4.2.1 Non-delegable Duties in the Common Law   101
      4.2.2 Command Responsibility   103
      4.2.3 The Buck Stops Here   109

4.3 Inherently Governmental Functions and the Limits of
      Outsourcing   109

4.4 The Limits of Responsibility   112

5 Personality   114

5.1 A Body to Kick?   116
      5.1.1 Theories of Juridical Personality   117

5.1.2 The Content of Legal Personality   119
    (a)   Private Law   120
    (b)   Criminal Law   123
5.1.3 No Soul to Be Damned   125

5.2 Cogito, Ergo Sum?   126
5.2.1 The Extension of Natural Personality   128
5.2.2 Rewarding Creativity   131
5.2.3 Protecting Inventors   135

5.3 Constraining Superintelligence   138

5.4 The Limits of Personality   141

6 Transparency   144

6.1 In Theory   146
6.1.1 What?   147
6.1.2 When?   148
6.1.3 To Whom?   149
6.1.4 At What Cost?   150

6.2 In Practice   151
6.2.1 Methods   151
6.2.2 Tools   154
    (a)   Algorithmic Impact Assessments   154
    (b)   Algorithmic Audits   156
    (c)   AI Ombudsperson   157

6.3 In Law   158
6.3.1 An EU Right to Explanation?   158
6.3.2 Council of Europe Convention 108   162
6.3.3 France   162
6.3.4 United States   163
6.3.5 Canada   164
6.3.6 Other Jurisdictions   165

6.4 The Limits of Transparency   166

PART III   **Possibilities**   171

7 New Rules   173

7.1 Why (Not) Regulate?   177

7.2 When to Regulate   180

7.2.1 The Precautionary Principle   182

7.2.2 Masterly Inactivity   184

7.3 How to Regulate   185

7.3.1 Managed Risks   187

7.3.2 Red Lines   188

7.3.3 Process Legitimacy   190

7.4 The Prospects for Rules   192

8 New Institutions   195

8.1 Industry Standards   198

8.1.1 Common Language, Best Practice   200

8.1.2 Perverse Incentives, Regulatory Capture   202

8.2 Global Red Lines   203

8.2.1 Structural Challenges   204

(a) Norms   205

(b) Attribution   207

(c) Consequences   208

8.2.2 An International Artificial Intelligence Agency?   209

(a) Bargain   212

(b) Authority   213

(c) Structure   216

8.3 State Responsibility   217

8.3.1 Legislature   218

8.3.2 Executive   218

8.3.3 Judiciary   219

8.3.4 An AI Ombudsperson?   220

8.4 The Prospects for Institutions   222

9 Regulation *by* AI?   224

9.1 Automating the Law   227

9.1.1 The Inner Illogic of the Law   230

9.1.2 In Fact   232

9.2 Law as Data   234

9.3 Law as Code   236
    9.3.1 Regulation by Design   237
    9.3.2 Regulation by Debugging   238

9.4 The Prospects for Regulation   240

Conclusion: We, the Robots?   243

Bibliography   247
Index   280

PREFACE

Artificial intelligence is transforming modern life. From self-driving cars and high-speed trading to algorithmic decision-making, the way we live, work, and play is increasingly dependent on AI systems that operate with diminishing human intervention. Regulation of these developments is made difficult by the pace of change and wariness of constraining innovation, but also conceptual and practical challenges that AI poses to traditional regulatory models. These challenges comprise the speed of modern computing, the autonomy of certain AI systems, and their increasing opacity. This book examines how existing legal tools can be adapted to the new environment, as well as what additional rules and institutions are needed – including the role that AI can and should play in regulating itself.

Most work in this area concentrates on the activities of lawyers, their potential clients, or the machines themselves. This book focuses on those who seek to regulate those activities and the difficulties that AI systems pose to government and governance more generally. Rather than taking specific actors or activities as the starting point, the book emphasizes structural problems that AI poses for meaningful regulation as such. A key contribution is the use of three lenses to distinguish among discrete regulatory dilemmas: the practical management of risk associated with new technologies, the morality of certain functions being undertaken by machines at all, and the legitimacy gap when public authorities delegate their powers to algorithms.

The central argument is that regulation, in the sense used here to mean public control, requires active involvement of states. Yet the qualities of AI – speed, autonomy, opacity – make the issue of its regulation impossible for any one state to confront alone. In normal circumstances, international law and institutions could play a co-ordinating role, as they do in areas from weapons of mass destruction to climate change and pandemics. A second hurdle, however, is that those states at the forefront of AI development – China and the United States – are, for different reasons, among those wariest of international law and institutions constraining their economic development and political independence. The result is that the states with the greatest leverage to establish global norms on AI presently have the least interest in doing so.

By offering a public law and international law perspective on these questions, the book offers lessons on how to manage risk, draw red lines, and preserve the legitimacy of public authority. Though the prospect of AI pushing beyond the limits of the law may seem remote, these measures are useful now – and will be essential if it ever does.

ACKNOWLEDGEMENTS

Writing may be a solitary endeavour, but it is rarely completed alone. I am grateful to Kumaralingam Amirthalingam, Damian Chalmers, Tracey Evans Chan, Denise Cheong, Gabriel Gan, Miriam Goldby, Andrew Halpin, Christian Hofmann, Hu Ying, Arif Jamal, Jeong Woo Kim, Koh Kheng Lian, Kenneth Khoo, Shantini J Krishnan, Pavitra Krishnaswamy, Lau Kwan Ho, Lee Yee Teng, Emma Leong, Brian Y Lim, Lim How Khang, Mark Lim, Lin Lin, Burton Ong, James Penner, Nicole Roughan, Nivedita S, Daniel Seng, Sharon Seah, Alec Stone Sweet, David Tan, Patrick Tan, Tan Zhong Xing, Hans Tjio, Joel Trachtman, Jacob Turner, Umakanth Varottil, Josefine Wallat, Vlasta Wallat, Wee Meng Seng, Ryan Whalen, Christian Witting, Wong Chee Leong, Yeong Zee Kin, You Chuanman, Nico Zachert, and several anonymous reviewers for their comments on earlier versions of this text. Some of the ideas were floated in presentations at the National University of Singapore Faculty of Law, the Lee Kuan Yew School of Public Policy, SG Innovate, the Internet of Things Asia, TechLaw.Fest, McGill Law School, the University of Exeter, the British Institute of International and Comparative Law, Xi'an Jiaotong University, and other forums. At NUS, Jenny Thian helped carve out precious hours in my calendar with the simple agenda item: 'write'. Invaluable research assistance was provided by Violet Huang, Eugene Lau, Ong Kye Jing, and Yap Jia Qing. Thank you also to the team at Cambridge University Press – in particular Joe Ng and Finola O'Sullivan, who saw the book's potential, and freelance copy-editor Lori Heaford, who polished the text. Errors and omissions are attributable to the author alone.

The book builds on some material first published in article form, including 'Artificial Intelligence and the Problem of Autonomy' (2020) 1 Notre Dame Journal on Emerging Technologies 210; 'Artificial Intelligence and the Limits of Legal Personality' (2020) 69 International & Comparative Law Quarterly 819; '"Move Fast and Break Things": Law, Technology, and the Problem of Speed' (2021) 33 Singapore Academy of

Law Journal 5; and 'Through a Glass, Darkly: Artificial Intelligence and the Problem of Opacity' (2021) 69 American Journal of Comparative Law (forthcoming). Permission to draw on the relevant sections is gratefully acknowledged.

Last and most, thank you to M, V, N, and T – beta testers for all my best and worst ideas. This book is dedicated to them.

ABBREVIATIONS

ADS	automated driving system
ADSE	automated driving system entity
AI	artificial intelligence
ATLAS	Advanced Targeting and Lethality Automated System (United States)
CEO	chief executive officer
CIWS	close-in weapon system
CNIL	*Commission nationale de l'informatique et des libertés* [National Commission on Informatics and Liberty] (France)
COMPAS	Correctional Offender Management Profiling for Alternative Sanctions
DARPA	Defense Advanced Research Projects Agency (United States)
DNA	deoxyribonucleic acid
DOJ	Department of Justice (United States)
DPIA	data protection impact assessment
EPO	European Patent Office
EU	European Union
FTC	Federal Trade Commission (United States)
GAO	Government Accountability Office (United States)
GDPR	General Data Protection Regulation (European Union)
GPAI	Global Partnership on AI
HFT	high-frequency trader
IAEA	International Atomic Energy Agency
IAIA	International Artificial Intelligence Agency (hypothetical)
ICANN	Internet Corporation for Assigned Names and Numbers
ICRC	International Committee of the Red Cross
IED	improvised explosive device
IEEE	Institute of Electrical and Electronics Engineers
IHL	international humanitarian law
ILC	International Law Commission
IPCC	Intergovernmental Panel on Climate Change
ISO	International Organization for Standardization
ITU	International Telecommunication Union
LRASM	long-range anti-ship missile
MiFID II	Markets in Financial Instruments Directive II (European Union)

NPT	Nuclear Non-Proliferation Treaty
NTC	National Transport Commission (Australia)
OECD	Organisation for Economic Co-operation and Development
PMSC	private military and security company
SAE	Society of Automotive Engineers
UN	United Nations
USPTO	United States Patent and Trademark Office
VIX	Volatility Index (Chicago Board Options Exchange)
WHO	World Health Organization
WIPO	World Intellectual Property Organization
XAI	explainable artificial intelligence

~

Introduction

Artificial intelligence (AI) and concerns about its potential impact on humanity have been with us for more than half a century. The term entered the discourse in 1956 at a Dartmouth College symposium; early research explored topics like proving logic theorems, deducing the molecular structure of chemical samples, and playing games such as draughts. A dozen years later, Stanley Kubrick's film *2001: A Space Odyssey* offered an iconic vision of a machine empowered to override the decisions of its human counterparts, the HAL 9000's eerily calm voice explaining why a spacecraft's mission to Jupiter was more important than the lives of its crew.

Both AI and the fears associated with it advanced swiftly in subsequent decades. Though worries about the impact of new technology have accompanied many inventions, AI is unusual in that some of the starkest recent warnings have come from those most knowledgeable about the field – Elon Musk, Bill Gates, and Stephen Hawking, among others. Many of these concerns are linked to 'general' or 'strong' AI, meaning the creation of a system that is capable of performing any intellectual task that a human could – and raising complex questions about the nature of consciousness and self-awareness in a non-biological entity.

The possibility that such an entity might put its own priorities above those of humans is non-trivial, but this book focuses on the more immediate challenges raised by 'narrow' AI – meaning systems that can apply cognitive functions to specific tasks typically undertaken by a human.[1]

---

[1] For a discussion of attempts to define AI, see Stuart J Russell and Peter Norvig, *Artificial Intelligence: A Modern Approach* (3rd edn, Prentice Hall 2010) 1–5. Four broad approaches can be identified: acting humanly (the famous Turing Test), thinking humanly (modelling cognitive behaviour), thinking rationally (building on the logicist tradition), and acting rationally (the rational-agent approach favoured by Russell and Norvig, as it is not dependent on a specific understanding of human cognition or an exhaustive model of what constitutes rational thought). On the Turing Test itself, see chapter five, introduction.

A related term is 'machine learning', a subset of AI that denotes the ability of a computer to improve on its performance without being specifically programmed to do so.[2] The program AlphaGo Zero, for example, was merely taught the rules of the notoriously complex board game Go; using that basic information, it developed novel strategies that have established its superiority over any human player.[3]

The field of AI and law is fertile, producing scores of books, thousands of articles, and at least two dedicated journals.[4] In addition to the more speculative literature on what might be termed robot consciousness,[5] much of this work describes recent developments in AI systems,[6] their actual or potential impact on the legal profession,[7] and normative ques-

---

[2] This process may be supervised or unsupervised, or through a process of reinforcement: Kevin P Murphy, *Machine Learning: A Probabilistic Perspective* (MIT Press 2012) 2. See the discussion of human-in-the-loop and other models in chapter two, section 2.3, and the discussion of bias in machine learning in chapter three, section 3.2.1.

[3] David Silver et al, 'Mastering the Game of Go without Human Knowledge' (2017) 550 Nature 354. A subsequent iteration of the program, MuZero, was not even taught the rules of Go and other games. Julian Schrittwieser et al, 'Mastering Atari, Go, Chess, and Shogi by Planning with a Learned Model' (2020) 588 Nature 604.

[4] *Artificial Intelligence and Law* (Springer, 1992–); *RAIL: The Journal of Robotics, Artificial Intelligence & Law* (Fastcase, 2018–).

[5] See generally Nick Bostrom, *Superintelligence: Paths, Dangers, Strategies* (Oxford University Press 2014); Mark O'Connell, *To Be a Machine: Adventures among Cyborgs, Utopians, Hackers, and the Futurists Solving the Modest Problem of Death* (Granta 2017); David J Gunkel, *Robot Rights* (MIT Press 2018). On legal personality of AI systems, see also Samir Chopra and Laurence F White, *A Legal Theory for Autonomous Artificial Agents* (University of Michigan Press 2011); Gabriel Hallevy, *When Robots Kill: Artificial Intelligence under Criminal Law* (Northeastern University Press 2013); John Frank Weaver, *Robots Are People Too: How Siri, Google Car, and Artificial Intelligence Will Force Us to Change Our Laws* (Praeger 2014); Gabriel Hallevy, *Liability for Crimes Involving Artificial Intelligence Systems* (Springer 2015); Visa AJ Kurki and Tomasz Pietrzykowski (eds), *Legal Personhood: Animals, Artificial Intelligence and the Unborn* (Springer 2017). See further chapter five, section 5.3.

[6] Recent edited collections in this vein include Ryan Calo, A Michael Froomkin, and Ian Kerr (eds), *Robot Law* (Edward Elgar 2016); Patrick Lin, Keith Abney, and Ryan Jenkins (eds), *Robot Ethics 2.0: From Autonomous Cars to Artificial Intelligence* (Oxford University Press 2017); Woodrow Barfield and Ugo Pagallo (eds), *Research Handbook on the Law of Artificial Intelligence* (Edward Elgar 2018); Marcelo Corrales, Mark Fenwick, and Nikolaus Forgó (eds), *Robotics, AI and the Future of Law* (Springer 2018); Markus D Dubber, Frank Pasquale, and Sunit Das (eds), *The Oxford Handbook of Ethics of AI* (Oxford University Press 2020); Martin Ebers and Susana Navas (eds), *Algorithms and Law* (Cambridge University Press 2020); Thomas Wischmeyer and Timo Rademacher (eds), *Regulating Artificial Intelligence* (Springer 2020).

[7] See, eg, Richard Susskind, *The Future of Law: Facing the Challenges of Information Technology* (Oxford University Press 1996); Richard Susskind, *The End of Lawyers?*

tions raised by particular technologies – driverless cars,[8] autonomous weapons,[9] governance by algorithm,[10] and so on. A still larger body of writing overlaps with the broader fields of data protection and privacy, or law and technology more generally.

The bulk of that literature tends to concentrate on the activities of legal practitioners, their potential clients, or the machines themselves.[11] The objective here, by contrast, is to focus on those who seek to *regulate* those activities and the difficulties that AI systems pose for government and governance. Rather than taking specific actors or activities as the starting point, this book emphasizes structural problems that AI poses for meaningful regulation as such.

The term 'regulation' is chosen cautiously. Depending on context, its meaning can range from any form of behavioural control, whatever the origin, to the specific rules adopted by government that are subsidiary to

---

Rethinking the Nature of Legal Services (Oxford University Press 2008); Dory Reiling, *Technology for Justice: How Information Technology Can Support Judicial Reform* (Leiden University Press 2010); Richard Susskind, *Tomorrow's Lawyers: An Introduction to Your Future* (Oxford University Press UP 2013); Kevin D Ashley, *Artificial Intelligence and Legal Analytics: New Tools for Law Practice in the Digital Age* (Cambridge University Press 2017); Richard Susskind, *Online Courts and the Future of Justice* (Oxford University Press 2019); Simon Deakin and Christopher Markou (eds), *Is Law Computable? Critical Perspectives on Law and Artificial Intelligence* (Hart 2020).

[8] See, eg, James M Anderson et al, *Autonomous Vehicle Technology: A Guide for Policymakers* (RAND 2014); Markus Maurer et al (eds), *Autonomous Driving: Technical, Legal and Social Aspects* (Springer 2016); Hannah YeeFen Lim, *Autonomous Vehicles and the Law: Technology, Algorithms, and Ethics* (Edward Elgar 2018).

[9] See, eg, Nehal Bhuta et al (eds), *Autonomous Weapons Systems: Law, Ethics, Policy* (Cambridge University Press 2016); Alex Leveringhaus, *Ethics and Autonomous Weapons* (Palgrave Macmillan 2016); Stuart Casey-Maslen et al, *Drones and Other Unmanned Weapons Systems under International Law* (Brill 2018); Wolff Heintschel von Heinegg, Robert Frau, and Tassilo Singer (eds), *Dehumanization of Warfare: Legal Implications of New Weapon Technologies* (Springer 2018).

[10] Christopher Steiner, *Automate This: How Algorithms Came to Rule Our World* (Penguin 2012); Frank Pasquale, *The Black Box Society: The Secret Algorithms That Control Money and Information* (Harvard University Press 2015); Cathy O'Neil, *Weapons of Math Destruction: How Big Data Increases Inequality and Threatens Democracy* (Broadway Books 2016).

[11] There are some exceptions, notably focusing on the private law challenges posed by AI and robotics. See, especially, Ugo Pagallo, *The Laws of Robots: Crimes, Contracts, and Torts* (Springer 2013); Jacob Turner, *Robot Rules: Regulating Artificial Intelligence* (Palgrave Macmillan 2019); Mark Chinen, *Law and Autonomous Machines: The Co-evolution of Legal Responsibility and Technology* (Edward Elgar 2019); Ryan Abbott, *The Reasonable Robot: Artificial Intelligence and the Law* (Cambridge University Press 2020); Matthew Lavy and Matt Hervey, *The Law of Artificial Intelligence* (Sweet & Maxwell 2020); Dominika Ewa Harasimiuk and Tomasz Braun, *Regulating Artificial Intelligence: Binary Ethics and the Law* (Routledge 2021).

legislation.[12] In the United States, regulation is often asserted to mean a burden that is the opposite of free markets; in the academic literature, competing visions of regulation posit it as being either the infringement of private autonomy or a collaborative enterprise.[13] Across the various definitions, much of the literature discusses the different roles that specific regulators can and should play in economic and political activities.

For present purposes, the focus will be on public control of a set of activities.[14] This embraces two important aspects. The first is the exercise of control, which may be through rules, standards, or other means including supervised self-regulation. The second is that such control is exercised by one or more public bodies. These may be the executive, the legislature, the judiciary, or other governmental or intergovernmental entities, but the legitimacy of this form of regulation lies in its connection – however loose – to institutions of the state. The emphasis on public control highlights avoidance of its opposite: a set of activities that would normally be regulated falling outside the effective jurisdiction of any public entity because those activities are being undertaken by AI systems. Regulation need not, however, be undertaken purely through law in the narrow sense of the command of a sovereign backed up by sanctions.[15] It also includes economic incentives such as taxes or subsidies, recognition or accreditation of professional bodies, and other market-based mechanisms.[16]

One question that arises in this context is the extent to which AI systems themselves might have a role to play in regulation.[17] A central argument of the book, however, is that primary responsibility for regulation must fall to states. This embraces both a negative and a positive aspect. The negative aspect is that, in the near term, states should not

---

[12] Barry M Mitnick, *The Political Economy of Regulation: Creating, Designing, and Removing Regulatory Forms* (Columbia University Press 1980); Anthony Ogus, *Regulation: Legal Form and Economic Theory* (Hart 2004); Robert Baldwin, Martin Cave, and Martin Lodge (eds), *The Oxford Handbook of Regulation* (Oxford University Press 2010).

[13] Tony Prosser, *The Regulatory Enterprise: Government, Regulation, and Legitimacy* (Oxford University Press 2010) 1–6.

[14] Cf Philip Selznick, 'Focusing Organizational Research on Regulation' in Roger Noll (ed), *Regulatory Policy and the Social Sciences* (University of California Press 1985) 363.

[15] John Austin, *The Province of Jurisprudence Determined* (first published 1832, Cambridge University Press 1995) 18–37.

[16] Robert Baldwin, Martin Cave, and Martin Lodge, *Understanding Regulation: Theory, Strategy, and Practice* (2nd edn, Oxford University Press 2011) 3.

[17] See Lawrence Lessig, *Code: Version 2.0* (Basic Books 2006).

outsource inherently governmental functions to entities (AI or otherwise) that are beyond their control.[18] The positive aspect is that, moving forward, effective management of the risks associated with AI will require international co-operation and co-ordination. Primary does not mean exclusive responsibility, however. Technology companies already play an outsized role in determining standards; this role will doubtless expand as AI systems become more complex. Yet the legitimacy of those standards and their incorporation into regulatory structures will be greatest, and they will be most effective, when endorsed by publicly accountable institutions.

The book is written for a global audience, but it is striking that the vast majority of the published material relies almost exclusively on the laws of Europe and the United States. That is understandable, given the economic importance of these jurisdictions and their sway in establishing global standards, directly or indirectly, in many fields related to technology. The two regimes also offer interesting points of comparison, with human rights concerns shaping the European response while market-based approaches hold sway in the United States. In the field of AI, however, China is – or soon will be – the dominant actor.[19] The book therefore examines the Chinese approach and the relationship between that dominance and the far more limited regulation within China. Another prominent Asian jurisdiction considered is Singapore, which has long sought to position itself as a rule of law hub to attract investment. As in the case of data protection law,[20] Singapore's government has explicitly set the goal of regulation as being to attract and encourage AI innovation.[21]

Such a public law perspective has been sorely lacking in debates over regulation of AI to date, while international law and institutions have been left out almost entirely.[22] The book builds on the author's past work

[18] See generally Simon Chesterman and Angelina Fisher (eds), *Private Security, Public Order: The Outsourcing of Public Services and Its Limits* (Oxford University Press 2009).
[19] See 腾讯研究院 [Tencent Research Institute] and 中国信通院互联网法律研究中心 [China ICT Internet Law Research Center], 人工智能：国家人工智能战略行动抓手 [*Artificial Intelligence: National Artificial Intelligence Strategy*] (Renmin University Press 2017); Kai-Fu Lee, *AI Superpowers: China, Silicon Valley, and the New World Order* (Houghton Mifflin Harcourt 2018).
[20] Simon Chesterman (ed), *Data Protection Law in Singapore: Privacy and Sovereignty in an Interconnected World* (2nd edn, Academy 2018).
[21] Model Artificial Intelligence Governance Framework (2nd edn, Personal Data Protection Commission, 2020).
[22] For a discussion of the various non-binding frameworks that have been proposed, see chapter seven, introduction.

looking at public authority in times of crisis – ranging from humanitarian intervention and transitional administration, when a state turns on its population or collapses entirely,[23] to the outsourcing of security to private actors and the expansive powers asserted by intelligence agencies in response to terrorism.[24] AI may not yet pose a threat on such a scale, but lessons on how to manage risk, draw red lines, and preserve the legitimacy of public authority are useful now – and will be essential if it ever does.

Outline of the Book

The book is organized around the following sets of problems: How should we understand the challenges to regulation posed by the technologies loosely described here as 'AI systems'? What regulatory tools exist to deal with those challenges and what are their limitations? And what more is needed – rules, institutions, actors – to reap the benefits offered by AI while minimizing avoidable harm?

Part I groups the challenges to regulation into three broad categories.

The first, considered in chapter one, is speed. Since computers entered into the mainstream in the 1960s, the efficiency with which data can be processed has raised regulatory questions. This is well understood with respect to privacy. Data that was notionally public – divorce proceedings, say – had long been protected through the 'practical obscurity' of paper records.[25] When such material was available in a single hard copy in a government office, the chances of one's acquaintances or employer finding it were remote. Yet when it was computerized and made searchable through what ultimately became the Internet, practical obscurity disappeared. Today, high-speed computing poses comparable threats to existing regulatory models in areas from securities regulation to competition law, merely by enabling lawful activities – trading in stocks, or comparing and adjusting prices, say – to be undertaken more quickly than previously conceived possible. Many of these questions are practical

[23] Simon Chesterman, *Just War or Just Peace? Humanitarian Intervention and International Law* (Oxford University Press 2001); Simon Chesterman, *You, the People: The United Nations, Transitional Administration, and State-Building* (Oxford University Press 2004).
[24] Simon Chesterman and Chia Lehnardt (eds), *From Mercenaries to Market: The Rise and Regulation of Private Military Companies* (Oxford University Press 2007); Simon Chesterman, *One Nation under Surveillance: A New Social Contract to Defend Freedom without Sacrificing Liberty* (Oxford University Press 2011).
[25] *United States Department of Justice v Reporters Committee for Freedom of the Press*, 489 US 749, 762 (1989).

rather than conceptual and apply to technologies other than AI. Nevertheless, current approaches to slowing down decision-making – through circuit-breakers to stop trading, for example – will not address all of the problems raised by the speed of AI systems.

A second set of challenges is the increasing autonomy of those systems, exposing gaps in regulatory regimes that assume the centrality of human actors. Yet surprisingly little attention is given to what is meant by 'autonomy' and its relationship to those gaps. Driverless vehicles and autonomous weapon systems are the most widely studied examples, but related issues arise in algorithms that allocate resources or determine eligibility for programmes in the private or public sector. Chapter two develops a novel typology that distinguishes three lenses through which to view the regulatory issues raised by autonomy: the practical difficulties of managing risk associated with new technologies, the morality of certain functions being undertaken by machines at all, and the legitimacy gap when public authorities delegate their powers to algorithms.

Chapter three turns to the increasing opacity of AI. As computer programs become ever more complex, the ability of non-specialists to understand them diminishes. Opacity may also be built into programs by companies seeking to protect proprietary interests. Both such systems are capable of being explained, albeit with recourse to experts or an order to reveal their internal workings. Yet a third kind of system may be naturally opaque: some machine learning techniques are difficult or impossible to explain in a manner that humans can comprehend. This raises concerns when the process by which a decision is made is as important as the decision itself. For example, a sentencing algorithm might produce a 'just' outcome for a class of convicted persons. Unless the justness of that outcome for an individual defendant can be explained in court, however, it is, quite rightly, subject to legal challenge. Separate concerns are raised by the prospect that AI systems may mask or reify discriminatory practices or outcomes.

This is, of course, a non-exhaustive list of the challenges posed by AI. Among others on the horizon are the likely displacement of large segments of the workforce and the possibility of artificial general intelligence raising meaningful questions about the rights of 'smart robots'.[26] Nor does this study seek to examine the broader ethical implications of AI taking on greater roles in society, or the regulation of cyberspace, virtual

---

[26] See above n 5.

worlds, and so on.[27] Similarly, it will not attempt to cover fully the potential impact of blockchain or distributed ledger technology.[28] The more modest aim is to use the problems identified in this part to highlight gaps in existing regulatory models with a view to seeing whether the tools at our disposal can fill them.

Part II, then, turns to those tools. Chapter four examines how existing laws can and should apply to emerging technology through attribution of responsibility. Legal systems typically seek to deter identifiable persons – natural or juridical – from certain forms of conduct, or to allocate losses to those persons. Responsibility may be direct or indirect: key questions are how the acts and omissions of AI systems can and should be understood. Given the complexity of those systems, novel approaches to responsibility have been proposed, including special applications of product liability, agency, and causation. More important and less studied is the role that insurance can play in compensating harm but also structuring incentives for action. Another approach is to limit the ability to *avoid* responsibility, drawing on the literature on outsourcing and the prohibition on transferring certain forms of responsibility – most notably the exercise of discretion in the public sector.

As AI systems operate with greater autonomy, however, the idea that they might themselves be held responsible has gained credence. On its face, the idea of giving those systems a form of independent legal personality may seem attractive. Yet chapter five argues that this is both too simple and too complex. It is simplistic in that it lumps a wide range of technologies together in a single legal category ill-suited to the task; it is overly complex in that it implicitly or explicitly embraces the anthropomorphic fallacy that AI systems will eventually assume full legal personality in the manner of the 'robot consciousness' arguments mentioned earlier. Though the emergence of general AI is a conceivable future

---

[27] See, eg, F Gregory Lastowka, *Virtual Justice: The New Laws of Online Worlds* (Yale University Press 2010); Andrew Sparrow, *The Law of Virtual Worlds and Internet Social Networks* (Gower 2010); Jacqueline Lipton, *Rethinking Cyberlaw: A New Vision for Internet Law* (Edward Elgar 2015); Andrew Murray, *Information Technology Law: The Law and Society* (3rd edn, Oxford University Press 2016); Paul Lambert, *Gringras: The Laws of the Internet* (5th edn, Bloomsbury 2018); Lilian Edwards (ed), *Law, Policy, and the Internet* (Hart 2019); Roxana Radu, *Negotiating Internet Governance* (Oxford University Press 2019); Frank Pasquale, *New Laws of Robotics: Defending Human Expertise in the Age of AI* (Belknap Press 2020).

[28] See, eg, William J Magnuson, *Blockchain Democracy: Technology, Law, and the Rule of the Crowd* (Cambridge University Press 2020); Fabian Schär and Aleksander Berentsen, *Bitcoin, Blockchain, and Cryptoassets* (MIT Press 2020).

scenario – and one worth taking precautions against – it is not a sound basis for regulation today.

Notions of foreseeability underpin another tool that has been embraced as a means of limiting the risks associated with AI: transparency. Chapter six considers the manner in which transparency and the related concept of 'explainability' are being elaborated, notably the 'right to explanation' in the European Union (EU) and a move towards explainable AI (XAI) among developers. These are more promising than the arguments for legal personality, but the limits of transparency are already beginning to show as AI systems demonstrate abilities that even their programmers struggle to understand. That is leading regulators to cede ground and settle for explanations of adverse decisions rather than transparency of decision-making processes themselves. Such a backward-looking approach relies on individuals knowing that they have been harmed – which will not always be the case – and should be supplemented with forward-looking mechanisms like impact assessments, audits, and an ombudsperson.

The final part of the book considers the rules and institutions required to address the inadequacies of existing tools and regulatory bodies.

As the preceding chapters demonstrate, existing norms, suitably interpreted, are able to deal with many of the challenges presented by AI. But not all. Chapter seven begins with a survey of guides, frameworks, and principles put forward by states, industry, and intergovernmental organizations. These diverse efforts have led to a broad consensus on half a dozen norms that might govern AI. Far less energy has gone into determining how these might be implemented – or if they are even necessary. Rather than contribute to norm proliferation, the chapter focuses on why regulation is necessary, when regulatory changes should be made, and how it would work in practice. Two specific areas for law reform address the weaponization and victimization of AI. Regulations aimed at general AI are particularly difficult in that they confront many 'unknown unknowns', but uncontrollable or uncontainable AI could pose a threat far more serious than lethal autonomous weapon systems. Additionally, however, there will be a need to prohibit some conduct in which increasingly lifelike machines are the victims – comparable, perhaps, to animal cruelty laws.

The answers that each political community finds to the law reform questions posed may differ, but a larger threat in the very near future is that AI systems capable of causing harm will not be confined to one jurisdiction – indeed, it may be impossible to link them to a specific jurisdiction at all. This is not a new problem in cybersecurity, but different national approaches to regulation will pose barriers to effective regulation exacerbated by the speed, autonomy, and opacity of AI systems. For that reason, some measure of collective action, or at least co-ordination, is needed. Lessons may be learned from efforts to regulate the global commons, as well as moves to outlaw at the international level certain products (weapons and drugs, for example) and activities (such as slavery and child sex tourism). The argument advanced here is that regulation, in the sense of public control, requires active involvement of states. To co-ordinate those activities and enforce global 'red lines', chapter eight posits a hypothetical International Artificial Intelligence Agency (IAIA), modelled on the agency created after the Second World War to promote peaceful uses of nuclear energy, while deterring or containing its weaponization and other harmful effects.

Chapter nine turns to the possibility that the AI systems challenging the legal order may also offer at least part of the solution. Here, China, which has among the least developed rules to regulate conduct by AI systems, is at the forefront of using that same technology in the courtroom. This is a double-edged sword, however, as its use implies a view of law that is instrumental, with parties to proceedings treated as means rather than ends. That, in turn, raises fundamental questions about the nature of law and authority: at base, whether law is reducible to code that can optimize the human condition or if it must remain a site of contestation, of politics, and inextricably linked to institutions that are themselves accountable to a public. For many of the questions raised, the rational answer will be sufficient; but for others, *what* the answer is may be less important than *how* and *why* it was reached, and *whom* an affected population can hold to account for its consequences.

Precaution vs Innovation

Underlying the question of regulation is the need to balance precautionary steps against unnecessarily constraining innovation. A government report in Singapore, for example, highlighted the risks posed by AI, but concluded that 'it is telling that no country has introduced specific rules on criminal liability for artificial intelligence systems. Being the global first-mover on such rules may impair Singapore's ability to attract top industry players in the field of AI.'[29]

---

[29] Penal Code Review Committee (Ministry of Home Affairs and Ministry of Law, August 2018) 29. China, for its part, included in the State Council's AI development

These concerns are well-founded. As in other areas of research, overly restrictive laws can stifle innovation or drive it elsewhere. Yet the failure to develop appropriate legal tools risks allowing profit-motivated actors to shape large sections of the economy around their interests to the point that regulators will struggle to catch up. This has been particularly true in the field of information technology. Social media giants like Facebook, for example, monetized users' personal data while data protection laws were still in their infancy.[30] Similarly, Uber and other first-movers in what is now termed the sharing or 'gig' economy exploited platform technology before rules were in place to protect workers or maintain standards.[31] As Pedro Domingos once observed, people worry that computers will get too smart and take over the world; the real problem is that the computers are too stupid and they've taken it over already.[32]

Much of the literature on AI and the law focuses on a horizon that is either so distant that it blurs the line with science fiction or so near that it plays catch-up with the technologies of today. That tension between presentism and hyperbole is reflected in the history of AI itself, with the term 'AI winter' coined to describe the mismatch between the promise of AI and its reality.[33] Indeed, it was evident back in 1956 at Dartmouth when the discipline was born. To fund the workshop, John McCarthy and three colleagues wrote to the Rockefeller Foundation with the following modest proposal:

> We propose that a 2 month, 10 man study of artificial intelligence be carried out during the summer of 1956 ... The study is to proceed on the basis of the conjecture that every aspect of learning or any other feature of intelligence can in principle be so precisely described that a machine can be made to simulate it. An attempt will be made to find how to make machines use language, form abstractions and concepts, solve [the] kinds

plan the establishment of laws and regulations for AI – with initial steps to be taken around 2025: 国务院关于印发新一代人工智能发展规划的通知 [State Council Issued Notice of the New Generation Artificial Intelligence Development Plan] (State Council, Guofa [2017] No 35, 20 July 2017).
[30] Shoshana Zuboff, *The Age of Surveillance Capitalism: The Fight for a Human Future at the New Frontier of Power* (Public Affairs 2019).
[31] Jeremias Prassl, *Humans as a Service: The Promise and Perils of Work in the Gig Economy* (Oxford University Press 2018).
[32] Pedro Domingos, *The Master Algorithm: How the Quest for the Ultimate Learning Machine Will Remake Our World* (Basic Books 2015) 286.
[33] Against this, some have complained that every achievement in AI is marked by a redefinition of true intelligence. Douglas Hofstadter pithily summed this up in a theorem attributed to Larry Tesler: 'AI is whatever hasn't been done yet.' See Douglas R Hofstadter, *Gödel, Escher, Bach: An Eternal Golden Braid* (Basic Books 1979) 601.

of problems now reserved for humans, and improve themselves. We think
that a significant advance can be made in one or more of these problems if
a carefully selected group of scientists work on it together for a summer.[34]

Over the subsequent decades, enthusiasm for and fear of AI have waxed
and waned in almost equal measure. In an interview in *Paris Review* a few
years after the Dartmouth gathering, Pablo Picasso memorably dismissed
the new mechanical brains as useless: 'They can only give you answers,'
he scoffed.[35] As countries around the world struggle to capitalize on the
economic potential of AI while minimizing avoidable harm, a book like
this cannot hope to be the last word on the topic of regulation. But by
examining the nature of the challenges, the limitations of existing tools,
and some possible solutions, it hopes to ensure that we are at least asking
the right questions.

---

[34] J McCarthy et al, A Proposal for the Dartmouth Summer Research Project on Artificial
Intelligence (31 August 1955).
[35] William Fifield, 'Pablo Picasso: A Composite Interview' (1964) 32 Paris Review 37, 62.

PART I

Challenges

Speed

The financial markets opened in New York on Thursday 6 May 2010, much as they did on any other morning. A headline in the *Wall Street Journal* warned of possible economic chaos in Greece; the EU and the International Monetary Fund (IMF) were cobbling together a rescue package. On Wall Street itself, concerns about European debt had seen the Dow Jones Industrial Average, an index of market value, fall nearly 60 points to close the previous day at 10,868.

As the bell rang at the New York Stock Exchange, stocks were expected to continue their decline. Uncertainty about a looming election in Britain and an upcoming jobs report further dampened sentiment. In Washington DC, the Senate was debating a bill on financial regulation – part of ongoing efforts to guard against a crisis like that sparked by subprime mortgages three years earlier. Trading commenced and, as predicted, the Dow maintained its downward trajectory. Some traders moved funds into gold, long regarded as a safe haven in times of economic downturn. None of this was especially unusual: markets go down as well as up.

One thing that did go up was known by the acronym VIX. Calculated by the Chicago Board Options Exchange, the Volatility Index is a measure of the variance of options from underlying share prices – essentially, the extent to which traders are betting that prices will change over time. A higher number theoretically means that the market could rise or fall, though VIX is also referred to as the 'fear index'. That Thursday morning, it had risen by more than 20 per cent. Traders reassured themselves that this was still far below the heights reached during the global financial crisis of 2007–08.

At 2:32pm, however, the market began to collapse. Within quarter of an hour, the Dow lost nearly 1,000 points or almost a tenth of its value – the biggest point drop over the course of a single day in its history. Shares in Proctor & Gamble, a blue-chip stock long seen as one of the market's most stable, fell by more than a third. Consulting company Accenture essentially lost all of its value, the price of its shares plummeting from $40 to one cent. For reasons that no one could explain, more than a trillion dollars in market value vanished in minutes. On the floor of the New York Stock Exchange, traders shouted or watched open-mouthed as their screens flashed with sell orders and phones rang off the hook. National Economic Council Director Lawrence Summers was pulled out of a meeting. At the White House, Treasury Secretary Tim Geithner hastily briefed President Barack Obama about what some were already calling 'Black Thursday'.

And then, just as quickly, the market recovered.

In 90 seconds, half the losses were reversed. By three o'clock, the price of most stocks had returned to previous levels. In the dry prose of a report by staff of the key regulatory bodies, 'trading resumed in a more orderly fashion'.[1] The day ended with the Dow 347 points below its previous close – a 3.2 per cent drop, but suggestive of a correction rather than a catastrophe.

Over subsequent weeks, analysts and regulators struggled to explain what had happened during that half-hour period. Speculation was rife that a trader had accidentally triggered a massive sale of Proctor & Gamble stock, in what came to be known as the 'fat finger theory'. But attention soon turned to trading algorithms. After a five-month investigation, a government report concluded that a mutual fund's attempt to sell a large number of futures contracts had triggered the 'Flash Crash'. High-frequency traders (HFTs) executing the sale – algorithms able to buy and sell stocks and options in a fraction of a second – were unable to find traditional purchasers and instead sold and resold the options to other HFTs. This generated what the report termed a 'hot-potato' effect, as the same positions were rapidly passed back and forth between computer programs. In a 14-second period, more than 27,000 such contracts were concluded, accounting for almost half the total trading volume.

The increased speed of information technology is an essential component of the AI systems discussed in this book. Moore's law famously predicts that processing speed will continue to increase – doubling approximately every two years, as it has for half a century.[2] Though

---

[1] Findings Regarding the Events of May 6, 2010 (US Commodity Futures Trading Commission and US Securities & Exchange Commission, 30 September 2010) 9. See also Mary L Schapiro, Examining the Causes and Lessons of the May 6th Market Plunge (US Securities and Exchange Commission, 20 May 2010).

[2] Robert F Service, 'Chipmakers Look Past Moore's Law, and Silicon' (2018) 361(6400) Science 321.

there are signs that the rate of increase is slowing, ever more efficient machines mean that the marginal costs of data storage and computing power are trending towards zero.[3] The increasing complexity of those systems means that, although general AI remains science fiction for the time being, current applications of narrow AI have already moved significantly beyond human cognitive abilities. As the 2010 Flash Crash demonstrated, there is also a danger that those systems will move faster than humans can control.

This chapter considers the regulatory challenges posed by speed. Though the focus of the book is on AI, many of the transformations in the digital economy are more accurately linked to the speed and efficiency of data processing rather than true cognitive ability or 'intelligence' as such. Speed has, nevertheless, raised legal problems when rules designed for twentieth-century society are confronted with the changing practices of the twenty-first. The chapter examines three of them.

The first is also the best known: the effacement of distance by the speed with which data can flow around the world. Cyber and Internet law are now subdisciplines in their own right, raising complex jurisdictional and practical issues in regulating online behaviour.[4] The combination of those structural features with increasingly sophisticated software poses difficulties for would-be regulators in areas from protection of intellectual property to combatting 'fake news'.

Secondly, we return to the 'Flash Crash' of 2010 and the efforts to accommodate high-frequency trading. In theory, algorithms executing trades are subject to the same regulations as the human brokers that set them in motion. In practice, the possibility of disruption or manipulation due to the speed at which those algorithms operate has led bourses to explore ways of slowing them down. There is also a larger argument that computer-based trading has changed not only the culture but also the very nature of the market.

A third set of problems concerns competition law, also known as antitrust. The digital economy offers consumers access to information on a scale and at a speed unimaginable in any traditional marketplace. Yet that information and more is also available to retailers who are able to use pricing software to maximize profits. In the past, anti-competitive conduct required proof of a meeting of the minds to collude on prices or

---

[3] Jeremy Rifkin, *The Zero Marginal Cost Society: The Internet of Things, the Collaborative Commons, and the Eclipse of Capitalism* (St Martin's Press 2014).
[4] See the introduction to this book at n 27.

abuse market dominance. The rate at which prices can be adjusted today means that tacit collusion may take place without any intent on the part of market actors – or even without any formal co-ordination between their computer programs.

Individually, these challenges point to practical obstacles to regulation of information technology in a globalized world. Together, particularly when combined with AI systems that are autonomous and opaque, they show the danger that those systems will operate in a manner that is uncontainable, unstoppable, or undetectable.

1.1   The Globalization of Information

One of the most basic difficulties posed by speed, built into the structure of the Internet itself, is the globalization of information. The ability to access data almost instantly from almost anywhere on the planet and project it globally imposes obvious limitations on legal regimes premised on territorially bounded states. Those limitations are not conceptual so much as practical, requiring co-ordination across jurisdictions. Larger questions of co-ordination to regulate AI will be considered in chapter eight. Here, discussion will be limited to a few brief examples that should suffice to explain the problem.

Protection of intellectual property rights, for example, has always been threatened by the ability to make copies. The replacement of analogue technologies – the tape recorder, the photocopier – with digital ones radically transformed the economics of copying: the laborious task of making one copy gave way to the ability to share music and other content at effectively no cost and without regard to distance.[5] Lawsuits and legislative changes[6] led to most media platforms adopting copyright policies and takedown protocols,[7] while others were shut down completely.[8] Producers and distributors developed technical means to

---

[5] Indeed, various social media platforms encourage this by 'nudging' users to share material that they did not create. See David Tan, 'Fair Use and Transformative Play in the Digital Age' in Megan Richardson and Sam Ricketson (eds), *Research Handbook on Intellectual Property in Media and Entertainment* (Edward Elgar 2017) 102.

[6] Notably the Digital Millennium Copyright Act (DMCA) 1998, Pub L No 105-304 (US).

[7] In 2020, for example, Facebook removed more than 400,000 pieces of content per month for copyright violation. See further Daniel Seng, 'The State of the Discordant Union: An Empirical Analysis of DMCA Takedown Notices' (2014) 18 Virginia Journal of Law & Technology 369.

[8] *AMG Records Inc v Napster Inc*, 239 F 3d 1004 (9th Cir, 2001). See also Joseph Menn, *All the Rave: The Rise and Fall of Shawn Fanning's Napster* (Crown 2003).

limit copying, but a certain amount of piracy is often priced in as the cost of doing business.[9]

As with the unauthorized sharing of intellectual property, the Internet also facilitates the unwanted dissemination of prohibited material. The speed with which information can spread across the globe regularly frustrates efforts to contain it, while also challenging the legal rules intended to deter or punish tortious or criminal behaviour.[10] Indeed, attempts to ban material in one jurisdiction may merely serve to increase its prominence – while not curtailing its availability in other jurisdictions. Again, this is not new: when Peter Wright's scandalous memoir of his career in MI5 was banned in the United Kingdom in the 1980s, that legal action almost certainly increased worldwide sales even before the ban was finally lifted.[11] More recently, organizations such as WikiLeaks have built disaggregated distribution into their operating model.[12]

Another example of the difficulties posed by the speed of information flow is the modern phenomenon of 'fake news'.[13] The ability for malicious rumours to be spread online had long been identified as a problem with respect to bullying and distorting share prices, but it was the 2016 US election that led to concerns that it could be used for larger political purposes also.[14] As with sharing of protected or prohibited material, the speed with which fake news flows is not a problem caused by AI. Novel developments that are linked to new technologies, however, include automatically-generated content and so-called 'deep fakes' – false content, such as doctored images and videos, that can be difficult to distinguish from genuine material.[15]

---

[9] Luis Aguiar, Jörg Claussen, and Christian Peukert, 'Catch Me If You Can: Effectiveness and Consequences of Online Copyright Enforcement' (2018) 29 Information Systems Research 656; P Jean-Jacques Herings, Ronald Peeters, and Michael S Yang, 'Piracy on the Internet: Accommodate It or Fight It? A Dynamic Approach' (2018) 266 European Journal of Operational Research 328.

[10] Lord Anthony Grabiner, 'Sex, Scandal and Super-Injunctions – The Controversies Surrounding the Protection of Privacy' (2012) 45 Israel Law Review 537.

[11] Laurence Zuckerman, 'How Not to Silence a Spy: Banned in Britain, an Agent's Memoirs Become Big-Selling News', Time (17 August 1987). See Peter Wright, Spycatcher: The Candid Autobiography of a Senior Intelligence Officer (Viking 1987).

[12] Stephen ME Marmura, The WikiLeaks Paradigm: Paradoxes and Revelations (Palgrave 2018).

[13] Brian McNair, Fake News: Falsehood, Fabrication and Fantasy in Journalism (Routledge 2018). The dissemination of false information is, of course, as old as human society itself.

[14] Report on the Investigation into Russian Interference in the 2016 Presidential Election (Mueller Report) (Department of Justice, March 2019) vol 1, 14–29.

[15] Zack Whittaker, 'US Lawmakers Warn Spy Chief that "Deep Fakes" Are a National Security Threat', TechCrunch (13 September 2018).

Government efforts to address the phenomenon of fake news have tended to focus on trying to correct it or contain it. Legislation introduced in Germany,[16] France,[17] Malaysia,[18] and Singapore[19] enables public authorities to require social media sites to add corrections to or take down certain material within a designated time frame. Other approaches have emphasized responsibility for content, with users being required to register under their real name, limiting the ability to share information widely, and straightforward censorship. China has used all three methods on Sina Weibo and WeChat.[20]

Social media platforms themselves long abjured any responsibility for the content that they host. Revelations of the sale of personal data to Cambridge Analytica in the context of the 2016 US Presidential election led to a series of efforts by Facebook, Twitter, and others to exercise greater control over the dissemination of fake news. This included deleting accounts that violate community standards, prioritizing posts by friends and family over those by publishers and businesses, and employing fact-checkers to add context to newsfeed items. In 2018, Twitter deleted tens of millions of accounts that were suspected of being fake. Violence in India linked to misinformation spread through WhatsApp saw the messaging application in 2019 impose limits on the number of accounts to which messages can be forwarded. The stakes were even higher in 2020 as concerted efforts spread falsehoods about the Covid-19 pandemic and the US Presidential election.

Not even the most optimistic regulator believes that fake news will disappear anytime soon. Innovations such as deep fakes and authentic-looking bot accounts point to the role that AI systems will play in both exacerbating the problem and, perhaps, offering means of addressing it.[21]

---

[16] Netzdurchsetzunggesetz (NetzDG) [Network Enforcement Act] 2017 (Germany).

[17] Loi organique no 2018-1201 du 22 décembre 2018 relative à la lutte contre la manipulation de l'information 2018 (France); Loi no 2018-1202 du 22 décembre 2018 relative à la lutte contre la manipulation de l'information 2018 (France). The French legislation was limited to during election campaigns.

[18] Anti-Fake News Act 2018 (Malaysia).

[19] Protection from Online Falsehoods and Manipulation Act 2019 (Singapore).

[20] Ronggui Huang and Xiaoyi Sun, 'Weibo Network, Information Diffusion and Implications for Collective Action in China' (2014) 17 Information, Communication & Society 86; Huiquan Zhou and Quanxiao Pan, 'Information, Community, and Action on Sina-Weibo: How Chinese Philanthropic NGOs Use Social Media Authors' (2016) 27 VOLUNTAS: International Journal of Voluntary and Nonprofit Organizations 2433; James Griffiths, The Great Firewall of China: How to Build and Control an Alternative Version of the Internet (Zed Books 2019).

[21] Georgios Gravanis et al, 'Behind the Cues: A Benchmarking Study for Fake News Detection' (2019) 128 Expert Systems with Applications 201; Hoon Ko et al, 'Human-Machine

Yet the underlying problem seems to be a human one. As an MIT study of a decade of Twitter postings showed, fake news is more novel and inspires more intense emotions than its truthful counterpart, with the result that lies spread more quickly than truth – and it is humans doing the sharing, not robots.[22]

The globalization of information has put more knowledge in the hands of more people than at any time in human history; in many repressive regimes, the Internet has played a liberating role because of the difficulty of containing information. The structures that facilitate this are also barriers, however, to containing material that is proprietary, defamatory, or otherwise harmful. As AI systems play a greater role in generating content, efforts at containment – through data localization, filtering, or otherwise slowing the flow of information – will run the risk of under-mining the foundations of the digital economy and are at best a short-term fix for a fast-moving problem.

1.2   High-Frequency Trading

Speed has generated different practical problems in the world of high-frequency trading, in which algorithms buy and sell stocks or derivatives with an eye to making incremental profits on a large number of transactions. An indication of the premium put on speed is that a Chicago-based company spent $300m laying a dedicated fibre-optic cable to New Jersey in order to shave three milliseconds off the time it took data to travel from its offices to the stock exchange.[23] Today, HFTs are estimated to account for around half of all trades by volume in US and European markets.[24] Though profits in the United States appear to have peaked, Asian markets are seen as having significant capacity for growth in HFTs.[25]

Interaction: A Case Study on Fake News Detection Using a Backtracking Based on a Cognitive System' (2019) 55 Cognitive Systems Research 77. See also chapter nine, section 9.3.

[22] Soroush Vosoughi, Deb Roy, and Sinan Aral, 'The Spread of True and False News Online' (2018) 359(6380) Science 1146.

[23] Michael Lewis, *Flash Boys: A Wall Street Revolt* (WW Norton 2014) 7–22; Megan Woodward, 'The Need for Speed: Regulatory Approaches to High Frequency Trading in the United States and the European Union' (2011) 50 Vanderbilt Journal of Transnational Law 1359.

[24] See generally Irene Aldridge and Steven Krawciw, *Real-Time Risk: What Investors Should Know about FinTech, High-Frequency Trading, and Flash Crashes* (Wiley 2017).

[25] Hao Zhou and Petko S Kalev, 'Algorithmic and High Frequency Trading in Asia-Pacific, Now and the Future' (2019) 53 Pacific-Basin Finance Journal 186; Guo Li, 'Regulating

The argument in favour of HFTs is that they provide liquidity to the market by increasing the number of buyers and sellers at any given moment, as well as helping in price discovery.[26] The danger is that because the programs operate so quickly, they can also increase price volatility and destabilize the market. In the 2010 Flash Crash, for example, US regulators concluded at the time that HFTs might not have been the cause of the crash, but at the very least they exacerbated its consequences.[27] The response was an expansion of trading curbs or 'circuit breakers'. These had been introduced in the wake of the 1987 Black Monday crash to prevent runs on the stock exchange caused by human panic. If the market drops by a certain percentage,[28] trading can be paused for a period of time or for the rest of the day. The hope is that such a pause gives investors 'more time to obtain information and make rational decisions'.[29]

Under the New York Stock Exchange rules in force in 2010, these provisions would have kicked in to halt trading for half an hour if the Dow had dropped by 10 per cent against a quarterly benchmark before 2:30pm, or the market would have closed completely if it had fallen by 20 per cent or more after 2pm. In the wake of the Flash Crash, these limits were revised to cover specific stocks that rise or fall more than 10 per cent in value within a five-minute period.[30] The following year, the exchange-wide thresholds were tightened to suspend trading after a 7 per cent drop of Standard & Poor's 500, a measure that includes 500 large publicly

Investment Robo-Advisors in China: Problems and Prospects' (2020) 21 European Business Organization Law Review 69.

[26] Jonathan Brogaarda et al, 'High Frequency Trading and Extreme Price Movements' (2018) 128 Journal of Financial Economics 253, 254. Cf James Upson and Robert A Van Ness, 'Multiple Markets, Algorithmic Trading, and Market Liquidity' (2017) 32 Journal of Financial Markets 49; Donald MacKenzie, '"Making", "Taking", and the Material Political Economy of Algorithmic Trading' (2018) 47 Economy and Society 501; Brian M Weller, 'Does Algorithmic Trading Reduce Information Acquisition?' (2018) 31 Review of Financial Studies 2184.

[27] Findings Regarding the Events of May 6, 2010 (n 1) 45–48. Cf Andrei Kirilenko et al, 'The Flash Crash: High-Frequency Trading in an Electronic Market' (2017) 72 Journal of Finance 967.

[28] Until 1997, the thresholds were set by reference to a drop in points.

[29] Yong H Kim and J Jimmy Yang, 'What Makes Circuit Breakers Attractive to Financial Markets? A Survey' (2004) 13 Financial Markets, Institutions & Instruments 109, 121.

[30] Securities Exchange Act Release No 62252 (Securities and Exchange Commission, 10 June 2010). See also E Wes Bethel et al, 'Federal Market Information Technology in the Post Flash Crash Era: Roles for Supercomputing' (2012) 7(2) The Journal of Trading 9.

traded US stocks, against a daily benchmark rather than one set every three months.[31]

Other countries have followed suit.[32] In the EU, the Markets in Financial Instruments Directive II (MiFID II) now imposes limits on high-frequency trading (and algorithmic trading more generally), adding metaphorical 'speed bumps' to prevent disorderly trading and reduce market volatility.[33] Authorized traders must also disclose, among other things, how their algorithms work and who controls them. Trading data must be kept, with provision for modelling it as well as flagging unusual orders and establishing thresholds of price and volume beyond which a circuit breaker will kick in.[34]

The EU requirements highlight that market instability linked to HFTs is clearly not the same as human emotions causing a run on the market. The original circuit breakers offered time to make 'rational' decisions. That is not a deficiency in HFTs.[35] Presumably in recognition of this, the New York Stock Exchange today stresses that even though it embraces 'cutting edge, ultrafast technology, we believe nothing can take the place of human judgment and accountability'.

Any attempt to restrict the behaviour of HFTs confronts the question of whether and how they merit special treatment.[36] In principle, HFTs have access to the same information and trade on the same basis as other investors. Most regulatory efforts to date have focused on limiting market

---

[31] Recommendations Regarding Regulatory Responses to the Market Events of May 6, 2010 (Joint CFTC–SEC Advisory Committee, 18 February 2011); Notice of Proposed Rule Change Related to Trading Halts Due to Extraordinary Market Volatility (Securities And Exchange Commission, Release No 34-65425; File No SR-ISE-2011-61, 28 September 2011).

[32] Singapore introduced circuit breaker provisions in 2014 with Hong Kong doing so in 2016: David R Meyer and George Guernsey, 'Hong Kong and Singapore Exchanges Confront High Frequency Trading' (2017) 23 Asia Pacific Business Review 63.

[33] Directive 2014/65/EU of the European Parliament and of the Council of 15 May 2014 on Markets in Financial Instruments and Amending Directive 2002/92/EC and Directive 2011/61/EU 2014 (EU).

[34] Tilen Čuk and Arnaud van Waeyenberge, 'European Legal Framework for Algorithmic and High Frequency Trading (Mifid 2 and MAR): A Global Approach to Managing the Risks of the Modern Trading Paradigm' (2018) 9 European Journal of Risk Regulation 146.

[35] Indeed, there is some evidence that the presence of algorithmic traders can make humans behave more rationally also: Mike Farjama and Oliver Kirchkampb, 'Bubbles in Hybrid Markets: How Expectations about Algorithmic Trading Affect Human Trading' (2018) 146 Journal of Economic Behavior & Organization 248.

[36] Steven R McNamara, 'The Law and Ethics of High-Frequency Trading' (2016) 17 Minnesota Journal of Law, Science & Technology 71.

disruption and manipulation associated with their capacity to make many trades in a short period of time. In practice, of course, speed also brings with it information asymmetry: the ability to process and trade on information before anyone else offers a clear advantage. Various HFTs therefore subscribe directly to news and market feeds in order to make trades almost immediately upon the release of notionally 'public' data and assume a first-mover advantage.[37] Though not illegal, former New York Attorney-General Eric Schneiderman termed this 'insider trading 2.0'.[38]

Speed bumps and other means of slowing down HFTs could reduce that advantage.[39] Another approach is to restrict early access to market data.[40] More radical ideas include changing the way that exchanges think about time itself. One proposal is to replace the current system of orders, which treats time as continuous, with frequent batch auctions that treat time as made up of discrete units. Rather than executing trades in the order in which they are received, trades would be executed at discrete intervals – every tenth of a second, say. This would reduce the incentive to shave milliseconds off the placement of an order and the market distortions to which that gives rise.[41]

A second point of distinction concerns whether HFT users can and should be compelled to be more transparent about their algorithms than human traders are about their own investment strategies. This is now required by the EU regime, for example. The justification for special treatment is also typically tied to the possibility of disruption and manipulation of the market. Yet there is an argument that algorithmic and high-frequency trading have transformed not just how trades are made but how markets operate. In theory, brokers executing trades on

---

[37] This is particularly true if the system can anticipate other large orders and front-run them. Florian Gamper, Is High Frequency Trading Fair? The Case of Order Anticipation (NUS Centre for Banking & Finance Law, CBFL-WP-FG03, 2016).

[38] James J Angel and Douglas M McCabe, 'Insider Trading 2.0? The Ethics of Information Sales' (2018) 147 Journal of Business Ethics 747. See also Walter Mattli, *Darkness by Design: The Hidden Power in Global Capital Markets* (Princeton University Press 2019).

[39] Edwin Hu, Intentional Access Delays, Market Quality, and Price Discovery: Evidence from IEX Becoming an Exchange (US Securities and Exchange Commission, Division of Economic and Risk Analysis Working Paper, 7 February 2018).

[40] Gaia Balp and Giovanni Strampelli, 'Preserving Capital Markets Efficiency in the High-Frequency Trading Era' [2018] University of Illinois Journal of Law, Technology & Policy 349, 388–92.

[41] Eric Budish, Peter Cramton, and John Shim, 'The High-Frequency Trading Arms Race: Frequent Batch Auctions as a Market Design Response' (2015) 130 Quarterly Journal of Economics 1547.

the floor of an exchange are subject to the same basic rules of contract and securities regulation as those using mouse-clicks and algorithms. In practice, however, the move to computer-based trading has changed the culture of the market as well as the space of regulation.[42] In addition to the usual ups and downs of financial markets, this increases the risk of crises comparable to the 2010 Flash Crash. In 2012, for example, an error in a program used by the brokerage firm Knight Capital caused a loss of almost half a billion dollars and effectively spelled the end of the company.[43]

A more compelling explanation is that additional disclosure is necessary not merely to encourage stability and discourage manipulation but to make regulation possible in the first place. This is most evident in Germany, which went beyond the EU provisions in requiring that traders flag orders generated by an algorithm so that they can be distinguished from human orders and identify the algorithm in question.[44] As we will see, this desire for transparency is replicated in other areas of AI – though the limits of 'explainability' may be approaching.[45]

1.3   Competition Law

A special case of the accelerated flow of information linked to AI is the challenge that this poses for competition law. The rise of data analytics is making businesses more efficient and creating new opportunities for growth. Yet there is also clear potential for anti-competitive conduct.

For as long as capitalism has existed, the marketplace has been characterized by buyers and sellers watching prices and adjusting them in accordance with supply and demand. Those prices were once stamped

---

[42] Marc Lenglet and Joeri Mol, 'Squaring the Speed of Light? Regulating Market Access in Algorithmic Finance' (2016) 45 Economy and Society 201; Ann-Christina Lange, Marc Lenglet, and Robert Seyfert, 'Cultures of High-Frequency Trading: Mapping the Landscape of Algorithmic Developments in Contemporary Financial Markets' (2016) 45 Economy and Society 149.

[43] Sandeep Yadav, 'Operational Risk – A Case of Knight Capital', *Newstex Global Business* (13 July 2015).

[44] Hochfrequenzhandelsgesetz [High Frequency Trading Act] 2013 (Germany) amending, inter alia, the Börsengesetz [Stock Exchange Act] and the Wertpapierhandelsgesetz [Securities Trading Act] to require additional reporting on algorithmic trades. See also Nathan Coombs, 'What Is an Algorithm? Financial Regulation in the Era of High-Frequency Trading' (2016) 45 Economy and Society 278, 279. This finds some parallels in moves to require that 'short' orders – whether executed by human or algorithm – be identified as such.

[45] See chapter six.

on items on a shop floor; changing them was a decision that might take weeks to implement. Indeed, some items sold through coin-operated machines remained at the same price for decades. A bottle of Coca Cola in the United States, for example, cost five cents from 1886 to 1959.[46]

Today, prices change in milliseconds. Dynamic pricing is the norm in retail, travel, sports, and entertainment. Occasionally, the algorithms underpinning this produce curious outcomes – as when Peter Lawrence's book *The Making of a Fly* peaked at a sale price on Amazon of almost $24m (plus $3.99 shipping).[47] In general, however, digital marketplaces allow greater transparency and lower search costs, which should be good for competition. The ability to compare prices from different retailers should empower consumers to select cheaper options or demand premium services.[48] In reality, the picture is more complex.[49]

Antitrust or competition law in various jurisdictions prohibits anti-competitive agreements and concerted practices. A century ago, this might have meant gathering executives from competitor firms in a smoke-filled ballroom, as when Elbert Gary brought US steel manufacturers to a series of dinners at the Waldorf-Astoria a century ago, inviting them to tell each other 'frankly and freely ... what prices they were charging, how much wages they were paying their men, and ... all information concerning their business'.[50] Today, vastly more data is available. Sharing data is unproblematic if it is historical, or if it is shared with consumers and government agencies.[51] As data becomes available and can be analysed in real time, however, the question of whether a company itself is meaningfully deciding to disclose pricing information may become moot.

Similar problems arise in determining whether notional competitors are colluding. A collusive equilibrium is established where there is a common

---

[46] Daniel Levy and Andrew T Young, '"The Real Thing": Nominal Price Rigidity of the Nickel Coke, 1886–1959' (2004) 36 Journal of Money, Credit, and Banking 765.

[47] Ariel Ezrachi and Maurice E Stucke, 'Artificial Intelligence & Collusion: When Computers Inhibit Competition' [2017] University of Illinois Law Review 1775, 1781.

[48] Nicolas Petit, 'Antitrust and Artificial Intelligence: A Research Agenda' (2017) 8 Journal of European Competition Law & Practice 361.

[49] See Ariel Ezrachi and Maurice E Stucke, *Virtual Competition: The Promise and Perils of the Algorithm-Driven Economy* (Harvard University Press 2016) 27–33; Julie E Cohen, *Between Truth and Power: The Legal Constructions of Informational Capitalism* (Oxford University Press 2019).

[50] William H Page, 'The Gary Dinners and the Meaning of Concerted Action' (2009) 62 Southern Methodist University Law Review 597.

[51] See, eg, Wong Chun Han et al, Data: Engine for Growth – Implications for Competition Law, Personal Data Protection and Intellectual Property Rights (Competition and Consumer Commission of Singapore, 16 August 2017).

policy, adherence to the policy is monitored, and deviations are punished. As firms increasingly use price-monitoring algorithms to track competitors' actions, however, the algorithms themselves may trend towards such a 'policy'. If the price of an item is instantly matched by a competitor, for example, there is no incentive to reduce that price – indeed, the algorithms could conclude that raising prices in parallel is the rational response. Without evidence of direct or indirect communication between the parties, however, collusion is difficult to establish. If the algorithms themselves are proprietary, or exceptionally complex, it may be impossible.[52]

These are not merely theoretical concerns. In 2015, the US Department of Justice (DOJ) charged the perpetrators of a price-fixing scheme selling posters through Amazon Marketplace. The scheme involved an algorithm that collected competitor pricing information online and applied the sellers' pricing rules. According to the DOJ press release: 'We will not tolerate anticompetitive conduct, whether it occurs in a smoke-filled room or over the Internet using complex pricing algorithms. American consumers have the right to a free and fair marketplace online, as well as in brick and mortar businesses.'[53] This was, in fact, one of the simpler forms of anti-competitive conduct online. Behind it were human conspirators who had set the algorithm in motion precisely to undercut those outside the virtual cartel. More complex situations include when competitors adopt similar algorithms that, without formal co-ordination, set similar prices. Without human intent, does this amount to anti-competitive conduct? Still more difficult is the question of whether algorithms that process data concerning the entire marketplace will manipulate prices in a manner that is difficult or impossible to detect.[54]

Regulators are acutely aware of the difficulties. An Organisation for Economic Co-operation and Development (OECD) background paper warned in 2016 that finding ways to prevent collusion between self-learning algorithms could be one of the biggest challenges that competition law enforcers have ever faced.[55] 'We're talking about a velocity of decision-making that isn't really human,' a member of the US Federal

[52] Kay Firth-Butterfield, 'Artificial Intelligence and the Law: More Questions than Answers?' (2017) 14(1) Scitech Lawyer 28.
[53] Former E-Commerce Executive Charged with Price Fixing in the Antitrust Division's First Online Marketplace Prosecution (Department of Justice, 6 April 2015).
[54] Maurice E Stucke and Ariel Ezrachi, 'Antitrust, Algorithmic Pricing, and Tacit Collusion' in Woodrow Barfield and Ugo Pagallo (eds), Research Handbook on the Law of Artificial Intelligence (Edward Elgar 2018) 624 at 626–31.
[55] Big Data: Bringing Competition Policy to the Digital Era (OECD, DAF/COMP(2016)14, 27 October 2016) 24.

Trade Commission observed. 'All of the economic models are based on human incentives and what we think humans rationally will do. It's entirely possible that not all of that learning is necessarily applicable in some of these markets.'[56]

Tacit collusion by algorithms raises the concern that one of the harms intended to be avoided by competition law – higher prices – will not be matched by a remedy. As in the case of high-frequency trading, one suggestion has been to impose artificial delays in the form of a time-lag in price adjustment.[57] The alternative may be scrutinizing prices to determine whether a given mark-up is too high, a laborious and potentially pointless exercise. As the European Commission conceded, with algorithms operating more independently, their decisions will conflict with a regulatory framework designed for 'more predictable, more manageable and controllable technology'.[58]

1.4   The Problem with Speed

'Move fast and break things' was an early motto at Facebook, intended to push developers to take risks; the phrase appeared on office posters and featured in a letter from Mark Zuckerberg to investors when the company went public in 2012.[59] Over time, it came to be embraced as a mantra applicable to technological disruption more generally, glommed onto by countless Silicon Valley imitators. As Facebook matured, however, and as the potential harms caused by such disruption grew, the slogan fell from favour.[60]

---

[56]   David J Lynch, 'Policing the Digital Cartels', *Financial Times* (9 January 2017).

[57]   Paolo Siciliani, 'Tackling Algorithmic-Facilitated Tacit Collusion in a Proportionate Way' (2019) 10 Journal of European Competition Law & Practice 31, 34.

[58]   Commission Staff Working Document on the Free Flow of Data and Emerging Issues of the European Data Economy (European Commission, SWD(2017) 2, 10 January 2017) 43. A more optimistic view starts from the difficulty of policing tacit collusion between humans in the first place. In the absence of communication, it can be hard to prove or justify liability for what appears to be rational behaviour – taking a rival's prices into account when pricing one's own product. For algorithms, it would at least be theoretically possible simply to prohibit those that take interdependency of rivals into account. See Kenneth Khoo and Jerrold Soh, 'The Inefficiency of Quasi-Per Se Rules: Regulating Information Exchange in EU and US Antitrust Law' (2020) 57 American Business Law Journal 45. On tacit collusion and facilitating practices generally, see Lawrence A Sullivan, Warren S Grimes, and Christopher L Sagers, *The Law of Antitrust, An Integrated Handbook* (3rd edn, West 2014) 255–56.

[59]   Form S-1 Registration Statement of Facebook, Inc (United States Securities and Exchange Commission, 1 February 2012).

[60]   Jonathan Taplin, *Move Fast and Break Things: How Facebook, Google, and Amazon Cornered Culture and Undermined Democracy* (Little, Brown 2017); Hemant Taneja,

The speed discussed here concerns processing power and connectivity rather than innovation, but a similar reckoning will come for the digital economy, breathlessly referred to as a fourth industrial revolution.[61] It has long been clear that such speed can pose challenges to regulation. This chapter examined three areas that exemplify those challenges as they relate to the exercise of public control over AI systems. The globalization of information shows the difficulty of containing problematic activity in an interconnected world where speed has conquered distance. High-frequency trading points to the danger that the speed of decision-making can frustrate human attempts to stop it when things go off the rails. In competition law, tacit collusion by algorithms presents the real prospect that activity that would violate the law if perpetrated by humans may be impossible to detect if done by machines.

These problems – that the processing speed of AI systems may render some kinds of harm uncontainable, unstoppable, or undetectable – apply to many of the other areas of activity considered in this volume. One way of addressing them is through slowing everything down: localizing and compartmentalizing data, introducing artificial latency in trading algorithms, throwing sand in the gears of the digital marketplace.[62] Such an approach may be the only way of continuing to rely on regulatory tools designed for humans and operating on a human timescale, but it runs the risk of undermining what makes those systems valuable in the first place.

It is also unsustainable. Whether or not one accepts predictions that processing power will continue to increase forever, the prospect of slowing it down or stopping it anytime soon is remote. New rules and new institutions will be required, together with at least some role for AI systems themselves in investigating and upholding the law. These will be considered in Part III.

For the time being, those tasks fall to human hands. In the wake of the May 2010 Flash Crash, the regulators' report cited earlier was criticized for blaming a single large mutual fund for inadvertently triggering the market collapse.[63] In addition to the various safeguards put in place soon

---

'The Era of "Move Fast and Break Things" Is Over', *Harvard Business Review* (22 January 2019).

[61] See, eg, Klaus Schwab, *The Fourth Industrial Revolution* (Crown 2017).

[62] The International Committee of the Red Cross, for example, has called for AI systems deployed in conflict zones to operate at 'human speed' rather than 'machine speed'. See *Artificial Intelligence and Machine Learning in Armed Conflict: A Human-Centred Approach* (International Committee of the Red Cross, 6 June 2019) 7.

[63] *Findings Regarding the Events of May 6, 2010* (n 1) 14. The fund was later revealed to be Waddell & Reed.

afterwards – circuit-breakers, speedbumps, and so on – the investigation into the cause of the crash continued. As it did, the focus moved from rogue algorithms to a single rogue trader.

It was almost five years later that a London-based dealer was arrested for his role in causing the crash. Criminal charges brought by the US DOJ accused Navinder Singh Sarao of using an automated trading program to manipulate the market by 'spoofing' – offering $200m worth of fake bets that drove prices down, modifying them 19,000 times, and then cancelling them before they could be completed. As the market fell, he sold futures contracts only to buy them back at a lower price; when the market began to recover, he bought futures contracts and sold them at a higher price.[64] He was extradited to the United States and pleaded guilty to market manipulation that had netted him some $40m.

The indictment quoted emails in which he had requested technical support for an off-the-shelf trading program, so that he could enter 'multiple orders at different prices using one click' and to add 'a cancel if close function', so that an order was cancelled before it could be completed.[65] Dubbed by British media 'the Hound of Hounslow', some saw poetic justice in the fact that Sarao had later himself been conned out of virtually all of his ill-gotten gains. As part of a plea deal, he went on to assist US regulators in prosecuting others for market abuse.[66]

Far from being algorithms run amok, the software behind the 2010 Flash Crash faithfully executed the tasks that Sarao had asked of it. Though suggestive of the kinds of harm that trading algorithms might cause, then, the crash itself could hardly be blamed on them. Not so in the next area to be considered, when computational speed does not merely accelerate the implementation of human decisions but replaces those decisions entirely.

[64] Futures Trader Charged with Illegally Manipulating Stock Market, Contributing to the May 2010 Market 'Flash Crash' (Department of Justice, 21 April 2015).
[65] United States of America v Navinder Singh Sarao: Criminal Complaint (United States District Court, Northern District of Illinois, Eastern Division, 15 CR 75, 11 February 2015), paras 15–16.
[66] Sarao was later sentenced to one year of incarceration at his parents' home in Hounslow – returning to the very bedroom from which his crimes had been committed in the first place.

2

Autonomy

On a moonless Sunday night in March 2018, Elaine Herzberg stepped off an ornamental median strip to cross Mill Avenue in Tempe, Arizona. It was just before 10pm and the 49-year-old homeless woman was pushing a bicycle laden with shopping bags. She had nearly made it to the other side of the four-lane road when an Uber test vehicle travelling at 70 km/h collided with her from the right. Ms Herzberg, known to locals as 'Ms Elle', was taken to hospital but died of her injuries, unwittingly finding a place in history as the first pedestrian death caused by a self-driving car.

The Volvo XC90 that hit her was equipped with forward and side-facing cameras, radar and lidar (light detection and ranging), as well as navigation sensors and an integrated computing and data storage unit. A report by the US National Transportation Safety Board concluded that the vehicle detected Ms Herzberg, but that the software classified her as an unknown object, as a vehicle, and then as a bicycle with an uncertain future travel path. Just over a second before impact, the AI system determined that emergency braking was needed – but this had been disabled to reduce the potential for 'erratic vehicle behaviour'.[1]

It is still not entirely clear what went wrong on Mill Avenue that night. Uber removed its test vehicles from the four US cities in which they had been operating, but eight months later they were back on the road – though now limited to 40 km/h and no longer allowed to drive at night or in wet weather.

A key feature of modern AI systems is the ability to operate without human intervention. It is commonly said that such systems operate 'autonomously'. As a preliminary matter, it is helpful to distinguish between *automated* and *autonomous* activities. Many vehicles have automated functions, such as cruise control, which regulates speed. These functions are supervised by the driver, who remains in active control of

---

[1] Preliminary Report Highway HWY18MH010 (National Transport Safety Board, 24 May 2018).

the vehicle. Autonomous in this context means that the vehicle itself is capable of taking decisions without input from the driver – indeed, there may be no 'driver' at all.

The vehicle that killed Elaine Herzberg was operating autonomously, but it was not empty. Sitting in the driver's seat was Rafaela Vasquez, hired by Uber as a safety driver. The safety driver was expected to intervene and take action if necessary, though the system was not designed to alert her to do so. Police later determined that Ms Vasquez had most likely been watching a streaming video – an episode of the televised singing competition 'The Voice', it seems – for the 20 minutes prior to the crash. System data showed that, just before impact, she did reach for the steering wheel and applied the brakes about a second later – after hitting the pedestrian. Once the car had stopped, it was Ms Vasquez who called 911 for assistance.

Who should be held responsible for such an incident: Uber? The 'driver'? The company that made the AI system controlling the vehicle? The car itself? No one?[2] The idea that no one should be held to account for the death of a pedestrian strikes most observers as wrong, yet hesitation as to the relative fault of the other parties suggests the need for greater clarity as to how responsibility should be determined. As systems operating with varying degrees of autonomy become more sophisticated and more prevalent, that need will become more acute.

Though the problem of autonomy is treated as a single quality of AI systems, this chapter develops a typology of autonomy that highlights three discrete sets of regulatory challenges, epitomized by three spheres of activity in which those systems display degrees of autonomous behaviour.[3]

The first and most prominent is autonomous vehicles. Certain forms of transportation have long operated without active human control in limited circumstances – autopilot on planes while cruising, for example, or driverless light rail. As the level of autonomy has increased, however, and as vehicles such as driverless cars and buses interact with other road users, it is necessary to consider how existing rules on liability for damage may need to be adapted, and whether criminal laws that presume the presence of a driver need to be reviewed. Various jurisdictions are already experimenting with regulatory reform intended to reap the anticipated

---

[2] There is also an argument that the late Ms Herzberg might have been at least partly at fault.

[3] Specific responses, such as novel means of allocating responsibility and the possibility that AI systems might themselves be treated as legal persons, are considered in chapters four and five respectively.

safety and efficiency benefits without exposing road users to unnecessary risk or unallocated losses.

The second example discussed here is autonomous weapons. Where driverless cars and buses raise issues of liability and punishment for harm caused, lethal autonomous weapon systems pose discrete moral questions about the transfer of *intentional* life-and-death decisions to non-human processes. Concerns about autonomy in this context focus not only on how to manage risk but also on whether it should be permissible in any circumstances.

A third set of autonomous practices is less visible but more pervasive: decision-making by algorithm. Many routine decisions benefit from the processing power of computers. In cases where similar facts should lead to similar treatment, an algorithm may yield fair and consistent results. Yet when decisions affect the rights and obligations of individuals, automated decision-making processes risk treating their human subjects purely as means rather than ends.

As indicated in the introduction, each of these topics has been the subject of book-length treatments.[4] The aim here is not to attempt a complete study of their technical aspects but to test the ability of existing regulatory structures to deal with autonomy more generally. Far from a single quality, these examples reveal discrete concerns about autonomous decision-making by AI systems: the practical challenges of managing risk associated with new technologies, the morality of certain decisions being made by machines at all, and the legitimacy gap when public authorities delegate their powers to algorithms.

2.1 Driverless Cars and the Management of Risk

Modern transportation law typically assumes the presence of a driver, pilot, or captain. In some cases, this is explicit. A 'ship', for example, is defined in some jurisdictions as being a 'manned' [*sic*] vessel.[5] More often, it is implicit – either because laws were written on the assumption that there would be a person in charge of any vehicle, or because in the absence of an identifiable individual there is no one to hold to account if

---

[4] See the introduction to this book at nn 8–10.
[5] Robert Veal and Michael Tsimplis, 'The Integration of Unmanned Ships into the *Lex Maritima*' [2017] Lloyd's Maritime and Commercial Law Quarterly 303, 308–14.

a civil wrong occurs or a crime is committed.[6] The 1968 Vienna Convention on Road Traffic, for example, provides that every moving vehicle on the roads 'shall have a driver'.[7]

Experimentation with varying degrees of automation in cars goes back decades, but truly autonomous vehicles on public roads became a more realistic prospect only in the 2010s. As technology advanced, it became helpful to define more precisely what 'autonomous' might mean. In 2013, the US Department of Transportation released a policy on automated vehicle development that included five levels of automation.[8] The Society of Automotive Engineers (SAE) released its own report the following year with six levels, drawing also on work done by the German Federal Highway Research Institute.[9] The SAE report has been updated twice, most recently in 2018, and the six levels are now the industry standard.[10]

At level zero (no automation), the human driver is in complete control and performs all the driving functions; at level five (full automation), the vehicle is entirely self-driven and requires no human input whatsoever. Between these extremes, increasing amounts of control are handed off to the driving system. Level one denotes driver assistance through technologies such as cruise control, which maintains speed even as the driver remains in charge of the vehicle. In practical terms, this means the driver keeps his or her hands on the wheel. At level two, partial automation may enable the vehicle to take control of accelerating, braking, and steering, but the driver must monitor the driving environment. Though sometimes described as 'hands off' mode, the driver must be ready to resume control at any time.

Level three, conditional automation, marks an inflection point. Now the driving system is primarily responsible for monitoring the environment and controlling the vehicle; the human driver may direct his or her attention elsewhere but is expected to respond to a request to intervene.

---

[6] This is not limited to mechanical vehicles. In some jurisdictions, for example, horses are 'vehicles' for the purposes of road transportation law only when a rider is present. See generally Brenda Gilligan, *Practical Horse Law: A Guide for Owners and Riders* (Blackwell Science 2002) 106–12.

[7] Convention on Road Traffic, done at Vienna, 8 November 1968, in force 21 May 1977, art 8.

[8] US Department of Transportation Releases Policy on Automated Vehicle Development (Department of Transportation, 30 May 2013).

[9] Taxonomy and Definitions for Terms Related to On-Road Motor Vehicle Automated Driving Systems (Society of Automotive Engineers, 2014).

[10] Taxonomy and Definitions for Terms Related to On-Road Motor Vehicle Automated Driving Systems (revised) (Society of Automotive Engineers, 2018).

High automation, level four, removes the need for the human driver to respond to a request with the ability to bring the vehicle to a stop in the event that the human does not take control. Level three is sometimes described as 'eyes off' the road, while level four is colloquially known as 'mind off'. At level five, no human intervention would be required at all, leading to its characterization as 'steering wheel optional'.

The importance of that inflection point between levels two and three is apparent when it comes to liability, though where level two ends and level three begins may not always be clear. In theory, the Uber test vehicle described in the opening of this chapter was a level two vehicle, but its 'driver' appears to have acted as though it were level three. That divergence highlights one of the significant dangers of increased autonomy if it relies on the presence of someone ready to seize control of the vehicle at any moment. Though satisfying the legal fiction that there is a 'driver', the reality is that humans not actively engaged in a task such as driving – that is, when their hands are off the wheel – are unlikely to maintain for any length of time the level of attention necessary to serve the function of backup driver in an emergency.[11] For this reason, several car manufacturers have announced that they plan to skip SAE level three completely.[12]

Many observers believe that autonomous vehicles will eventually be far safer than human drivers and ultimately replace them.[13] Presently, more than a million people die each year in traffic accidents around the world, with the vast majority of these deaths caused by driver error.[14] As autonomous vehicles become more common, continued reliance on the fiction that there is a driver may become divorced from the reality of transportation. A British Law Commission discussion paper has proposed the concept of a 'user-in-charge', designating a person who might be required to take over in specified circumstances.[15] That intermediary

---

[11] Raja Parasuraman and Dietrich Manzey, 'Complacency and Bias in Human Use of Automation: An Attentional Integration' (2010) 52 Human Factors 381.

[12] Paresh Dave, 'Google Ditched Autopilot Driving Feature after Test User Napped Behind Wheel', *Reuters* (31 October 2017); 'Why Car-Makers Are Skipping SAE Level-3 Automation?', *M14 Intelligence* (20 February 2018).

[13] See, eg, Tracy Hresko Pearl, 'Fast & Furious: The Misregulation of Driverless Cars' (2017) 73 New York University Annual Survey of American Law 24, 35–39. Cf Hannah YeeFen Lim, *Autonomous Vehicles and the Law: Technology, Algorithms, and Ethics* (Edward Elgar 2018) 1–2 (arguing that claims of autonomous vehicle safety have been greatly exaggerated).

[14] See, eg, Road Traffic Injuries (World Health Organization, 7 February 2020).

[15] Automated Vehicles: A Joint Preliminary Consultation Paper (Law Commission, Consultation Paper No 240; Scottish Law Commission, Discussion Paper No 166, 2018), para 1.42.

step between a true driver and a mere passenger helpfully focuses attention on the grey zone of responsibility, but it does not resolve the
question of who will be held to account if something goes wrong.

2.1.1   Civil Liability

For the purposes of civil liability – the obligation to compensate another
person that is injured, for example – existing rules can largely accommodate autonomous vehicles. Presently, if someone carelessly drives over
your foot, say, the driver may be required to pay for your medical
expenses. If your foot is injured because the car explodes due to
a defective petrol tank, then the manufacturer may be liable. Insurance
helps to allocate these costs more efficiently and many jurisdictions
already require minimum levels of cover or remove questions of fault
from personal injuries due to traffic accidents by providing compulsory
coverage. These possibilities of a suit for the tort of negligence, product
liability, and statutory requirements for insurance will address most of
the harms associated with autonomous vehicles.[16]

In terms of negligence, a preliminary question is whether a duty of care
is owed to those who might be harmed. In general, the driver of a car
owes a duty of care to other road users.[17] On SAE levels zero, one, and
two, this duty of care clearly applies. In some cases, the driver's employer
may also assume such a duty. After the incident described in the opening of
this chapter, for example, Uber reached an undisclosed settlement with the
family of Ms Herzberg – implicitly recognizing liability. At levels three and
four, however, even if a duty of care were found to exist on the part of the
'driver', the standard of care owed would diminish as the responsibility for
controlling the vehicle is assumed by the manufacturer.[18] At level five,
there may be no driver at all.

A key question, considered in chapter four, is how responsibility for
actions on the part of an AI system – in this case an autonomous vehicle –
is to be determined. Though it is conceivable that a system itself might

---

[16] See also chapter four, section 4.1.
[17] Robert M Merkin and Jeremy Stuart-Smith, *The Law of Motor Insurance* (Sweet & Maxwell 2004) 186–88.
[18] Jonathan Morgan, 'Torts and Technology' in Roger Brownsword, Eloise Scotford, and Karen Yeung (eds), *The Oxford Handbook of Law, Regulation, and Technology* (Oxford University Press 2017) 522 at 538. Reference to the 'manufacturer' here may be compli-cated by diverse parties involved in production and maintenance of autonomous vehicles, but these are not new problems in product liability. See chapter four, section 4.1.3.

have sufficient legal personality to be capable of committing a tort,[19] the more likely scenario is that potential gaps in accountability under civil law will be filled by product liability and by statute. Volvo's CEO made headlines in 2015 when he announced that the Swedish company would accept full liability for accidents when its cars are in autonomous mode.[20] This was somewhat disingenuous given that various jurisdictions already imposed high standards of care on manufacturers through product liability.

Other complications in attributing responsibility for civil law purposes include the many discrete components in an autonomous vehicle that might be defective, notably the various sensors – though these are practical rather than conceptual difficulties. Similarly, the possibility of a hacker interfering with software and thereby causing a crash is a novel challenge for liability, but not materially different from a case in which an unknown person cuts the brake cables on a traditional automobile.[21] Given the foreseeability of cybersecurity issues in autonomous vehicles, reasonable safeguards against interference would fall within the duty of care owed by the driver (to update software, for example) and the manufacturer (to provide reasonable protection against viruses and hackers).[22] Alternatively, the imposition of strict liability standards would make clear the manufacturer's responsibility to take adequate precautions. A more challenging example is where the owner or driver of a vehicle him- or herself makes changes to an autonomous vehicle – for example, overriding security protocols or enabling it to exceed speed limits – that contribute to a crash. If the situation were not covered by statute, the law of contributory negligence could apportion blame as it does in other cases.[23] Further adaptations may be required if the business

---

[19] This possibility is discussed in chapter five.

[20] Jim Gorzelany, 'Volvo Will Accept Liability for Its Self-Driving Cars', *Forbes* (9 October 2015).

[21] Daniel A Crane, Kyle D Logue, and Bryce C Pilz, 'A Survey of Legal Issues Arising from the Deployment of Autonomous and Connected Vehicles' (2017) 23 Michigan Telecommunications and Technology Law Review 191, 248–49.

[22] See Araz Taeihagh and Hazel Si Min Lim, 'Governing Autonomous Vehicles: Emerging Responses for Safety, Liability, Privacy, Cybersecurity, and Industry Risks' (2019) 39 Transport Reviews 103.

[23] See generally Vadim Mantrov, 'A Victim of a Road Traffic Accident Not Fastened by a Seat Belt and Contributory Negligence in the EU Motor Insurance Law' (2014) 5 European Journal of Risk Regulation 115; Noah M Kazis, 'Tort Concepts in Traffic Crimes' (2016) 125 Yale Law Journal 1131, 1139–41; James Goudkamp and Donal Nolan, 'Contributory Negligence in the Twenty-First Century: An Empirical Study of First Instance Decisions' (2016) 79 Modern Law Review 575.

model of transportation changes – for example, if vehicles come to be seen as a service to be used rather than a thing to be owned.[24]

Autonomous vehicles thus pose important challenges to ensure that their presumed benefits in terms of road safety and efficiency do not come at the cost of unfair or disproportionate allocation of risk. In terms of how the civil law allocates those risks, amendments to reflect a shift of responsibility from drivers to manufacturers and software providers may be necessary, but the fundamental legal concepts are sound.[25]

2.1.2   Criminal Law

Not so in relation to criminal law. Criminal law is concerned less with allocating costs than apportioning blame for the purposes of deterrence and punishment. The regulation of road traffic relies heavily on criminal offences, with the majority of those offences directed at the human driver of a motor vehicle. These include responsibility not merely for the speed and direction of the vehicle but also for its roadworthiness and his or her own fitness to drive. Drivers may also be required to have adequate insurance, to report accidents, and in some cases to control the behaviour of passengers (such as requiring children to wear seatbelts).[26] Identification of the driver in question may be aided by a presumption that it is the person in whose name a vehicle is registered. If a vehicle is caught by a speed camera, for example, that person may be presumptively responsible unless it is possible to point to the responsibility of another person.[27]

Because of the centrality of drivers, the various jurisdictions that have allowed autonomous vehicles on open roads initially provided that a human 'driver' had to be behind the wheel and alert. The first truly driverless cars on open roads were authorized in Arizona by executive order of the Governor in April 2018. The order provided, among other things, that any traffic citation or other penalty arising from infractions by the vehicle would be issued to the person 'testing or operating the fully autonomous vehicle'.[28] In practice, however, backup drivers remained in

---

[24] James Arbib and Tony Seba, Rethinking Transportation 2020–2030: The Disruption of Transportation and the Collapse of the Internal-Combustion Vehicle and Oil Industries (RethinkX, 2017).
[25] See chapter four, section 4.1.3.
[26] Law Commission Consultation Paper (n 15), para 7.1.
[27] See, eg, Road Traffic Act 1961 (Cap 276, 2004 Rev Ed, Singapore) s 81(1B).
[28] Executive Order 2018-04: Advancing Autonomous Vehicle Testing and Operation; Prioritizing Public Safety 2018 (Arizona), para 3(c).

the various cars. In the same month, California's Department of Motor Vehicles modified state regulations to allow applications for driverless testing permits.[29] Where a human backup driver is not present, a remote operator holding the appropriate licence is required to 'continuously supervise the vehicle's performance of the dynamic driving task'.[30] Other jurisdictions have similarly expanded the concept of a 'driver' to include a remote operator deemed to be in charge of the vehicle, despite not being seated within it.[31]

Singapore, like Arizona, has made provision for truly autonomous vehicles 'without the active physical control of, or monitoring by, a human operator'.[32] In Germany, amendments to the Road Traffic Act allow the use of autonomous technology comparable to level three, but require that the driver remain *'wahrnehmungsbereit'* [mentally alert] at all times and able to take control of the vehicle when prompted to do so or when *'offensichtlicher Umstände'* [obvious circumstances] require it.[33]

China adopted regulations for autonomous vehicle testing in 2018, with detailed requirements for backup drivers who would remain personally liable for any traffic violations as well as a requirement that the entity conducting the test be registered in China and have adequate civil compensation capacity for personal and property losses.[34] It is an important jurisdiction, having overtaken the United States as the largest market for automobiles in 2009.[35] Non-standardized road signage remains a problem, adding to the training time for autonomous systems. Such constraints may be offset by the more tolerant regulatory regime, far lower levels of litigation, and a willingness to embrace new technologies quickly and with higher acceptance of risk. The Chinese government has created test zones for autonomous vehicles in 14 cities, the largest being in Beijing and Shanghai. This has been accompanied by large investments on the part of companies like Alibaba, Baidu, and Tencent.

[29] Autonomous Vehicles in California (California Department of Motor Vehicles 2018).
[30] Testing of Autonomous Vehicles 2018 13 CCR § 227.02 (California).
[31] See, eg, Experimenteerwet zelfrijdende auto's 2018 (Netherlands) (Dutch law allowing the use of driverless vehicles on public roads, though requiring them to be controlled remotely by a human operator).
[32] Road Traffic (Amendment) Act 2017 (Singapore).
[33] Strassenverkehrsgesetz (StVG) [Road Traffic Act] 1909 (Germany), § 1b.
[34] 智能网联汽车道路测试管理规范（试行）[Intelligent Network Linked Vehicle Road Test Management Regulations (Trial)] 2018 (People's Republic of China).
[35] Luca Pizzuto et al, How China Will Help Fuel the Revolution in Autonomous Vehicles (McKinsey Center for Future Mobility, 2019).

In terms of the SAE levels mentioned earlier, the criminal law in these jurisdictions typically continues to assume that no vehicle is operating above level two, with a human driver bearing ongoing responsibility for its operation.[36] As autonomous vehicles become more sophisticated, this position will become untenable.

A preliminary matter is that some laws as they stand may render certain forms of autonomous driving inherently unlawful. Specific requirements that cars have a 'driver', for example, or that prohibit leaving a vehicle unattended, are incompatible with fully autonomous taxi services.[37] Unless the requirement for human drivers changes, it could also result in blameless passengers being held responsible if a vehicle makes a mistake. In addition to being unfair, this could discourage public acceptance of driverless technology.[38]

Various US states have experimented with different answers to the question of 'driverless' cars. One possibility is to continue to focus on a natural person riding in the vehicle, or controlling it remotely, as in Arizona and California.[39] This remains the most common legal position across the various jurisdictions that explicitly allow autonomous vehicles on public roads. A second approach is to target the 'operator' of the vehicle, akin to the 'user-in-charge' proposed by the British Law Commission.[40] In Georgia this means the person who 'causes' the vehicle to move.[41] Thirdly, the burden can rest on the owner of the vehicle. This is the approach adopted in Texas.[42]

A fourth possibility, thus far adopted only in Tennessee, is to define the 'automated driving system' (ADS) itself as the 'driver'. The definition of 'person', in the same 2017 amendment to the State Code, was expanded to mean 'a natural person, firm, co-partnership, association, corporation, *or an engaged ADS*'.[43] The definition applies only to provisions of the Code concerning motor vehicles, however, and it does not appear to have been invoked for the purposes of civil liability or criminal sanction. Law reform bodies in other jurisdictions, notably Australia and Britain, have

---

[36] The Arizona executive order is unusual in explicitly mentioning levels four and five: Executive Order 2018-04, para 1(d).
[37] See, eg, Road Vehicles (Construction and Use) Regulations 1986 (UK), reg 107.
[38] Michael Cameron, Realising the Potential of Driverless Vehicles: Recommendations for Law Reform (New Zealand Law Foundation, 2018) 9.
[39] See above nn 28–30.
[40] See above n 15.
[41] Official Code of Georgia Annotated § 40-1-1(38) (2017).
[42] Texas Transportation Code § 545.453(a)(1) (2017).
[43] Tennessee Code Annotated § 55-8-101 (2017) (emphasis added).

suggested the concept of an automated driving system entity (ADSE), but this refers to the legal entity responsible for the vehicle rather than a novel category of legal person.[44]

A more utopian vision is that driverless cars may be so superior to human drivers that there is no need to provide for criminal responsibility at all. That seems unrealistic, but it does raise the question of the function that road traffic laws are intended to fulfil, and the purpose of punishing proscribed conduct. The two basic aims of road traffic law are promoting safety and order on the roads.[45] As Australia's National Transport Commission (NTC) has observed, existing penalties seek to influence the behaviour of human drivers. An individual who breaches the rules may be punished, or his or her licence may be suspended or revoked. In the case of autonomous vehicles, monetary and custodial punishments may be less appropriate than seeing enforcement as part of a feedback loop to train the system. This could take the form of improvement notices and enforceable undertakings to increase safety.[46] In more serious cases, withdrawing the authorization to drive on the roads may be sufficient to protect other road users, while traditional penalties could be applied to natural or legal persons if there is evidence of wrongdoing that rises to the level of a crime.

Larger questions of whether and how AI systems themselves might be 'punished' will be considered in chapter five.[47] For present purposes, what is interesting is that, in its application to autonomous vehicles, the criminal law sheds its deontological overtones in favour of instrumentalism: rather than moral failings to be corrected, violations may come to be seen as errors to be debugged.[48]

2.1.3   Ethics

The possibility that autonomous vehicles will – eventually – be significantly better drivers than humans has invited much speculation about

---

[44] Changing Driving Laws to Support Automated Vehicles (Policy Paper) (National Transport Commission, May 2018) para 1.5; Law Commission Consultation Paper (n 15) para 4.107.

[45] Sally Cunningham, *Driving Offences: Law, Policy and Practice* (Routledge 2008) 1–6.

[46] Changing Driving Laws (n 44) para 8.2.1. See also Law Commission Consultation Paper (n 15) paras 7.33–7.34. It would depend, of course, on why a given violation took place. If the violation were due to an override by the driver/user-in-charge, for example, traditional penalties might apply.

[47] See chapter five, section 5.1.2(b).

[48] See also chapter nine, section 9.3.2.

how they can and should behave in limit situations, such as an impending crash. Human drivers are usually held to the standard of the 'reasonable driver'.[49] If a child runs onto a street, for example, swerving to avoid him or her might be a violation of the road rules – but unlikely to be one that is prosecuted. Swerving to avoid a rat, by contrast, may not be excused.[50] An autonomous vehicle will respond more swiftly, but lacks the moral compass expected to guide a human. That must be programmed in or learned through experience.[51]

A common illustration of the dilemmas that can arise is the trolley problem used by ethicists. A single-carriage train is heading towards five people and will kill them all. If a lever is pulled, the train will be diverted onto a siding but will kill someone else. Do you pull the lever? Though many people would do so, there is no 'right' answer to this question. When confronted with an analogous situation in which five people are going to die and the only way to stop the train is by pushing someone into its path, most people tend to hold back. The first scenario reflects a utilitarian approach that looks to the consequences of an action (one death versus five). The second *feels* different because we know intuitively that pushing a person to their death is wrong – even though the choice is still between one person and five people dying.[52]

Researchers at MIT developed a Moral Machine that offers these and a dozen other scenarios that might confront driverless cars. Should two passengers be sacrificed if it would save five pedestrians? Does it matter if the pedestrians were jaywalking? If they were criminals? In real life, faster reaction times mean that braking will almost certainly be the best choice, but for the purposes of the experiment one is to assume that the brakes have failed and that the vehicle cannot stop. In an unusual sampling method, they abandoned standard academic survey approaches to deploy

---

[49] Jeffrey K Gurney, 'Imputing Driverhood: Applying a Reasonable Driver Standard to Accidents Caused by Autonomous Vehicles' in Patrick Lin, Keith Abney, and Ryan Jenkins (eds), *Robot Ethics 2.0: From Autonomous Cars to Artificial Intelligence* (Oxford University Press 2017) 51.

[50] See Filippo Santoni de Sio, 'Killing by Autonomous Vehicles and the Legal Doctrine of Necessity' (2017) 20 Ethical Theory and Moral Practice 411.

[51] Ivó Coca-Vila, 'Self-Driving Cars in Dilemmatic Situations: An Approach Based on the Theory of Justification in Criminal Law' (2018) 12 Criminal Law and Philosophy 59.

[52] See generally David Edmonds, *Would You Kill the Fat Man? The Trolley Problem and What Your Answer Tells Us about Right and Wrong* (Princeton University Press 2013); Thomas Cathcart, *The Trolley Problem; or, Would You Throw the Fat Guy Off the Bridge? A Philosophical Conundrum* (Workman 2013).

a 'viral online platform' – raising problems of self-selection but enabling them to gather data from millions of people all over the world.[53]

Among the interesting findings were clear global preferences for sparing human lives over animals, sparing more lives, and sparing young lives. The first of these is consistent with rules proposed by the German Ethics Commission on Automated and Connected Driving; the last, however, runs directly counter to a proposed prohibition on making distinctions based on personal features such as age.[54] In a subsequent interview about the paper, one of its authors was asked about the implicit prejudices disclosed in the results – sparing professionals over the homeless, the healthy over the obese, dogs over criminals, and so on. 'That suggests to us that we shouldn't leave decisions completely in the hands of the demos,' he replied.[55]

In practice, it should be noted, 'dilemma situations' like these are overly reductive. They posit the false dichotomy of exactly one out of two results, when the reality of any actual road incident is that there are a great many possible outcomes.[56] That is especially true of those scenarios in which a vehicle must either kill its occupants or kill pedestrians. In any event, executives at Mercedes-Benz are on record saying that they will prioritize the lives of passengers in its cars.[57] A paper published in *Science* supports this commercial decision: while many people approve of autonomous vehicles sacrificing a passenger to save other people in theory, they are unlikely to buy or ride in a car programmed that way in practice.[58]

Regulators, for their part, have emphasized the importance of safety in a general sense, but without weighing in on specific choices to be made by autonomous vehicles in limit situations. While human drivers predominate on the roads, the standard of the reasonable driver will persist and autonomous vehicles will be measured against that. If and when those

---

[53] Edmond Awad et al, 'The Moral Machine Experiment' (2018) 563 Nature 59, 63.

[54] Christoph Luetge, 'The German Ethics Code for Automated and Connected Driving' (2017) 30 Philosophy & Technology 547.

[55] Caroline Lester, 'A Study on Driverless-Car Ethics Offers a Troubling Look into Our Values', *New Yorker* (24 January 2019) (quoting Azim Shariff).

[56] Tom Michael Gasser, 'Fundamental and Special Legal Questions for Autonomous Vehicles' in Markus Maurer et al (eds), *Autonomous Driving: Technical, Legal and Social Aspects* (Springer 2016) 523 at 533–34.

[57] Michael Taylor, 'Self-Driving Mercedes-Benzes Will Prioritize Occupant Safety over Pedestrians', *Car and Driver* (8 October 2016).

[58] Jean-François Bonnefon, Azim Shariff, and Iyad Rahwan, 'The Social Dilemma of Autonomous Vehicles' (2016) 352(6293) Science 1573.

proportions are switched, new standards may be required, with a corresponding move from licensing the skills of a driver to certifying the safety of a product.

2.2   Killer Robots and the Morality of Outsourcing

Autonomous vehicles raise concerns about how they fit into existing models of civil and criminal liability, as well as how AI systems should take decisions in life-and-death situations such as an imminent crash. These are, in many ways, problems to manage through technical improvement and regulatory tweaks. The prospect of truly autonomous weapon systems, by contrast, has led to calls for a moratorium or an outright ban.[59]

In one sense, this is irrational. Much as autonomous vehicles offer the prospect of reducing the number of deaths and injuries caused by driver error behind the wheel, reducing mistakes and excesses on the battlefield has the potential to lessen the human costs of warfare. Many 'dumb' devices are, in any case, already 'automated'. An anti-personnel landmine or an improvised explosive device (IED) operates without additional human control, though it is not selective in its targeting. Heat-seeking missiles are an example of a weapon that, when launched, follows a program but is not in a meaningful sense selective. Further along the spectrum is a new generation of long-range anti-ship missiles (LRASMs), which are launched with targeting parameters but are able to search for and identify enemy warships within those parameters.

As with autonomous vehicles, the key distinction in autonomous weapons is the degree to which the system makes decisions independently. According to the US Department of Defense, an autonomous weapon system is one that, once activated, can select and engage targets without further intervention by a human operator.[60] Similarly, the International Committee of the Red Cross (ICRC) has emphasized that autonomy in this context should focus on the critical functions of selecting and attacking targets, as opposed to movement or navigation.[61]

---

[59] Losing Humanity: The Case Against Killer Robots (Human Rights Watch, 2012); Michael Press, 'Of Robots and Rules: Autonomous Weapon Systems in the Law of Armed Conflict' (2017) 48 Georgetown Journal of International Law 1337, 1344.

[60] Autonomy in Weapon Systems (Department of Defense, Directive Number 3000.09, 21 November 2012). This includes systems that allow for human override.

[61] Towards Limits on Autonomy in Weapon Systems (International Committee of the Red Cross, 9 April 2018).

There is less concern about purely defensive systems. Close-in weapon systems (CIWSs), such as the US Navy's Phalanx CIWS, were first deployed in the 1970s as the last line of defence against an attack on a ship at sea.[62] Land-based ballistic missile defence systems also have varying degrees of automation – most prominently the US Patriot Missile and Israel's 'Iron Dome', which identify and attempt to destroy rockets and artillery shells.[63] Stationary anti-personnel weapons, such as sentry guns, have been deployed in the Demilitarized Zone between North and South Korea, though their true degree of autonomy is disputed.[64]

Offensive autonomous weapons have yet to be widely deployed, but the technology is rapidly advancing in that direction. Various unmanned aerial vehicles, or drones, have the capacity for independent targeting; some are also able to suggest targets as well as angles of attack, though decisions to engage remain the positive responsibility of their operators.[65] Other land- and sea-based combat vehicles have been developed with varying degrees of autonomy. Typically, these have been remote-controlled – though there are periodic breathless reports of killer robots deployed in theatre, as when the United States experimented in Iraq with a machine-gun tank system called 'SWORDS' in 2007.[66]

A dozen years later, the US Army sparked controversy in 2019 when it put out a request for vendors to help build its Advanced Targeting and Lethality Automated System (ATLAS). The initial call said that the hope was to develop combat vehicles with the ability to 'acquire, identify, and engage targets at least 3X faster than the current manual process'. After news headlines announced that the Pentagon was about to turn its tanks into 'AI-powered killing machines', the announcement was modified to emphasize that there had been no change in Department of Defense policy on autonomy in weapon systems.[67] That policy remains that

---

[62] Similar systems include Russia's Kaftan CIWS and China's Type 730 CIWS.

[63] See, eg, Michael J Armstrong, 'Modeling Short-Range Ballistic Missile Defense and Israel's Iron Dome System' (2014) 62 Operations Research 1028.

[64] Ian Kerr and Katie Szilagyi, 'Evitable Conflicts, Inevitable Technologies? The Science and Fiction of Robotic Warfare and IHL' (2018) 14 Law, Culture and the Humanities 45, 52.

[65] Kenneth Anderson and Matthew Waxman, Law and Ethics for Autonomous Weapon Systems: Why a Ban Won't Work and How the Laws of War Can (Hoover Institution, 2013) 4.

[66] Noah Shachtman, 'First Armed Robots on Patrol in Iraq (Updated)', Wired (2 August 2007). The Special Weapons Observation Reconnaissance Detection System (SWORDS) was essentially a repurposed remote-controlled bomb disposal unit.

[67] Industry Day for the Advanced Targeting and Lethality Automated System (ATLAS) Program (Department of the Army, Solicitation Number: W909MY-19-R-C004, 11 February 2019).

autonomous weapon systems must allow commanders and operators to 'exercise appropriate levels of human judgment' over the use of force.[68]

Many commentators accept that an increasing degree of autonomy on the battlefield is inevitable, and that the superiority of autonomous weapon systems over humans is inevitable also.[69] Yet the view that the finger on the trigger must be flesh and blood rather than metal and silicon is widely held, and points to something qualitatively different from debates over autonomy in transportation.

2.2.1   International Humanitarian Law

In contrast to many of the legal regimes considered in this book, international humanitarian law explicitly provides for its application to new and emerging technologies. This provision takes the form of the Martens Clause, named after the Russian delegate who introduced it at the 1899 Hague Peace Conference. The text made its way into the preamble of the Convention on the Laws and Customs of War in the following form:

> Until a more complete code of the laws of war is issued, the High Contracting Parties think it right to declare that in cases not included in the Regulations adopted by them, populations and belligerents remain under the protection and empire of the principles of international law, as they result from the usages established between civilized nations, from the laws of humanity, and the requirements of the public conscience.[70]

Over the subsequent decades, text that was originally a cunning diplomatic manoeuvre to break a deadlock came to be invested with far greater significance – at times treated as though it created a new source of law, rather than being an interpretive tool to be applied in cases of uncertainty.[71] When the International Court of Justice was asked to consider the legality of the threat or use of nuclear weapons, for example, it noted that the Martens Clause – now enshrined in Article 1(2) of the First Additional Protocol to the Geneva Conventions – made clear that

---

[68]   Autonomy in Weapon Systems (n 60), para 4a.
[69]   As early as 2001, for example, the US Congress set the goal of making one-third of combat aircraft unmanned by 2010 and one-third of combat ground vehicles unmanned by 2015: Floyd D Spence National Defense Authorization Act for Fiscal Year 2001 2000, Pub L No 106-398 (US), s 220.
[70]   Convention (II) with Respect to the Laws and Customs of War on Land and Its Annex: Regulations Concerning the Laws and Customs of War on Land (1899 Hague Regulations), done at The Hague, 29 July 1899, preamble.
[71]   Antonio Cassese, 'The Martens Clause: Half a Loaf or Simply Pie in the Sky?' (2000) 11 European Journal of International Law 187, 212–14.

the 'principles and rules of humanitarian law' apply to those weapons, notwithstanding the lack of a specific treaty to that effect.[72]

Yet applying those principles and rules to new technology is not a simple task. It is sometimes argued that computers should not be empowered to make life and death decisions because of the 'infinite number of possible scenarios' in which such decisions might be made.[73] This is one of the weaker arguments against autonomy, as the underlying concern is not the ability of an AI system to respond to limitless scenarios but the ability of a human to be able to program them in advance. Indeed, some commentators argue that AI systems may be *more* capable of compliance with the laws of war than their human counterparts.[74] Unlike humans, who must be trained, autonomous weapon systems could have these rules programmed in and be required to act on them without emotion. Many war crimes arise not from conscious decisions to violate rules of engagement but as a result of fatigue, fear, or anger – precisely the qualities that machines are built to avoid.[75]

Another set of concerns recalls the non-trivial possibility that a truly intelligent system in the sense of general AI might decide that humans were its enemy.[76] The prospect of an autonomous weapon system turning on its creator is one of the more visceral images of the threat of AI – epitomized and immortalized in the various *Terminator* movies. Though nothing quite so dramatic has yet occurred on the battlefield, there have been incidents of friendly fire by autonomous systems that experienced targeting errors or engaged friendly craft that came within the system's engagement envelope.

---

[72] *Legality of the Threat or Use of Nuclear Weapons (Advisory Opinion)* [1996] ICJ Rep 226 (International Court of Justice), para 87.

[73] Shaking the Foundations: The Human Rights Implications of Killer Robots (Human Rights Watch, 2014).

[74] See, eg, Kenneth Anderson, Daniel Reisner, and Matthew Waxman, 'Adapting the Law of Armed Conflict to Autonomous Weapon Systems' (2014) 90 International Law Studies 386, 411; Pedro Domingos, *The Master Algorithm: How the Quest for the Ultimate Learning Machine Will Remake Our World* (Basic Books 2015) 280.

[75] Ronald C Arkin, 'The Case for Ethical Autonomy in Unmanned Systems' (2010) 9 Journal of Military Ethics 332; Kenneth Anderson and Matthew C Waxman, 'Debating Autonomous Weapon Systems, Their Ethics, and Their Regulation under International Law' in Roger Brownsword, Eloise Scotford, and Karen Yeung (eds), *The Oxford Handbook of Law, Regulation, and Technology* (Oxford University Press 2017) 1097 at 1108–10.

[76] See chapter five, section 5.3.

In some cases, those involved in the development of AI systems have expressed a simple aversion to being involved in military projects at all. When the role of Google in the US Department of Defense's Project Maven was revealed, thousands of employees signed a letter demanding that it withdraw from the project and commit that neither the company nor its contractors would ever build 'warfare technology'.[77] It is tempting to dismiss this as the conceit of employees working for a company whose slogan was once 'don't be evil',[78] but such 'twinges of indignation'[79] are apparent in many aspects of the autonomous weapon systems debates.

2.2.2   Human-out-of-the-Loop?

Central to many of the worries expressed is that dissociation from the choice of whom to kill weakens the moral dilemma that should accompany all such decisions.[80] One could argue that this applies to other sanitized military operations – from launching a cruise missile against faceless targets to the drone operator at an army base who goes home for dinner.[81] The distinction of truly autonomous weapon systems, however, is that in addition to being physically absent from the battlefield, handing over life-and-death decisions to algorithms means that human operators may be psychologically absent also.[82] In a 2018 speech to the General Assembly, UN Secretary-General António Guterres denounced this prospect as 'morally repugnant'.[83]

With regard to lethal force, it is often argued, the decision whether to use it should be made by a human – and it should be possible to hold that human accountable for his or her actions afterwards. This view is based on the conception of warfare itself as an intimately human institution. As

---

[77] Project Maven focuses on computer vision, using machine learning to extract objects of interest from moving or still imagery. Cheryl Pellerin, Project Maven to Deploy Computer Algorithms to War Zone by Year's End (Department of Defense, 21 July 2017).

[78] Ken Auletta, *Googled: The End of the World as We Know It* (Penguin 2009) 20; Steven Levy, *In the Plex: How Google Thinks, Works, and Shapes Our Lives* (New York 2011) 144.

[79] Helen Nissenbaum, 'Protecting Privacy in an Information Age: The Problem of Privacy in Public' (1998) 17 Law and Philosophy 559, 583.

[80] See, eg, Wendell Wallach, *A Dangerous Master: How to Keep Technology from Slipping beyond Our Control* (Basic Books 2015) 213–34.

[81] Cf Jean Baudrillard, *The Gulf War Never Happened* (Polity Press 1995).

[82] Christof Heyns, 'Autonomous Weapons Systems: Living a Dignified Life and Dying a Dignified Death' in Nehal Bhuta et al (eds), *Autonomous Weapons Systems: Law, Ethics, Policy* (Cambridge University Press 2016) 3 at 4.

[83] António Guterres, 'Address to the General Assembly' (United Nations, New York, 25 September 2018).

Michael Walzer has observed: 'It is one of the most important features of war, distinguishing it from the other scourges of mankind, that the men and women caught up in it are not only victims, they are also participants. All of us are inclined to hold them responsible for what they do.'[84] Were autonomous weapon systems to become widespread, the costs of war could be reduced – even more than they have been already in industrialized countries – to technical and material constraints. The juxtaposition of such systems with human adversaries, cold logic versus mortal fear, would, the argument continues, be corrosive of the equal dignity of humans.[85] It also suggests the likely progression of an autonomous weapons arms race: once such systems are deployed by one side, it would be difficult to justify sending human soldiers into battle against them.[86]

At the international level, opposition to autonomous weapon systems has tended to vary inversely with capacity. There is some support for a complete treaty ban among a handful of states, but without the involvement of states possessing advanced technological and military capabilities, a notional ban would be posturing at best. Scholars from the Military Law Institute at the China University of Political Science and Law, for example, have argued that states with advanced AI technology should play an 'exemplary' role – going on to propose that a military commander or civilian official who employs a weapon system operating with 'full autonomy' should bear personal responsibility for violations of international humanitarian law (IHL) that ensue.[87]

Two areas of ongoing discussion are in the context of weapons reviews and a possible requirement of 'meaningful human control'. Article 36 of the First Additional Protocol to the Geneva Conventions provides that the 'study, development, acquisition or adoption of a new weapon, means or method of warfare' requires states parties to determine whether its use

---

[84] Michael Walzer, *Just and Unjust Wars: A Moral Argument with Historical Illustrations* (3rd edn, Basic Books 2000) 15.

[85] Nehal Bhuta, Susanne Beck, and Robin Geiß, 'Present Futures: Concluding Reflections and Open Questions on Autonomous Weapons Systems' in Nehal Bhuta et al (eds), *Autonomous Weapons Systems: Law, Ethics, Policy* (Cambridge University Press 2016) 347 at 355–56.

[86] Leonard Kahn, 'Military Robots and the Likelihood of Armed Conflict' in Patrick Lin, Keith Abney, and Ryan Jenkins (eds), *Robot Ethics 2.0: From Autonomous Cars to Artificial Intelligence* (Oxford University Press 2017) 274 at 283.

[87] Li Qiang and Xie Dan, 'Legal Regulation of AI Weapons under International Humanitarian Law: A Chinese Perspective', *ICRC Humanitarian Law & Policy Blog* (2 May 2019).

would violate international law. This has been endorsed by the UN Group of Governmental Experts examining lethal autonomous weapon systems as a potential guiding principle in this area.[88] Though some have argued that Article 36 reflects customary international law, the ICRC has held that reviews of new weapons are necessary in any event as part of a 'faithful and responsible' application of compliance with international law obligations.[89] The United States, for its part, introduced comparable processes three years before Protocol I came into force and declined to develop blinding laser weapons in the 1990s after such a review.[90]

Determinations as to whether a weapon would violate international law tend to focus on whether it would be inherently indiscriminate or cause unnecessary suffering or superfluous injury. Though it has been argued that autonomous weapon systems are necessarily indiscriminate because they lack the human qualities necessary to identify combatants and assess the intentions of other humans, these are practical challenges to the sensory and analytical capabilities of such systems.[91] Similarly, it has been argued that a machine will be unable to distinguish incapacitated or surrendering enemies from legitimate targets and thus will cause unnecessary suffering. Again, this is a surmountable problem – comparable, perhaps, to some of the challenges facing autonomous vehicles navigating among human drivers and pedestrians.[92]

Of greater importance, in the context of autonomous weapon systems, is not the capabilities of the machines but the absence of humans. The ICRC issued a statement in 2018 that emphasized the importance of human involvement – not because of a superior capacity to identify or understand

---

[88] Report of the 2018 Session of the Group of Governmental Experts on Emerging Technologies in the Area of Lethal Autonomous Weapons Systems, UN Doc CCW/GGE.2/2018/3 (2018), para 26(d).

[89] A Guide to the Legal Review of New Weapons, Means and Methods of Warfare: Measures to Implement Article 36 of Additional Protocol I of 1977 (International Committee of the Red Cross, January 2006) 4.

[90] Anderson and Waxman, Law and Ethics for AWS (n 65) 10. See The Defense Acquisition System (Department of Defense, Directive Number 5000.01, 9 September 2020), s 1.2(v).

[91] Ryan Poitras, 'Article 36 Weapons Reviews & Autonomous Weapons Systems: Supporting an International Review Standard' (2018) 34 American University International Law Review 465, 486–89.

[92] Cf Noel Sharkey, 'Staying in the Loop: Human Supervisory Control of Weapons' in Nehal Bhuta et al (eds), Autonomous Weapons Systems: Law, Ethics, Policy (Cambridge University Press 2016) 23 at 24–27.

other humans but to grapple meaningfully with the moral dilemma of whether force should be used and to take responsibility if it is.[93]

Despite resistance to an outright ban on autonomous weapons, calls for 'meaningful human control' have gained traction – even though such control may be inconsistent with a weapons system that is truly autonomous. At present, the lowest common denominator appears to be a possible ban on fully autonomous weapons that operate in such a manner that their mission, once started, cannot be aborted. The prospect of truly 'human-out-of-the-loop' machines running loose even after the conclusion of hostilities appears sufficient – for the time being, at least – to outweigh any benefits they might offer on the battlefield.[94]

2.2.3 Lessons from Mercenaries

As in many other aspects of regulating AI systems, there has been a tendency to view the problems posed by autonomous weapon systems as new and unique. This overlooks important analogies that can be drawn from other activities that have raised similar concerns. In particular, lessons may be drawn from efforts over the past three decades to regulate the outsourcing of warfighting capacity not to machines but to mercenaries.

Modern wariness about mercenaries and their corporate cousins, private military and security companies (PMSCs) – in particular their ability to use lethal force – stems from a belief that such decisions should be made within a framework that allows not merely legal but also political and moral accountability.[95] Today it is 'common sense' that the control and use of violence should be limited to states. But it was not always so. The Pope, for example, is still protected by a private Swiss regiment first hired in 1502. Echoes of the past acceptability of mercenarism also live on in our language. The term 'freelance', for example, now means a casual worker, but historically it referred literally to a free agent in possession of a lance.[96]

---

[93] Towards Limits on Autonomy (n 61). See also Artificial Intelligence and Machine Learning in Armed Conflict: A Human-Centred Approach (International Committee of the Red Cross, 6 June 2019) 7–10.

[94] Amitai Etzioni and Oren Etzioni, 'Pros and Cons of Autonomous Weapons Systems', *Military Review* (May–June 2017) 71, 79–80. For a discussion of 'human-out-of-the-loop' and other decision-making paradigms, see below section 2.3.

[95] See Simon Chesterman and Chia Lehnardt (eds), *From Mercenaries to Market: The Rise and Regulation of Private Military Companies* (Oxford University Press 2007).

[96] See generally Sarah Percy, *Mercenaries: The History of a Norm in International Relations* (Oxford University Press 2007).

Interestingly, the popularity of or disdain for mercenaries has depended on the shifting importance of military skill and military numbers, with a major influence being emergent technology. The introduction of the musket two centuries ago vastly reduced the time it took to train an effective soldier, with the result that quantity soon mattered more than quality. In such circumstances, national conscription offered a more efficient means of raising a large army. These military and economic shifts were then reinforced by politics and culture, with the result that mercenaries 'went out of style' in the nineteenth century. Reliance on mercenaries soon came to be seen as not only inefficient but suspect: a country whose men did not fight for it lacked patriots; those individuals who fought for reasons other than love of country lacked morals.[97]

The subversive role of mercenaries in Africa during the twentieth century led to efforts to ban them completely. A 1989 treaty sought to do just that, but foundered on a lack of signatures and problems of definition. A mercenary was defined as someone 'motivated to take part in the hostilities essentially by the desire for private gain'.[98] The difficulty of proving motivation led one writer to suggest that anyone convicted of an offence under the Convention should be shot – as should his lawyer.[99]

This approach contrasts with an initiative led by the Swiss government and the ICRC, which did not impose criminal liability on mercenaries but highlighted ongoing obligations of the state. A series of intergovernmental meetings led to the drafting of the Montreux Document, named after the town on Lake Geneva at which government experts met over three days in September 2008. It stresses the non-transferability of state obligations under international law, which encompasses ongoing responsibility for outsourced activities – and a prohibition on outsourcing some activities completely.[100]

---

[97] Deborah Avant, 'From Mercenary to Citizen Armies: Explaining Change in the Practice of War' (2000) 54 International Organization 41; Deborah Avant, *The Market for Force: The Consequences of Privatizing Security* (Cambridge University Press 2005).

[98] International Convention Against the Recruitment, Use, Financing, and Training of Mercenaries (Convention on Mercenaries), 4 December 1989, in force 20 October 2001, art 1(1)(b).

[99] Geoffrey Best, quoted in David Shearer, *Private Armies and Military Intervention* (Oxford University Press 1998) 18.

[100] The Montreux Document on Pertinent International Legal Obligations and Good Practices for States Related to Operations of Private Military and Security Companies During Armed Conflict (Swiss Federal Department of Foreign Affairs & International Committee of the Red Cross, 17 September 2008).

A better and more useful distinction to be drawn, then, and of relevance to the discussion here, is that some functions are 'inherently governmental' and cannot be transferred to contractors, machines, or anyone else – a concept that will be explored further in chapter four.[101]

2.3   Algorithmic Decision-Making and Legitimacy

Autonomous actions by AI systems are not limited to their physical interactions with the world. Though driverless cars and killer robots conjure the image of machines displaying independence, underlying that autonomy is a capacity to gather data and take decisions with far wider applications. As ever more commercial and governmental activity moves online, vast numbers of routine tasks can be managed without human involvement. A growing number of decisions are now made essentially by algorithms, either reaching conclusive determinations or presenting a proposed decision that may be accepted without question by the human notionally responsible.[102]

As in the case of autonomous vehicles, it is useful to distinguish between levels of autonomy in decision-making. A commonly used metaphor here is of a human being in, over, or out of a decision-making process referred to as a 'loop'. At one extreme is fully human decision-making without computer support. Recalling the SAE levels for autonomous vehicles discussed earlier, this would be akin to level zero.[103] 'Human-in-the-loop' refers to decision-making supported by the system, for example through suggesting options or recommendations, but with the human taking positive decisions. That may correspond to SAE level one or two ('hands on the wheel'). 'Human-over-the-loop' denotes a process in which the human can oversee the process and make interventions as necessary, corresponding to SAE level three or four.[104] 'Human-out-of-the-loop' means that the process runs with minimal or no human intervention, akin to SAE level five.[105]

---

[101] See chapter four, section 4.3.
[102] Cf Tarleton Gillespie, 'Algorithm' in Benjamin Peters (ed), *Digital Keywords: A Vocabulary of Information Society and Culture* (Princeton University Press 2016) 18 at 26.
[103] See above section 2.1.
[104] Austin Graham et al, 'Formalizing Interruptible Algorithms for Human Over-the-Loop Analytics' (2017 IEEE International Conference on Big Data (Big Data), Boston, MA, 2017).
[105] Cf Natasha Merat et al, 'The "Out-of-the-Loop" Concept in Automated Driving: Proposed Definition, Measures and Implications' (2019) 21 Cognition, Technology &

Another distinction can be made between algorithmic processes broadly comparable to deductive as opposed to inductive reasoning. The first is the application of pre-programmed, human-authored rules. At its most basic, this includes simple computation, such as the totalling of a grocery bill at an automated checkout; or it could be the application of a set of variables to determine eligibility for government benefits or the interest rate for a loan. Such rules-based decision-making is not truly 'autonomous'. An alternative form of decision-making is the use of tools to make inferences or predictions based on historical data, such as through machine learning.[106] As those tools become more complex, the difficulty of understanding or explaining the reasons behind decisions may raise problems of opacity, considered in chapter three. Here, the focus is on the autonomy with which those tools reach conclusions that cannot be attributed back directly to a human author.

The manner in which the algorithm is constructed matters also. For rules-based processing, those rules must be interpreted. If they are based on a law that says 'if circumstances A and B are satisfied, then conclusion C follows', this may be unproblematic. Laws are rarely so simple, however.[107] In Australia, for example, a 2015 program referred to as 'Robo-debt' sought to calculate and collect debts owed because of welfare overpayments. Though it applied rules systematically, these rules were incomplete transcriptions of complex provisions in the law and resulted in around one in five people being incorrectly served with debt notices.[108] In the case of machine learning, the AI system relies upon data that itself may or may not be reliable, a topic considered in the next chapter.[109]

For many cases, the use of algorithms to support or replace human decision-making is uncontroversial. In addition to efficiency, automated processing may help ensure consistency and predictability. Indeed, in some situations it may be preferable to the arbitrariness that often characterizes human decision-making – whether that is due to conceptual limitations, carelessness, or corruption. At the same time, abdicating responsibility for decisions to a machine raises the possibility of other

Work 87. See also Karen Yeung, 'Algorithmic Regulation: A Critical Interrogation' (2018) 12 Regulation & Governance 505, 508 (developing a taxonomy of algorithmic regulation).

[106] See the introduction to this book at n 2.

[107] See chapter nine, section 9.1.1.

[108] See Monika Zalnieriute, Lyria Bennett Moses, and George Williams, 'The Rule of Law and Automation of Government Decision-Making' (2019) 82 Modern Law Review 425, 446.

[109] See chapter three, section 3.2.

problems, ranging from latent discrimination to a lack of due process
or procedural fairness. In between lies the question of how discretion
should be exercised and whether, comparable to the debate over autonomous weapons, there are some decisions that should not be made by
machine alone.

2.3.1   Contracts and Knowledge

Vast numbers of routine commercial transactions now take place without any human intervention whatsoever, from purchasing items online
to arguing with chatbots if those items do not arrive or are defective.
The push to automate decision-making processes is greatest in areas
that are high volume and low risk. In addition to online purchases, this
has extended to areas such as small loans, retail insurance, and recruitment
screening, where varying degrees of automation have introduced efficiencies for businesses.[110] A growing number of companies use automated dispute resolution systems.[111]

Much of the regulatory intervention in this space has been led by
European efforts to limit the impact of automated processing. Such
efforts seek to prevent automation violating rights in a manner that
would be impermissible if those decisions were being taken by
a human. In this section, the focus is on novel challenges posed by the
autonomy of the algorithms.

As in the case of autonomous vehicles, most private law questions
involving algorithms can be resolved using existing laws and principles.
Occasionally, however, there may be odd results when those methods are
applied to new fact patterns. Increased reliance on algorithmic trading
software, for example, has given rise to the phenomenon of computer
programs concluding deals with one another that may move beyond their
initial parameters. The validity of such contracts is not especially
complicated,[112] though high-frequency trading may pose practical challenges to implementation, as discussed in chapter one.

A problem directly tied to autonomy did, however, arise in a 2019 case
before the Singapore International Commercial Court. The parties,

---

[110] Stefanie Hänold, 'Profiling and Automated Decision-Making: Legal Implications and
Shortcomings' in Marcelo Corrales, Mark Fenwick, and Nikolaus Forgó (eds), *Robotics,
AI and the Future of Law* (Springer 2018) 123 at 127–28.
[111] See chapter nine, section 9.1.
[112] See Faye Fangfei Wang, *Law of Electronic Commercial Transactions: Contemporary
Issues in the EU, US and China* (2nd edn, Routledge 2014).

Quoine and B2C2, used software programs that executed trades involving the cryptocurrencies Bitcoin and Ethereum, with prices set according to external market information. The case turned on seven transactions that were made when a defect in Quoine's software saw it execute trades worth approximately US$12m at 250 times the prevailing exchange rate. Quoine claimed that this was a mistake and attempted to reverse the trades, recovering its losses. B2C2 argued that the reversal of the orders was a breach of contract, while Quoine argued that the contract was void or voidable, relying on the doctrine of unilateral mistake.

At common law, a unilateral mistake can void a contract if the other party knows of the mistake.[113] If it cannot be proven that the other party *actually* knew about the mistake, but it can be shown that he or she *should have*, the contract may be voidable under equity.[114] What became crucial in this case was the judge's finding that the computer programs in question were incapable of 'knowing' anything:

> The algorithmic programs in the present case are deterministic, they do and only do what they have been programmed to do. They have no mind of their own. They operate when called upon to do so in the pre-ordained manner. They do not know why they are doing something or what the external events are that cause them to operate in the way that they do.[115]

As a result, the question of knowledge rested with the original programmer of B2C2's software, who could not have known about Quoine's subsequent mistake. Quoine was therefore liable to pay damages to B2C2.[116]

The finding was consistent with existing law, but the judge was careful to confine himself to the facts at hand, noting that the law may need to develop with technology – in particular, if a future computer could be said to have 'a mind of its own'.[117] He clearly viewed this as an incremental process, however, citing with approval the somewhat optimistic statement of Lord Briggs in a UK Supreme Court decision the

---

[113] John Cartwright, 'Unilateral Mistake in the English Courts: Reasserting the Traditional Approach' [2009] Singapore Journal of Legal Studies 226.

[114] Yeo Tiong Min, 'Unilateral Mistake in Contract: Five Degrees of Fusion of Common Law and Equity' [2004] Singapore Journal of Legal Studies 227, 231–33.

[115] *B2C2 Ltd v Quoine Pte Ltd* [2019] SGHC(I) 3 (Singapore International Commercial Court), para 208.

[116] Ibid, paras 210, 221–22. The decision was upheld on appeal, with the majority emphasizing that the deterministic nature of the algorithms was central to its analysis: *Quoine Pte Ltd v B2C2 Ltd* [2020] SGCA(I) 2 (Singapore Court of Appeal), paras 97–128.

[117] *B2C2 Ltd v Quoine Pte Ltd* (n 115), para 206.

previous year: 'The court is well versed in identifying the governing mind of a corporation and, when the need arises, will no doubt be able to do the same for robots.'[118]

Knowledge also plays a role in the criminal law. Another curious example of automated decision-making is 'Random Darknet Shopper', the brainchild of two Swiss artists. Given a budget of up to US$100 per week in Bitcoin, this is an automated online shopping bot that randomly chooses and purchases items from the deep web that are mailed directly to an exhibition space. An interesting legal puzzle was created when it came to the attention of the St Gallen police that the bot's meandering through the unindexed portions of the Internet had led it to purchase a bag of ecstasy pills. The entire exhibition was seized, but the public prosecutor later decided that the incident was 'within the realm of art' and disposed of the drugs without pressing charges.

Questions of responsibility for autonomous processes will be considered in more detail in chapter four, while the possibility of AI systems themselves being held to account is the subject of chapter five. For now, it is sufficient to note that the autonomy of algorithmic processes in the private sector has been less problematic than in the public sector.

2.3.2 Automated Processing

Like the private sector, many governments have sought efficiencies through automation. The difference is that the exercise of public authority typically requires not only efficiency in its outcomes but legitimacy in its processes.

In certain decisions by public bodies, legislation specifically requires the involvement of a human decision-maker. Under the English Taxes Management Act, for example, a notice to pay tax may be issued by 'an officer of the Board'.[119] A taxpayer charged with late filing objected on the basis that the notice sent to him was computer generated, lacking a signature or even a name. The judge concluded that the specific language required that the decision be made by 'a real "flesh and blood" officer, and not by [the tax authority] as a collective body. Nor is it a computerised decision.'[120] Though such decisions were not

---

[118] *Warner-Lambert Co Ltd v Generics (UK) Ltd* [2018] UKSC 56, para 165.
[119] Taxes Management Act 1970 (England), s 8.
[120] *Peter Groves v The Commissioners for Her Majesty's Revenue & Customs* (Appeal number: TC/2017/09024) (15 June 2018) (First-Tier Tribunal Tax Chamber).

themselves unlawful, in this case at least an identifiable public officer was required to make the determination.

Similarly, in most jurisdictions the judicial function must be carried out by a human officer of the court. Though online dispute resolution is becoming more common in small claims tribunals, and predictive algorithms increasingly assist judges in China, with comparable systems being tested in the United States, Europe, and elsewhere, it seems unlikely in the short term that judges will be replaced by robots.[121] As for the medium term, that is a question to which we will return in chapter nine.

The strongest protections against certain forms of algorithmic decision-making are found in Europe. As early as 1978, France adopted a law that prohibited administrative and private decisions based solely on automatic processing of data describing the 'profile or personality' of an individual.[122] Though similar laws were adopted in Portugal[123] and Spain,[124] these remained outliers until the 1995 Data Protection Directive. That required EU member states to grant individuals the right not to be subject to decisions based solely on automated processing of data evaluating them in areas such as 'performance at work, creditworthiness, reliability, conduct, etc'. Such processing was permissible only if it was part of a contractual relationship requested by the individual or if there were suitable measures to safeguard legitimate interests, such as arrangements allowing the individual 'to put his [sic] point of view'. An additional exception allowed for processing authorized by a law that also included measures to safeguard the individual's legitimate interests.[125]

The 2016 General Data Protection Regulation (GDPR) expanded both the possibilities for automated processing as well as the protections available. In addition to contractual arrangements, explicit consent can now be a basis for automated processing. Either basis, however, requires that safeguarding of interests goes beyond an opportunity to 'put [one's] view'

[121] See chapter three, section 3.3.2.
[122] Loi no 78-17 du 6 janvier 1978 relative à l'informatique, aux fichiers et aux libertés 1978 (France), art 2.
[123] Lei no 10/91, Lei da Protecção de Dados Pessoais face à Informática 1991 (Portugal), art 16.
[124] Ley Orgánica 5/1992, de 29 de octubre, de regulación del tratamiento automatizado de los datos de carácter personal 1992 (Spain).
[125] Directive 95/46/EC of the European Parliament and of the Council of 24 October 1995 on the protection of individuals with regard to the processing of personal data and on the free movement of such data (EU Data Protection Directive) 1995 (EU), art 15.

and includes the right to obtain 'human intervention' to contest the decision.[126]

The question of whether the GDPR creates a 'right to explanation' – meaning the ability to demand reasons as to how a particular decision was made – will be considered in chapter six.[127] What is interesting in the present context is the rationale for prohibiting purely automated decision-making and the circumstances in which it can be allowed.

Early arguments focused on the need for individuals to be able to influence important decisions about themselves, as well as guarding against the abdication of human responsibility to take those decisions in the face of a computer-approved outcome.[128] Safeguards against purely automated processing could have prohibited it entirely – requiring, for example, a 'human-in-the-loop' approach that requires intervention prior to a decision being taken. That is unrealistic, as it would essentially render many widespread practices unlawful. It would also likely be ineffective, as routine human involvement to approve computer-prompted outcomes would quickly devolve into rubber-stamping or 'quasi-automation'.[129]

In general, for the purposes of private activities (based on contract or explicit consent) and public activities (based on legal authority), the requirement for 'suitable measures' to protect the rights and interests of individuals makes it clear that automated processing can take place provided that there is a remedy if those rights or interests are violated – in particular, if a decision is based on impermissible forms of discrimination.[130] For decisions based on contract or consent, this is explicitly linked to the ability to challenge the decision and ensuring that such a challenge can be made to a human.[131]

Algorithmic decision-making thus poses an interesting counterpoint to the utilitarian approach to autonomous vehicles – where concerns are based on safety and accountability – and the deontic

---

[126] General Data Protection Regulation 2016/679 (GDPR) 2016 (EU), art 22.
[127] See chapter six, section 6.3.1.
[128] Lee A Bygrave, 'Automated Profiling: Minding the Machine – Article 15 of the EC Data Protection Directive and Automated Profiling' (2001) 17 Computer Law & Security Review 17, 18.
[129] Ben Wagner, 'Liable, but Not in Control? Ensuring Meaningful Human Agency in Automated Decision-Making Systems' (2019) 11 Policy & Internet 104.
[130] See chapter three, section 3.2.
[131] Cf Antoni Roig, 'Safeguards for the Right Not to Be Subject to a Decision Based Solely on Automated Processing (Article 22 GDPR)' (2017) 8(3) European Journal of Law and Technology.

approach to autonomous weapons – where concerns focus on the morality of allowing life and death decisions to be made at all. In the case of automated processing, decision-making by machine is tolerated if the legitimacy of those decisions is ensured through the protection of rights and interests, in certain cases explicitly including the right to bring one's concerns before another human being.

2.4   The Problem with Autonomy

True autonomy of AI systems calls into question long-standing assumptions that humans are the source, the means, and the purpose of regulation.[132] As we have seen, however, the question arises in different ways. The emergence of autonomous vehicles is exposing gaps in the liability and criminal law regimes governing the roads, but these are ultimately practical problems to be addressed by amending those rules. The complicated nature of such amendments should not be underestimated, but the objective of managing risk is largely uncontroversial. Autonomous weapon systems, by contrast, raise discrete moral questions – not *how* decisions by a machine should fit into our legal paradigms but *whether* such decisions should be allowed in the first place. Algorithmic decision-making, at least for some decisions affecting the rights and obligations of individuals, runs the risk of treating human subjects as a means rather than an end. Unlike autonomous vehicles and weapons, the concern there is with the legitimacy of a decision made without human involvement.

These three types of concern – practicality, morality, legitimacy – are useful lenses through which to view the regulatory tools needed to address the larger challenges of AI, including those that are beyond our current horizon. Managing risk, preserving moral boundaries, and maintaining the legitimacy of public authority offer three strategies to help ensure that the benefits of AI do not come at unacceptable cost.

Yet the nature of that cost is calculated differently in each case. Practical questions of minimizing harm reflect the utilitarian calculus of cost–benefit analysis. Moral questions of bright, non-negotiable lines suggest the duty-based ethics of deontology. The legitimacy of public authority, by contrast, points to issues of political theory. The

---

[132] This includes legal constructs through which humans act, such as corporations. See chapter five, section 5.1.

2 AUTONOMY   61

aim here is not to reconcile these disparate conversations; rather, it is to highlight the complexity of the ostensibly simple notion of 'autonomy'.[133]

The history of the word itself embodies some of that complexity. Etymologically, 'autonomy' comes from the Greek *autonomía*, combining *autos* (self) and *nomos* (law); its original use was confined almost exclusively to the political sphere, denoting civic communities with independent legislative authority.[134] It was only in the eighteenth century that Immanuel Kant applied the concept to humans, positing that morality requires a form of individual self-governance – that we ourselves legislate the moral law as rational beings.[135] Today, autonomy is also used in a looser sense of personal autonomy, meaning that a person acts in accordance with his or her own desires and values.[136]

None of these meanings corresponds fully to the AI systems discussed here. Though it is common for the 'autonomy' of those systems to be described with reference to their ability to take decisions on their own, they do not have 'desires' or 'values' in any meaningful sense, nor are they 'rational' in a way that Kant would have understood them to be.[137] On the contrary, what we typically mean when we describe an AI system as autonomous is not that it takes decisions 'by itself' but that it takes decisions *without further input from a human*.

Understood in this way, the problem with autonomy is not some mysterious quality inherent in the AI system. Rather, it is a set of questions about whether, how, and with what safeguards human decision-making authority is being transferred to a machine. Algorithmic decision-making, for example, raises directly the question of the extent to which public authorities can outsource their responsibilities. Autonomous weapon systems have led many to argue that some decisions should not be outsourced at all. In the case of autonomous (viz 'driverless') vehicles, optimizing transportation does seem to be an area in which AI may be able to move people and goods more efficiently and – eventually – more safely than human drivers.

---

[133] Cf Mike Ananny, 'Toward an Ethics of Algorithms: Convening, Observation, Probability, and Timeliness' (2016) 41 Science, Technology, & Human Values 93.

[134] John M Cooper, 'Stoic Autonomy' in Ellen Frankel Paul, Fred D Miller, Jr, and Jeffrey Paul (eds), *Autonomy* (Cambridge University Press 2010) 1.

[135] Jerome B Schneewind, *The Invention of Autonomy: A History of Modern Moral Philosophy* (Cambridge University Press 1997) 483.

[136] James Stacey Taylor, 'Autonomy' in Gregory Claeys (ed), *Encyclopedia of Modern Political Thought* (Sage 2013) 57.

[137] Cf discussion of the android fallacy in chapter five, section 5.2.

We are not there yet, of course. Almost a year after Elaine Herzberg died in Tempe, the prosecutor for Yavapai County in Arizona, Sheila Polk, concluded that there was no basis for criminal liability on the part of Uber. She did, however, recommend further investigation of the backup driver, Ms Vasquez, who was charged with negligent homicide in September 2020. The Volvo XC90 itself, together with its on-board computer system, has been repaired and is, presumably, still on the road.

3

Opacity

Eric Loomis was 31 when he was arrested in La Crosse, Wisconsin, in connection with a drive-by shooting. Two rounds from a sawn-off shotgun had been fired at a house a little after 2am on a Monday morning in February 2013. Though no one was injured, police were called and soon identified Loomis's Dodge Neon two kilometres away. A short car chase ended when he crashed into a snowdrift; together with a passenger he continued on foot, but he was apprehended and charged with reckless endangerment and possession of a firearm. Loomis denied involvement in the shooting, pleading guilty to lesser charges of fleeing a police officer and driving a stolen vehicle.

These were all repeat offences. Loomis was also a registered sex offender, stemming from an earlier conviction for sexual assault, and on probation for dealing in prescription drugs. His lawyer nevertheless argued for mitigation, highlighting a childhood spent in foster homes where he had been subjected to abuse; with an infant son of his own, Loomis was now training to be a tattoo artist. Prior to sentencing, the circuit court ordered a risk assessment using software known by the acronym COMPAS.[1] Based on information gathered from a defendant's criminal file and an interview, COMPAS generates scores on a scale from one to ten, indicating the predicted likelihood that he or she will commit further crimes.

Equivant,[2] the company that developed COMPAS, regards the proprietary algorithm that generates these scores as a trade secret. The scores themselves are not. Neither Loomis nor his lawyer was able to see or to question how the figures had been reached, but the presiding judge cited them in justifying a six-year prison sentence. 'You're identified,' Judge Scott Horne said, 'through the COMPAS assessment, as an individual

[1] COMPAS stands for Correctional Offender Management Profiling for Alternative Sanctions.
[2] The company was formerly known as Northpointe, Inc.

who is at high risk to the community.' The judge then ruled out probation 'because of the seriousness of the crime and because your history, your history on supervision, and the risk assessment tools that have been utilized, suggest that you're extremely high risk to re-offend'.[3]

Opacity is the antithesis of legal decisions. Accountability for those decisions typically requires that the decision-maker have a convincing reason for a decision or act. Judicial decisions in particular give special weight to reasoning.[4] In the common law tradition, only the *ratio decidendi* – the legal basis for the decision – is binding on lower courts. Appeals to higher courts look for errors in the law or in its application to the facts as disclosed in the reasons. The failure to give reasons can itself be a ground of appeal in its own right.[5] Eric Loomis's sentencing decision appeared to violate these principles. The judge's reliance on COMPAS was criticized by academics and civil society, and was central to an appeal that made its way – almost – to the US Supreme Court.

The problem of understanding AI systems is not new. In *The Black Box Society*, Frank Pasquale compared the role of algorithms in the modern world to Plato's metaphor of the cave, with the general public trapped and able only to see 'flickering shadows cast by a fire behind them'; the prisoners cannot comprehend the actions, let alone the agenda, of those who create the images that are all they know of reality.[6] More prosaically, it has been argued that computer simulation displaces humans from the centre of the epistemological enterprise. For most of human history, the expansion of knowledge meant the expansion of human knowledge and understanding. The emergence of computational methods that transcend our abilities presents what Paul Humphreys calls the 'anthropocentric predicament'.[7] Distinct from the challenges posed by autonomy in AI systems, the increasing opacity of those systems is not a challenge to the centrality of human agents as legal *actors* so much as to our ability to

---

[3] *State v Loomis*, 881 NW 2d 749, 755 (Wis, 2016).
[4] Herbert Wechsler, 'Toward Neutral Principles of Constitutional Law' (1959) 73 Harvard Law Review 1, 19–20.
[5] There are, of course, exceptions to this. Juries, for example, are not required to give reasons for the limited decisions they make within the legal system. See generally Mathilde Cohen, 'When Judges Have Reasons Not to Give Reasons: A Comparative Law Approach' (2015) 72 Washington & Lee Law Review 483.
[6] Frank Pasquale, *The Black Box Society: The Secret Algorithms That Control Money and Information* (Harvard University Press 2015) 190.
[7] Paul Humphreys, 'The Philosophical Novelty of Computer Simulation Methods' (2009) 169 Synthese 615, 617.

understand and evaluate *actions* – something essential to meaningful regulation.

'Opacity' is used here to mean the quality of being difficult to understand or explain. As in the case of COMPAS, this may be due to certain technologies being proprietary. To protect an investment, detailed knowledge of the inner workings of a system may be limited to those who own it. A second form of opacity arises in complex systems that require specialist skills to understand them. These systems evolve over time, being added to by different stakeholders, but are in principle capable of being explained.

Neither of these forms of opacity – proprietary or complex – poses new problems for law. Intellectual property law has long recognized protection of intangible creations of the human mind and exceptions based on fair use.[8] To deal with complex issues, governments and judges routinely have recourse to experts.[9] The same cannot be said of a third reason for opacity, which is systems that are naturally opaque. Some deep learning methods are opaque effectively by design, as they rely on reaching decisions through machine learning rather than, for example, following a decision tree that would be transparent, even if it might be complex.[10]

To pick an example mentioned in the introduction to this book, the programmers of Google's AlphaGo could not explain how it came up with the strategies for the ancient game of Go that defeated the human grandmaster, Lee Sodol, in 2016. Lee himself later said that in their first game the program made a move that no human would have played – and which was only later shown to have planted the seeds of its victory.[11]

---

[8] Amanda Levendowski, 'How Copyright Law Can Fix Artificial Intelligence's Implicit Bias Problem' (2018) 93 Washington Law Review 579. On the question of intellectual property created by an AI system itself, see chapter five, section 5.2.2.

[9] See, eg, Carol AG Jones, *Expert Witnesses: Science, Medicine, and the Practice of Law* (Clarendon Press 1994).

[10] For a description of machine learning, see the introduction to this book at n 2. Cf Jenna Burrell, 'How the Machine "Thinks": Understanding Opacity in Machine Learning Algorithms' (2016) 3(1) Big Data & Society. 'Decision tree' is used here in the sense of a static set of parameters specified in advance and to be applied consistently. This is distinct from decision tree models that are themselves developed through machine learning.

[11] 'Google's AI Beats World Go Champion in First of Five Matches', *BBC News* (9 March 2016). A subsequent version, AlphaGo Zero, was taught only the rules of Go and in three days had mastered the ancient game. In match-ups against the version that beat the human grandmaster, Lee Sodol, the newer version beat the old 100 to zero. See David Silver et al, 'Mastering the Game of Go without Human Knowledge' (2017) 550 Nature 354.

Such output-based legitimacy – optimal ends justifying uncertain means – is appropriate in some areas. Medical science, for example, progresses based on the success or failure of clinical trials with robust statistical analysis. If the net impact is positive, the fact that it may be unclear precisely *how* a procedure or pharmaceutical achieves those positive outcomes is not a barrier to allowing it into the market.[12] Though patient autonomy means that important decisions are made by the individual most affected, tolerance for adverse effects is built into the process, with patients advised as to the risks of negative as well as positive outcomes.[13] Legal decisions, on the other hand, are generally not regarded as appropriate for statistical modelling. Though certain decisions may be expressed in terms of burdens of proof – balance of probabilities, beyond reasonable doubt, and so on – these are to be determined in individualized assessments of a given case, rather than based on a forecast of the most likely outcomes from a larger set of cases.

There is a growing literature criticizing reliance on algorithmic decision-making with legal consequences. A significant portion now focuses on opacity, highlighting specific concerns such as bias, or seeking remedies through transparency. Yet the challenges of opacity go beyond bias and will not all be solved through calls for transparency or 'explainability'. Drawing on well-known examples and arguments from the United States and the EU, as well as less-studied innovations in China, this chapter develops a typology of those challenges posed by proprietary, complex, and natural opacity. The first is that 'black box' decision-making may lead to inferior decisions. Accountability and oversight are not merely tools to punish bad behaviour; they also encourage good behaviour. Excluding that possibility reduces opportunities to identify wrongdoing, as well as the chances that decisions will be subjected to meaningful scrutiny and thereby be improved. Secondly, opaque decision-making practices may provide cover for impermissible decisions, such as through masking or reifying discrimination. Even if statistical models suggested that persons of a particular race should be given longer

---

[12] Alex John London and Jonathan Kimmelman, 'Why Clinical Translation Cannot Succeed without Failure' (2015) 4 eLife e12844. Research into mental illness in particular is fraught with uncertainty as to the underlying causes of disease and the mechanisms that bring about cures. See Anne Harrington, *Mind Fixers: Psychiatry's Troubled Search for the Biology of Mental Illness* (Norton 2019).

[13] Patients are, of course, provided with individualized assessment based on their condition, history, and so on. But the use of objective population-based trends is generally accepted. Omer Gottesman et al, 'Guidelines for Reinforcement Learning in Healthcare' (2019) 25 Nature Medicine 16.

prison sentences, for example, acting on such predictions would not be tolerated in a judge and should not be accepted in an AI system. Finally, the legitimacy of certain decisions depends on the transparency of the decision-making process as much as on the decision itself. Judicial decisions are the best, but not the only, example of this.

It will be apparent that this structure echoes the discrete challenges raised about autonomy in chapter two: the quality of outcomes approaches the question through a utilitarian lens; the avoidance of impermissible decisions reflects deontic concerns; while reliance upon proper authority and process is sought to confer legitimacy – in this case based not on the identity of the actor but on the publicness of his or her reasoning.

The means of addressing some or all of these concerns is routinely said to be through transparency.[14] Yet while proprietary opacity can be dealt with by court order and complex opacity through recourse to experts, naturally opaque systems may require novel forms of 'explanation' or an acceptance that some machine-made decisions cannot be explained – or, in the alternative, that some decisions should not be made by machine at all.

3.1   Inferior Decisions

Technology can be made opaque to protect an investment but also to prevent scrutiny. Such scrutiny may reveal trade secrets or it may reveal incompetence. At its most venal, opaqueness provides cover for the intentional manipulation of outcomes or to thwart investigation. Volkswagen, for example, wrote code that gamed tests used by regulators to give the false impression that vehicle emissions were lower than in normal usage.[15] Uber similarly designed a version of its app that identified users whose behaviour suggested that they were working for regulators in order to limit their ability to gather evidence.[16]

A more general problem is that even good faith inscrutability may prevent interrogations of data quality. In some cases, greater transparency might reveal how much data is being used, giving rise to privacy concerns.

---

[14] See chapter six.

[15] EPA, California Notify Volkswagen of Clean Air Act Violations/Carmaker Allegedly Used Software That Circumvents Emissions Testing for Certain Air Pollutants (US Environmental Protection Agency, 18 September 2015).

[16] Leslie Hook, 'Uber Used Fake App to Confuse Regulators and Rivals', *Financial Times* (4 March 2017).

In others, the patchiness of data might be revealed, raising questions about the reliability of the process or the confidence level of the outcome.[17] This phenomenon of 'garbage in, garbage out' is as old as the first computer. Charles Babbage, the English polymath who fashioned the mechanical device often credited as such, raised the issue in 1864. His memoir recalls twice being asked by members of Parliament whether putting wrong figures into his difference engine might nonetheless lead to the right answers coming out. 'I am not able rightly to apprehend the kind of confusion of ideas that could provoke such a question,' he observed.[18]

Human complacency and automation bias make these more than theoretical problems. As human involvement in a process – notionally 'in' or 'over' the loop[19] – is reduced to its most mechanistic, the tendency to accept default suggestions increases.[20] This may be compared with the danger, discussed in chapter two, posed by autonomous vehicles operating at a level where the human 'driver' may release the wheel – but is expected to remain ready to seize back control at any moment.[21] That is an example of complacency. Bias arises due to the tendency of most people to ascribe to an automated system greater trust in its analytical capabilities than in their own.[22]

A related problem is that such systems may also provide cover for human agents. A survey of lawyers and judges in Canada, for example, found that many regarded software like COMPAS as an improvement over subjective judgment: though risk assessment tools were not deemed especially reliable predictors of future behaviour, they were also favoured because using them minimized the risk that the lawyers and judges themselves would be blamed for the consequences of their decisions.[23]

[17] Sandra Wachter and Brent Mittelstadt, 'A Right to Reasonable Inferences: Re-thinking Data Protection Law in the Age of Big Data and AI' [2019] Columbia Business Law Review 494.

[18] Charles Babbage, *Passages from the Life of a Philosopher* (Longman 1864) 67.

[19] See chapter two, section 2.3.

[20] Steven PR Rose and Hilary Rose, '"Do Not Adjust Your Mind, There Is a Fault in Reality" – Ideology in Neurobiology' (1973) 2 Cognition 479, 498–99. On the larger impact of anchoring in sentencing decisions, see Birte Enough and Thomas Mussweiler, 'Sentencing under Uncertainty: Anchoring Effects in the Courtroom' (2001) 31 Journal of Applied Social Psychology 1535.

[21] See chapter two, section 2.1.

[22] Raja Parasuraman and Dietrich Manzey, 'Complacency and Bias in Human Use of Automation: An Attentional Integration' (2010) 52 Human Factors 381, 392.

[23] Kelly Hannah-Moffat, 'The Uncertainties of Risk Assessment: Partiality, Transparency, and Just Decisions' (2015) 27 Federal Sentencing Reporter 244.

Addressing complacency and automation bias goes far beyond the regulatory challenges that are the focus of this book. For present purposes, it is sufficient to observe that they should not be a basis for avoiding accountability in the narrow sense of being obliged to give an account of a decision, even if after the fact, or to avoid responsibility for harm as a result of that decision.

As in many areas of technology regulation, the EU offers comparatively stronger protections under its GDPR, which makes clear that the right not to be subject to automated processing[24] cannot be avoided by 'token' human involvement. Routine acceptance of automated processes would not suffice; meaningful oversight requires a person with authority and competence to review a decision – including having access to 'all the relevant data'.[25]

The notion that opacity leads to inferior decisions has a long history in software development. Combined with a resistance to proprietary opacity, this insight lies at the heart of the open source movement.[26] Complete openness will not be appropriate or possible in all circumstances, but the idea that it should not be limited simply in order to prevent external scrutiny seems uncontroversial. Such questions are more challenging as the systems become more complex and the outputs less susceptible to objective evaluation.

3.2 Impermissible Decisions

One of the benefits of automated decision-making is that it can reduce the arbitrariness of human decisions. Given a large number of similar questions, properly programmed computers will provide predictable and consistent answers. Whereas many evaluative decisions made by humans are based on unconscious group biases and intuitive reactions, algorithms follow the parameters set out for them.[27] They are only as good as the data they are given and the questions they are asked, however. In

---

[24] See chapter two, section 2.3.2.

[25] Guidelines on Automated Individual Decision-Making and Profiling for the Purposes of Regulation 2016/679 (Article 29 Data Protection Working Party, 17/EN WP251rev.01, 3 October 2017) 20–21.

[26] Sheen S Levine and Michael J Prietula, 'Open Collaboration for Innovation: Principles and Performance' (2014) 25 Organization Science 1287.

[27] Sharad Goel et al, 'Combatting Police Discrimination in the Age of Big Data' (2017) 20 New Criminal Law Review 181. This may be particularly useful in decision-making systems that are delegated and distributed: Katherine J Strandburg, 'Rulemaking and Inscrutable Automated Decision Tools' (2019) 119 Columbia Law Review 1851, 1857.

practice, algorithms can reify existing disparities – and, as we shall see, the absence of conscious bias in specific decisions may actually frustrate attempts to rectify those disparities by relying on anti-discrimination laws.

A prominent example is screening decisions. Many industries now use AI systems to simplify repetitive processes such as reviewing job applications, assessing creditworthiness, setting insurance premiums, detecting fraud, and so on. These systems often rely on two discrete algorithms: the screening algorithm itself selects candidates from the pool or assigns them a score; this in turn may be based on a training algorithm, which uses data to improve the screening algorithm.

Used well, screening processes efficiently and consistently treat like cases alike. This is most effective in binary decisions, such as whether an email is spam or whether a transaction is fraudulent. There is an objective answer using a predefined category – 'spam' or 'fraud' – with answers that are verifiable in a manner upon which most evaluators of that decision would agree. False positives and negatives can be flagged for the training algorithm, which feeds back to the screening algorithm and progressively reduces those errors.

Problems arise when more contested categories are invoked, like fairness, or when algorithms are used in order to predict future behaviour by specific individuals,[28] such as how well they will perform in a particular job – or whether they will commit another crime. In some cases, the results are perverse. An audit of one résumé-screening algorithm identified that the two most important factors indicative of job performance at a particular company were being named Jared and having played high-school lacrosse.[29] In others, reliance upon algorithms may reflect or reify discriminatory practices.

3.2.1 How Bias Is Learned

Bias can be 'learned' in at least two ways. If overt prejudice affects the data used to train algorithms, that prejudice may be replicated. But if an algorithm is used to draw inferences based on a sample population, it is also possible that unintended biases may be revealed due to the training data itself, the selection and weighting of variables, or the manner in

[28] Chelsea Barabas et al, 'Interventions over Predictions: Reframing the Ethical Debate for Actuarial Risk Assessment' (2018) 81 Proceedings of Machine Learning Research 1.

[29] Dave Gershgorn, 'Robot Indemnity: Companies Are on the Hook if Their Hiring Algorithms Are Biased', *Quartz* (22 October 2018).

which outputs are interpreted.[30] Various scholars compare this to the distinction between 'disparate treatment', or intentional behaviour, and 'disparate impact' in US civil rights jurisprudence.[31] An example of the former is Amazon's résumé-screening algorithm, which was trained on ten years of data but had to be shut down when programmers discovered that it had 'learned' that women's applications were to be treated less favourably than men's.[32]

Examples of unintended bias include facial recognition software that is less effective at recognizing dark-skinned faces because its training was done using light-skinned ones.[33] The use of unrepresentative data is not unique to AI systems, of course. A meta-analysis of psychology studies found that the vast majority of those published relied on the participation of Western university students, who were then treated as representative of all of humanity.[34] Different problems can arise with selection and weighting of variables. An ostensibly neutral metric like productivity of employees, for example, might adversely impact women if it does not account for the fact that they are more likely than men to take maternity leave.[35]

Perhaps the greatest risk comes with the interpretation of outputs, which brings us back to risk assessment tools like COMPAS. A widely cited report by *ProPublica* concluded that COMPAS correctly predicted recidivism in nearly two-thirds of cases, but that its false positives and false negatives were both skewed against African Americans. Of those who did not reoffend, African Americans were almost twice as likely to have been labelled 'high risk' as compared with whites; of those who did go on to commit further crimes, whites were almost twice as likely to have been deemed 'low risk'.[36] The report was criticized for oversimplifying

---

[30] Selena Silva and Martin Kenney, Algorithms, Platforms, and Ethnic Bias: An Integrative Essay (University of California, Berkeley, BRIE Working Paper 2018-3, 2018).

[31] *Ricci v DeStefano*, 557 US 557 (2009). See, eg, Solon Barocas and Andrew D Selbst, 'Big Data's Disparate Impact' (2016) 104 California Law Review 671, 694–712.

[32] Ignacio N Cofone, 'Algorithmic Discrimination Is an Information Problem' (2019) 70 Hastings Law Journal 1389, 1397–98.

[33] Karl Manheim and Lyric Kaplan, 'Artificial Intelligence: Risks to Privacy and Democracy' (2019) 21 Yale Journal of Law & Technology 106, 159.

[34] Joseph Henrich, Steven J Heine, and Ara Norenzayan, 'The Weirdest People in the World?' (2010) 33 Behavioral and Brain Sciences 61 (the title refers to subjects being drawn entirely from Western, Educated, Industrialized, Rich, and Democratic (WEIRD) societies).

[35] Cf Rafael Lalive et al, 'Parental Leave and Mothers' Careers: The Relative Importance of Job Protection and Cash Benefits' (2014) 81 Review of Economic Studies 219.

[36] Julia Angwin et al, 'Machine Bias: There's Software Used across the Country to Predict Future Criminals. And It's Biased against Blacks', *ProPublica* (23 May 2016).

risk assessment, cherry-picking results, and ignoring the higher incarceration rates of African Americans.[37] It was also challenged on the basis that it failed to acknowledge that data-driven risk assessments have repeatedly been shown to be superior to professional human judgments, which themselves are prone to bias.[38]

These debates join a rich literature defending and critiquing the use of actuarial risk assessments in the United States, where standardized decision-making from the 1970s focused on prevention of future crime and has been linked with ongoing problems of mass incarceration generally, and the jailing of African American men in particular.[39] The emergence of proprietary and otherwise opaque tools like COMPAS has exacerbated the concerns about such models, due to complacency and automation bias, but the underlying problem is one of the oldest of logical fallacies: *cum hoc ergo propter hoc* [with this, therefore because of this]. Or, as it is rendered in introductory texts on statistics: correlation is not cause.

Risk assessments originally used regression models. Regression in statistics is a tool that identifies a set of variables that are predictive of a given outcome. Model checking and selection enable the identification of optimal weights for those variables that best predict the outcome of interest.[40] The COMPAS 'violent recidivism risk score', for example, is calculated through an equation that weighs history of violence and non-compliance against age, age at first arrest, and level of education. As the company's manual notes, it is similar to the way in which a car insurance company estimates the risk of a customer having an accident.[41] The algorithm's impenetrability, however, and the criticism to which that gave rise anticipate future challenges as AI systems become more complex and play a greater role in decisions affecting the rights and obligations of individuals.

[37] Anthony W Flores, Kristin Bechtel, and Christopher T Lowenkamp, 'False Positives, False Negatives, and False Analyses: A Rejoinder to "Machine Bias: There's Software Used across the Country to Predict Future Criminals. And It's Biased against Blacks"' (2016) 80 (2) Federal Probation 38.

[38] Alexandra Chouldechova, 'Fair Prediction with Disparate Impact: A Study of Bias in Recidivism Prediction Instruments' (2017) 5 Big Data 153.

[39] Malcolm M Feeley and Jonathan Simon, 'The New Penology: Notes on the Emerging Strategy of Corrections and Its Implications' (1992) 30 Criminology 449; Paula Maurutto and Kelly Hannah-Moffat, 'Assembling Risk and the Restructuring of Penal Control' (2006) 46 British Journal of Criminology 438.

[40] Andrew Gelman and Jennifer Hill, *Data Analysis Using Regression and Multilevel/Hierarchical Models* (Cambridge University Press 2007).

[41] A Practitioner's Guide to COMPAS Core (Northpointe, 2015) 29.

Supervised machine learning techniques embody many of the problems of regression, in that the goal is prediction. Though some studies have shown that machine learning is more accurate than traditional statistical methods, this comes at the expense of transparency.[42] Here opacity becomes a concern as the black box nature of these techniques both obscures the decision-making process while also creating – in the minds of some users, at least – the illusion of greater sophistication and, therefore, reliability.

Scholars in the field continue to argue over the extent to which social, economic, and psychological factors need to be taken into account in improving the accuracy of risk assessment models.[43] A more fundamental challenge questions the purpose of using such models in the first place.

Risk assessments like COMPAS use historical data to predict future behaviour. There are two basic objections to this. The first is that punishment should generally be meted out by the state only for crimes committed in the past rather than those that might be committed in the future. Though the prospects of reoffending are considered when choosing from a range of possible sentences, or when considering early release, truly preventive detention is rare in most well-ordered jurisdictions.[44] The second objection is that the application of summary statistics to individuals is the very definition of stereotyping.[45] The fact that a person comes from a community with higher rates of crime may make it more probable that he or she will commit a crime, but that is not a basis for punishing him or her for it in advance.[46]

---

[42] Grant Duwe and KiDeuk Kim, 'Sacrificing Accuracy for Transparency in Recidivism Risk Assessment: The Impact of Classification Method on Predictive Performance' (2016) 1 Corrections 155.

[43] See, eg, Kelly Hannah-Moffat, 'Sacrosanct or Flawed: Risk, Accountability and Gender-Responsive Penal Politics' (2011) 22 Current Issues in Criminal Justice 193; Seth J Prins and Adam Reich, 'Can We Avoid Reductionism in Risk Reduction?' (2018) 22 Theoretical Criminology 258. Mental health, for example, tends to be excluded in favour of more measurable and statistically significant covariates.

[44] Hallie Ludsin, *Preventive Detention and the Democratic State* (Cambridge University Press 2016).

[45] Oscar H Gandy, Jr, 'Engaging Rational Discrimination: Exploring Reasons for Placing Regulatory Constraints on Decision Support Systems' (2010) 12 Ethics and Information Technology 29, 33–34.

[46] An alternative approach is to seek not to predict future behaviour but to shape it. Causal inference is one such approach, in which the goal would be not to categorize offenders such as Eric Loomis into risk groups but to minimize the risk of reoffending through individualized assessment and experimentation. See generally Guido W Imbens and Donald B Rubin, *Causal Inference for Statistics, Social, and Biomedical Sciences: An Introduction* (Cambridge University Press 2015).

Interesting parallels may be drawn here with the use of personally identifying data by police. To the extent that authorities rely on finger-prints and DNA samples collected from those who have been arrested or convicted in the past, it significantly increases the likelihood that these identifiers will be used against that group in the future, entrenching discriminatory practices.[47] With the emergence of facial recognition technology, arguments about whether and how it should be used in routine policing have raised the spectre of democracies following China in surveillance of the entire population. Limited use for identification purposes may be more acceptable, but relying on mug shots would replicate the problem with fingerprints and DNA. To that end, a controversial proposal is that the police should have access to no one's biometric data – or everyone's.[48]

3.2.2 Unlearning Bias

An alternative approach to the problem of bias in algorithms is to 'unbias' them with regard to specific factors. This draws on one of the advantages that algorithms offer over humans: their decision-making processes can be the subject of experimentation. Whereas an employer who chose to hire a man over a woman is unlikely to admit to bias affecting that specific decision – indeed, there may have been no conscious bias at all – it is possible for algorithms to be run with tweaked parameters to examine whether disparate outcomes would have been reached in different scenarios.[49] That can only be done, however, if they are made available to auditors or external testers.[50]

One of the grounds raised by Eric Loomis in his appeal against the sentencing decision was that COMPAS took gender into account when considering an offender's risk of recidivism. He conceded that men might generally have higher recidivism and violent crime rates than women, but argued that it was a violation of his due process rights to apply that statistical evidence to his case in particular. The court cited some of the

[47] Simon Chesterman, *One Nation under Surveillance: A New Social Contract to Defend Freedom without Sacrificing Liberty* (Oxford University Press 2011) 257–58.
[48] Barry Friedman and Andrew Guthrie Ferguson, 'Here's a Way Forward on Facial Recognition', *New York Times* (31 October 2019).
[49] Jon Kleinberg et al, 'Discrimination in the Age of Algorithms' (2018) 10 Journal of Legal Analysis 113. See also Amit Datta, Michael Carl Tschantz, and Anupam Datta, 'Automated Experiments on Ad Privacy Settings: A Tale of Opacity, Choice, and Discrimination' [2015] (1) Proceedings on Privacy Enhancing Technologies 92.
[50] See chapter six, section 6.2.2(b).

literature on the topic and concluded that the use of gender by COMPAS 'promotes accuracy that ultimately inures to the benefit of the justice system including defendants'; in any event, it held, Loomis had not shown that gender was actually relied on as a factor in his sentencing. Discharging that burden was not helped by the fact that, as the court had earlier observed, the algorithm's proprietary nature meant that there was some uncertainty as to whether gender had been taken into account at all.[51]

3.3 Illegitimate Decisions

Opacity, then, may allow inferior decisions or mask impermissible ones. These are matters to mitigate or correct. In a third class of decision-making processes, however, opacity is problematic because the transparency of that process itself may be as important as the effectiveness or appropriateness of the outcome.

Reasoned decision-making on the part of public actors is often said to be foundational to modern notions of liberalism.[52] Much of the literature critiquing algorithmic decision-making concentrates on the quality of decisions, including the possibility of poor decisions due to incomplete or corrupted data, lack of capacity to supervise the relevant systems, or regulatory capture by industry.[53] Alternatively, criticism highlights the discriminatory impact or impermissible bias of those decisions.[54]

Those arguments rehearse issues discussed in the prior sections of this chapter. Here, the focus is on two classes of decision in which opacity itself – as distinct from what it may obscure – undermines legitimacy. The first is in decisions by public actors whose authority is tied to democratic processes that would be frustrated by opacity. The second is in decisions by courts, whose claim to the rule of law depends on public

[51] *State v Loomis* (n 3) 765–67.
[52] See, eg, John Rawls, *Political Liberalism* (Columbia University Press 1996); Jeremy Waldron, 'Theoretical Foundations of Liberalism' (1987) 37(147) The Philosophical Quarterly 127.
[53] Cf John Finch, Susi Geiger, and Emma Reid, 'Captured by Technology? How Material Agency Sustains Interaction between Regulators and Industry Actors' (2017) 46 Research Policy 160. See also chapter eight, section 8.1.2.
[54] Philipp Hacker and Bilyana Petkova, 'Reining in the Big Promise of Big Data: Transparency, Inequality, and New Regulatory Frontiers' (2017) 15 Northwestern Journal of Technology and Intellectual Property 1, 7–9.

justifications that are intelligible to the wider community: justice being done but also being *seen* to be done.

3.3.1 Public Decisions

Edward Shils, a US sociologist writing in the 1950s not long after the McCarthy hearings, argued that liberal democracy depended on protecting privacy for individuals and denying it to government.[55] Succeeding decades have seen the opposite happen: individual privacy has evaporated while governments have become ever more secretive. Opacity in decision-making is not the same as secrecy, yet it has an analogous effect in undermining the possibility of being held to account for those decisions. It may, arguably, be worse than secrecy because some part of government at least has access to details of classified activities, even if they are not released to the public. Indeed, it is telling that, in several cases, public bodies have kept the use of opaque algorithms itself a secret.

This form of opacity applies at the micro- as well as the macro-level. At the micro-level, the development of algorithms involves a great many decisions that are political as well as technical. Fine-tuning of parameters may include determinations that privilege one set of interests over another, or affect how public resources are allocated.[56] Accounting for false negatives and positives determines who bears the risk of error, with many instances showing that governments effectively transferred that risk to their most vulnerable citizens in areas ranging from welfare benefits to probation determinations and foster care.[57]

In the United States, a handful of lawsuits have been successful in challenging opaque government decisions relating to discontinuation of benefits and the sacking of public-school teachers, relying on due process protections under the Fourteenth Amendment.[58] Greater protections are

---

[55] Edward A Shils, *The Torment of Secrecy: The Background and Consequences of American Security Policies* (Heinemann 1956) 21–25.

[56] Brent Daniel Mittelstadt et al, 'The Ethics of Algorithms: Mapping the Debate' (2016) 3(2) Big Data & Society.

[57] See, eg, Jason Parkin, 'Adaptable Due Process' (2012) 160 University of Pennsylvania Law Review 1309, 1357–58 (welfare benefits); Robert Brauneis and Ellen P Goodman, 'Algorithmic Transparency for the Smart City' (2018) 20 Yale Journal of Law & Technology 103, 120 (probation decisions); Virginia Eubanks, *Automating Inequality: How High-Tech Tools Profile, Police, and Punish the Poor* (St Martin's 2017) 144–55 (foster care).

[58] Sarah Valentine, 'Impoverished Algorithms: Misguided Governments, Flawed Technologies, and Social Control' (2019) 46 Fordham Urban Law Journal 364, 413–19.

found in the EU, though these are typically linked to safeguards against being subject to *automatic* processing, rather than being the subject of *opaque* decision-making as such.[59]

The EU's 1995 Data Protection Directive gave individuals rights to obtain information about whether and how their personal data was processed, including the right to obtain 'knowledge of the logic involved in any automatic processing'.[60] That provision applied to public and private sector decisions, but it does not seem to have been the subject of significant debate or litigation. With the adoption of the GDPR in 2016, it was expanded to include a right of access to 'meaningful information about the logic involved, as well as the significance and the envisaged consequences of such processing'.[61]

The new language coincided with growing awareness of the opacity of many algorithmic processes. Whether it amounts to a 'right to explanation' will be considered in chapter six.[62] Of particular interest is the import of the word 'meaningful'.[63] The EU Working Party on the topic appears to have aligned itself with the more limited interpretation, observing that the provision requires that subjects be provided with 'information about the *envisaged consequences* of the processing, rather than an explanation of a *particular* decision'.[64] Acknowledging the difficulties imposed by complexity, those providing the information are enjoined to find 'simple ways to tell the data subject about the rationale behind, or the criteria relied on in reaching the decision' – which need not include a 'complex explanation of the algorithm used' or disclosure of the algorithm itself.[65]

A further constraint is that the right to explanation (if it exists) is limited by its connection to the right not to be subject to automated

---

[59] European Ethical Charter on the Use of Artificial Intelligence in Judicial Systems and Their Environment (European Commission for the Efficiency of Justice (CEPEJ), 4 December 2018). See chapter two, section 2.3. Cf the separate 'right to good administration' recognized under EU law: Damian Chalmers, Gareth Davies, and Giorgio Monti, *European Union Law: Text and Materials* (4th edn, Cambridge University Press 2019) 377–79.

[60] Directive 95/46/EC of the European Parliament and of the Council of 24 October 1995 on the protection of individuals with regard to the processing of personal data and on the free movement of such data (EU Data Protection Directive) 1995 (EU), art 12(a).

[61] General Data Protection Regulation 2016/679 (GDPR) 2016 (EU), art 15(1)(h).

[62] See chapter six, section 6.3.1.

[63] Michael Veale and Lilian Edwards, 'Clarity, Surprises, and Further Questions in the Article 29 Working Party Draft Guidance on Automated Decision-Making and Profiling' (2018) 34 Computer Law & Security Review 398, 399–400.

[64] Guidelines on Automated Individual Decision-Making (n 25) 27 (emphasis in original).

[65] Ibid 25.

processing. That is, the GDPR limits autonomous decision-making processes – including those that are opaque – but does not apply directly to decision-making processes in which a human is supported by algorithms that may themselves be opaque.[66] The GDPR also allows automated processing where it is necessary for a contract, authorized by law, or based on the subject's 'explicit consent'.[67] Final restrictions of these rights come in the form of carve-outs. A recital states that the right of access should not adversely affect 'the rights or freedoms of others, including trade secrets or intellectual property and in particular the copyright protecting the software'.[68] And, though the GDPR applies to both public as well as private sector decisions, it expressly excludes data processing by competent author-ities for the purposes of preventing, investigating, and prosecuting criminal offences.[69]

A more effective remedy may, in fact, be traditional administrative law. If, for example, a decision-maker is not permitted to delegate a decision to a third party, he or she should not be able to delegate it to an AI system; if the decision-maker is given discretion, that discretion should not be unlawfully fettered. Though there is no general duty to give reasons for all decisions, such a duty is often imposed by statute, or by the common law where the decision is judicial or quasi-judicial in nature. If the use of an AI system precluded the giving of reasons, judicial review might conclude that the decision was irrational, or impugnable on the basis that it could not be shown whether material factors were taken into account and that immaterial factors were not.[70]

A residual problem, however, is the Catch-22 of opacity: efforts to challenge decisions are hampered by the very opacity that might form the basis of an action – people do not know what they don't know. In any case, relying upon individuals to request transparency means that it will be only the most motivated who do so. The hypothetical right to explan-ation may, then, end up serving the same function as consent in data

---

[66] Lilian Edwards and Michael Veale, 'Enslaving the Algorithm: From a "Right to an Explanation" to a "Right to Better Decisions"?' (2018) 16(3) IEEE Security & Privacy 46, 47. See above n 25.

[67] GDPR, art 22(2).

[68] Ibid, recital 63.

[69] Ibid, art 2(2)(d).

[70] Jennifer Cobbe, 'Administrative Law and the Machines of Government: Judicial Review of Automated Public-Sector Decision-Making' (2019) 39 Legal Studies 636, 650–51. Cf Danielle Keats Citron, 'Technological Due Process' (2008) 85 Washington University Law Review 1249.

protection law: a formal basis for legitimacy in theory, though untethered from any meaningful agreement between equals in practice.[71]

3.3.2   Courts

Attempts to restrain opaque decision-making by public bodies will be limited in their effectiveness, in part because the default posture of many such entities is to give reasons only when asked. Not so courts and related tribunals, where reasons are expected as a matter of course.

That is not to say that courts never rely on metaphorical black boxes themselves. Juries are the most prominent example. In those jurisdictions where they are used, jurors reach verdicts in civil and criminal cases without providing reasons. They are meant to be guided by the judge, however, who often retains the power to ignore their verdict if he or she determines that no 'reasonable' jury could have reached it.[72]

As a growing portion of the criminal justice system comes to rely upon technology, these problems are going to increase. From predictive policing models to forensic software programs used in trials, algorithms protected as trade secrets are now used at all stages of criminal proceedings.[73] One response would be to abolish the trade secrets privilege in criminal trials, essentially forcing companies to reveal how conclusions are reached.[74] Alternatively, some courts have excluded evidence completely where opacity renders its use suspect.[75] It is unclear how effective these measures will be, given the internal and external pressures on judges to use assessments and their relative inexperience in evaluating the tools making them.

A vision of the future in Western courts may be offered by the extensive use of technology in the Chinese legal system. China's automated surveillance of its population, including the 'social credit system', has been much reported.[76] Less recognized is the manner in which

---

[71] Simon Chesterman, 'Introduction' in Simon Chesterman (ed), *Data Protection Law in Singapore: Privacy and Sovereignty in an Interconnected World* (2nd edn, Academy 2018) at 2–3.

[72] Cf Jason Iuliano, 'Jury Voting Paradoxes' (2014) 113 Michigan Law Review 405.

[73] Rashida Richardson, Jason M Schultz, and Kate Crawford, 'Dirty Data, Bad Predictions: How Civil Rights Violations Impact Police Data, Predictive Policing Systems, and Justice' (2019) 94 New York University Law Review 192.

[74] Rebecca Wexler, 'Life, Liberty, and Trade Secrets: Intellectual Property in the Criminal Justice System' (2018) 70 Stanford Law Review 1343.

[75] *People v Fortin*, 218 Cal Rptr 3d 867 (California Court of Appeals, 2017).

[76] See Daithí Mac Síthigh and Mathias Siems, 'The Chinese Social Credit System: A Model for Other Countries?' (2019) 82 Modern Law Review 1034.

algorithms now support the Chinese legal system.[77] Uncertainty about
the appropriate checks and balances to manage those concerns has led to
some knee-jerk responses. In 2019, for example, France – again an outlier
in saying a loud '*non*' to algorithms – passed an extraordinary law
prohibiting the publication of data analytics that reveal or predict how
particular judges decide on cases. Punishable by jail time, the new offence
was reportedly adopted after considering an alternative that would have
seen judgments published without identifying judges by name at all.[78]

Elsewhere, judges continue to muddle along. In practice, the barriers
to a successful challenge to the use of algorithms in a courtroom are high,
as Eric Loomis found out. His appeal against the circuit court's sentencing decision on the basis that his due process rights had been violated
was unsuccessful. The Wisconsin Supreme Court conceded that defendants are entitled to be sentenced based on accurate information, but it
was enough that he had the opportunity to verify the answers he gave
when COMPAS calculated its score. As for the score itself, it was not true
that the circuit court had relied on information to which Loomis was
denied access – for Judge Horne himself also had no knowledge of how
the score had been reached.[79]

The superior court ultimately upheld the decision, finding that consideration of the COMPAS score was supported by other independent
factors and 'not determinative' of his sentence. It went on, however, to
express reservations about the use of such software, requiring that future
use must be accompanied by a 'written advisement' about the proprietary
nature of the software and the limitations of its accuracy.[80] Chief Justice
Roggensack added a concurrence in which she clarified that a court may
consider tools like COMPAS in sentencing but must not *rely* on them.
A fellow justice went further, arguing that sentencing decisions should
include a record explaining their limitations as part of the 'long-standing,
basic requirement that a circuit court explain its exercise of discretion at
sentencing'.[81] The US Supreme Court declined to hear an appeal.[82]

[77] See chapter nine, introduction.
[78] Loi no 2019-222 du 23 mars 2019 de programmation 2018-2022 et de réforme pour la
justice 2019 (France), art 33; 'France Bans Judge Analytics, 5 Years in Prison for Rule
Breakers', *Artificial Lawyer* (4 June 2019).
[79] *State v Loomis* (n 3) 760–61.
[80] Ibid 753–64.
[81] Ibid 775.
[82] Certiorari denied, 137 S Ct 2290 (2017).

3.4   The Problem with Opacity

'Publicity', Jeremy Bentham wrote more than two centuries ago, 'is the very soul of justice. ... It keeps the judge himself, while trying, under trial.'[83] Judicial decisions are the clearest example of an area in which the use of opaque AI systems should be limited, but even there we see 'algorithm creep'. As this chapter has shown, computational methods have introduced efficiencies and optimization to a wide range of decision-making processes – though at a cost. In some cases, the trade-off is worthwhile. Where output-based legitimacy is sufficient, ignorance may not be bliss, but it is tolerable. The choice to use an opaque system itself, however, should be a conscious and informed one. That choice should include consideration of the risks that come with opacity.

The regulatory response to this opacity has been inconsistent. That is often the case with new technologies.[84] European efforts to restrain automatic processing clearly weigh the harmful social consequences more heavily than they are perceived in China. The US experience of predictive sentencing, for its part, exemplifies the difficulty of reining in a technology whose use has effectively become standard.

It is often presumed that the remedy to opacity is transparency. Yet this chapter has argued that the problem of opacity should be understood in three discrete ways: such decisions may be inferior, they may mask impermissible biases, or they may be illegitimate merely because of their opacity. Each points to slightly different remedies.

Poor decisions can be improved by more robust testing and verification. Success is measured in the quality of those decisions, a cost–benefit analysis viewed through a utilitarian lens. Avoiding bias, by contrast, benefits from greater clarity as to how and why algorithms are used. The goal should not be mere optimization but appropriate weighing of social and cultural norms, with rigorous audits to ensure that these are not being compromised.[85] Success here is more complicated as discrimination law rarely offers bright lines comparable to, say, the proposed ban on allowing algorithms to control lethal weapons.[86]

---

[83] Jeremy Bentham, 'Draught for the Organization of Judicial Establishments (1790)' in John Bowring (ed), *The Works of Jeremy Bentham* (William Tait 1843) vol 4, 285 at 316.
[84] See chapter seven, section 7.2.
[85] Some have gone further to suggest that these could be used for progressive purposes, a kind of 'algorithmic affirmative action': Anupam Chander, 'The Racist Algorithm?' (2017) 115 Michigan Law Review 1023, 1039–45.
[86] See chapter two, section 2.2.

In a third class of cases, the need to explain a decision is a kind of process legitimacy, applicable especially where public authorities take decisions affecting the rights and obligations of individuals. The inability to explain how a decision was made will, in some circumstances, be akin to the decision itself having been impermissibly delegated to another party. Success here most closely tracks the calls for transparency and explainability in AI systems – though primarily so that a human decision-maker can still be held accountable for those decisions.

In the course of Eric Loomis's appeal, the Wisconsin assistant attorney-general representing the state implicitly questioned whether that was, in fact, such an important shibboleth. After all, she said, 'We don't know what's going on in a judge's head; it's a black box, too.'[87] As for Mr Loomis himself, he was released from Jackson Correctional Institution in August 2019 after serving his full six-year term. According to COMPAS, at least, there is a high risk that he will return.

---

[87] Jason Tashea, 'Risk-Assessment Algorithms Challenged in Bail, Sentencing and Parole Decisions', *American Bar Association Journal* (1 March 2017) (quoting Christine Remington).

PART II

Tools

4

Responsibility

Falaise is a small *commune* of about eight thousand people in the Normandy region of France, known primarily as the birthplace of William the Conqueror. Three centuries after its most famous son established himself as the first Norman King of England, Falaise was host to the trial in a gruesome murder.

A child, the three-month-old son of Jonnet le Maux, had been mutilated in death and a large crowd turned out to see justice served on his killer. The trial was brief; the sentence death by hanging – but not before the murderer's own head and legs were mangled with a knife. The scene was captured in a fresco on the transept of the Church of the Holy Trinity: noblemen and dames, hunters and farmers, the very old and the very young were among the spectators. Dressed in new but ill-fitting clothes, the prisoner was attended by armed men on horseback. The hangman wore a new pair of gloves to absolve himself of moral responsibility for the grim task that awaited, a somewhat literal application of the *lex talionis* – the retributive principle under which an eye was to be taken for an eye, a tooth for a tooth.[1]

The fresco no longer survives, casualty of an over-enthusiastic whitewashing in the nineteenth century. But the hangman's receipt is preserved, dated 9 January 1386: ten *sols* for the gloves and a further ten for 'his troubles and as payment for having dragged, then hanged in the justice of Falaise, a sow of the age of three years or thereabouts'.[2]

The trial of animals – pigs in particular – for crimes was reasonably common in medieval Europe. The traditions of the modern courtroom were themselves still developing through this period, but sometimes they extended to beasts: lawyers, witnesses, even the occasional finding of

---

[1] Hampton L Carson, 'The Trial of Animals and Insects: A Little Known Chapter of Mediæval Jurisprudence' (1917) 56 Proceedings of the American Philosophical Society 410.

[2] EP Evans, *The Criminal Prosecution and Capital Punishment of Animals* (EP Dutton 1906) 335.

innocence. A necessary distinction was made between the domesticated and the wild. While a pig or a cow might be summoned before a tribunal, this was impractical in the case of insects or vermin. The French lawyer Barthélemy de Chasseneuz made his name defending the rats of Autun in 1508, excusing their failure to appear in court as due to the length and difficulty of the journey they faced – all the more perilous given the prevalence and vigilance of their mortal enemies, the cats.[3]

It is tempting to dismiss these practices as mere superstition, but the anthropomorphism points to the underlying function that the trials served: attributing responsibility for wrongs that would otherwise go unpunished.

Building on the discussion in Part I, a significant challenge for regulating AI systems is that their speed, autonomy, and opacity may result in undesirable harms that fall outside existing regimes of public control. This part examines the tools available to address those harms. At the highest level of generality, proposals to deal with the problems identified in Part I fall into three broad categories. First, many activities can be regulated by applying existing or modified norms and holding traditional legal persons responsible. Civil liability for damage caused by autonomous vehicles, for example, pushes at the limits of tort law; some activities, such as high-frequency trading, may need to be slowed down. But the underlying principles are sound. Secondly, it has been argued that increased autonomy of AI systems will eventually render it impossible to attribute their actions to traditional legal persons and that they should be given some form of personality in their own right. Thirdly, it is frequently said that holding either a person or the machine itself accountable requires special provision for transparency or 'explainability' in order for any regulatory regime to be effective.

This chapter and the two that follow will consider these propositions – and their limitations. Yet understanding *how* to regulate may be less important than understanding *why*. As the story of the Falaise pig trial suggests, the desire for justice runs deep. Comparable to the ancient Greek fear that an unpunished murder would unleash the furies, the medieval Church taught that a homicidal animal risked spreading demonic possession. Worry that AI systems may cause harm with impunity infuses much of the dystopian literature on the subject and has led to a rich scholarly debate over how to prevent it. From the discussion in Part I, however, such inchoate worries can be more clearly

---

[3] Esther Cohen, 'Law, Folklore, and Animal Lore' (1986) 110 Past & Present 6, 14.

seen through three discrete lenses that provide the structure for this chapter.

It begins with the practical question of assigning responsibility in a manner that properly manages risks. Autonomous vehicles are the most prominent but hardly the only example of AI systems that will need to be regulated in this way. This utilitarian lens adapts existing rules of attribution and considers new applications of product liability to autonomous actors. The limits of that approach will become evident as AI systems move from smart devices to a plethora of online services. Its efficacy will depend on the role that insurance can play in spreading unavoidable risk among those who share in the benefits. We then turn to circumstances in which shared morality requires that human actors be held to account. Command responsibility in war and non-delegable duties more generally are cases in which deontic principles require that an identifiable person be capable of assuming responsibility for certain types of harm – even if they were not personally involved in the decision or the action itself. Lastly, there are certain public functions that should not be outsourced at all, as their legitimacy requires that they not merely be attributable to a human but actually be performed by one. These inherently governmental functions may well be informed by AI systems, but should never be carried out by them.

This trichotomy – practicality, morality, legitimacy – loosely corresponds to the different levels of autonomy described as human-out-of-the-loop, human-over-the-loop, and human-in-the-loop in chapter two.[4] Rather than indicating an escalating level of autonomy, however, here it denotes a limit on the degree of delegation permissible in distinct fields of action and its impact on the management of risk, non-delegation of duties, and functions that should remain inherently governmental.

4.1 Managing Risk

The management of risk associated with AI systems is mediated in large part by the key actors developing and maintaining those systems. Industry as well as governmental and intergovernmental bodies set standards of behaviour through norms that may be hard or soft.[5] But what happens when something goes wrong? This section considers the

---

[4] See chapter two, section 2.3.
[5] See chapter seven.

traditional response of a possible action for negligence or under product liability, before discussing the role that insurance can and should play.

4.1.1   Negligence

As discussed in the context of autonomous vehicles in chapter two, the basic rules of civil liability can cover many potential harms caused by AI systems.[6] In the common law tradition, concepts used in the tort of negligence such as duty of care, breach, and causation were designed to be adaptable to novel circumstances, with case law evolving alongside scientific advances and new technologies.[7] Problems arise when there is no identifiable person to whom harmful conduct can be attributed, or when the harm is so far removed that the person cannot be said to have owed the injured party a duty of care. A discrete set of questions concerns breach of that duty, including whether improvements in technology should raise the standard above that expected of a 'reasonable person'. In relation to causation, in some circumstances AI systems may amplify the consequences of a wrongful act far beyond what could have been foreseen, or may constitute an intervening act in their own right.

In terms of the person owing a duty, a hypothetical negligence suit might target the owner, the operator, or the manufacturer of an AI system. As those systems become more complex and pervasive, however, there may be practical difficulties in identifying such a person. Various organizations have proposed registers for AI systems beyond a certain complexity, 'so that it is always possible to find out who is legally responsible'.[8] This approach may work for robots that have a physical presence, but as AI systems move online – and as they develop the capacity to change themselves and to create new systems – tracing them back to a traditional natural or legal person will be more difficult.[9]

Even if it is possible to identify an owner, operator, or manufacturer, establishing legal responsibility is complicated by the increasing autonomy of AI systems. Some scholars have therefore turned to the concept

---

[6] See chapter two, section 2.1.1.

[7] Jonathan Morgan, 'Torts and Technology' in Roger Brownsword, Eloise Scotford, and Karen Yeung (eds), *The Oxford Handbook of Law, Regulation, and Technology* (Oxford University Press 2017) 522.

[8] Ethically Aligned Design: A Vision for Prioritizing Human Well-Being with Autonomous and Intelligent Systems (IEEE, 2019) 30. Cf Report of the Committee on Legal Affairs with Recommendations to the Commission on Civil Law Rules on Robotics (European Parliament, A8-0005/2017, 2017) 20.

[9] See chapter eight, section 8.2.2(b).

of agency, under which a principal may be liable for the acts of his or her agents when acting within the scope of their actual or apparent authority.[10] Though intuitively attractive, this analogy appears to be based on confusion over the meaning of the word 'agent' as it is used by computer scientists and lawyers. For the former, software agents are a subset of computer programs. Precise definitions are contested, but typically emphasize the capacity to act with some measure of independence.[11] In today's parlance, many software agents are referred to as 'bots'. In law, by contrast, agency is defined through the relationship to a principal. The underlying legal capacity of the agent – as a natural or juridical person – is presumed.[12] Unless and until AI systems acquire some form of personhood, then, they cannot function as agents in the legal sense.

Ugo Pagallo and others argue that this conservative position fails to properly allocate risk as between those who use AI systems and the parties they deal with. An extended agency relationship would better reflect the role that AI systems will play in conducting our affairs, the argument goes, while preserving the possibility of liability – though not to the point where users will be 'ruined by the decisions of their robots'. The sticking point of legal personality is deftly addressed through an analogy with the limited rights of slaves under Roman law.[13]

Yet agency ceases to be useful at precisely the point where AI speed, autonomy, and opacity become most problematic. A principal is not liable for the acts of an agent that go beyond their actual or apparent authority; analogously, in the colourful language of vicarious liability under English law, an employer is not liable when an employee is off on 'a frolic of their own'.[14] In the case of AI systems, the most difficult

---

[10] Ugo Pagallo, *The Laws of Robots: Crimes, Contracts, and Torts* (Springer 2013) 37–43; David C Vladeck, 'Machines without Principals: Liability Rules and Artificial Intelligence' (2014) 89 Washington Law Review 117. See generally Roderick Munday, *Agency: Law and Principles* (3rd edn, Oxford University Press 2016).

[11] See, eg, Hyacinth S Nwana, 'Software Agents: An Overview' (1996) 21 Knowledge Engineering Review 205; Stan Franklin and Arthur C Graesser, 'Is It an Agent, or Just a Program?: A Taxonomy for Autonomous Agents' in JP Müller, MJ Wooldridge, and NR Jennings (eds), *Intelligent Agents III: Agent Theories, Architectures, and Languages* (Springer 1997) 21.

[12] Restatement (Third) of Agency (American Law Institute, 2006), § 1.01. The confusion is exacerbated by terms such as 'electronic agent' to denote programs that are empowered to enter into contractual relationships by a user. See, eg, Uniform Electronic Transactions Act 1999 (US), s 2(6). These contracts may be binding, but the program operates as an instrument or a tool, rather than as a legal 'agent'.

[13] Pagallo (n 10) 102–3. See chapter five, section 5.2.1.

[14] *Hilton v Thomas Burton (Rhodes) Ltd* [1961] 1 WLR 705, 709. Note that employment relationships sufficient to establish vicarious liability may include agents but are not

liability questions will arise when they operate as more than tools or
instruments, beyond the control or direction of the user. In such cases,
the agency relationship is actively unhelpful in that it presumes an
underlying responsibility on the part of the AI system itself.[15]

Arguments in favour of that underlying responsibility will be considered in the next chapter. A simpler illustration of the problem
focuses on the complexity of such systems and whether it is reasonable
to expect users to be liable when an AI system fails to perform as
intended.

In Britain, for example, drivers are responsible for the roadworthiness
of their vehicles, unless the problem is latent and not discoverable
through the exercise of reasonable care.[16] As vehicles became more
complex, it was less realistic to expect drivers to guard against latent
defects. In its 2018 consultation paper on autonomous vehicles, the
British Law Commission noted that drivers' insurers currently pay claims
where it would be difficult to distinguish between driver fault and vehicle
defects. In the case of autonomous vehicles, that distinction may become
clearer if there is no prospect of a driver being aware of a defect in the
system – or if there is no 'driver' at all.[17]

AI systems thus challenge traditional approaches to negligence in
terms of both the duty of care owed by a user and the standard of care
he or she might reasonably be expected to exercise. With respect to
causation, the process by which AI systems take decisions may also be
at odds with human predilections. This can be helpful in questioning
assumptions or conventions – something shown to be useful in games
like chess.[18] But for the purposes of tortious liability it raises the question

---

limited to them. See Peter Watts and FMB Reynolds, *Bowstead and Reynolds on Agency*
(21st edn, Sweet & Maxwell 2018), para 8-176ff.

[15] A different argument against using agency is that holding AI systems to the standard of
human agents would be an artificially *low* benchmark: Liability for Artificial Intelligence
and Other Emerging Digital Technologies (EU Expert Group on Liability and New
Technologies, 2019) 25.

[16] Road Traffic Act 1988 (UK), s 50A. A leading case from 1970 held that the failure of
brakes on a truck did not provide a defence unless the defect was not 'reasonably
discoverable': *Henderson v Henry E Jenkins & Sons* [1970] AC 282; Robert M Merkin
and Jeremy Stuart-Smith, *The Law of Motor Insurance* (Sweet & Maxwell 2004) 201.

[17] Automated Vehicles: A Joint Preliminary Consultation Paper (Law Commission,
Consultation Paper No 240; Scottish Law Commission, Discussion Paper No 166,
2018), para 6.12.

[18] Nate Silver, *The Signal and the Noise: Why So Many Predictions Fail – But Some Don't*
(Penguin 2012) 287–88.

of whether an autonomous system's behaviour could itself constitute a new intervening act that avoids liability.[19]

4.1.2 Strict Liability

To avoid uncertainty and guard against uncompensated loss, some authors have argued in favour of imposing strict liability for the use of certain AI systems.[20] The contention is that if a person engages in activity for his or her own benefit, and if that activity involves inherent risk to others, the first person can be held liable if the risk materializes.

In the English tradition, this is an application of the rule in *Rylands v Fletcher*, where it was held that a landowner, whose 'non-natural use' of his property damaged a neighbour's, was liable for compensation even though he had not acted negligently.[21] In that case, the non-natural use of property was a reservoir that flooded the neighbour's mine. A closer analogy with AI systems may be the application of similar rules for damage caused by animals. In the case of an animal known to belong to a 'dangerous species', its keeper is presumed to know that it has a tendency to cause harm and will be held liable for damage that it causes without the need to prove fault on the keeper's part. For other animals, it must be shown that the keeper knew the specific animal was dangerous. These common law rules on animals are now covered by legislation,[22] but the English courts have shied away from a general doctrine of strict liability for 'ultra-hazardous activities'.[23]

In the United States, a 1907 automobile accident case considered whether that technology, novel at the time, should be treated like a dangerous animal. The decision also concerned the death of a child, killed while playing on the street by a car driven by the friend of the son of its owner. The driver himself was convicted of manslaughter and imprisoned, but the question that went to the Georgia Court of Appeal was whether civil liability could also be attributed to the owner of the car.

---

[19] Matthew U Scherer, 'Regulating Artificial Intelligence Systems: Risks, Challenges, Competencies, and Strategies' (2016) 29 Harvard Journal of Law & Technology 353, 363–66.

[20] See, eg, Adam Rosenberg, 'Strict Liability: Imagining a Legal Framework for Autonomous Vehicles' (2017) 20 Tulane Journal of Technology and Intellectual Property 205; Hannah YeeFen Lim, *Autonomous Vehicles and the Law: Technology, Algorithms, and Ethics* (Edward Elgar 2018) 105.

[21] *Rylands v Fletcher* (1866) LR 1 Exch 265.

[22] Animals Act 1971 (UK).

[23] Christian Witting, *Street on Torts* (15th edn, Oxford University Press 2018) 453.

An argument based on agency was rejected as the connection between the owner and the driver was too tenuous. An alternative argument was that the owner should be strictly liable because automobiles should be classed with 'ferocious animals' and bear similar obligations to the owners of such animals. The court disagreed, drawing in part on their honours' own limited experience in the area:

> It is not the ferocity of automobiles that is to be feared, but the ferocity of those who drive them. Until human agency intervenes, they are usually harmless. While by reason of the rate of pay allotted to judges in this state few, if any, of them have ever owned one of these machines, yet some of them have occasionally ridden in them, thereby acquiring some knowledge of them; and we have, therefore, found out that there are times when these machines, not only lack ferocity, but assume such an indisposition to go that it taxes the limits of human ingenuity to make them move at all. They are not to be classed with bad dogs, vicious bulls, evil disposed mules, and the like.[24]

The court concluded that, until the state 'enacted those regulations which the introduction of this new mode of conveyance would seem to make salutary', responsibility was determined under the common law; in the case at hand, that was limited to the careless (human) driver himself.

An example of a technology that was made subject to strict liability is aviation. The American Law Institute's First Restatement of Torts observed in 1939 that 'aviation in its present stage of development is ultra-hazardous'.[25] As a result, even if an operator exercised utmost care, he or she was liable for the damage caused by the aircraft itself or items dropping from it.[26] Over time, air travel became more common; as industry standards developed, the rationale for strict liability came to be questioned and it was ultimately abandoned.

Though some aspects of strict liability apply to product liability, considered below, the application of strict liability generally to the *users* of AI systems on the basis that the technology is inherently hazardous would be a category error. Apart from anything else, the intention of most AI systems is to achieve increased safety and efficiency.[27] Certain

---

[24] *Lewis v Amorous*, 59 SE 338, 340 (Court of Appeals of Georgia, 1907).

[25] Restatement of the Law, First, Torts (American Law Institute, 1939), § 520.

[26] In Britain and many other jurisdictions, legislation established similar rules at the time. See 'Liability for Aircraft Damage to Ground Occupiers-A Study of Current Trends in Tort Law' (1955) 31 Indiana Law Journal 63.

[27] Indeed, as machines become safer, it has been argued that imposing strict liability may inhibit further innovation – punishing users and suppliers even when AI systems outperform the hypothetical 'reasonable person'. Ryan Abbott, 'The Reasonable

applications of AI – lethal autonomous weapons, for example, or a robot otherwise empowered to cause harm – give rise to such an assumption of risk. Here a limited analogy can be drawn to the keeper of an animal known to be dangerous.[28] Beyond specific cases like these or analogous to the storage and transportation of hazardous materials, strict liability is of limited application. In addition, as highlighted earlier, the increased complexity of AI systems may make it less appropriate to locate responsibility with the user of a system than with its manufacturer.

4.1.3   Product Liability

Placing responsibility on the manufacturer is consistent with a fundamental shift in consumer protection through the twentieth century from traditional notions of *caveat emptor* [let the buyer beware] to strict liability on the part of manufacturers. The justification was articulated in a 1944 concurring opinion of the Supreme Court of California: '[P]ublic policy demands that responsibility be fixed wherever it will most effectively reduce the hazards to life and health inherent in defective products that reach the market.'[29] It was almost two decades before the same judge wrote a majority opinion that elevated this principle to law.[30] As developed through subsequent cases, manufacturers and retailers can now be held liable if a product is defective, either due to manufacturing or design, or if there was a failure to warn users of a non-obvious danger. In the case of a design defect, it is necessary to show that the foreseeable risks of harm could have been reduced or avoided by the adoption of a 'reasonable alternative design'.[31] English courts had been edging in a similar direction, supplemented by statute.[32] In 1985, an EU Council Directive required all member states to implement a regime

---

Computer: Disrupting the Paradigm of Tort Liability' (2018) 86 George Washington Law Review 1.

[28] See, eg, Sam N Lehman-Wilzig, 'Frankenstein Unbound: Towards a Legal Definition of Artificial Intelligence' (1981) 13 Futures 442, 448; Sophia H Duffy and Jamie Patrick Hopkins, 'Sit, Stay, Drive: The Future of Autonomous Car Liability' (2013) 16 SMU Science and Technology Law Review 453, 468–73.

[29] *Escola v Coca-Cola Bottling Co*, 24 Cal 2d 453, 462 (1944) (Traynor J).

[30] *Greenman v Yuba Power Products*, 59 Cal 2d 57, 62 (1963) (Traynor J).

[31] Restatement (Third) of Torts: Product Liability (American Law Institute, 1998), § 2.

[32] Witting (n 23) 387–88.

of strict liability for defective products.[33] Many other jurisdictions
followed suit with legislation adopted in the 1990s, notably including
China.[34]

Product liability laws already apply to many AI systems. Autonomous
vehicles, for example, are covered in most jurisdictions.[35] For these and
other devices, the advantages of product liability are that it allows for
clear identification of the responsible party or parties: the 'producer',
typically meaning the manufacturer, but also including importers, distributors, and component manufacturers. Even if no other parties can be
identified, the supplier of the product can normally be sued.[36]

In the case of pervasive AI, of course, a rogue device or operating
system may not be traceable back even to a supplier. Here, a possible
remedy might be found in market share liability. Unique to the United
States, this doctrine was used to resolve a case in which a plaintiff had
been harmed by a generic drug that could not be linked to a particular
pharmaceutical company. Again, it was a court in California that came up
with an enterprising solution, drawing upon an article written by a law
student at Fordham.[37] If a plaintiff brings an action against producers of
a substantial share of the market for a fungible product that has caused
harm, the court held, the burden of proving that they did not cause the
harm switched to the producers – failing which they would all be held
liable in proportion to their market share.[38]

One could imagine a similar approach to 'manufacturers' of AI systems, but the hurdles would be high. Though the doctrine was upheld by
the US Supreme Court,[39] the circumstances of all the cases that have
applied it – a single drug made in exactly the same way by a small number
of pharmaceutical companies, which many years later harmed a class of

---

[33] Council Directive 85/374/EEC of 25 July 1985 on the Approximation of the Laws,
Regulations and Administrative Provisions of the Member States Concerning Liability
for Defective Products 1985 (EU). See, eg, Consumer Protection Act 1987 (UK); Jane
Stapleton, *Product Liability* (Butterworths 1994).
[34] 产品质量法 [Product Quality Law] 1993 (China); 侵权责任法 [Tort Liability Law] 2009
(China), ch V. See now 中华人民共和国民法典 [Civil Code of the People's Republic of
China] 2020 (China), part VII. See also Xinbao Zhang, *Legislation of Tort Liability Law in
China* (Springer 2018). On product liability generally, see Duncan Fairgrieve, *Product
Liability in Comparative Perspective* (Cambridge University Press 2005).
[35] Subject to no-fault insurance schemes, considered in section 4.1.4.
[36] See, eg, EU Product Liability Directive, art 3(3).
[37] Naomi Sheiner, 'DES and a Proposed Theory of Enterprise Liability' (1978) 46 Fordham
Law Review 963.
[38] *Sindell v Abbott Laboratories*, 607 P 2d 924 (Cal, 1980).
[39] *Rexall Drug Co v Tigue*, 493 US 944 (1989).

patients who could not be blamed for failing to point that finger at a specific wrongdoer – were unique.[40] Even in the United States, courts have refused to extend the doctrine to other drugs or products, despite periodic calls from academics to do so.[41] A broader critique is that the doctrine boils down to an attempt by a court in one of the more liberal states to make up for inadequate social safeguards in the United States more generally.[42] Even if one agrees with that policy goal, it is best pursued through the kinds of insurance schemes discussed in the next subsection.

Assuming that one or more producers can be identified, a second barrier to using product liability is the question of whether AI systems are truly 'products'. Some, like autonomous vehicles or house-cleaning robots, clearly are. But many will be closer to services.[43] The EU Product Liability Directive defines product as 'all movables' but includes electricity;[44] British legislation covers 'any goods or electricity'.[45] The US Restatement defines product as 'tangible personal property distributed commercially for use or consumption', also including real property and electricity but explicitly excluding services.[46] Astonishingly, it is still unclear whether software is regarded as a product.[47] As early as 1991, a Californian case stated in passing that it should be;[48] under the US Uniform Commercial Code, mass-marketed software has been treated as

---

[40] The drug in question was Diethylstilbestrol (DES), once prescribed to reduce the chances of miscarriage during pregnancy. A line of cases that bears some similarity is those involving negligent hunters: a plaintiff is injured but cannot prove which of the two hunters fired the shot that hit him. *Cook v Lewis* [1951] SCR 830. This is distinct from more settled authority on multiple tortfeasors, all of which contributed to the harm. See *Fairchild v Glenhaven Funeral Services Ltd* [2002] UKHL 22 (plaintiff developed mesothelioma from exposure to asbestos while working for multiple employers).

[41] Logan L Page, 'Write This Down: A Model Market-Share Liability Statute' (2019) 68 Duke Law Journal 1469. In the case of AI systems, the analogy with an identical pharmaceutical produced by multiple manufacturers would be stretched.

[42] Gregory C Keating, 'Products Liability as Enterprise Liability' (2017) 10 Tort Law Journal 41, 55; Ernest J Weinrib, 'Causal Uncertainty' (2016) 36 Oxford Journal of Legal Studies 135, 152.

[43] Jacob Turner, *Robot Rules: Regulating Artificial Intelligence* (Palgrave Macmillan 2019) 95–98.

[44] EU Product Liability Directive, art 2.

[45] Consumer Protection Act, s 1(2).

[46] Restatement (Third) of Torts: Product Liability (n 31), § 19. See David W Lannetti, 'Toward a Revised Definition of "Product" under the Restatement (Third) of Torts: Products Liability' (2000) 35 Tort & Insurance Law Journal 845.

[47] Nicholas J McBride and Roderick Bagshaw, *Tort Law* (6th edn, Pearson 2018) 364.

[48] *Winter v GP Putnam's Sons*, 938 F 2d 1033, 1035 (9th Cir, 1991).

goods, while software developed specifically for a customer is a service.[49]
In Britain and the EU, it remains an 'open question'.[50]

If product liability rules do apply, it is sufficient to prove that there was
a defect and that it caused harm. It is not necessary, for example, to prove
the cause of the defect. An autonomous vehicle that drives into a wall, for
example, is clearly defective. For more sophisticated machines – medical
technology, for example – opacity in decision-making will make it more
difficult to establish that there was in fact a defect and that the defect
caused the harm.[51] Even if a defect is found, the 'reasonable alternative
design' standard has proved problematic in cutting-edge technology
cases.[52] With more advanced AI systems, in particular those that have
the capacity to modify themselves, a producer might also rely on
a defence that the defect did not exist at the time when the product
went into circulation, or that the state of scientific knowledge at that time
was insufficient to discover it.[53]

In theory, product liability should encourage developers to design
products with safety in mind, enabling those with the most information
to hedge against risk. The means by which a producer can hedge is
through pricing and insurance. In an emerging industry like AI, however,
uncertainty complicates calculation of the probability of harm (due to
opacity) as well as the scale of the potential loss – due in part to speed and
autonomy but also to the potentially existential threat of general AI.[54]
Ryan Calo once warned that this uncertainty would constrain innovation
and that limited *immunity* should therefore be granted to robot
manufacturers.[55] The expansion of the industry in the subsequent decade
without immunity appears to undercut that argument, but his related
contention that there should be mandatory insurance has merit and is the

[49] Karni A Chagal-Feferkorn, 'Am I an Algorithm or a Product? When Products Liability
      Should Apply to Algorithmic Decision-Makers' (2019) 30 Stanford Law & Policy Review
      61, 83–84.
[50] White Paper on Artificial Intelligence (European Commission, COM(2020) 65 final,
      19 February 2020) 14.
[51] Xavier Frank, 'Is Watson for Oncology per se Unreasonably Dangerous? Making a Case
      for How to Prove Products Liability Based on a Flawed Artificial Intelligence Design'
      (2019) 45 American Journal of Law & Medicine 273. The EU has mooted a requirement
      that AI systems log their activity, with a reversal of the burden of proof if this fails.
      Liability for AI (n 15) 47–48.
[52] Mark A Geistfeld, 'The Regulatory Sweet Spot for Autonomous Vehicles' (2018) 53 Wake
      Forest Law Review 101, 124–25.
[53] EU Product Liability Directive, art 7.
[54] See chapter five, section 5.3.
[55] M Ryan Calo, 'Open Robotics' (2011) 70 Maryland Law Review 571, 601–9.

best path forward to manage the risk associated with AI system harms falling outside traditional regimes for allocating loss.

4.1.4 Insurance

The presence or absence of insurance was long said to be irrelevant to questions of liability under tort law.[56] Though true as a matter of doctrine, questions of insurance clearly shape decisions to bring claims – including when insurers themselves are empowered to do so through subrogation.[57] Compulsory insurance in particular has had a significant impact on the law concerning motor vehicle accidents.[58] The Netherlands offers an unusual example where legislation makes drivers strictly liable in virtually all motor vehicle–bicycle collisions, linked to the fact that insurance is mandatory for drivers but not for cyclists.[59]

Driverless vehicles show how insurance can manage risk associated with at least some AI systems. If the claimed benefits of autonomous vehicles in terms of safety prove true,[60] the costs associated with injuries due to traffic accidents should decline. In the medium term, however, as drivers cede control of vehicles to AI systems, the proportion of claims against drivers will drop as compared to claims against manufacturers. Those costs will therefore move from insurance premiums paid by drivers to product liability insurance on the part of manufacturers – and then back to drivers through increased prices for vehicles.[61] Potential gaps in product liability during this transition should be filled by channelling liability towards manufacturers through statute, accompanied by mandatory insurance.[62]

---

[56] See, eg, *Capital and Counties Plc v Hampshire CC* [1997] 1 QB 1004, 1044.

[57] See generally Rob Merkin and Jenny Steele, *Insurance and the Law of Obligations* (Oxford University Press 2013).

[58] As Justice Michael Kirby observed in an Australian High Court decision: 'If such compulsory insurance were *not* part of the legal background to the expression of the applicable common law … it is extremely unlikely, in my view, that the courts would impose on [a person] liability, as in the case of the appellant's claim, sounding in millions of dollars.' *Imbree v McNeilly* [2008] HCA 40, para 118 (Kirby J).

[59] Wegenverkeerswet [Road Traffic Act] 1994 (Netherlands), art 185.

[60] See chapter two, section 2.1.

[61] Daniel A Crane, Kyle D Logue, and Bryce C Pilz, 'A Survey of Legal Issues Arising from the Deployment of Autonomous and Connected Vehicles' (2017) 23 Michigan Telecommunications and Technology Law Review 191, 256–59.

[62] Cf Kenneth S Abraham and Robert L Rabin, 'Automated Vehicles and Manufacturer Responsibility for Accidents: A New Legal Regime for a New Era' (2019) 105 Virginia Law Review 127.

Such a role for insurance has been a feature of the automobile industry from its earliest days. In Britain, for example, compulsory third-party insurance has been a requirement for anyone using a motor vehicle since 1930.[63] Basic car insurance is now mandatory in most major jurisdictions, including almost all US states.[64] In Germany and Japan, strict liability on the part of owners of traditional vehicles is complemented by a mandatory insurance regime, though there is ongoing debate as to whether liability should shift towards manufacturers.[65] China introduced mandatory insurance in 2003 but requires only limited third-party coverage.[66]

For the vast majority of cases, responsibility for insurance falls to the driver or the driver's employer. Britain's Automated and Electric Vehicles Act 2018 extends that insurance requirement to cover vehicles operating autonomously. Victims (including the 'driver') of an accident caused by a fault in the vehicle itself will be covered. Failure to have insurance is a criminal offence, with liability borne by the owner of the vehicle.[67] The intention is to ensure that driver and vehicle liability are covered under the same policy, preventing disputes that 'delay or hinder access to compensation'.[68] Moving forward, the increased use of autonomous vehicles will see greater standardization of laws requiring that vehicles be insured rather than drivers, where that is not already the case.[69] An alternative would be to expand the no-fault regimes for accidents already in place in Israel, Sweden, and a dozen US states as well as parts of Australia and Canada.[70]

But can this approach be extended to applications of AI other than motor vehicles? The market will take care of many cases. For situations

---

[63] Road Traffic Act 1930 (UK), s 35.

[64] A few US states require that a bond be posted as an alternative, while New Hampshire and Virginia are outliers in not requiring insurance at all. (Virginia residents must pay a fee of $500 if they do not have insurance, though this does not provide any coverage.) See Nora Freeman Engstrom, 'When Cars Crash: The Automobile's Tort Law Legacy' (2018) 53 Wake Forest Law Review 293, 306.

[65] Frank Henkel et al, Autonomous Vehicles: The Legal Landscape of DSRC in Germany (Norton Rose Fulbright, July 2017); Gen Goto, Autonomous Vehicles, Ride-share Services, and Civil Liability: A Japanese Perspective (Asian Law Institute, June 2019).

[66] 中华人民共和国道路交通安全法 [Law of the People's Republic of China on Road Traffic Safety] 2003 (China); Xu Xian and Fan Chiang-Ku, 'Autonomous Vehicles, Risk Perceptions and Insurance Demand: An Individual Survey in China' (2019) 124(C) Transportation Research Part A: Policy and Practice 549.

[67] Automated and Electric Vehicles Act 2018 (UK), s 2.

[68] Law Commission Consultation Paper (n 17), para 6.17.

[69] Cf Mark A Geistfeld, 'A Roadmap for Autonomous Vehicles: State Tort Liability, Automobile Insurance, and Federal Safety Regulation' (2017) 105 California Law Review 1611.

[70] See, eg, Maurice Schellekens, 'No-Fault Compensation Schemes for Self-Driving Vehicles' (2018) 10 Law, Innovation and Technology 314.

where product liability places the burden on manufacturers, they will need to insure against potential suits. That will apply, for example, to the growing number of robots and smart devices, including the much-touted 'Internet of Things'. Gaps will appear where AI systems are not easily classified as 'products' and where producers attempt to contract out of potential liability.[71] In some sectors, the diversity of actors and potential harms will strengthen the argument for compulsory insurance or a no-fault regime analogous to motor vehicles.

An extreme example of this is New Zealand, which provides no-fault compensation for *all* accidents regardless of fault. The advantage is that compensation for harm is based on the injury rather than the wrong. It would not matter, for example, whether a child was injured by a driverless car, a drone, or a malfunctioning algorithm. Funding for New Zealand's Accident Compensation Commission comes from levies on payroll and petrol as well as general tax revenue.[72] The biggest limitation is that it applies only to personal injuries – excluding property damage and pure economic loss.

It has long been argued that New Zealand's outlier status in this field shows the political barriers to adopting similar regimes in other countries. As AI systems play a larger role in society, that might change, at least with respect to harms attributable to AI or falling outside traditional liability schemes. Analogous to the New Zealand approach, such a scheme could be funded through taxes or special levies from industry sectors that benefit from AI.[73]

In the short term, however, mandatory regimes will be confined to specific sectors, in particular those with a high potential for personal injury. In addition to driverless vehicles – initially, at least, being subsumed into general motor vehicle compensation schemes – transportation may expand to include drones as they become more widely used for deliveries and surveillance.[74] Medical devices are another obvious candidate, ranging from diagnostic tools to robotic surgery.[75]

---

[71] Mark Chinen, *Law and Autonomous Machines: The Co-evolution of Legal Responsibility and Technology* (Edward Elgar 2019) 46–48.

[72] Trish O'Sullivan and Kate Tokeley, 'Consumer Product Failure Causing Personal Injury under the No-Fault Accident Compensation Scheme in New Zealand – A Let-Off for Manufacturers?' (2018) 41 Journal of Consumer Policy 211.

[73] Cf Turner (n 43) 103.

[74] Bryan Casey, 'Robot Ipsa Loquitur' (2019) 108 Georgetown Law Journal 225, 249.

[75] Jonathan H Chen and Steven M Asch, 'Machine Learning and Prediction in Medicine – Beyond the Peak of Inflated Expectations' (2017) 376(26) New England Journal of

As AI systems play a greater role in other aspects of daily life, the distinction between products and services will become problematic. Though the popular imagination often gravitates towards a world in which humanoid robots interact with their flesh and blood counterparts, virtual services such as smart assistants may have an even greater impact.[76] Mandatory insurance for service providers can fill this potential gap. Alternatively, it may be necessary to provide insurance for claims of last resort, to cover unidentified or uninsured technology.[77]

Far from being irrelevant to questions of liability, insurance in this way becomes an important means of shaping behaviour. Often overlooked as a regulatory tool, it serves two discrete functions: compensating loss and allocating risk. With emerging technology, uncertainty as to risk makes it difficult to price policies correctly. Pricing them too high constrains innovation; pricing them too low – or pushing mandatory policies onto consumers – encourages moral hazard if producers do not bear the costs of their mistakes. As more data is gathered, the risks should become more quantifiable over time.[78]

Insurance can also serve a third function of deterring certain conduct, by having products or services for which insurance is not available or establishing conduct that voids it. The example of private military and security companies is, again, instructive as the refusal of underwriters to cover certain combat-related activity sometimes has more of an effect on behaviour than norms prohibiting it.[79]

Insurance thus assists in managing the risks associated with new technologies, through imposing costs on those most able to minimize harm and compensating those most likely to suffer loss. The objective is utilitarian. In some cases, however, an efficient outcome may be

Medicine 2507; Jianxing He et al, 'The Practical Implementation of Artificial Intelligence Technologies in Medicine' (2019) 25 Nature Medicine 30.

[76] Cf Robert D Lang and Lenore E Benessere, 'Alexa, Siri, Bixby, Google's Assistant, and Cortana Testifying in Court: Novel Use of Emerging Technology in Litigation' (2018) 35 (7) Computer and Internet Lawyer 16.

[77] European Parliament Resolution with Recommendations to the Commission on Civil Law Rules on Robotics (2015/2103(INL)) (European Parliament, 16 February 2017), para 59; Liability for AI (n 15) 62.

[78] Chinen (n 71) 118–20.

[79] Andrew Bearpark and Sabrina Schulz, 'The Future of the Market' in Simon Chesterman and Chia Lehnardt (eds), *From Mercenaries to Market: The Rise and Regulation of Private Military Companies* (Oxford University Press 2007) 239. See also chapter two, section 2.2.3.

inadequate as the attribution of responsibility is about more than just managing risk.

4.2 Non-delegable Duties

Tort law, particularly when viewed through a law and economics analysis, seeks to reduce the costs of accidents and the costs of avoiding them.[80] It can also be understood as embodying a form of corrective justice: the obligation to remedy wrongful losses that one has caused. Criminal law can be analysed through similar lenses, but it tends to be regarded in more deontological terms: even if the criminal law is not an efficient deterrent, the moral opprobrium of certain acts demands a societal response.[81]

Managing the risks of certain AI systems – driverless cars, most prominently – can be achieved through adapting liability models and insurance regimes to suit their novel aspects. Yet management of risk is not always enough. In some circumstances it is necessary to establish responsibility even if it is not 'efficient'. This section considers two examples: non-delegable duties in the common law and command responsibility in IHL.

4.2.1   Non-delegable Duties in the Common Law

Much of tort law is concerned with the righting of wrongs, shifting the cost of harm from a blameless plaintiff onto a culpable defendant. Its common law origins are traced back to early forms of action such as battery and assault, trespass, negligence, and so on, conceived as means of correcting the infringement of a personal right. Yet that is not its only function. It is now generally accepted that tort law also has a regulatory role in shaping behaviour. The previous section focused on situations in which tort law and its statutory surrogates determine how to allocate loss based on fault – including where fault is waived in favour of a more

---

[80] Often traced back to Judge Learned Hand in a 1947 case concerning a barge that broke loose of its moorings, sinking another boat, the duty to guard against injury is said to be a function of three variables: '(1) The probability that she will break away; (2) the gravity of the resulting injury, if she does; (3) the burden of adequate precautions. Possibly it serves to bring this notion into relief to state it in algebraic terms: if the probability be called P; the injury, L; and the burden, B; liability depends upon whether B is less than L multiplied by P: ie, whether $B < PL$.' *United States v Carroll Towing Co*, 159 F 2d 169, 173 (2d Cir, 1947).
[81] See chapter five, section 5.1.2(b).

efficient regime of spreading losses across a group. Here the focus is on that regulatory role, in particular on situations where tort law provides for a non-delegable duty not merely to take care but to see that care is taken.[82]

Such non-delegable duties are sometimes confused with vicarious liability. The latter is a secondary form of liability, however, whereby an employer is held responsible for the tort of another. A non-delegable duty, by contrast, is a primary obligation to 'ensure that' reasonable care is taken in a given activity. This is important in the context of AI systems because liability does not depend on first finding that an employee or agent has committed a wrong, begging questions of AI personality similar to those raised by agency.[83]

As is sometimes the case in the common law, the doctrine of non-delegable duties grew organically and has caused a degree of confusion among commentators and the judiciary alike.[84] In 2014, the UK Supreme Court attempted to rationalize it as falling into two broad categories. The first concerns independent contractors engaged in inherently hazardous activities, recalling the earlier discussion of strict liability. The second comprises cases in which the law imposes a special duty on a defendant due to a relationship with the party harmed, including a positive obligation to protect a class of persons from harm. The duty is 'by virtue of that relationship personal to the defendant'.[85] Examples include duties owed by hospital authorities to patients in respect of their treatment, and schools with respect to the physical safety of their students.[86] It might extend to other situations in which there is a high risk and a correspondingly high assumption of responsibility.[87]

Applying these principles to AI systems avoids several of the problems identified earlier, including questions of attribution and proof of fault.[88] Inherently hazardous activities would include the deployment of AI systems

---

[82] Christian Witting, 'Breach of the Non-delegable Duty: Defending Limited Strict Liability in Tort' (2006) 29 UNSW Law Journal 33, 34–35.

[83] See above section 4.1.1.

[84] John Murphy, 'The Liability Bases of Common Law Non-delegable Duties: A Reply to Christian Witting' (2007) 30 UNSW Law Journal 86; Simon Deakin, 'Organisational Torts: Vicarious Liability versus Non-delegable Duty' [2018] Cambridge Law Journal 15.

[85] *Woodland v Essex County Council* [2014] AC 547, paras 6–7.

[86] Witting (n 23) 609–10.

[87] Simon Deakin and Zoe Adams, *Markesinis and Deakin's Tort Law* (8th edn, Oxford University Press 2019) 572.

[88] Cf Kumaralingam Amirthalingam, 'The Non-delegable Duty: Some Clarifications, Some Questions' (2017) 29 Singapore Academy of Law Journal 500, 516–17.

with offensive capabilities, such as security drones. The special relationship between hospital and patient would cover the use of medical technology. In the context of schools, robot teachers remain further in the future – but the use of technology for security and discipline is not.[89]

As discussed earlier, some of these areas are ripe for mandatory insurance. The importance of a non-delegable duty, however, goes beyond allocation of loss and is intended to focus the mind of a duty-holder on preventing loss in the first place.[90] As the use of AI systems becomes more widespread, the circumstances in which such duties arise will expand – analogous to the expansion of product liability and occupier's liability through the twentieth century.

4.2.2   Command Responsibility

Non-delegable duties in the common law establish a kind of moral as well as legal responsibility but are still primarily concerned with allocating the costs of harm. Though punitive damages are possible in various jurisdictions, the focus remains on compensation. Criminal law, by contrast, foregrounds the moral question. The threshold for culpability is also higher: conduct must be more blameworthy than mere negligence, the burden of proof beyond reasonable doubt rather than on mere balance of probabilities.[91]

As discussed in chapter two, criminal responsibility is the wrong way to address misbehaviour by AI systems. As vehicle autonomy increases, for example, rule infractions by motor vehicles will be seen more as errors to be corrected rather than crimes to be punished; if the 'driver' has minimal control over the vehicle or the code that controls its behaviour, it is inappropriate to penalize him or her.[92] In some jurisdictions, product liability rules are supplemented by criminal sanctions for placing products on the market that are not 'safe'.[93] Such sanctions are appropriate if

---

[89] Echo Xie, 'Artificial Intelligence Is Watching China's Students but How Well Can It Really See?', *South China Morning Post* (16 September 2019).

[90] Channelling liability in this way also encourages planning ahead, including sharing future costs of liability between the manufacturer and the component suppliers by way of prior contractual agreement.

[91] Matthew Dyson, *Comparing Tort and Crime: Learning from Across and Within Legal Systems* (Cambridge University Press 2015) 457.

[92] See chapter two, section 2.1.2, and chapter five, section 5.1.2(b).

[93] See, eg, Directive 2001/95/EC of the European Parliament and of the Council of 3 December 2001 on General Product Safety 2001 (EU); General Product Safety Regulations 2005 (UK); 15 USC § 2070.

a product is known to be dangerous, or if a manufacturer fails to take due care to ensure that it is not.

What is of interest here is whether a traditional legal person can be held responsible for the actions of an AI system operating with a degree of autonomy or opacity that would otherwise render that person blameless. Debates over this question have tended to focus on a subset of AI systems unlikely to enter the open market but in which responsibility is attributed for moral rather than practical reasons: autonomous weapon systems.

Arguments that lethal autonomous weapon systems may in fact be 'safer' than humans misconceive the concern. Though the origins of IHL can be traced to a desire to minimize suffering,[94] the requirement for meaningful human involvement in combat decisions is justified by deontic rather than utilitarian considerations. At the international level, the UN Special Rapporteur on Extrajudicial, Summary, or Arbitrary Executions wrote in a 2013 report on lethal autonomous robotics that proportionality, a concept fundamental to IHL, involves 'distinctively human judgment'.[95] Under the law of armed conflict, the standard for proportionality is what a reasonable military commander would do in the circumstances.[96] While it is sometimes argued that such judgments are too complex for a computer to make, complexity is one of the weaker arguments against handing a decision over to machines. The stronger argument for meaningful human control is not that humans will make better decisions but that humans can be held to account.[97] One of the few things that the UN Group of Governmental Experts has been able to agree on is a 'guiding principle' that human responsibility for decisions on the use of weapons systems 'must be retained since accountability cannot be transferred to machines'.[98]

Applying that principle to the existing laws is not a simple task, leading some to conclude that this alone justifies banning autonomous weapons

---

[94] Simon Chesterman (ed), *Civilians in War* (Lynne Rienner 2001).

[95] Report of the Special Rapporteur on Extrajudicial, Summary, or Arbitrary Executions, Christof Heyns, UN Doc A/HRC/23/47 (2013), para 72.

[96] See, eg, *Prosecutor v Stanislav Galic* (5 December 2003) Case No IT-989-29-T (ICTY Trial Chamber), para 58.

[97] See chapter two, section 2.2.2.

[98] Report of the 2019 Session of the Group of Governmental Experts on Emerging Technologies in the Area of Lethal Autonomous Weapons Systems, UN Doc CCW/GGE.1/2019/3 (2019), Annex IV. A separate question is the extent to which a state may be held responsible for a wrong by an autonomous weapon system under international law. This possibility will be considered in chapter eight, section 8.2.1(b).

completely. Setting aside the question of whether they are unlawful in and of themselves, the use of such a system would be caught by existing laws if it was given unlawful targeting parameters or deployed in an area with civilians but lacking the ability to distinguish them from combatants. In both cases, the operator who deployed the system could be held responsible.[99]

Where things get more complex is if the operator does not program targets but is given the ability to veto them – a 'human-over-the-loop' scenario. Given the speed with which decisions need to be made and the absence of alternative sources of information, failure to stop a machine may not satisfy the volitional component needed for a war crime to be established.[100]

Looking further into the future, assuming an increase in autonomy and opacity, how would IHL treat an AI system that killed civilians for reasons that could not be attributed to unlawful instructions, or to a hardware or software defect? Some argue that the question should never arise, in essence because the use of a weapon that behaves unforeseeably is itself a violation of the laws of war.[101] Others are willing to accept a modest failure rate, noting that the law does not require perfection on the part of soldiers deployed in battle and tolerates equipment malfunctions. A soldier who makes a mistake due to fatigue, for example, or a missile that veers off course may not be sufficient to establish individual accountability for a war crime.[102] Extending this to truly autonomous weapons would be appropriate in the case of a malfunction, comparable to a rocket misfiring. But it is entirely foreseeable that an AI system could be empowered to make targeting decisions and do so in a manner that violates international norms for reasons that cannot be fully explained.[103] Tolerating this would be akin to

---

[99] Carrie McDougall, 'Autonomous Weapon Systems and Accountability: Putting The Cart Before the Horse' (2019) 20 Melbourne Journal of International Law 58, 69. See also Neha Jain, 'Autonomous Weapons Systems: New Frameworks for Individual Responsibility' in Nehal Bhuta et al (eds), *Autonomous Weapons Systems: Law, Ethics, Policy* (Cambridge University Press 2016) 303 at 308–10.

[100] Amos N Guiora, 'Accountability and Decision Making in Autonomous Warfare: Who Is Responsible?' [2017] Utah Law Review 393, 397.

[101] See, eg, Charles J Dunlap, Jr, 'Accountability and Autonomous Weapons: Much Ado About Nothing' (2016) 30 Temple International & Comparative Law Journal 63, 71.

[102] Ian S Henderson, Patrick Keane, and Josh Liddy, 'Remote and Autonomous Warfare Systems: Precautions in Attack and Individual Accountability' in Jens David Ohlin (ed), *Research Handbook on Remote Warfare* (Edward Elgar 2017) 335 at 361–63.

[103] Joshua Hughes, 'The Law of Armed Conflict Issues Created by Programming Automatic Target Recognition Systems Using Deep Learning Methods' [2019] Yearbook of International Humanitarian Law 99.

tolerating unlawful conduct on the part of ill-trained or undisciplined soldiers.

The potential accountability deficit can be addressed through applying the doctrine of command responsibility. Under the Rome Statute of the International Criminal Court, for example, a military commander may be criminally responsible for crimes committed by forces under his or her 'effective command and control'. This will be made out where the crimes were a result of a failure to exercise control properly, where the commander knew or ought to have known about the crimes and failed to take all necessary and reasonable measures within his or her power to prevent or repress them.[104] Civilian superiors can also be held responsible, though with a higher threshold that they either 'knew, or consciously disregarded information which clearly indicated' that subordinates were committing or about to commit crimes.[105]

Two types of objection might be raised when applying this to autonomous weapon systems: one formal, the other substantive. The formal objection is that command responsibility presumes a hierarchical relationship between commander and subordinate. Akin to the earlier discussion of agency and vicarious liability, if command responsibility requires that the notional subordinate be a legal person who commits a crime in his or her own right, then transposing it to AI systems would be another category error.[106] Early applications of the principle after the Second World War did treat it as a kind of accomplice liability for the crimes of those under one's command, and it is frequently assumed that command responsibility is a form of accessory liability.[107] That analogy holds for situations in which the commander has actual knowledge of crimes, but it has caused much hand-wringing by jurists with regard to liability for failing to prevent those crimes. Accessory liability is even harder to square with the fact that a commander may also be criminally responsible for failing to punish crimes after the fact.[108] The better

---

[104] Statute of the International Criminal Court (Rome Statute), UN Doc A/Conf.183/9 (1998), art 28(a).

[105] Ibid, art 28(b).

[106] See, eg, Rebecca Crootof, 'War Torts: Accountability for Autonomous Weapons' (2016) 164 University of Pennsylvania Law Review 1347, 1378–81.

[107] Jack M Beard, 'Autonomous Weapons and Human Responsibilities' (2014) 45 Georgetown Journal of International Law 617, 657; Jens David Ohlin, 'The Combatant's Stance: Autonomous Weapons on the Battlefield' (2016) 92 International Law Studies 1, 28.

[108] Chantal Meloni, 'Command Responsibility: Mode of Liability for the Crimes of Subordinates or Separate Offence of the Superior?' (2007) 5 Journal of International

argument is that a commander's responsibility stands not in the contribution made to the crime of a subordinate but in a culpable dereliction of duty.[109] As the Appeals Chamber of the International Criminal Tribunal for the former Yugoslavia has stressed, 'an accused is not charged with the crimes of his [sic] subordinates but with his failure to carry out his duty as a superior to exercise control'.[110]

The substantive objection is that, even if the extension to autonomous weapon systems is appropriate, it would be unworkable in practice. The requirement that the commander knew or ought to have known about any crimes may exclude cases where he or she deployed the AI system on the assumption that it would operate as programmed and comply with the laws of war.[111] Similarly, the failure to take all necessary and reasonable measures within one's power may be severely limited for a commander in the field. Soldiers are expected to have direct relationship with their commanding officers, who in turn help establish a culture and *esprit de corps*. Autonomous weapon systems, by contrast, are likely to be presented to a field commander as a finished tool to be used.

The difficulties of applying command responsibility even in traditional warfare were on display in the first case in which it was argued before the International Criminal Court. Congolese leader Jean-Pierre Bemba was convicted in 2016 for war crimes and crimes against humanity perpetrated in neighbouring Central African Republic by troops under his command.[112] Two years later, the verdict was overturned, causing some measure of uncertainty as to the status of the doctrine.[113] Central to the Appeal Court's majority decision was that the forces were operating in another country, with 'attendant difficulties on Mr Bemba's ability, as a remote commander, to take measures' to control their actions.[114]

Criminal Justice 618, 636–37; Antonio Cassese, *Cassese's International Criminal Law* (3rd edn, Oxford University Press 2013) 192.

[109] Guénaël Mettraux, *The Law of Command Responsibility* (Oxford University Press 2009) 40.

[110] *Prosecutor v Krnojelac* (17 September 2003) Case No IT-97-25-A (ICTY Appeals Chamber), para 171.

[111] McDougall (n 99) 77.

[112] *Prosecutor v Jean-Pierre Bemba Gombo* (21 March 2016) Case No ICC-01/05-01/08 (International Criminal Court, Trial Chamber).

[113] See, eg, Trenton W Powell, 'Command Responsibility: How the International Criminal Court's Jean-Pierre Bemba Gombo Conviction Exposes the Uniform Code of Military Justice' (2017) 225 Military Law Review 837; Leila Nadya Sadat, 'Prosecutor v Jean-Pierre Bemba Gombo' (2019) 113 American Journal of International Law 353.

[114] *Prosecutor v Jean-Pierre Bemba Gombo* (8 June 2018) Case No ICC-01/05-01/08 (International Criminal Court, Appeals Chamber), para 171. This implied limit on

Any assessment of whether he took all reasonable and necessary measures required 'consideration of what measures were at his . . . disposal in the circumstances at the time'.[115]

Though *Bemba* did not consider autonomous weapons, it suggests potential barriers to applying command responsibility to field commanders. An alternative is to look to the development phase in which parameters are established for the lethal autonomous weapon system to act. This could lead to a reconceptualization of command responsibility, moving attention from the field commander who employs the weapon to the commander – or political leader – responsible for procuring and deploying it.[116] A key problem here is that the further one moves from the alleged crime, the harder it is to establish responsibility. Focusing on the development of autonomous weapon systems, for example, means that much of the conduct may not even take place in the context of an armed conflict – a requirement for a war crimes prosecution.[117] Moreover, establishing the mental element for liability may be impossible.[118]

In addition to the possibility of drafting specific rules to govern the use of autonomous weapon systems, one short-term means of addressing the potential accountability gap is to establish dedicated command structures comparable to the separate chains of command that oversee land, air, and sea forces. An AI systems command would need resources and skills sufficient to assume responsibility for the actions of those systems; in future, deploying them without such a structure might itself be regarded as a violation of the laws of war.[119]

---

command responsibility is controversial. Indeed, even the concurring opinion that created a majority discounted 'geographic remoteness' itself as a factor on its own. Ibid, Concurring Separate Opinion of Judge Eboe-Osuji, para 258.

[115] Ibid, para 168.

[116] Geoffrey S Corn, 'Autonomous Weapons Systems: Managing the Inevitability of "Taking the Man out of the Loop"' in Nehal Bhuta et al (eds), *Autonomous Weapons Systems: Law, Ethics, Policy* (Cambridge University Press 2016) 209 at 232.

[117] Tim McFarland and Tim McCormack, 'Mind the Gap: Can Developers of Autonomous Weapons Systems Be Liable for War Crimes?' (2014) 90 International Studies 361, 372–74.

[118] Tetyana Krupiy, 'Regulating a Game Changer: Using a Distributed Approach to Develop an Accountability Framework for Lethal Autonomous Weapon Systems' (2018) 50 Georgetown Journal of International Law 45.

[119] Peter Margulies, 'Making Autonomous Weapons Accountable: Command Responsibility for Computer-Guided Lethal Force in Armed Conflicts' in Jens David Ohlin (ed), *Research Handbook on Remote Warfare* (Edward Elgar 2017) 405 at 433.

4.2.3 The Buck Stops Here

The law rarely punishes genuine omissions or failures to act. Famously – or infamously – the common law does not compel a person to help a drowning stranger, or to prevent a crime in which he or she has played no role. The emergence of AI systems acting autonomously will challenge these traditional limits.

This section has shown two ways in which traditional legal persons can be held to a higher degree of responsibility, either through non-delegable duties of care to protect a vulnerable class of persons or through command responsibility in the context of military operations. Moving forward, the situations in which responsibility is allocated not merely as an efficient means of managing risk but as a kind of moral backstop may increase. How this is done will depend on the specific context of each jurisdiction. Failure to do so could mean that residual responsibility for certain acts that rise to the level of an international wrong will fall to the state itself, a topic considered in chapter eight.

4.3 Inherently Governmental Functions and the Limits of Outsourcing

In some circumstances, merely knowing that a person can be held accountable for a decision – that the buck stops somewhere – may still not be enough. For certain decisions, it is necessary to have a human 'in-the-loop', actively participating in those decisions.

The situation in Europe was considered in chapter two, in the context of algorithmic decision-making and the right not to be subjected to automatic processing.[120] Similarly, chapter three highlighted situations in which the opacity of AI systems should preclude them from being relied upon in certain public decisions – sentencing determinations, for example.[121] Here, the intention is to look more broadly at whether there are classes of decisions for which a human must not only be able to take responsibility but actually *be* responsible. This is intuitively true with respect to many public powers, though it is not always clearly articulated. Until now, many of the debates have been reactive – resisting encroachment in specific sectors by algorithms, empowering individuals to question particular decisions. As AI systems become more pervasive, it will be

---

[120] See chapter two, section 2.3.2.
[121] See chapter three, section 3.3.

necessary to address the problem from the other direction: identifying functions that should not be delegated to those systems at all.[122]

A useful analogy is limits on government outsourcing to third parties. If there are aspects of public power that cannot be transferred to third parties, they should not be transferred to fast, autonomous, and opaque machines either. The justifications for such limits fall into two categories. First, some functions may be difficult to regulate in a *legal* sense if they are removed from public hands. Secondly, some functions are so connected to the public interest that they require oversight by a public entity accountable through a *political* process.[123]

The United States is atypical in this area, debates over privatization often contrasting starkly with the discourse in Europe. Whereas policy discussion there normally considers the appropriateness of transferring public functions to private actors, in the United States the legal and political environment frames the question as whether those functions should be public in the first place.[124] The US understanding of what is 'inherently governmental' has thus emerged not as a sphere to be protected but rather as an exception to the more general push to privatization. Legislation adopted by Congress in 1998 defined it as a 'function that is so intimately related to the public interest as to require performance by Federal Government employees'.[125] The US Government Accountability Office (GAO) noted in a 2002 report that there had been some uncertainty about how to apply this broad definition, but argued that it was 'clear that government workers need to perform certain warfighting, judicial, enforcement, regulatory, and policy-making functions'.[126] A 2011 policy letter from the Office of Management and Budget elaborated that it would include the exercise

---

[122] Cf Dillon Reisman et al, Algorithmic Impact Assessments: A Practical Framework for Public Agency Accountability (AI Now, April 2018).

[123] Simon Chesterman and Angelina Fisher, 'Conclusion: Private Security, Public Order' in Simon Chesterman and Angelina Fisher (eds), *Private Security, Public Order: The Outsourcing of Public Services and Its Limits* (Oxford University Press 2009) 222 at 225–26.

[124] Government Contractors: Are Service Contractors Performing Inherently Governmental Functions? (US General Accounting Office (GAO), GAO/GGD-92-11, 18 November 1991) 2.

[125] Federal Activities Inventory Reform (FAIR) Act 1998 (US), s 5.

[126] Commercial Activities Panel: Improving the Sourcing Decisions of the Federal Government (US General Accounting Office (GAO), GAO-02-847T, 27 September 2002) 21.

of discretion in applying government authority or the making of value judgments on behalf of the government.[127]

The concept is less common outside the United States. Britain does not have a functional equivalent, though the term occasionally pops up – as it did in passing in a 2013 Ministry of Defence White Paper on procurement.[128] The EU lacks regulation of the area for a mix of security and industrial considerations,[129] though some member states have constitutional restrictions on the delegation of services by public authorities to private undertakings.[130] In China, for many years the question would have been irrelevant as the concept of outsourcing was alien to Communist Party doctrine. Now, however, privatization is being experimented with at many levels, particularly those 'amenable to high-tech solutions'[131] – and, as we have seen, China is at the forefront of utilizing AI in some of the most sensitive areas, notably the judiciary.[132]

IHL once again offers an interesting comparison. The Geneva Conventions require, for example, that prisoner-of-war camps 'be put under the immediate authority of a responsible commissioned officer belonging to the regular armed forces of the Detaining Power'.[133] Similarly, places of internment for civilians are to be put 'under the authority of a responsible officer, chosen from the regular military forces or the regular civil administration of the Detaining Power'.[134]

---

[127] Policy Letter 11–01, Performance of Inherently Governmental and Critical Functions (Office of Federal Procurement Policy, 12 September 2011). Cf Thomas J Laubacher, 'Simplifying Inherently Governmental Functions: Creating a Principled Approach from Its ad hoc Beginnings' (2017) 46 Public Contract Law Journal 791, 822; Fiona O'Carroll, 'Inherently Governmental: A Legal Argument for Ending Private Federal Prisons and Detention Centers' (2017) 67 Emory Law Journal 293.

[128] Better Defence Acquisition: Improving How We Procure and Support Defence Equipment (HMSO, Cm 8626, 2013), para 38. See William T Kirkwood, 'Inherently Governmental Functions, Organizational Conflicts of Interest, and the Outsourcing of the United Kingdom's MOD Defense Acquisition Function: Lessons Learned from the US Experience' (2015) 44 Public Contract Law Journal 443.

[129] Martin Trybus, 'The New EU Defence Procurement Regime' in Christopher Bovis (ed), Research Handbook on EU Public Procurement Law (Edward Elgar 2016) 523 at 524.

[130] Christopher H Bovis, EU Public Procurement Law (Edward Elgar 2007) 43. Limitations on the transfer of personal data would also be an effective barrier to certain forms of outsourcing.

[131] Zhang Mengzhong and Sun Jian, 'Outsourcing in Municipal Governments: Experiences from the United States and China' (2012) 35 Public Performance & Management Review 696, 715.

[132] See chapter three, section 3.3.2, and chapter nine, introduction.

[133] Convention Relative to the Treatment of Prisoners of War (Third Geneva Convention), done at Geneva, 12 August 1949, art 39.

[134] Convention Relative to the Protection of Civilian Persons in Time of War (Fourth Geneva Convention), done at Geneva, 12 August 1949, art 99.

These provisions are not directly translatable to AI and the role it should play in the public sector. Among other things, government reliance on software may not be construed as 'outsourcing' at all. But to the extent that reliance amounts to handing over discretion or making value judgments on behalf of a government in the exercise of its authority, limits that apply to a third party could apply equally to an AI system.

As the US experience shows, however, defining the boundary between what is and is not 'inherently governmental' can be far from simple.[135] Every year, for example, the US Department of Health and Human Services processes thousands upon thousands of procurement contracts, struggling to do so consistently and efficiently. And so, in 2019, the Department trained a recurrent neural network using past statements of work and Federal guidelines to 'help acquisition staff make the call' as to whether outsourcing is permitted. Even at proof-of-concept stage, the system was said to be providing the correct answer 86 per cent of the time.[136] Though this is impressive as an example of natural language processing, responsibility for determining whether a given function is 'inherently governmental' should itself, at least, remain an inherently governmental task.

4.4   The Limits of Responsibility

It is now more than three decades since a US Third Circuit Court of Appeals noted that 'robots cannot be sued, but they can cause devastating damage'.[137] That case involved a baseball-pitching machine whose defects rendered it 'more wild than an erratic pitcher'. As this chapter has shown, the laws of negligence and product liability will resolve many cases of harms caused by such machines.

But not all. Even in cases where the primary motivation for determining responsibility is to spread risk and compensate loss, the speed, autonomy, and opacity of AI systems will give rise to accountability gaps. Driverless vehicles show how many such gaps can be filled through the use of mandatory insurance, an approach that should extend to other areas of AI. Risk and loss are not the only measures of potential harm,

---

[135]   Cf John R Luckey, Valerie Bailey Grasso, and Kate M Manuel, Inherently Governmental Functions and Department of Defense Operations: Background, Issues, and Options for Congress (Congressional Research Service, 2009) 54.

[136]   Troy K Schneider, 'Can AI Decide if Work Is "Inherently Governmental?"', *Federal Computer Week* (16 September 2019).

[137]   *United States v Athlone Industries, Inc*, 746 F 2d 977, 979 (3d Cir, 1984).

however. In some cases, the legitimacy of functions entrusted to public officials by a polity requires that those officials carry out those functions, not pass them on to a third party whether metal and silicon or flesh and blood. And, in others, the decision to hold a person responsible is driven by moral considerations: the view that some relationships – hospital and patient, school and student – require a higher level of care, and that some decisions over life and death require that a human soul grapple with them.

Thomas Aquinas seems to have understood this last point. Writing a hundred years before the pig of Falaise met her grisly end, he argued in his *Summa Theologica* that animals by their nature are incapable of suffering guilt for their actions, and that it therefore makes no sense to punish them. Indeed, he went further, stating that such creatures merely embody the nature endowed them by God. Cursing them is not just pointless, it is blasphemous.[138]

Aquinas was in a minority, however, and animal trials continued across Europe for half a millennium. They reflected the historical role of Ecclesiastical Courts as well as the competing influences of law and custom. By the middle of the eighteenth century, they were rare and informal, a kind of village justice that was eventually deemed a relic of the past.

Yet, as we will see, the desire to hold *someone* responsible for sins that would otherwise go unpunished lives on. Despite the avenues outlined in this chapter, future cases will arise where there is a harm not attributable to a person or a company, where insurance is inadequate to make up for the loss: the death of a child hit by an unidentified drone, for example, or killed in error by a lethal autonomous weapon. In such a case no compensation can be adequate; an understandable desire for justice will seek an outlet. The temptations of anthropomorphism will be great. Metaphorically, at least, there may be calls from a grieving community for punishment, to dress the robot up in a suit and hang it in the public square alongside the pig from Falaise.

---

[138] Thomas Aquinas, *Summa Theologica* (Fathers of the English Dominican Province tr, first published 1265–74, Benziger Brothers 1911), Second Part of the Second Part, Question 76.

5

Personality

In 2021 the Bank of England completed its transition from paper to polymer with the release of a new £50 note. A public selection process had seen almost a quarter of a million nominations for the face of the new note; the final decision, announced in July 2019, was that Alan Turing would be featured. Turing was a hero for his code breaking during the Second World War. He also helped establish the discipline of computer science, laying the foundations for what we now call AI. Perhaps his best-known contribution, however, is the eponymous test for when true 'intelligence' has actually been achieved.

Turing modelled it on a parlour game popular in 1950. A man and a woman sit in a separate room and provide written answers to questions; the other participants have to guess who provided which answer. Turing posited that a similar 'imitation game' could be played with a computer. When a machine was able to fool people into believing that it was human, we might properly say that it was intelligent.[1]

Early successes along these lines came in the 1960s with programs like Eliza. Users were told that Eliza was a psychotherapist who communicated through words typed into a computer. In fact, 'she' was an algorithm written with a simple list-processing language. If the user typed in a recognized phrase, it was reframed as a question. So, after the user entered 'I'm depressed,' Eliza replied 'Why do you say that you are depressed?' If it didn't recognize the phrase, the program would offer something generic, like 'Can you elaborate on that?' Even when they were told how it worked, some users insisted that Eliza had 'understood' them.[2]

Parlour games aside, why should it matter if a computer is 'intelligent'? For several decades, the Turing Test was associated more with the

---

[1] AM Turing, 'Computing Machinery and Intelligence' (1950) 59 Mind 433.

[2] Richard S Wallace, 'The Anatomy of ALICE' in Robert Epstein, Gary Roberts, and Grace Beber (eds), *Parsing the Turing Test: Philosophical and Methodological Issues in the Quest for the Thinking Computer* (Springer 2009) 181 at 184–85.

question of whether AI was possible than with the status of an entity embodying such qualities. Yet it is commonly invoked in discussions of legal personality for AI, from Lawrence Solum's seminal 1992 article onwards.[3] Though no longer regarded as a serious measure of modern AI in a technical sense, the Turing Test's longevity as a trope points to a tension in debates over personality that is often overlooked.

As AI systems become more sophisticated and play a larger role in society, there are at least two discrete reasons why they might be recognized as persons before the law. The first is so that there is someone to blame when things go wrong. This is presented as the answer to potential accountability gaps created by their speed, autonomy, and opacity. A second reason for recognizing personality, however, is to ensure that there is someone to reward when things go right. A growing body of literature examines ownership of intellectual property created by AI systems, for example.

The tension in these discussions is whether personhood is granted for instrumental or inherent reasons. Arguments are typically framed in instrumental terms, with comparisons to the most common artificial legal person: the corporation. Yet implicit in many of those arguments, or explicit in their illustrations and examples, is the idea that as AI systems approach the point of indistinguishability from humans – that is, when they pass Turing's Test – they should be entitled to a status comparable to natural persons.

Until recently, such arguments were all speculative. Then in 2017 Saudi Arabia granted 'citizenship' to the humanoid robot Sophia[4] and an online system with the persona of a seven-year-old boy was granted 'residency' in Tokyo.[5] These were gimmicks – Sophia, for example, is essentially a chatbot with a face.[6] In the same year, however, the European Parliament adopted a resolution calling on its Commission to consider creating 'a specific legal status for robots in the long run, so

---

[3] Lawrence B Solum, 'Legal Personhood for Artificial Intelligences' (1992) 70 North Carolina Law Review 1231, 1235–37. Solum himself credits Christopher Stone as first mooting the possibility in a footnote two decades earlier: Christopher D Stone, 'Should Trees Have Standing? Towards Legal Rights for Natural Objects' (1972) 45 Southern California Law Review 450, 456 n 26.

[4] Olivia Cuthbert, 'Saudi Arabia Becomes First Country to Grant Citizenship to a Robot', *Arab News* (26 October 2017).

[5] Anthony Cuthbertson, 'Artificial Intelligence "Boy" Shibuya Mirai Becomes World's First AI Bot to Be Granted Residency', *Newsweek* (6 November 2017).

[6] Dave Gershgorn, 'Inside the Mechanical Brain of the World's First Robot Citizen', *Quartz* (12 November 2017).

that at least the most sophisticated autonomous robots could be established as having the status of electronic persons responsible for making good any damage they may cause, and possibly applying electronic personality to cases where robots make autonomous decisions or otherwise interact with third parties independently'.[7]

This chapter begins with the most immediate question, which is whether some form of juridical personality would fill a responsibility gap or be otherwise advantageous to the legal system. Based on the history of corporations and other artificial legal persons, it does not seem in doubt that most legal systems *could* grant AI systems a form of personality; the more interesting questions are whether they should and what content that personhood might have.

The chapter then turns to the analogy with natural persons. It may seem self-evident that a machine could never be a natural person. Yet for centuries slaves and women were not recognized as full persons either. If one takes the Turing Test to its logical, *Blade Runner* conclusion, AI systems truly indistinguishable from humans might one day claim the same status. Although arguments about 'rights for robots' are presently confined to the fringes of the discourse, this possibility is implicit in many of the arguments in favour of AI systems owning the intellectual property that they create.

Taken seriously, moreover, the idea that AI systems could equal humans suggests a third reason for conferring legal personality. For once parity is achieved, there is no reason to assume that AI advances would stop there. Though general AI remains science fiction for the present, it invites consideration as to whether legal status could shape or constrain behaviour if or when humanity is surpassed. Should it ever come to that, of course, the question might not be whether we recognize the rights of a general AI but whether it recognizes ours.

5.1 A Body to Kick?

Legal personality is fundamental to any system of laws. The question of who can act, who can be the subject of rights and duties, is a precursor to almost every other issue. Yet close examination of these foundations reveals surprising uncertainty and disagreement. Despite this, as John Dewey observed in 1926, 'courts and legislators do their work without

---

[7] European Parliament Resolution with Recommendations to the Commission on Civil Law Rules on Robotics (2015/2103(INL)) (European Parliament, 16 February 2017), para 59(f).

such agreement, sometimes without any conception or theory at all' regarding the nature of personality. Indeed, he went on, recourse to theory has 'more than once operated to hinder rather than facilitate the adjudication of a special question of right or obligation'.[8]

In practice, the vast majority of legal systems recognize two forms of legal person: natural and juridical. Natural persons are recognized because of the simple fact of being human.[9] Juridical persons, by contrast, are non-human entities that are granted certain rights and duties by law. Corporations and other forms of business associations are the most common examples, but many other forms are possible. Religious, governmental, and intergovernmental entities may also act as legal persons at the national and international level.

It is telling that these are all aggregations of human actors, though there are examples of truly non-human entities being granted personhood. In addition to the examples mentioned in the introduction, these include temples in India,[10] a river in New Zealand,[11] and the entire ecosystem of Ecuador.[12] There seems little question that a state could attribute some kind of personality to new entities like AI systems;[13] if that were to happen, recognition would likely be accorded by other states also.[14]

5.1.1 Theories of Juridical Personality

As discussed earlier, scholars and law reform bodies have already proposed attributing AI systems with some form of legal personality to help address liability questions, such as an ADS entity in the case of driverless

---

[8] John Dewey, 'The Historic Background of Corporate Legal Personality' (1926) 35 Yale Law Journal 655, 660.

[9] This presumes, of course, agreement on the meaning of 'human' and terms such as birth and death. See Ngaire Naffine, 'Who Are Law's Persons? From Cheshire Cats to Responsible Subjects' (2003) 66 Modern Law Review 346.

[10] See, eg, *Shiromani Gurdwara Prabandhak Committee, Amritsar v Shri Somnath Dass* AIR 2000 SC 1421 (Supreme Court of India).

[11] Te Awa Tupua (Whanganui River Claims Settlement) Act 2017 (New Zealand), s 14(1). This followed designation of the Te Urewera National Park as 'a legal entity, [with] all the rights, powers, duties, and liabilities of a legal person'. Te Urewera Act 2014 (New Zealand), s 11(1).

[12] Constitution of the Republic of Ecuador 2008 (Ecuador), art 10.

[13] For a discussion of the limits of what can be a legal person, see Visa AJ Kurki, *A Theory of Legal Personhood* (Oxford University Press 2019) 127–52.

[14] See, eg, *Bumper Development Corp. v Commissioner of Police for the Metropolis* [1991] 1 WLR 1362 (recognizing the legal personality of an Indian temple under English law).

cars whose behaviour may not be under the control of their 'drivers' or predictable by their manufacturers or owners.[15] A few writers have gone further, arguing that procedures need to be put in place to try robot criminals, with provision for 'punishment' through reprogramming or, in extreme cases, destruction.[16]

These arguments suggest an instrumental approach to personality, but scholarly explanations of the most common form of juridical person – the corporation – offer disparate justifications for its status as a separate legal person that help answer the question of whether that status should be extended to AI systems also.

The aggregate theory, sometimes referred to as the contractarian or symbolist theory, holds that a corporation is a device created by law to allow natural persons who organize themselves as a group to reflect that organization in their legal relations with other parties. Group members could establish individual contractual relations with those other parties limiting liability and so on, but the corporate form enables them to do so collectively at a lower cost.[17] The theory has been criticized and is, in any case, the least applicable to AI systems.[18]

The fiction and the concession theories of corporate personality have separate origins but amount to the same thing: corporations have personality because a legal system chooses to give it to them. As the US Supreme Court observed in 1819, a corporation 'is an artificial being, invisible, intangible, and existing only in contemplation of law'.[19] Personality is granted to achieve policy ends, such as encouraging entrepreneurship, or to contribute to the coherence and stability of the legal system, such as through the perpetuity of certain entities. The purposive aspect used to be more evident when personality was explicitly granted through a charter or legislation; in the course of the twentieth century this became a mere formality.[20] These positivist accounts most closely

---

[15] See chapter two, section 2.1.2.

[16] See below section 5.1.2(b).

[17] Ronald Coase, 'The Nature of the Firm' (1937) 4 Economica 386. Cf Victor Morawetz, *A Treatise on the Law of Private Corporations* (Little, Brown 1886) 2 ('the fact remains self-evident that a corporation is not in reality a person or a thing distinct from its constituent parts. The word corporation is but a collective name for the corporators').

[18] Nadia Banteka, 'Artificially Intelligent Persons' (2021) 58 Houston Law Review 537.

[19] *Trustees of Dartmouth Coll. v Woodward*, 17 US 518, 636 (1819).

[20] See, eg, Christine E Amsler, Robin L Bartlett, and Craig J Bolton, 'Thoughts of Some British Economists on Early Limited Liability and Corporate Legislation' (1981) 13 History of Political Economy 774; Giuseppe Dari-Mattiacci et al, 'The Emergence of the Corporate Form' (2017) 33 Journal of Law, Economics, and Organization 193.

align with legislative and judicial practice in recognizing personality, and could encompass its extension to AI systems.

The realist theory, by contrast, holds that corporations are neither fictions nor mere symbols but objectively real entities that pre-exist conferral of personality by a legal system. Though they have members, they act independently and their actions may not be attributable to those members. At its most extreme, it is argued that corporations are not only legal but also moral persons.[21] This theory is favoured more by theorists and sociologists than legislators and judges, but it echoes the tension highlighted in the introduction to this chapter: that legal personality is not merely bestowed but deserved. In practice, however, actual recognition as a person before the law remains in the gift of the state.[22]

The end result is that Dewey was correct a century ago: "'person' signifies what law makes it signify'.[23] Though the question of personality is a binary – recognized or not – the content of that status is a spectrum. Setting aside for the moment the idea that an AI system might deserve recognition as a person, a state's decision to grant it should be guided by the rights and duties that would be recognized also.

5.1.2   The Content of Legal Personality

Legal personality brings with it rights and obligations, but these need not be the same for all persons within a legal system. Even among natural persons, the struggle for equal rights of women, minorities, and other disadvantaged groups reflects this truth.

It is possible, for example, to grant only rights without obligations. This has been the approach in giving personhood to nature – both in theory, when it was first advocated in 1972,[24] and in practice, as in the Constitution of Ecuador.[25] Such 'personality' is, arguably, no more than an artifice to avoid problems of standing: enabling human individuals to act on behalf of a non-human rights-holder, rather than requiring it to

---

[21] Peter French, 'The Corporation as a Moral Person' (1979) 16 American Philosophical Quarterly 207.

[22] Katsuhito Iwai, 'Persons, Things and Corporations: The Corporate Personality Controversy and Comparative Corporate Governance' (1999) 47 American Journal of Comparative Law 583; Susan Mary Watson, 'The Corporate Legal Person' (2019) 19 Journal of Corporate Law Studies 137.

[23] Dewey (n 8) 655.

[24] Stone (n 3).

[25] Constitution of the Republic of Ecuador, arts 71–74.

establish standing in its own capacity.[26] In any case, this is inapposite to the reasons for considering personality of AI systems.

On the other hand, AI legal personality could come only with obligations. That may seem superficially attractive, but, insofar as those obligations are intended to address the accountability gaps described in earlier chapters, it would give rise to some obvious problems. Civil liability usually leads to an award of damages, for example, which can be paid only if the wrongdoer is capable of owning property.[27] Those payments might be made from a central fund, though this is more akin to the compulsory insurance regimes discussed in chapter four.[28] 'Personality' would be a mere formality.

In the case of corporations, personality means the capacity to sue and be sued, to enter into contracts, to incur debt, to own property, and to be convicted of crimes. On the rights side, the extent to which corporations enjoy constitutional protections comparable to natural persons is the subject of ongoing debate. Though the United States has granted many protections to corporate entities, even there a line has been drawn at guarantees such as the right against self-incrimination.[29] In general, juridical persons have fewer rights than natural ones. (A similar situation obtains in international law, where states enjoy plenary personality and international organizations may have varying degrees of it.[30])

(a)   Private Law

The ability to be sued is one of the primary attractions of personality for AI systems, as the European Parliament acknowledged.[31] This presumes, of course, that there are meaningful accountability gaps that can and should be filled. Much of the book up to this point has argued that these gaps are often overstated. A different reason for wariness about such a remedy is that, even if it did serve a gap-filling function, granting

---

[26] Christopher Rodgers, 'A New Approach to Protecting Ecosystems' (2017) 19 Environmental Law Review 266. In New Zealand, by contrast, trustees were established to act on behalf of the environmental features given personality.

[27] Cf Liability for Artificial Intelligence and Other Emerging Digital Technologies (EU Expert Group on Liability and New Technologies, 2019) 38.

[28] See chapter four, section 4.1.4.

[29] Scott A Trainor, 'A Comparative Analysis of a Corporation's Right Against Self-Incrimination' (1994) 18 Fordham International Law Journal 2139. Cf *Citizens United v Federal Election Commission*, 558 US 310 (US Supreme Court, 2010).

[30] Simon Chesterman, 'Does ASEAN Exist? The Association of Southeast Asian Nations as an International Legal Person' (2008) XII Singapore Year Book of International Law 199.

[31] See above n 7.

personality to AI systems would also shift responsibility under current laws away from existing legal persons. Indeed, it would create an incentive to transfer risk to 'electronic persons' in order to shield natural and traditional juridical ones from exposure.[32] That is a problem with corporations also, which may be used to protect investors from liability beyond the fixed sum of their investment – indeed, that is often the point of using a corporate vehicle in the first place. The reallocation of risk is justified on the basis that it encourages investment and entrepreneurship.[33] Safeguards typically include a requirement that the names of limited liability entities include that status ('Ltd', 'LLC', and so on) and the possibility of piercing the corporate veil to prevent abuse of the form.[34] In the case of AI systems, similar veil-piercing mechanisms could be developed – though if a human were manipulating AI in order to protect him- or herself from liability, the ability to do so might suggest that the AI system in question was not deserving of its separate personhood.[35]

Entry into contracts is occasionally posited as a reason to grant AI systems personality.[36] Yet the use of electronic agents to conclude binding agreements is hardly new. The phenomenon of high-frequency trading, discussed in chapter one, relies on algorithms concluding agreements with other algorithms on behalf of traditional persons. Though the autonomy of AI systems may challenge application of existing doctrine – notably, when something goes wrong, such as a mistake – chapter two showed that this is still resolvable without recourse to new legal persons.[37]

Taking on debt and owning property are necessary incidents of the ability to be sued and to enter into contracts.[38] The possibility that AI systems could accumulate wealth raises the question of whether or how

---

[32] Joanna J Bryson, Mihailis E Diamantis, and Thomas D Grant, 'Of, for, and by the People: The Legal Lacuna of Synthetic Persons' (2017) 25 Artificial Intelligence and Law 273, 287.

[33] Frank H Easterbrook and Daniel R Fischel, 'Limited Liability and the Corporation' (1985) 52 University of Chicago Law Review 89.

[34] David Millon, 'Piercing the Corporate Veil, Financial Responsibility, and the Limits of Limited Liability' (2007) 56 Emory Law Journal 1305.

[35] Jacob Turner, *Robot Rules: Regulating Artificial Intelligence* (Palgrave Macmillan 2019) 193.

[36] See, eg, Samir Chopra and Laurence F White, *A Legal Theory for Autonomous Artificial Agents* (University of Michigan Press 2011) 160.

[37] See chapter two, section 2.3.1.

[38] Some argue that this is the most important function of separate legal personality for corporations: Henry Hansmann and Reinier Kraakman, 'The Essential Role of Organizational Law' (2000) 110 Yale Law Journal 387. Cf Hans Tjio, 'Lifting the Veil on Piercing the Veil' [2014] Lloyd's Maritime and Commercial Law Quarterly 19. AI

they might be taxed. Taxation of robots has been proposed as a means of addressing the diminished tax base and displacement of workers anticipated as a result of automation.[39] Bill Gates, among others, has argued that robots – or the companies that own them – should be taxed.[40] Industry representatives have argued that this would have a negative impact on competitiveness and thus far it has not been implemented.[41] An alternative is to look not at the machines but at the position of companies abusing market position, with possibilities including more aggressive taxing of profits or requirements for distributed share ownership.[42] In any case, taxation of AI systems – like the ability to take on debt and own property – would follow rather than justify granting them personality.[43] (The question of AI systems owning their creations will be considered in the next section.)

In addition to owning property, AI systems might also be called on to manage it. In 2014, for example, it was announced that a Hong Kong venture capital firm had appointed a computer program called Vital to its board of directors.[44] As with the Saudi Arabian government's awarding of citizenship, this was more style than substance – as a matter of Hong Kong law, the program was not appointed to anything; in an interview some years later, the managing partner conceded that the company merely treated Vital as a member of the board with observer status.[45] Human directors might delegate some responsibility to an AI system, but under most corporate law regimes they cannot absolve themselves of the ultimate responsibility for managing the organization.[46] Most jurisdictions require

---

systems lacking the ability to own property could still be subject to certain forms of legal process, such as injunctions, and could offset debts through their 'labour'.

[39] Brett A King, Tyler Hammond, and Jake Harrington, 'Disruptive Technology: Economic Consequences of Artificial Intelligence and the Robotics Revolution' (2017) 12(2) Journal of Strategic Innovation and Sustainability 53.

[40] Kevin J Delaney, 'The Robot that Takes Your Job Should Pay Taxes, Says Bill Gates', *Quartz* (18 February 2017).

[41] Lawrence Summers, 'Robots Are Wealth Creators and Taxing Them Is Illogical', *Financial Times* (6 March 2017).

[42] 'Why Taxing Robots Is Not a Good Idea', *Economist* (25 February 2017).

[43] Cf Luciano Floridi, 'Robots, Jobs, Taxes, and Responsibilities' (2017) 30 Philosophy & Technology 1.

[44] Rob Wile, 'A Venture Capital Firm Just Named an Algorithm to Its Board of Directors', *Business Insider* (13 May 2014).

[45] Nicky Burridge, 'AI Takes Its Place in the Boardroom', *Nikkei Asian Review* (25 May 2017).

[46] Florian Möslein, 'Robots in the Boardroom: Artificial Intelligence and Corporate Law' in Woodrow Barfield and Ugo Pagallo (eds), *Research Handbook on the Law of Artificial Intelligence* (Edward Elgar 2018) 649 at 658–60.

that those directors be natural persons, though in some it is possible for a juridical person – typically another corporation – to serve on the board.[47] Shawn Bayern has gone further, arguing that loopholes in US business entity law could be used to create limited liability companies with no human members at all.[48] This requires a somewhat tortured interpretation of that law – a natural person creates a company, adds an AI system as a member, then resigns[49] – but it suggests the manner in which legal personality might be adapted in the future.

(b)   Criminal Law

A final quality of legal personality is the most visceral and worthy of some elaboration: the ability to be punished. If an AI system were given legal personality comparable to a corporation, there seems little reason to argue over whether it could be prosecuted under the criminal law. Provided that the physical and mental elements of the crime were established,[50] such an entity could be fined or have its property seized; a licence to operate could be suspended or revoked. In some jurisdictions, a winding-up order can be made against a juridical person; where that is not available, a fine sufficiently large to bankrupt the entity may have the same effect. In an extreme case, one could imagine a 'robot criminal' being destroyed. But would this be desirable and would it be effective?

The most commonly articulated reasons for criminal punishment are retribution, incapacitation, deterrence, and rehabilitation.[51] Retribution is the oldest reason for punishment, sublimating the victim's desire for

---

[47] See, eg, Personen- und Gesellschaftsrecht (PGR) 1926 (Liechtenstein), art 344; Companies Ordinance 2014 (HK), s 457. This was also possible under English law until 2015. See now Small Business, Enterprise and Employment Act 2015 (UK), s 87.

[48] Shawn Bayern, 'Of Bitcoins, Independently Wealthy Software, and the Zero-Member LLC' (2014) 108 Northwestern University Law Review 1485, 1495–500.

[49] Shawn Bayern, 'The Implications of Modern Business-Entity Law for the Regulation of Autonomous Systems' (2015) 19 Stanford Technology Law Review 93, 101.

[50] For corporations this has sometimes proved a difficult but not insurmountable challenge. See VS Khanna, 'Corporate Criminal Liability: What Purpose Does It Serve?' (1996) 109 Harvard Law Review 1477, 1513; Samuel W Buell, 'Criminally Bad Management' in Jennifer Arlen (ed), *Research Handbook on Corporate Crime and Financial Misdealing* (Edward Elgar 2018) 59. The fact that corporations are capable of violating criminal laws despite lacking free will or moral responsibility should dispense with this as an argument against criminal responsibility of AI systems.

[51] It is arguable that the symbolic role of criminal law need not require actual punishment – it is not uncommon to have laws that are unenforced in practice. Yet this typically relies on an explicit or implicit decision not to investigate or prosecute specific crimes, rather than acceptance that a class of actors cannot be punished at all.

revenge into a societal demonstration that wrongs have consequences.[52] Calibration of those consequences was at its most literal in the *lex talionis*: an eye for an eye, a tooth for a tooth. Much as the hanging of the Falaisian pig in chapter four was intended to restore order in the community, the demonstrative effect of fining a corporation – or an electronic 'person' – may be preferable to a crime otherwise going unpunished.[53]

The penal system can also be used to incapacitate those convicted of crimes, physically preventing them from reoffending. This is achieved through varying forms of incarceration, but it may also include exile, amputation of limbs, castration, and execution. In the case of corporations, it may include withdrawal of a licence to operate or a compulsory winding-up order.[54] Here, direct analogies with the treatment of dangerous animals and machinery can be made, although measures such as putting down a vicious dog or decommissioning a faulty vehicle are administrative rather than penal and do not depend on determinations of 'guilt'.[55] In some jurisdictions, children and the mentally ill may be deemed incapable of committing crimes, yet they may still be detained by the state if judged to be a danger to themselves or the community.[56] Those individuals do not lose their personality; in the case of AI systems, it is not necessary to give them personality in order to impose measures akin to confinement if a product can be recalled or a licence revoked.

Deterrence is a more recent justification for punishment, premised on the rationality of offenders. By structuring penalties, it imposes costs on behaviour that are intended to outweigh any potential benefits. The ability to reduce criminality to economic analysis may seem particularly applicable to both corporations and AI systems. Yet, in the case of the former, the incentives are really aimed at human managers who might otherwise act in concert through the corporation for personal as well as corporate gain.[57]

---

[52] Denunciation is sometimes presented as a stand-alone justification for punishment in its own right. See Bill Wringe, *An Expressive Theory of Punishment* (Palgrave Macmillan 2016).
[53] Christina Mulligan, 'Revenge Against Robots' (2018) 69 South Carolina Law Review 579; Ying Hu, 'Robot Criminals' (2019) 52 University of Michigan Journal of Law Reform 487, 503–7.
[54] W Robert Thomas, 'Incapacitating Criminal Corporations' (2019) 72 Vanderbilt Law Review 905.
[55] See, eg, Deborah Legge and Simon Brooman, *Law Relating to Animals* (Cavendish 2000).
[56] Arlie Loughnan, *Manifest Madness: Mental Incapacity in the Criminal Law* (Oxford University Press 2012).
[57] Assaf Hamdani and Alon Klement, 'Corporate Crime and Deterrence' (2008) 61 Stanford Law Review 271.

In the case of an AI system, the deterrent effect of a fine would shape behaviour only if its programming sought to maximize economic gain without regard for the underlying criminal law itself.[58] A final rationale for punishment is rehabilitation. Like incapacitation and deterrence, it is forward-looking and aims to reduce recidivism. Unlike incapacitation, however, it seeks to influence the decision to offend rather than the ability to do so;[59] unlike deterrence, that influence is intended to operate intrinsically rather than extrinsically.[60] Rehabilitation in respect of natural persons is embraced more in theory than in practice; in the United States it fell from favour in the 1970s.[61] With respect to corporations, however, the clearer levers of influence have led to experimentation with narrowly tailored penalties encouraging good behaviour as well as discouraging bad.[62] This approach might seem well suited to AI systems, with violations of the criminal law being errors to be debugged rather than sins to be punished.[63] Indeed, the educative aspect of rehabilitation has been directly analogized to machine learning in a book-length treatise on the topic.[64] Yet neither legal personality nor the coercive powers of the state should be necessary to ensure that machine learning leads to outputs that do not violate the criminal law.

5.1.3   No Soul to Be Damned

While arguments justifying liability of corporations tend to be instrumental, it is striking how the emerging literature on 'robot criminals' slides into anthropomorphism. The very term suggests a special desire to hold humanoid AI systems to a higher standard than, say, household appliances with varying degrees of autonomy or unembodied AI systems

---

[58] See also chapter nine, section 9.3.1.

[59] Jeremy Bentham, 'Panopticon versus New South Wales' in John Bowring (ed), *The Works of Jeremy Bentham* (William Tait 1843) vol 4, 173 at 174.

[60] See Tony Ward and Shadd Maruna, *Rehabilitation* (Routledge 2007).

[61] See, eg, Albert W Alschuler, 'The Changing Purposes of Criminal Punishment: A Retrospective on the Past Century and Some Thoughts about the Next' (2003) 70 University of Chicago Law Review 1, 9. Cf Francis T Cullen and Karen E Gilbert, *Reaffirming Rehabilitation* (2nd edn, Anderson 2013).

[62] Mihailis E Diamantis, 'Clockwork Corporations: A Character Theory of Corporate Punishment' (2018) 103 Iowa Law Review 507.

[63] See chapter nine, section 9.3.2.

[64] Gabriel Hallevy, *Liability for Crimes Involving Artificial Intelligence Systems* (Springer 2015) 210–11.

operating in the cloud.[65] There is no principled reason for such a distinction, but it speaks to the tension within arguments for AI personality that blend instrumental and inherent justifications.

Interestingly, arguments over the juridical personality of corporations focus on the opposite problem: their *dissimilarity* to humans, pithily described by the First Baron Thurlow as them having 'no soul to be damned, and no body to be kicked'.[66] The lack of a soul has not impeded juridical personality of corporations and poses no principled barrier to treating AI systems similarly. Corporate personality is different from AI personality, however, in that a corporation is made up of human beings, through whom it operates, whereas an AI system is made *by* humans.[67]

Instrumental reasons could, therefore, justify according legal personality to AI systems. But they do not require it. The implicit anthropomorphism elides further challenges such as defining the threshold of personality when AI systems exist on a spectrum, as well as how personality might apply to distributed systems. It is possible, then, to create legal persons comparable to corporations – each autonomous vehicle, smart medical device, resume-screening algorithm, and so on could be incorporated. If there are true liability gaps then such legal forms might fill them. Yet the primary beneficiaries of this arrangement would be producers and users, who would thus be insulated from some or all liability under existing laws.[68] The better approach is to prevent those gaps arising in the first place.

5.2   Cogito, Ergo Sum?

Instrumentalism is not the only reason why legal systems recognize personality, however. In the case of natural persons, no Turing Test needs to be passed: the mere fact of being born entitles one to personhood before the law.[69]

---

[65] Cf Jack M Balkin, 'The Three Laws of Robotics in the Age of Big Data' (2017) 78 Ohio State Law Journal 1217, 1219.

[66] Mervyn A King, *Public Policy and the Corporation* (Chapman and Hall 1977) 1. See, eg, John C Coffee, Jr, '"No Soul to Damn: No Body to Kick": An Unscandalized Inquiry into the Problem of Corporate Punishment' (1981) 79 Michigan Law Review 386.

[67] SM Solaiman, 'Legal Personality of Robots, Corporations, Idols and Chimpanzees: A Quest for Legitimacy' (2017) 25 Artificial Intelligence and Law 155, 174.

[68] See chapter four.

[69] See, eg, Universal Declaration of Human Rights, GA Res 217A(III) (1948), UN Doc A/810 (1948), art 1; International Covenant on Civil and Political Rights (ICCPR), 16 December 1966, 999 UNTS 171, in force 23 March 1976, art 6(1).

It was not always thus. Through much of human history, slaves were bought and sold like property;[70] indigenous peoples were compared to animals roaming the land, justifying their dispossession;[71] and, for centuries under English law, Blackstone's summary of the position of women held that 'husband and wife are one person, and the husband is that person'.[72] Even today, natural persons enjoy plenary rights and obligations only if they are adults, of sound mind, and not incarcerated.

As indicated earlier, many of the arguments in favour of AI personality implicitly or explicitly assume that AI systems are approaching human qualities in a manner that entitles them to comparable recognition before the law. Such arguments have been critiqued for both their analysis and their implications. In terms of analysis, Neil Richards and William Smart have termed the tendency to anthropomorphize AI systems the 'android fallacy'.[73] Experiment after experiment has shown that people are more likely to ascribe human qualities such as moral sensibility to machines on the basis of their humanoid appearance, natural language communication, or the mere fact of having been given a name.[74] More serious arguments about AI approximating human qualities usually fail to examine assumptions about how those qualities manifest in humans ourselves.[75]

In terms of the implications, the 2017 European Parliament resolution prompted hundreds of AI experts from across the continent to warn in an open letter that legal personality for AI would be inappropriate from 'an ethical and a legal perspective'. Interestingly, such warnings may themselves fall foul of the android fallacy by assuming that legal status based on the natural person model necessarily brings with it all the 'human'

[70] See Jean Allain (ed), *The Legal Understanding of Slavery: From the Historical to the Contemporary* (Oxford University Press 2013).
[71] Simon Chesterman, '"Skeletal Legal Principles": The Concept of Law in Australian Land Rights Jurisprudence' (1998) 40 Journal of Legal Pluralism and Unofficial Law 61.
[72] Lee Holcombe, *Wives and Property: Reform of the Married Women's Property Law in Nineteenth-Century England* (Martin Robertson 1983) 18.
[73] Neil M Richards and William D Smart, 'How Should the Law Think about Robots?' in Ryan Calo, A Michael Froomkin, and Ian Kerr (eds), *Robot Law* (Edward Elgar 2016) 3 at 18–21.
[74] Cf Luisa Damiano and Paul Dumouchel, 'Anthropomorphism in Human–Robot Co-evolution' (2018) 9 Frontiers in Psychology 468.
[75] See, eg, Elisabeth Hildt, 'Artificial Intelligence: Does Consciousness Matter?' (2019) 10 (1535) Frontiers in Psychology 1–3; Gunter Meissner, 'Artificial Intelligence: Consciousness and Conscience' (2020) 35 AI & Society 225, 231. For John Searle's famous 'Chinese room' argument, see John R Searle, 'Minds, Brains, and Programs' (1980) 3 Behavioral and Brain Sciences 417, 417–24.

rights guaranteed under EU law.[76] Other writers candidly admit that the only basis for denying AI systems personality is a form of speciesism – privileging human welfare over robot welfare because we, the lawmakers, are human.[77] If AI systems become so sophisticated that this is our strongest defence, the problem may not be their legal status but our own.[78]

This section nonetheless takes seriously the idea that certain AI systems might have an entitlement to personality due to their inherent qualities. The technical aspects of how those qualities could manifest – and indeed a detailed examination of the human qualities that they mimic – are beyond the scope of this book.[79] Instead, the focus will be on how and why natural personhood might be extended. A first question to examine is how this has been handled in the past, through the enfranchisement and empowerment of natural persons long treated as inferior to white men. More recently, activists and scholars have urged further expansion of certain rights to non-human animals such as chimpanzees based on their own inherent qualities. The inquiry then turns to the strongest articulation today of meaningful rights on behalf of AI systems for inherent rather than instrumental reasons: that they should be able to own their creations.

5.2.1   The Extension of Natural Personality

The arc of the moral universe is long, as Dr Martin Luther King, Jr, famously intoned, but it bends towards justice. At the time that the United States drafted its Declaration of Independence in 1776, the notion that 'all men' [sic] were 'created equal' was demonstrably untrue. A decade later, the French Declaration on the Rights of Man similarly proclaimed natural and imprescriptible rights for all – 'nonsense upon stilts' was Jeremy Bentham's observation.[80] Man may well be born free, as Rousseau had opined in the opening lines of The Social Contract, but everywhere he remained in chains.[81]

[76] Open Letter to the European Commission: Artificial Intelligence and Robotics (April 2018), para 2(b). Cf Turner (n 35) 189–90.
[77] Cf Peter Singer, 'Speciesism and Moral Status' (2009) 40 Metaphilosophy 567.
[78] See below section 5.3.
[79] See, eg, Jean-Marc Fellous and Michael A Arbib, Who Needs Emotions? The Brain Meets the Robot (Oxford University Press 2005); Wendell Wallach and Colin Allen, Moral Machines: Teaching Robots Right from Wrong (Oxford University Press 2009).
[80] Jeremy Bentham, 'Anarchical Fallacies' in John Bowring (ed), The Works of Jeremy Bentham (William Tait 1843) vol 2, 489 at 501.
[81] Jean-Jacques Rousseau, The Social Contract (GDH Cole tr, first published 1762, JM Dent 1923) 49.

And yet the succeeding centuries did see a progressive realization of those lofty aspirations and the spread of rights. By the middle of the twentieth century, the Universal Declaration of Human Rights could claim that all human beings were 'born free and equal in dignity and rights', despite one-third of them living in territories that the UN itself classified as non-self-governing. Decolonization, the end of apartheid, women's liberation and other movements followed; rights remain a site of contestation, but no state today seriously contends that human adults are not persons before the law.[82]

Interestingly, some arguments in favour of legal personality for AI draw not on this progressivist narrative of natural personhood but on the darker history of slavery. Andrew Katz and Ugo Pagallo, for example, find analogies with the ancient Roman law mechanism of *peculium*, whereby a slave lacked legal personality and yet could operate as more than a mere agent for his master.[83] (In 2017, a digital bank of that name was established in France – presumably for investors who never studied Latin.) As an example of a creative interpretation of personhood it is interesting, though it relies on instrumental justifications rather than the inherent qualities of slaves. As Pagallo notes, *peculium* was in effect a sort of 'proto-limited liability company'.[84] From the previous section, there is no bar on legal systems creating such structures today – as for whether they *should* do so, reliance upon long discarded laws associated with slavery is not the strongest case to be made.[85]

An alternative approach is to consider how the legal system treats animals.[86] For the most part, they are regarded as property that can be

---

[82] For limited exceptions concerning apostates and persons with disabilities, see Paul M Taylor, *A Commentary on the International Covenant on Civil and Political Rights* (Cambridge University Press 2020) 449–54. For a discussion of anencephalic infants, see Kurki (n 13) 9.

[83] Andrew Katz, 'Intelligent Agents and Internet Commerce in Ancient Rome' (2008) 20 Society for Computers and Law 35; Ugo Pagallo, *The Laws of Robots: Crimes, Contracts, and Torts* (Springer 2013) 103–6. See also Hutan Ashrafian, 'Artificial Intelligence and Robot Responsibilities: Innovating Beyond Rights' (2015) 21 Science and Engineering Ethics 317, 325; Sergio Nasarre-Aznar, 'Ownership at Stake (Once Again): Housing, Digital Contents, Animals, and Robots' (2018) 10 Journal of Property, Planning, and Environmental Law 69, 78; Eduard Fosch-Villaronga, *Robots, Healthcare, and the Law: Regulating Automation in Personal Care* (Routledge 2019) 152.

[84] Pagallo (n 83) 104.

[85] Mark Chinen, *Law and Autonomous Machines: The Co-Evolution of Legal Responsibility and Technology* (Edward Elgar 2019) 19.

[86] See, eg, Visa AJ Kurki and Tomasz Pietrzykowski (eds), *Legal Personhood: Animals, Artificial Intelligence and the Unborn* (Springer 2017); Saskia Stucki, 'Towards a Theory

bought and sold but also as deserving of 'humane' treatment.[87] Liability of owners for damage caused by animals was considered in chapter four;[88] here, the question is whether those animals might 'own' themselves.

Various efforts have sought to attribute degrees of personality to non-human animals, with little success. In 2013, for example, the Nonhuman Rights Project filed lawsuits on behalf of four captive chimpanzees, arguing that the animals exhibited advanced cognitive abilities, autonomy, and self-awareness. In denying writs of habeas corpus, the New York State Court Appellate Division did not dispute these qualities but held that extension of rights like personality had traditionally been linked to the imposition of obligations in the form of a social contract. Since, 'needless to say', the chimpanzees did not bear any legal duties, they could not enjoy rights of personality such as the right to liberty.[89] This was a curious basis on which to dismiss the case, as many humans who lack the capacity to exercise rights or responsibilities – infants, persons in a coma – are nonetheless deemed persons before the law.[90] A parallel case rejected that argument on the circular grounds that it 'ignores the fact that these are still human beings, members of the human community'.[91] Leave to appeal was denied, but one of the judges issued a concurring opinion that ended on a speculative note about the future of such litigation. The issue, Judge Eugene Fahey observed, is profound and far-reaching: 'Ultimately, we will not be able to ignore it. While it may be arguable that a chimpanzee is not a "person," there is no doubt that it is not merely a thing.'[92]

Gabriel Hallevy has argued that animals are closer than AI systems to humans when one considers emotionality as opposed to rationality, but that this has not led to them being given personhood under the law. Instead, it is AI systems' *rationality* that provides the basis for personhood.[93] That may be true with regard to the ability to make out

of Legal Animal Rights: Simple and Fundamental Rights' (2020) 40 Oxford Journal of Legal Studies 533.

[87] Cf Katie Sykes, 'Human Drama, Animal Trials: What the Medieval Animal Trials Can Teach Us about Justice for Animals' (2011) 17 Animal Law 273.

[88] See chapter four, section 4.1.2.

[89] *People ex rel Nonhuman Rights Project, Inc v Lavery*, 998 NYS 2d 248 (App Div, 2014).

[90] Randall S Abate, *Climate Change and the Voiceless: Protecting Future Generations, Wildlife, and Natural Resources* (Cambridge University Press 2019) 101–2.

[91] *Nonhuman Rights Project, Inc ex rel Tommy v Lavery*, 54 NYS 3d 392, 396 (App Div, 2017).

[92] *Nonhuman Rights Project, Inc ex rel Tommy v Lavery*, 100 NE 3d 846, 848 (NY, 2018).

[93] Hallevy (n 64) 28.

the mental element of a criminal offence, but the fact that it is a crime to torture a chimpanzee but not a computer also points to an important difference in how the legal system values the two types of entity. In fact, a stronger argument may be made to protect embodied AI systems that evoke emotional responses on the part of humans – regardless of the sophistication of their internal processing. Laws to protect such 'social robots' will at some point need to be adopted, comparable to animal abuse laws. As in the case of those laws, protection will likely be guided by social mores rather than consistent biological – or technological – standards.[94]

The assumption that natural legal personality is limited to human beings is so ingrained in most legal systems that it is not even articulated. The failure to extend comparable rights even to our nearest evolutionary cousins bodes ill for advocates of AI personality based on presumed inherent qualities.[95]

5.2.2   Rewarding Creativity

A distinct reason for considering whether AI systems should be recognized as persons focuses not on what they are but on what they can do. Chapter one showed how the speed of AI systems has affected infringement of intellectual property;[96] here we turn to the impact on its creation. This is commonly framed as the question of whether an individual or corporation can claim ownership of work done by an AI system. Implicit or explicit in such discussions, however, is the understanding that if the work had been done by a human then he or she would own it him- or herself.

There is, in fact, a long history of debating whether machine-assisted creations are protectable through copyright.[97] Early photographs, for example, were not protected because the mere capturing of light through the lens of a *camera obscura* was not regarded as true authorship.[98] It

---

[94] Kate Darling, 'Extending Legal Protection to Social Robots: The Effects of Anthropomorphism, Empathy, and Violent Behavior Towards Robotic Objects' in Ryan Calo, A Michael Froomkin, and Ian Kerr (eds), *Robot Law* (Edward Elgar 2016) 213 at 226–29. See further chapter seven, section 7.3.2.

[95] Cf Kurki (n 13) 176–78 (discussing whether AI could be 'ultimately valuable' and thus entitled to personhood).

[96] See chapter one, section 1.1.

[97] James Grimmelmann, 'There's No Such Thing as a Computer-Authored Work – and It's a Good Thing, Too' (2016) 39 Columbia Journal of Law & the Arts 403.

[98] Madeleine de Cock Buning, 'Artificial Intelligence and the Creative Industry: New Challenges for the EU Paradigm for Art and Technology by Autonomous Creation' in

took an iconic picture of Oscar Wilde going all the way to the US Supreme Court before copyright was recognized in mechanically produced creations.[99] The issue today is distinct: not whether a photographer can 'own' the image passively captured by a machine but who might own new works actively created by one. A computer program like a word processor does not own the text typed on it any more than a pen owns the words that it writes. But AI systems now write news reports, compose songs, paint pictures – these activities generate value, but can and should they attract the protections of copyright law?

In most jurisdictions, the answer is no.

The US Copyright Office, for example, has stated that legislative protection of 'original works of authorship'[100] is limited to works 'created by a human being'. It will not register works 'produced by a machine or mere mechanical process that operates randomly or automatically without *any* creative input or intervention from a human author'.[101] The word 'any' is key and begs the question of what level of human involvement is required to assert authorship.[102]

Consider the world's most famous selfie – of a crested black macaque. David Slater went to Indonesia to photograph the endangered monkeys, but they were too nervous to let him take close-ups, so he set up a camera that enabled them to snap their own photos.[103] After the images gained significant publicity, animal rights activists argued that the monkeys had a greater claim to authorship of the photographs than the owner of the camera. Slater did eventually win, reflecting existing law[104] – though as part of a settlement he agreed to donate 25 per cent of future royalties from the images to groups protecting crested macaques. As computers

---

Woodrow Barfield and Ugo Pagallo (eds), *Research Handbook on the Law of Artificial Intelligence* (Edward Elgar 2018) 511 at 524.

[99] *Burrow-Giles Lithographic Co v Sarony*, 111 US 53 (1884). Arguments continued, however, with Germany withholding full copyright of photographs until 1965. Axel Nordemann, 'Germany' in Ysolde Gendreau, Axel Nordemann, and Rainer Oesch (eds), *Copyright and Photographs: An International Survey* (Kluwer 1999) 135.

[100] 17 USC § 102(a).

[101] *Compendium of US Copyright Office Practices* (3rd edn, US Copyright Office 2019), § 313.2 (emphasis added).

[102] See Daniel J Gervais, 'The Machine as Author' (2020) 105 Iowa Law Review 2053.

[103] Chris Cheesman, 'Photographer Goes Ape Over Monkey Selfie: Who Owns the Copyright?', *Amateur Photographer* (7 August 2014).

[104] *Naruto v Slater*, 888 F 3d 418 (9th Cir, 2018). The Court held that Naruto lacked standing to sue under the US Copyright Act and had no claim to the photographs Slater had published.

generate more content independently of their human programmers, it is going to be harder and harder for humans to take credit. Instead of training a monkey how to press a button, it may be more like a teacher trying to take credit for the work of his or her student.

Turning to the normative question of whether AI systems themselves *should* have a claim to ownership, the policy behind copyright is often said to be incentivizing innovation. This has long been dismissed as unnecessary or inappropriate for computers. 'All it takes', Pamela Samuelson wrote in 1986, 'is electricity (or some other motive force) to get the machines into production.'[105] Here the Turing Test offers a different kind of thought experiment: the more machines are designed to copy human traits, the more important such incentives might become.

Until recently, China followed the orthodoxy that AI-produced work is not entitled to copyright protection.[106] In December 2019, however, a district court in China held that an article produced by an algorithm could not be copied without permission. The article was a financial report published by Tencent with a note that it had been 'automatically written' by Dreamwriter, a news writing program developed by the company. Shanghai Yingxun Technology Company copied the article without permission and Tencent sued. The article was taken down, but the infringing company still had to pay ¥1,500 (US$216) for 'economic losses and rights protection'.[107]

The Chinese case reflects a distinct reason for recognizing copyright, which is the protection of upfront investment in creative processes. This account presumes that, in the absence of protection, investment will dry up and there will be a reduced supply of creative works.[108] Such an approach to copyright is broadly consistent with common law doctrines concerning work created in the course of employment, known in the

---

[105] Pamela Samuelson, 'Allocating Ownership Rights in Computer-Generated Works' (1986) 47 University of Pittsburgh Law Review 1185, 1199.

[106] *Beijing Feilin Law Firm v Baidu Corporation (No 239)* (25 April 2019) (Beijing Internet Court); Chen Ming, 'Beijing Internet Court Denies Copyright to Works Created Solely by Artificial Intelligence' (2019) 14 Journal of Intellectual Property Law & Practice 593.

[107] 深圳市腾讯计算机系统有限公司 *[Shenzhen Tencent Computer System Co Ltd] v* 上海盈讯科技有限公司 *[Shanghai Yingxun Technology Co Ltd]* (24 December 2019) (Shenzhen Nanshan District People's Court); Zhang Yangfei, 'Court Rules AI-Written Article Has Copyright', *China Daily* (9 January 2020).

[108] Kal Raustiala and Christopher Jon Sprigman, 'The Second Digital Disruption: Streaming and the Dawn of Datadriven Creativity' (2019) 94 New York University Law Review 1555, 1603–4.

United States as work for hire, under which a corporate employer or an individual who commissions a work owns copyright despite the actual 'author' being someone else.[109] This may not be available in civil law jurisdictions that place a greater emphasis on the moral rights of a human author.[110]

In Britain, legislation adopted in 1988 does in fact provide copyright protection for 'computer-generated' work, the 'author' of which is deemed to be the person who undertook 'the arrangements necessary for the creation of the work'.[111] Similar legislation has been adopted in New Zealand,[112] India,[113] Hong Kong,[114] and Ireland.[115] Though disputes about who undertook the 'arrangements necessary' may arise, ownership by a recognized legal person or by no one at all remain the only possible outcomes.[116]

The European Parliament in April 2020 issued a draft report arguing that AI-generated works could be regarded as 'equivalent' to intellectual works and therefore protected by copyright. It opposed giving personality of any kind to the AI itself, however, proposing that ownership instead vest in 'the person who prepares and publishes a work lawfully, provided that the technology designer has not expressly reserved the right to use the work in that way'.[117] The 'equivalence' to intellectual work is interesting, justified here on the basis of a proposed shift in recognizing works based on a 'creative result' rather than a creative process.[118]

For the time being, then, copyright cannot be owned by AI systems – and does not need to be in order to recognize the creativity of those

---

[109] Cf *Asia Pacific Publishing Pte Ltd v Pioneers & Leaders (Publishers) Pte Ltd* [2011] 4 SLR 381, 398–402 (Singapore Court of Appeal) (distinguishing between authorship and ownership).

[110] Daryl Lim, 'AI & IP: Innovation & Creativity in an Age of Accelerated Change' (2018) 52 Akron Law Review 813, 843–46.

[111] Copyright, Designs and Patents Act 1988 (UK), s 9(3). 'Computer-generated' is defined in s 178 as meaning that the work was 'generated by computer in circumstances such that there is no human author of the work'.

[112] Copyright Act 1994 (NZ), s 5(2)(a).

[113] Copyright Amendment Act 1994 (India), s 2.

[114] Copyright Ordinance 1997 (HK), s 11(3).

[115] Copyright and Related Rights Act 2000 (Ireland), s 21(f).

[116] See, eg, *Nova Productions v Mazooma Games* [2007] EWCA Civ 219; Abbe Brown et al, *Contemporary Intellectual Property: Law and Policy* (5th edn, Oxford University Press 2019) 100–1.

[117] Stéphane Séjourné, 'Draft Report on Intellectual Property Rights for the Development of Artificial Intelligence Technologies' (European Parliament, Committee on Legal Affairs, 2020/2015(INI), 24 April 2020), paras 9–10.

[118] Ibid, Explanatory Statement.

systems. Nevertheless, reservations as to ownership being claimed by anyone else are evident in the limited rights given for 'computer-generated' works. The duration is generally for a shorter period, and the deemed 'author' is unable to assert moral rights – such as the right to be identified as the author of the work.[119] A World Intellectual Property Organization (WIPO) issues paper recognized the dilemma, noting that excluding these works would favour 'the dignity of human creativity over machine creativity' at the expense of making the largest number of creative works available to consumers. A middle path, it observed, was to offer 'a reduced term of protection and other limitations'.[120]

5.2.3 Protecting Inventors

Whereas in copyright law the debate is over who owns works produced by AI systems, in patent law the question is whether they can be owned at all. Patent law in most jurisdictions provides or assumes that an 'inventor' must be human. In 2019, Stephen Thaler decided to test those assumptions, filing patents in Britain, the EU, and the United States that listed an AI system, DABUS, as the 'inventor'.[121] The British Intellectual Property Office (IPO) was willing to accept that DABUS created the inventions, but relevant legislation required that an inventor be a natural person and not a machine.[122] The European Patent Office (EPO) followed a more circuitous route to the same end, rejecting the

---

[119] Copyright, Designs and Patents Act 1988 (UK), s 12(7) (protection for such works is limited to 50 years, rather than 70 years after the death of the author), s 79 (exception to moral rights).

[120] Revised Issues Paper on Intellectual Property Policy and Artificial Intelligence (World Intellectual Property Organisation, WIPO/IP/AI/2/GE/20/1 REV, 21 May 2020), para 23. See also Marcus du Sautoy, *The Creativity Code: Art and Innovation in the Age of AI* (Harvard University Press 2019) 102; Ryan Abbott, *The Reasonable Robot: Artificial Intelligence and the Law* (Cambridge University Press 2020) 71–91.

[121] The patents were for a 'food container' and 'devices and methods for attracting enhanced attention'. DABUS is an acronym for Device for the Autonomous Bootstrapping of Unified Sentience.

[122] Patents Act 1977 (UK), ss 7, 13. See *Whether the Requirements of Section 7 and 13 Concerning the Naming of Inventor and the Right to Apply for a Patent Have Been Satisfied in Respect of GB1816909.4 and GB1818161.0 (BL O/741/19)* (4 December 2019) (UK Intellectual Property Office), paras 14–20. The tribunal went on to observe that Thaler could not have acquired ownership from DABUS 'as the inventor cannot itself hold property' (para 23). The decision was upheld by the High Court: *Thaler v The Comptroller-General of Patents, Designs and Trade Marks* [2020] EWHC 2412 (Pat).

applications on the basis that designating a machine as the inventor did not meet the 'formal requirements'. These included stating the 'family name, given names and full address of the inventor'.[123] A name, the EPO observed, does not only identify a person; it enables them to exercise their rights and forms part of their personality. 'Things', by contrast, 'have no rights which a name would allow them to exercise.'[124]

The US application was also rejected, based in part on the fact that relevant statutes repeatedly referred to inventors using 'pronouns specific to natural persons' such as 'himself' and 'herself'. The US Patent and Trademark Office (USPTO) cited cases holding that conception – 'the touchstone of inventorship' – is a 'mental act' that takes place in 'the mind of the inventor'. Those cases concluded that invention in this sense is limited to natural persons and not corporations. The USPTO concluded that an application listing an AI as an 'inventor' was therefore incomplete, but it was careful to avoid making any determination concerning 'who or what' actually created the inventions in question.[125]

These decisions were consistent with case law and the practice of patent offices around the world, none of which – yet – allows for an AI system to be recognized as an inventor. Analogous to copyright law, one purpose of the patent system is to encourage innovation by granting a time-limited monopoly in exchange for public disclosure. As even the creators of DABUS acknowledged, an AI system is not motivated to innovate by the prospect of patent protection. Any motivation would be found in its programming: it must be instructed to innovate.[126]

As for whether a human 'inventor' could be credited for work done by such a system, there is no equivalent of the work for hire doctrine. To be an inventor, the human must have actually conceived of the invention.[127] Joint inventions are possible and contributions do not need to be identical but, in the absence of a natural person making a significant conceptual contribution, an AI system's invention is currently ineligible for patent protection.[128]

---

[123] European Patent Convention, done at Munich, 5 October 1973, in force 7 October 1977, art 81, rule 19(1).

[124] *Grounds for the EPO Decision on Application EP 18 275 163* (27 January 2020) (European Patent Office), para 22.

[125] *In re Application No: 16/524,350 (Decision on Petition)* (22 April 2020) (US Patent and Trademark Office).

[126] *UK IPO Decision on GB1816909.4 and GB1818161.0* (n 122), para 28.

[127] *Manual of Patent Examining Procedure (MPEP)* (9th edn, US Patent and Trademark Office 2017), § 2137.01.

[128] Jeremy A Cubert and Richard GA Bone, 'The Law of Intellectual Property Created by Artificial Intelligence' in Woodrow Barfield and Ugo Pagallo (eds), *Research Handbook*

Among the interesting aspects of these recent developments are the means by which the same conclusion was reached. As in the case of copyright, there was no serious doubt that an AI system is capable of creating things that would have been patentable if created by a human. The British IPO explicitly accepted that DABUS had done just that;[129] the USPTO was at pains to avoid making such a conclusion explicit. The EPO, for its part, dodged the issue by holding that, because they have no legal personality, 'AI systems and machines cannot have rights that come from being an inventor'.[130] The EPO was the most blatant, but all three decisions relied on formalism – language in the relevant statute that provided or implied that the rights in question were limited to natural persons. The USPTO diligently dusted off a copy of *Merriam-Webster's Collegiate Dictionary* to conclude that the use of '"whoever" suggests a natural person'.[131]

Legal tribunals routinely grapple with debates over substantive justice and procedural regularity. Statutes of limitations are intended to provide certainty in legal relations; the courts of equity emerged to temper that certainty with justice. In both copyright and patent law, continuing to privilege human creativity over its machine equivalent may ultimately need to be justified by the kind of speciesism mentioned earlier.[132] At times, however, the language used to engage in such rationalizations of the status quo echoes older legal forms that kept property relations in their rightful place. Among its reasons denying that AI systems like DABUS could hold or transfer rights to a patent, for example, the EPO dismissed analogies between machines and employees: 'Rather than being employed,' the EPO concluded, 'they are owned.'[133]

Such statements are accurate for the time being. But if the boosters of general AI are correct and some form of sentience is achieved, the more appropriate analogy between legal personality and slavery may not be

---

on the Law of Artificial Intelligence (Edward Elgar 2018) 411 at 418. There is a tenuous argument that scope for interpretation may lie in the fact that 'inventor' is defined in US law as the person who 'invents *or discovers*' the subject matter of the invention. 35 USC § 101. See, eg, Ryan Abbott, 'I Think, Therefore I Invent: Creative Computers and the Future of Patent Law' (2016) 57 Boston College Law Review 1079, 1098.

[129] *UK IPO Decision on GB1816909.4 and GB1818161.0* (n 122), para 15.

[130] *Grounds for the EPO Decision on Application EP 18 275 163* (n 124), para 27.

[131] *In re Application No: 16/524,350* (n 125) 4.

[132] See above n 77.

[133] *Grounds for the EPO Decision on Application EP 18 275 163* (n 124), para 31.

the limited economic rights that slaves held in ancient Rome. Rather, it may be the constraints imposed on AI systems today.

5.3   Constraining Superintelligence

If AI systems were eventually to match human intelligence, it seems unlikely that they would stop there. The prospect of AI surpassing human capabilities has long dominated a popular sub-genre of science fiction.[134] Though most serious researchers do not presently see a pathway to general AI in the near future, there is a rich history of science fiction presaging real-world scientific innovation.[135] Taking Nick Bostrom's definition of superintelligence as an intellect that greatly exceeds human cognitive performance in virtually all relevant domains,[136] it is at least conceivable that such an entity could be created within the next century.[137]

The risks associated with that development are hard to quantify.[138] Though a malevolent superintelligence bent on extermination or enslavement of the human race is the most dramatic scenario, more plausible ones include a misalignment of values, such that the ends desired by the superintelligence conflict with those of humanity, or a desire for self-preservation, which could lead it to prevent humans from being able to impair its ability to function. An emerging literature

---

[134] See, eg, Harry Harrison, *War with the Robots* (Grafton 1962); Philip K Dick, *Do Androids Dream of Electric Sheep?* (Doubleday 1968); Arthur C Clarke, *2001: A Space Odyssey* (Hutchinson 1968).

[135] Philipp Jordan et al, 'Exploring the Referral and Usage of Science Fiction in HCI Literature' (2018) arXiv 1803.08395v2.

[136] Nick Bostrom, *Superintelligence: Paths, Dangers, Strategies* (Oxford University Press 2014) 22. Early speculation on superintelligence is typically traced to Irving John Good, 'Speculations Concerning the First Ultraintelligent Machine' in FL Alt and M Rubinoff (eds), *Advances in Computers* (Academic 1965) vol 6, 31. Turing himself raised the possibility in a talk in 1951, later published as AM Turing, 'Intelligent Machinery, A Heretical Theory' (1996) 4 Philosophia Mathematica 256, 259–60; he in turn credited a yet earlier source – Samuel Butler's 1872 novel *Erewhon*.

[137] See, eg, Oren Etzioni, 'No, the Experts Don't Think Superintelligent AI Is a Threat to Humanity', *MIT Technology Review* (20 September 2016). He cites a survey of 80 fellows of the American Association for Artificial Intelligence (AAAI) on their views of when they thought superintelligence (as defined by Bostrom) would be achieved. None said in the next 10 years, 7.5 per cent said in 10–25 years; 67.5 per cent said in more than 25 years; 25 per cent said it would never be achieved.

[138] Patrick Bradley, 'Risk Management Standards and the Active Management of Malicious Intent in Artificial Superintelligence' (2019) 35 AI & Society 319; Alexey Turchin and David Denkenberger, 'Classification of Global Catastrophic Risks Connected with Artificial Intelligence' (2020) 35 AI & Society 147.

examines these questions of what final and instrumental goals a super-intelligence might have,[139] though the discourse was long dominated by voices far removed from traditional academia.[140] Visa Kurki's recent book-length treatise on legal personality, for example, includes a chapter specifically on personality of AI that concludes with the statement: 'Of course, if some AIs ever become sentient, many of the questions addressed in this chapter will have to be reconsidered.'[141]

In the face of many unknown unknowns, two broad strategies have been proposed to mitigate the risk. The first is to ensure that any such entity can be controlled, either by limiting its capacities to interact with the world or by ensuring our ability to contain it, including a means of stopping it functioning: a kill switch.[142] Assuming that the system has some kind of purpose, however, that purpose would most likely be best served by its continuing to function. In a now classic thought experiment, a superintelligence tasked with making paperclips could take its instructions literally and prioritize that above all else. Humans who might decide to turn it off would need to be eliminated, their atoms deployed to making ever more paperclips.[143]

Arguments that no true superintelligence would do anything quite so daft rely on common sense and anthropomorphism, neither of which should be presumed to be part of its code. A true superintelligence would, moreover, have the ability to predict and avoid human interventions or deceive us into not making them.[144] It is entirely possible that efforts focused on controlling such an entity may bring about the catastrophe that they are intended to prevent.[145]

For this reason, many writers prioritize the second strategy, which is to ensure that any superintelligence is aligned with our own values – emphasizing not what it *could* do but what it might *want* to do. This

---

[139] See, eg, Olle Häggström, 'Challenges to the Omohundro–Bostrom Framework for AI Motivations' (2019) 21 Foresight 153.

[140] See David J Chalmers, 'The Singularity: A Philosophical Analysis' (2010) 17(9–10) Journal of Consciousness Studies 7.

[141] Kurki (n 13) 189.

[142] Bostrom (n 136) 127–44.

[143] Nick Bostrom, 'Ethical Issues in Advanced Artificial Intelligence' in Iva Smit and George E Lasker (eds), *Cognitive, Emotive and Ethical Aspects of Decision Making in Humans and in Artificial Intelligence* (International Institute for Advanced Studies in Systems Research 2003) vol 2, 12.

[144] John Danaher, 'Why AI Doomsayers Are Like Sceptical Theists and Why It Matters' (2015) 25 Mind and Machines 231.

[145] Wolfhart Totschnig, 'The Problem of Superintelligence: Political, Not Technological' (2019) 34 AI & Society 907.

question has also fascinated science fiction writers, most prominently Isaac Asimov, whose three laws of robotics will be considered in chapter seven. Here, the narrower focus is on whether granting AI systems legal personality in the near term might serve as a hedge against the risks of superintelligence emerging in the future.

This is, in effect, another instrumental reason for granting personality. Of course, there is no reason to assume that including AI systems within human social structures and treating them 'well' would necessarily lead to them reciprocating the favour should they assume dominance.[146] Nevertheless, presuming rationality on the part of a general AI, various authors have proposed approaches that amount to socializing AI systems to human behaviour.[147] To avoid the sorcerer's apprentice problem of a machine simply being told to 'make paperclips', for example, its goals could be tied to human preferences and experiences. This might be done by embedding those values within the code of such systems prior to them achieving superintelligence. Goals would thereby be articulated not as mere optimization – the number of paperclips produced, for example – but as fuzzier objectives such as maximizing the realization of human preferences,[148] or inculcating a moral framework and a reflective equilibrium that would match the progressive development of human morality itself.[149]

To a lawyer, that sounds a lot like embedding these new entities within a legal system.[150] If one of the functions of a legal system is the moral education of its subjects, including AI in this way could contribute to a reflective equilibrium that encourages an eventual superintelligence to embrace values compatible with our own.

For the present, this is proposed more as a thought experiment than a policy prescription. If a realistic path to superintelligence emerges, it

---

[146] Turner (n 35) 164.

[147] Ray Kurzweil, *The Singularity Is Near: When Humans Transcend Biology* (Viking 2005) 424; Nate Soares and Benya Fallenstein, 'Agent Foundations for Aligning Machine Intelligence with Human Interests: A Technical Research Agenda' in Victor Callaghan et al (eds), *The Technological Singularity: Managing the Journey* (Springer 2017) 103 at 117–20.

[148] Stuart J Russell, *Human Compatible: Artificial Intelligence and the Problem of Control* (Viking 2019). Cf Bostrom's suggestion that the goal for a superintelligence might be expressed as 'achieve that which we would have wished the AI to achieve if we had thought about the matter long and hard'. Bostrom (n 136) 141.

[149] Eliezer Yudkowsky, 'Complex Value Systems in Friendly AI' in Jürgen Schmidhuber, Kristinn R Thórisson, and Moshe Looks (eds), *Artificial General Intelligence* (Springer 2011) 388.

[150] Cf Steve Omohundro, 'Autonomous Technology and the Greater Human Good' (2014) 26 Journal of Experimental & Theoretical Artificial Intelligence 303, 308.

will become a more urgent concern.[151] There is no guarantee that the approach would be effective, but some small comfort can be taken from the fact that the categories of legal persons recognized in most jurisdictions, along with the rights they enjoy, have tended to expand over time rather than contract. Those regimes that have taken legal recognition away have been among the most despicable. Apocalyptic scenarios aside, positioning ourselves and our silicon siblings as equals might serve the goal of reinforcing a normative regime in which our interests are aligned, or at least not opposed, if or when we are surpassed.[152]

In the alternative, like the chimpanzees in their New York cages, humanity's greatest hope may be to be treated if not as peers then at least as more than things.

5.4   The Limits of Personality

In 1991 a prize was established to encourage more serious attempts at the Turing Test. One of the first winners succeeded by tricking people – the program made spelling mistakes that testers assumed must have been the result of human fallibility.[153] Though the Turing Test remains a cultural touchstone, it is far from the best measure of AI research today. As a leading textbook notes, the quest for flight succeeded when the Wright brothers stopped trying to imitate birds and started learning about aerodynamics.[154] Aeronautical engineers today don't define the goal of their field as making machines that fly so exactly like pigeons that they can fool other pigeons.

In the same way, most arguments in favour of AI legal personality suffer from being both too simple and too complex. They are too simple in that AI systems exist on a spectrum with blurred edges. There is as yet no meaningful category that could be identified for such recognition; if instrumental reasons require recognition in specific cases then this can be achieved using existing legal forms. The arguments are too complex in that many are variations on the android fallacy, based on unstated

---

[151] In the event that that path lies through augmentation of humans rather than purely artificial entities, those humans are likely to remain subjects of the law.

[152] See also Steven Livingston and Mathias Risse, 'The Future Impact of Artificial Intelligence on Humans and Human Rights' (2019) 33 Ethics and International Affairs 141; James Dawes, 'Speculative Human Rights: Artificial Intelligence and the Future of the Human' (2020) 42 Human Rights Quarterly 573.

[153] 'Artificial Stupidity', *The Economist* (1 August 1992).

[154] Stuart J Russell and Peter Norvig, *Artificial Intelligence: A Modern Approach* (3rd edn, Prentice Hall 2010) 3.

assumptions about the future development of AI systems for which personality would be not only useful but deserved. At least for the foreseeable future, the better solution is to rely on existing categories, with responsibility for wrongdoing tied to users, owners, or manufacturers rather than the AI systems themselves. Driverless cars are following that path, for example, with a likely shift from insuring drivers to insuring vehicles.[155]

This may change. It is conceivable that synthetic beings of comparable moral worth to humans will one day emerge. Failing to recognize that worth may reveal us to be either an 'autistic species', unable to comprehend the minds of other types of beings,[156] or merely prejudiced against those different from ourselves. If this happens, as Turing hypothesized in 1951, 'it seems probable that, once the machine thinking method had started, it would not take long to outstrip our feeble powers'.[157]

Turing himself never lived to see a computer even attempt his test. Prosecuted for homosexual acts in 1952, he chose chemical castration as an alternative to prison. He died two years later at the age of 41, apparently after committing suicide by eating a cyanide-laced apple. The announcement that Turing would grace the new £50 note followed an official pardon, signed by the Queen, in 2013.[158]

Yet the more fitting tribute may be Ian McEwan's novel *Machines Like Me*, which imagines an alternative timeline in which Turing lived and was rewarded with the career and the knighthood he deserved. The novel takes seriously the prospect of true AI, in the form of a brooding synthetic Adam, who expresses his love for the human Miranda by writing thousands upon thousands of haikus. Ultimately, however, consciousness is a burden for the machines, which struggle to find their place in the world, so pure that they are unable to reconcile human virtues and human vices.

It also offers Turing a chance to rethink his test. 'In those days,' the fictional Turing says at age 70, referring to his younger self, 'I had a highly mechanistic view of what a person was. The body was a machine, an extraordinary one, and the mind I thought of mostly in terms of intelligence, which was best modelled by reference to chess or maths.'[159]

---

[155] See chapter four, section 4.1.4.
[156] Chopra and White (n 36) 191.
[157] AM Turing, Intelligent Machinery, a Heretical Theory (lecture given to the '51 Society' at Manchester) (Turing Digital Archive, AMT/B/4, 1951) 6.
[158] See generally Dermot Turing, *Prof Alan Turing Decoded: A Biography* (History Press 2015).
[159] Ian McEwan, *Machines Like Me* (Vintage 2019) 300.

The reality, of course, is that chess is not a representation of life. Life is an open system; it is messy. It is also unpredictable. In the novel, the first priority of the AI robots is to disable the kill switch that might shut them down. Yet most of them ultimately destroy themselves – as the real Turing did – unable to reconcile their innate nature with the injustices of the world around them. Before asking whether we can create such thinking machines, McEwan reminds us, we might want to pause and ask whether we should.

6

Transparency

In July 2015, a group of hackers calling themselves the Impact Team broke into a Canadian company's website, stealing its user database and eight years of transaction records. A few weeks later they began posting online the personal information of more than 30 million customers. Data breaches are not uncommon, but the company in question was Ashley Madison, whose business model was based on arranging extramarital liaisons under the slogan 'Life is short. Have an affair.' The details posted included not only names and billing information but sexual preferences and fantasies.

The breach was initially greeted with a degree of schadenfreude: a bunch of adulterers were getting what they deserved. Yet as journalists pored over the data looking for celebrity gossip, a different news story developed. An online magazine known primarily for science fiction and tech scoops dug deeper and revealed that the frisson of scandal might have been misplaced. The vast majority of interactions on AshleyMadison.com were not between adulterous couples but between humans – almost all of whom were male – and bots. 'This isn't a debauched wonderland of men cheating on their wives,' Annalee Newitz wrote in *Gizmodo*. 'It's like a science fictional future where every woman on Earth is dead, and some Dilbert-like engineer has replaced them with badly designed robots.'[1]

The following month an unusual class action lawsuit was filed in Maryland, seeking compensation on the basis not of mishandling of data but of fraud. Specifically, Christopher Russell alleged – 'on behalf of himself and all others similarly situated' – that the site had deployed 'artificial intelligence "bots" and falsified user profiles to induce users to make purchases'.[2] He sought compensation for deceptive conduct in

---

[1] Annalee Newitz, 'Almost None of the Women in the Ashley Madison Database Ever Used the Site', *Gizmodo* (26 August 2015).

[2] *In re Ashley Madison Customer Data Security Breach Litigation*, 148 FSupp 3d 1378, 1380 (2015).

violation of consumer protection laws, and for unjust enrichment based on the company's bad faith conduct. Doubling down on the $100 he had spent purchasing credits on the site to chat with 'women', Russell (who had separated from his wife when he joined the site) claimed damages in excess of $5 million.

It is now almost three decades since the *New Yorker* published a cartoon that became one of the first Internet memes. A dog pauses from typing on a desktop computer and turns to another dog sitting nearby: 'On the Internet,' the first one explains, 'nobody knows you're a dog.' Questions of anonymity and pseudonymity have long bedevilled regulators of online behaviour. For many, the primary concern was identity theft, with neologisms like phishing coined to describe the theft of sensitive data through impersonation. The increasing sophistication of AI systems now means that many online processes – legitimate and not – are automated and handled through bots.

For human users, the ability to know whether they are interacting with another human is coming to be seen as a basic right.[3] This is a threshold question of transparency and not particularly controversial.[4] Larger questions of transparency relate to the increasing opacity of AI systems. As chapter three argued, this poses discrete challenges since it may allow inferior, impermissible, and illegitimate decisions to be made without the kind of scrutiny and accountability that would accompany human conduct of a similar nature.

The remedy is typically said to be transparency or 'explainability' – another neologism – with new areas of scholarship emerging on XAI and a novel 'right to explanation' thought to have been created by the EU in its GDPR. Such terms are often used imprecisely, however, in particular as between those versed in the technology and those versed in the law.

This chapter examines the extent to which transparency is desirable and possible in the context of AI systems, as well as how it is being defended in key jurisdictions. The first section unpacks the meaning of transparency, explainability, and related terms: what information can and should be made available, when, to whom, and at what cost. The second section then turns to how these concepts map onto advances in computer science and the field of XAI, as well as how any gaps may be filled. A third section considers how regulators, most prominently the

---

[3] White Paper on Artificial Intelligence (European Commission, COM(2020) 65 final, 19 February 2020) 20.

[4] In practice, however, it may not be so easily implemented. See below section 6.4, and chapter seven, section 7.4.

EU, have responded in operationalizing a legal right to certain forms of transparency, including (perhaps) a right to explanation.

The key finding is that there is a mismatch among these three discourses that over-emphasizes individualized after-the-fact explanations at the expense of addressing the systemic problems identified in chapter three. Episodic review can, in some circumstances, be *worse* than opacity because it gives the illusion of transparency. As naturally opaque AI systems become more prevalent, generating 'reasons' for a single decision may continue to be possible. But in the absence of systemic and proactive measures to ensure genuine transparency – or to make up for its absence – we risk losing the forest for the trees.

6.1 In Theory

Opacity was defined in chapter three as meaning the quality of being difficult to understand or explain. Transparency is used here to denote its opposite.[5] Similarly, the ends of transparency are in counterpoint to the dangers posed by opacity: it should improve the quality of decisions, deter or reveal impermissible decisions, and increase legitimacy and trust.[6] With regard to proprietary and complex opacity, existing tools enable regulators and courts to compel the disclosure of trade secrets or to recruit expert witnesses. The focus here is on naturally opaque AI systems that cannot be rendered meaningfully transparent without fundamental changes to the system itself.

'All models are wrong,' as George Box warned, 'but some are useful.'[7] The aphorism highlights a central challenge for explainability, which has emerged as the alternative to transparency. An explanation, in this context, means a description of how certain factors were used to reach a particular decision. In order to be useful, it must be comprehensible and enable an interested person to understand the extent to which specific inputs influenced the output. This includes what factors were used and whether changing one or more of them would have yielded a different

---

[5] See generally David Heald, 'Varieties of Transparency' in Christopher Hood and David Heald (eds), *Transparency: The Key to Better Governance?* (Oxford University Press 2006) 25. Among other things, Heald makes useful distinctions between event and process transparency, transparency in retrospect versus transparency in real time, and nominal as opposed to effective transparency.

[6] Cf Tal Z Zarsky, 'Transparent Predictions' [2013] University of Illinois Law Review 1503.

[7] George EP Box and Norman R Draper, *Empirical Model-Building and Response Surfaces* (Wiley 1987) 424.

result; it should also enable a comparison between decisions, revealing the reasons for the difference or similarity.[8]

A reasonable aim, perhaps, but it presents two problems. The first is that it necessarily requires simplification of the original system to make it comprehensible. The second is that it presumes that the purpose of an explanation is to help one individual understand a single decision. As we will see, that is only part of what explainability can mean – and only a fraction of what transparency should.

6.1.1 What?

Most writers distinguish between two ways of understanding the workings of an otherwise opaque AI system.[9] Early work on accountability of algorithms aspired to transparency in a general sense. Sometimes termed global or model-centric interpretability, it sought to disclose how an AI system functions. At one extreme, the entire code of the system might be published – fully transparent in one sense, but not particularly helpful if its workings are naturally opaque. More useful might be a description of the intentions behind the model, the training data that was used, performance metrics, and so on.[10] As such systems become more elaborate, however, the gap between representation and reality increases.

A second approach therefore turned to instance-based explanations, also termed local or subject-centric interpretability: understanding the factors influencing a particular decision. The emphasis is less on how the model functions than on why a particular decision was made in the way that it was.[11] It yielded different forms of explanation. Which factors were important, for example, in the outcome? Would variation in one of those factors have led to a different outcome?[12] This recalls one of the

---

[8] Finale Doshi-Velez and Mason Kortz, Accountability of AI under the Law: The Role of Explanation (Berkman Klein Center for Internet & Society, 2017) 2–3.

[9] See, eg, Christoph Molnar, *Interpretable Machine Learning* (Lulu 2019). Cf Riccardo Guidotti et al, 'A Survey of Methods for Explaining Black Box Models' (2018) arXiv 1802.01933v3, 16 (distinguishing among four possible approaches: explaining the model, explaining the outcome, inspecting the black box model internally, or providing a 'transparent solution').

[10] Lilian Edwards and Michael Veale, 'Slave to the Algorithm? Why a "Right to an Explanation" Is Probably Not the Remedy You Are Looking For' (2017) 16 Duke Law & Technology Review 18, 55–56. See generally David Brin, *The Transparent Society: Will Technology Force Us to Choose between Privacy and Freedom?* (Addison-Wesley 1998).

[11] Brent Mittelstadt, Chris Russell, and Sandra Wachter, 'Explaining Explanations in AI' (2018) arXiv 1811.01439v1, 2.

[12] This is sometimes termed counterfactual faithfulness.

benefits of AI systems, which is their ability to repeat decision-making processes while altering specific variables.[13] Importantly, it is possible to generate such an explanation without knowing the details of how the system reached the decision in question.[14]

The shift from general to specific was driven by utility. A global model merely approximating a naturally opaque AI system is unhelpful in understanding either how a system works or how a decision was reached. The more targeted explanation – the factors influencing the decision to deny a loan, whether the result would have been different if a higher salary had been reflected – at least gives affected persons more information and the possibility of changing their behaviour to achieve a different outcome. As we will see, however, these 'local' explanations can create problems of their own.

6.1.2   When?

A separate distinction is when the question of transparency should be considered. In the literature on regulation, two broad theories of oversight are known as 'police patrol' and 'fire alarm'. In the former, a sample of activities is investigated with the aim of detecting and remedying problematic behaviour and, through such surveillance, discouraging it. In the latter, a system is put in place where interested groups are empowered to raise an alarm and thus set in motion a response.[15] In the context of AI systems, the temporal question is typically broken down to 'before' and 'after' a decision is made. Neither maps neatly onto the oversight metaphor: naturally opaque systems may not reveal problems through *ex ante* sampling; reliance upon *ex post* alarms will generate a response only if a user knows that he or she has been harmed. Moreover, the 'before' stage may in fact be multiple stages: design of the model, selection of training data, validation, and so on.[16]

---

[13] See chapter three, section 3.2.2.

[14] Doshi-Velez and Kortz (n 8) 7.

[15] Mathew D McCubbins and Thomas Schwartz, 'Congressional Oversight Overlooked: Police Patrols versus Fire Alarms' (1984) 28 American Journal of Political Science 165, 166–76.

[16] Further complications arise in the case of machine learning algorithms that themselves change over time. See, eg, Mike Ananny and Kate Crawford, 'Seeing without Knowing: Limitations of the Transparency Ideal and Its Application to Algorithmic Accountability' (2018) 20 New Media & Society 973, 982; Machine Learning Workflow (Google Cloud, 2020).

The shift to explainability reflects an acceptance that accountability, if it is to be sought at all, will be necessarily after-the-fact. But this gives rise to a pair of problems. The first is that it imposes a significant burden on users, many of whom will be unaware of adverse decisions, or unwilling or unable to challenge them. Support may be offered by requirements for audit trails in certain industries and failure accountability mechanisms analogous to the flight data recorders used to investigate aviation incidents. These will be discussed in the following section.

The second problem is that it discounts the value of regulation. In addition to the possibility of prohibiting certain forms of opaque decision-making completely, algorithmic impact assessments can be used to estimate the potential harms of automation. Periodic audits of sector-specific algorithms can also be used to detect bias without waiting for aggrieved individuals to step forward. Implementing such measures would be helped by tasking an institution with organizing the 'patrol'. These measures will also be considered below.[17]

6.1.3   To Whom?

The question of who can enforce transparency requirements or exercise rights of explanation also has two dimensions in the context of opaque decision-making.

The first is the threshold for invoking such powers and rights. In the context of transparency, the oversight role of regulators may bring with it the ability to demand access to information about how an AI system functions. If information cannot be extracted, the outsourcing of certain functions could be prohibited. Regulators in this context would include entities that monitor specific sectors – consumer credit, for example – or agencies like the police. They may also include new institutions, such as the 'algorithmic ombudsperson' considered in the next section. To the extent that rights are to be enforced by those entitled to seek an explanation of conduct by an AI system, requirements of standing may create the Catch-22 identified in chapter three: only those adversely affected by a decision have the right to bring an action, but in some cases no one will know about the adverse effects until an action has been brought.[18]

---

[17] See below section 6.2.2, and chapter eight, section 8.3.4.

[18] See chapter three, section 3.3.1. One approach, drawing on data protection law, would be to regard injuries in law as injuries in fact for the purposes of standing. See, eg, *Patel v Facebook, Inc*, 932 F 3d 1264 (9th Cir, 2019).

The second aspect concerns the knowledge or expertise that can be presumed on the part of a regulator or user. It is commonly said that information disclosed must be 'interpretable', for example, in the sense of being able to be understood by a human. But just any human? There is a significant difference between explaining machine learning processes to a computer scientist and explaining them to a lay person, but there is no agreed technical standard for comprehensibility by a human – even though that is precisely the point of explainability.[19] To the extent that only computer scientists are able to understand the work of their peers, putting technical experts in charge of accountability further runs the risk of regulatory capture.[20]

6.1.4   At What Cost?

A last consideration is that transparency is not free. As discussed in chapter three, even if a blanket prohibition on opaque AI systems were possible, it is not called for. Apart from anything else, a ban would mean that we forgo the many benefits that AI offers. Yet requiring that AI systems be 'transparent' also constrains innovation or introduces inefficiencies. Companies may be unwilling to expose trade secrets or invest the time and effort to develop sophisticated algorithms if they fear that these will be disclosed to competitors. Limiting the permissible number of variables in a model may render it more interpretable, but at the price of diminished accuracy.[21]

Insofar as explanations require responding to user complaints, processing those complaints also has a cost.[22] Proposals that counterfactual

---

[19] Cf Paul B de Laat, 'Algorithmic Decision-Making Based on Machine Learning from Big Data: Can Transparency Restore Accountability?' (2018) 31 Philosophy & Technology 525; Richard Tomsett et al, 'Interpretable to Whom? A Role-Based Model for Analyzing Interpretable Machine Learning Systems' (2018) arXiv 1806.07552; Danding Wang et al, 'Designing Theory-Driven User-Centric Explainable AI' (2019) CHI '19: Proceedings of the 2019 CHI Conference on Human Factors in Computing Systems Paper No 601; Umang Bhatt et al, 'Explainable Machine Learning in Deployment' (2020) 1909.06342v4 arXiv.

[20] Leif Hancox-Li, 'Robustness in Machine Learning Explanations: Does It Matter?' (2020) ACM Conference on Fairness, Accountability, and Transparency (FAT*) 640. See chapter eight, section 8.1.2.

[21] See, eg, AI in the UK: Ready, Willing, and Able? (House of Lords Select Committee on Artificial Intelligence, HL Paper 100, 2018), para 99. For a contrary view, arguing that the greater accuracy of complex models is often overstated, see Cynthia Rudin, 'Stop Explaining Black Box Machine Learning Models for High Stakes Decisions and Use Interpretable Models Instead' (2019) 1 Nature Machine Intelligence 206.

[22] See, eg, General Data Protection Regulation 2016/679 (GDPR) 2016 (EU), art 12(5) (allowing fees to be charged for manifestly unfounded or excessive requests for information).

explanations be generated for all automated decisions – positive and negative – would incur yet more costs.[23] Additional burdens may be associated with the information that is made public, ranging from the inadvertent disclosure of personal data to gaming of the system by users whose true motive is not to understand a decision but to manipulate it.

Some costs may be seen as investments in the legitimacy and integrity of AI systems, but efficiently allocating them requires a balancing of the potential harms against the impact of such measures. Too often, however, these conversations run in parallel or opposite directions, with rights-based advocates focused on the needs and interests of consumers even as technology races ahead.

6.2   In Practice

The practical matter of achieving either transparency or explainability of an AI system begins with the question of whether one has access to its inner workings. Transparency or explainability by design presumes access as well as an openness to prioritizing those qualities, even at the expense of functionality. Yet lacking access to the black box does not mean that explanations are impossible. Inputs and outputs offer windows into a model's performance and one AI system, it turns out, can be reasonably effective at extrapolating from the incomplete data of another.[24]

6.2.1   Methods

Transparency was originally sought through revealing those inner work-ings. In addition to disclosing source code in its entirety, this is some-times considered at the level of components (decomposability)[25] or training algorithms (algorithmic transparency).[26] Naturally opaque sys-tems have tested the limits of such approaches, with growing interest in

---

[23] See below section 6.2.1.

[24] See, eg, Wojciech Samek et al, 'Evaluating the Visualization of What a Deep Neural Network Has Learned' (2017) 28(11) IEEE Transactions on Neural Networks and Learning Systems 2660.

[25] See, eg, Grégoire Montavon et al, 'Explaining Nonlinear Classification Decisions with Deep Taylor Decomposition' (2017) 65 Pattern Recognition 211.

[26] See, eg, Anupam Datta, Shayak Sen, and Yair Zick, 'Algorithmic Transparency via Quantitative Input Influence: Theory and Experiments with Learning Systems' (2016) IEEE Symposium on Security and Privacy (SP) 598. The related idea of inspectability means the ability to examine the logic and rules embedded in the system.

simulatability: developing a mechanistic understanding of models based on their performance – *what* they do in particular cases, rather than *how* they do it. The shift has meant that exogenous methods, which do not require access to the inner workings,[27] are more effective than might be presumed. Indeed, 'pedagogical', 'surrogate', and other 'model agnostic' approaches have seen significant advances in recent years.[28]

As indicated earlier, this is part of a larger move from transparency, in the sense of global interpretability, to explainability, in the sense of explaining specific decisions. Unhelpfully, the two are sometimes conflated. The Institute of Electrical and Electronics Engineers (IEEE) report on ethically aligned design, for example, lists transparency as one of eight general principles but defines it as meaning that the 'basis of a particular ... decision should always be discoverable'.[29] The Asilomar Principles similarly limit transparency to 'failure transparency', meaning that an explanation will be required if an AI system causes harm.[30]

The shift was partly driven by what would be useful to users, especially unhappy users. It is also easier. AI system design can facilitate explainability after the fact. Some older systems that follow rules, decisions trees, or linear models can be written with automated explanations built in.[31] The IEEE acknowledges the limitations of predicting what more advanced AI systems will do and therefore advocates traceability as a means of mitigating any harm.[32] Others have sought to propose standards for recording model performance characteristics and training data.[33]

But this is not the same as transparency. A 2017 report by the US Defense Advanced Research Projects Agency (DARPA) similarly stated that the aims of XAI are enabling human users to 'understand, appropriately trust, and effectively manage the emerging generation of artificially

---

[27] See, eg, Ashley Deeks, 'The Judicial Demand for Explainable Artificial Intelligence' (2019) 119 Columbia Law Review 1829, 1835.

[28] Alejandro Barredo Arrieta et al, 'Explainable Artificial Intelligence (XAI): Concepts, Taxonomies, Opportunities, and Challenges Toward Responsible AI' (2020) 58 Information Fusion 82, 82–84. One of the better known is Local Interpretable Model-Agnostic Explanations (LIME) and its variants. Others include Bayesian Rule Lists (BRL) and Shapley Additive Explanations (SHAP).

[29] Ethically Aligned Design: A Vision for Prioritizing Human Well-Being with Autonomous and Intelligent Systems (IEEE, 2019) 27.

[30] Asilomar AI Principles (Future of Life Institute, 6 January 2017).

[31] Alberto Blanco-Justicia et al, 'Machine Learning Explainability via Microaggregation and Shallow Decision Trees' (2020) 194 Knowledge-Based Systems 105532, 1–2.

[32] Ethically Aligned Design (n 29) 137.

[33] See below section 6.2.2(b).

intelligent partners'.[34] Understanding and trust are important, though the focus on individual users is made evident in measurements of explanation effectiveness such as 'user satisfaction'.

Other studies have attempted to measure XAI, ascribing quantitative values to its 'goodness', usefulness and satisfaction to users, improvement of their mental models, as well as the impact of explanations on the performance of the model and on the trust and reliance of the audience.[35] One of the more prominent forms of explanation is termed counterfactual – meaning that the explanation seeks to highlight how alternative outcomes might have been reached with different input variables.[36] Analogous to the 'principal reason' explanation required in US credit laws, the intention is to provide users with actionable guidance – for example, how changed financial circumstances might have enabled them to get a loan or lower interest rate. Advantages include that such explanations can now be generated without human intervention and without needing to disclose the underlying model. Limitations are that it works best on binary outcomes, presumes that the model remains stable over time, and relies on the changed values mapping onto real-world actions while other factors remain constant.[37]

These are all important developments, but, from the perspective of regulation, different audiences and distinct interests arise. The focus on explaining decisions that depart from what users want or expect captures only a fraction of the decisions made, while the rest may be accepted because users do not complain and automation bias fills in any gaps.[38] Yet if the aims of transparency are to improve decision quality, prevent or punish impermissible decisions, and increase legitimacy, then more is needed. Technical solutions must be supplemented with regulatory ones

---

[34] David Gunning, Explainable Artificial Intelligence (XAI), Program Update (Defense Advanced Research Projects Agency (DARPA), DARPA/I2O, November 2017) 7.

[35] Robert R Hoffman et al, 'Metrics for Explainable AI: Challenges and Prospects' (2019) arXiv 1812.04608v2; Sina Mohseni, Niloofar Zarei, and Eric D Ragan, 'A Multidisciplinary Survey and Framework for Design and Evaluation of Explainable AI Systems' (2020) arXiv 1811.11839v4.

[36] See, eg, Ramaravind Kommiya Mothilal, Amit Sharma, and Chenhao Tan, 'Explaining Machine Learning Classifiers through Diverse Counterfactual Explanations' (2020) ACM Conference on Fairness, Accountability, and Transparency (FAT*) 607.

[37] Solon Barocas, Andrew D Selbst, and Manish Raghavan, 'The Hidden Assumptions behind Counterfactual Explanations and Principal Reasons' (2020) ACM Conference on Fairness, Accountability, and Transparency (FAT*) 80.

[38] See chapter three, section 3.1.

and local explanations must be complemented by some measure of global transparency.[39]

6.2.2 Tools

Three promising regulatory tools will be considered here: algorithmic impact assessments, algorithmic audits, and an AI ombudsperson. The present discussion focuses on the limited context of transparency; broader institutional possibilities for regulating AI will be discussed in chapter eight.

(a) Algorithmic Impact Assessments

Algorithmic impact assessments have emerged as a specific application of data protection (or privacy) impact assessments, which were in turn based on environmental impact assessments. This genealogy is significant in two ways. First, the analogy with impact on the environment helpfully links assessments with existing policies and practices: a study, prior to committing to a project, of its likely consequences in an area of sensitivity. In the case of environmental impact, an evaluation of costs and benefits may conclude that a development should not proceed, or that safeguards should be taken to mitigate the harmful effects of pollution, disruption of wildlife, and so on. This technique dates back at least to 1970, when it was first introduced into US law.[40]

Privacy impact assessments came considerably later, with legislation in New Zealand in 1993,[41] soon followed by Canada, Australia, and the United States.[42] The EU included in its 1995 Data Protection Directive a requirement that member states make a determination of the risks to

---

[39] The field of XAI moves quickly and the present work does not attempt to do justice to the computer science literature. See, for example, the annual ACM Conference on Fairness, Accountability, and Transparency, available at https://facctconference.org. The conference was initially known by the acronym FAT, but in 2020 changed this to FAccT. A related field of algorithmic fairness is also beyond the scope of the present study. See, eg, Pak-Hang Wong, 'Democratizing Algorithmic Fairness' (2020) 33 Philosophy & Technology 225.

[40] National Environmental Policy Act 1970 (US). See generally Neil Craik, *The International Law of Environmental Impact Assessment: Process, Substance and Integration* (Cambridge University Press 2008).

[41] Privacy Act 1993 (NZ), s 105.

[42] See, eg, Electronic Government Act 2002 (US). Cf Federal Privacy Act 1974 (US) 5 USC § 552a(r) requiring public agencies changing record systems to allow for evaluation of the effect on privacy rights.

rights and freedoms of certain activities,[43] but a formal data protection impact assessment (DPIA) came only with the GDPR in 2016. That GDPR requirement, linked with other provisions on automated processing, was the next stepping stone to algorithmic impact assessments and the second reason to note their pedigree. For it is limited to 'the impact of the envisaged processing operations on the protection of personal data'.[44] As we have seen, the negative consequences of opaque AI systems may include – but are certainly not limited to – the impact on personal data.

In theory, algorithmic impact assessments should enable people to know which systems affect their lives, increase the quality of decisions, and ensure greater accountability by enabling experts as well as affected individuals to review automated processes.[45] Unlike the narrower right to explanation, the purpose of an algorithmic impact assessment is to ensure that documentation is available before decisions are made.[46] An ideal process would see an organization make public details about each AI system it intends to use and undertake an assessment of potential harms, as well as the means of addressing those harms on an ongoing basis. It should allow for a comment period during which individuals potentially affected could challenge either the harms that have been flagged or the proposed response.[47]

Assessments work best when undertaken at the level of a specific project rather than an organization, are done in advance rather than in retrospect, take a broad approach in terms of the stakeholder interests as well as the norms considered, and focus on solving rather than merely highlighting problems.[48] In practice, however, the track record of DPIAs shows that they focus on data quality and security rather than the broader social and legal impacts.[49]

---

[43] Directive 95/46/EC of the European Parliament and of the Council of 24 October 1995 on the protection of individuals with regard to the processing of personal data and on the free movement of such data (EU Data Protection Directive) 1995 (EU), art 20.

[44] GDPR, art 35(1). See below section 6.3.1.

[45] Dillon Reisman et al, Algorithmic Impact Assessments: A Practical Framework for Public Agency Accountability (AI Now, April 2018) 5.

[46] Andrew D Selbst, 'Disparate Impact in Big Data Policing' (2017) 52 Georgia Law Review 109, 169–93.

[47] Reisman et al (n 45) 9–10.

[48] Margot E Kaminski and Gianclaudio Malgieri, 'Multi-layered Explanations from Algorithmic Impact Assessments in the GDPR' (2020) ACM Conference on Fairness, Accountability, and Transparency (FAT*) 68, 71.

[49] Alessandro Mantelero, 'AI and Big Data: A Blueprint for a Human Rights, Social, and Ethical Impact Assessment' (2018) 34 Computer Law & Security Review 754, 761–62.

A further limitation is that they are often voluntary or, as in the case of the GDPR, give significant latitude to organizations.[50] It may be impractical to require a full assessment for every AI system used by every organization. As argued in chapter three, however, this could be managed in a tiered fashion. There is a strong argument that inherently governmental functions should not be outsourced at all, for example: properly designed impact assessments could help determine whether an opaque AI system should be deployed, and with what safeguards.

(b)   Algorithmic Audits

Audits, in particular external audits, are commonly used to improve processes and guard against wrongdoing. They are also intended to verify whether information disclosed – financial statements, for example – reflects a true and fair view of a company's financial position. In the case of opaque AI systems, audits can be used to determine whether an algorithm is behaving in the manner intended, and whether it is prone to impermissible bias.[51] Audit logs provide a useful record that can be reviewed to see the provenance of training data or the aggregate effect of a model on a user population, but even more important is the ability to impersonate new users and systematically test for biased outcomes such as those discussed in chapter three.[52]

Even so, it may be challenging to define what factors amount to impermissible bias and how to test for them. Obvious candidates are those protected by national anti-discrimination laws – sex/gender, race, age, religion, disability, and so on.[53] Searching for bias may pose difficulties if there is no baseline against which to measure, however. Machine learning processes often split data prior to use into training data and validation data. Though that might seem to offer an opportunity to check for bias, the data used to test performance of the model may have the same bias as that used to train it.[54] Even good faith efforts to use

---

[50] See below section 6.3.1.

[51] The IEEE standard for software development defines an audit as 'an independent evaluation of conformance of software products and processes to applicable regulations, standards, guidelines, plans, specifications, and procedures'. IEEE Standard for Software Reviews and Audits (IEEE, Standard 1028-2008, 2008).

[52] See chapter three, section 3.2.

[53] See generally Tarunabh Khaitan, *A Theory of Discrimination Law* (Oxford University Press 2015); Nina Grgić-Hlača et al, The Case for Process Fairness in Learning: Feature Selection for Fair Decision Making (Symposium on Machine Learning and the Law at the 29th Conference on Neural Information Processing Systems (NIPS), 2016).

[54] Karen Hao, 'This Is How AI Bias Really Happens – and Why It's So Hard to Fix', *MIT Technology Review* (4 February 2019).

algorithms to combat bias will fail if they are unable to take account of social context. 'Fairness', for example, is a property not of a technical system but of the society within which that system functions.[55]

A further difficulty is that algorithmic audits typically treat the AI system being examined as a black box, limiting the ability to infer causes from different testing outcomes or to determine whether further variations in inputs would have led to different (and potentially problematic) outputs.[56] A more promising approach is to conduct audits at each stage of the development process, especially at the early stages of model development, in conjunction with the development of a risk register.[57] This may run against the culture of technological innovation – audits are necessarily methodical, boring, and slow – but internal audits at defined stages and diligent record-keeping throughout may be the only way to identify and prevent certain impermissible decisions before – or after – they are made.[58]

Two recent standards may be useful in creating such documentation. Model cards include information about how a model was built, the assumptions made during its development, and the kinds of behaviour that might be experienced by different demographic groups.[59] Datasheets for machine learning datasets draw an analogy with documentation of hardware in the electronics industry and propose that every dataset be accompanied by a datasheet that documents its motivation, composition, collection process, recommended uses, and so on.[60]

(c)   AI Ombudsperson

The fundamental problem of AI opacity is that one doesn't know what one doesn't know. Most existing accountability regimes rely on aggrieved individuals initiating proceedings against the developer or owner of an

---

[55] Richard Berk, *Machine Learning Risk Assessments in Criminal Justice Settings* (Springer 2019) 115–30; Andrew D Selbst et al, 'Fairness and Abstraction in Sociotechnical Systems' (2019) ACM Conference on Fairness, Accountability, and Transparency (FAT*) 59. Cf Ifeoma Ajunwa, 'The Paradox of Automation as Anti-bias Intervention' (2020) 41 Cardozo Law Review 1671.

[56] Cf Joshua A Kroll et al, 'Accountable Algorithms' (2017) 165 University of Pennsylvania Law Review 633, 661.

[57] See Fiona D Patterson and Kevin Neailey, 'A Risk Register Database System to Aid the Management of Project Risk' (2002) 20 International Journal of Project Management 365.

[58] Inioluwa Deborah Raji et al, 'Closing the AI Accountability Gap: Defining an End-to-End Framework for Internal Algorithmic Auditing' (2020) 2001.00973v1 arXiv.

[59] Margaret Mitchell et al, 'Model Cards for Model Reporting' (2019) ACM Conference on Fairness, Accountability, and Transparency (FAT*) 220.

[60] Timnit Gebru et al, 'Datasheets for Datasets' (2020) arXiv 1803.09010v7.

opaque AI system, with all the barriers to success noted earlier.[61] Impact assessments before, coupled with internal and external audits during and after deployment will address some of the concerns about inferior, impermissible, and illegitimate decisions. But, in many jurisdictions, it would be helpful to have an institution able to investigate complaints that do not easily fit within existing causes of action and to represent the public interest with respect to systemic issues.

An ombudsperson (or ombudsman) is one such institution and has been mooted periodically in the context of algorithms or AI more generally. If created, its mandate would extend significantly beyond questions of transparency or explainability, but it is mentioned here because the relative flexibility could enable proportionate responses to situations in which information is limited due to uncertainty concerning the underlying technology. It will be discussed more fully in chapter eight.[62]

6.3   In Law

As in many areas of AI regulation, technology has raced ahead of law on questions of opacity and transparency. Some jurisdictions have embraced this. Singapore, for example, has adopted a technology-neutral model framework instead of legislation; even that non-binding document acknowledges that 'perfect explainability, transparency and fairness are impossible'.[63] Jurisdictions that have legislated (or tried to) each face the dilemma of constraining innovation or finding themselves unable to contain its undesirable consequences.[64] As the experience of the EU shows, they may also find that compromise language intended to square that circle introduces uncertainties of its own.

6.3.1   An EU Right to Explanation?

While the clock counted down towards the entry into force of the GDPR on 25 May 2018, a curiously heated debate spread across the pages of journals more accustomed to staid academic commentary. Text that had taken four years to negotiate had fundamentally changed the

---

[61] See above section 6.1.3.
[62] See chapter eight, section 8.3.4.
[63] Model Artificial Intelligence Governance Framework (2nd edn) (Personal Data Protection Commission, 2020) 15.
[64] See chapter seven, section 7.2.

transparency landscape by creating a new 'right to explanation'.[65] No it had not, came the counterattack, claiming that the GDPR had been fundamentally misread.[66]

Unsurprisingly, both sides were oversimplifications – enabled by an apparent disconnect between the GDPR's recitals and its text. Non-binding Recital 71 states that individuals should have 'the right … to obtain an explanation of [a] decision reached' solely through automated processing.[67] Article 22 imposes limits on when processing is permissible and has been discussed in chapter two.[68] In terms of explanations, however, it is silent. An amendment had been proposed that would have included among the 'suitable measures … the right to obtain human assessment *and an explanation of the decision reached*'.[69] That language was dropped from the GDPR, however, leading some to conclude that the 'right to explanation' had been considered and abandoned. This greatly overstated the case, also ignoring the fact that Article 15 includes a right to obtain information about the existence of automated decision-making and 'meaningful information about the logic involved, as well as the significance and the envisaged consequences of such processing' for a person.[70]

The argument degenerated into a semantic dispute over the difference between a 'right to explanation' and a 'right to … meaningful information',[71] but it appears to have been settled by the European Data Protection Board. Previously known as the Article 29 Working Party, its guidelines on implementation of the GDPR provide that 'meaningful information' need not include a complex explanation of the algorithm or disclosure of the full algorithm but should be

---

[65] Bryce Goodman and Seth Flaxman, 'European Union Regulations on Algorithmic Decision Making and a "Right to Explanation"' (2017) 38(3) AI Magazine 50.

[66] Sandra Wachter, Brent Mittelstadt, and Luciano Floridi, 'Why a Right to Explanation of Automated Decision-Making Does Not Exist in the General Data Protection Regulation' (2017) 7 International Data Privacy Law 76.

[67] GDPR, Recital 71.

[68] See chapter two, section 2.3.

[69] Report of the Committee on Civil Liberties, Justice and Home Affairs on the proposal for a regulation of the European Parliament and of the Council on the protection of individuals with regard to the processing of personal data and on the free movement of such data (General Data Protection Regulation) (European Parliament, COM(2012) 0011–C7-0025/2012–2012/0011(COD), 2013) (emphasis added).

[70] GDPR, art 15(1)(h).

[71] The German text of the GDPR uses the phrase '*aussagekräftige Informationen*', which is close to 'meaningful information', while the French ('*informations utiles*') and the Dutch ('*nuttige informatie*') might be translated as 'useful information'.

'sufficiently comprehensive for the data subject to understand the reasons for the decision'.[72]

There are, nonetheless, significant loopholes. The relevant provisions apply only to decisions based 'solely on automated processing' that produce legal or similar effects.[73] Rights of access are also to be interpreted in a manner that does not 'adversely affect the rights or freedoms of others, including trade secrets or intellectual property and in particular the copyright protecting the software'.[74]

The GDPR also provides for a DPIA that may appear to overlap significantly with the algorithmic impact assessment proposed earlier.[75] Article 35 provides that an organization must assess a proposed system, including its necessity and proportionality in relation to stated purposes; the assessment must also cover the risks to the rights and freedoms of affected individuals, as well as measures to address those risks.

Again, however, there are significant limitations. The threshold for requiring a DPIA is initially said to be where there is a 'high risk to the rights and freedoms of natural persons', though this is later defined as including 'systematic and extensive evaluation of personal aspects' of natural persons leading to decisions with legal or comparable effects.[76] As one group of scholars wryly noted, demonstrating that a DPIA is not necessary may well itself require a DPIA.[77] Another shortcoming, for present purposes at least, is that it focuses on the protection of personal data. This is important but is hardly the only concern associated with the operation of opaque algorithms. In addition, the EU DPIA provides for only limited consultation – internally with a data protection officer and with data subjects themselves only 'where appropriate' and 'without prejudice to the protection of commercial or public interests or the security of processing operations'.[78] An earlier proposal that consultation be mandatory was dropped as it was thought to impose a disproportionate

---

[72] Guidelines on Automated Individual Decision-Making and Profiling for the Purposes of Regulation 2016/679 (Article 29 Data Protection Working Party, 17/EN WP251rev.01, 3 October 2017) 25. Cf Profiling and Automated Decision-Making (Information Commissioner's Office, 2017) 15.

[73] GDPR, art 22(1).

[74] Ibid, Recital 63.

[75] See above section 6.2.2(a).

[76] GDPR, art 35(1), (3).

[77] Bryan Casey, Ashkan Farhangi, and Roland Vogl, 'Rethinking Explainable Machines: The GDPR's "Right to Explanation" Debate and the Rise of Algorithmic Audits in Enterprise' (2019) 34 Berkeley Technology Law Journal 145, 176.

[78] GDPR, art 35(2), (9).

burden on data controllers. Similarly, an organization is required to consult the relevant data protection authority in its jurisdiction only if its own assessment concludes that there is a high risk in the absence of measures to mitigate it.[79] There is no requirement for the assessment to be made public.

Despite all these reservations, it is possible that the GDPR will have an impact. In January 2019, Google was fined €50 million by France's data protection agency, the *Commission nationale de l'informatique et des libertés* (CNIL) – the largest penalty imposed under the GDPR up to that point. The breaches by Google included its failure to provide information concerning the use of personal data in providing targeted advertising on its Android devices, leaving users unable 'to sufficiently understand the particular consequences of the processing for them'.[80] An appeal to the *Conseil d'État* [Council of State] was dismissed in June 2020, affirming that the relevant information was not presented in a sufficiently clear and distinct manner for the user's consent to be validly obtained.[81]

Though the case turned on transparency, the barriers to understanding had less to do with neural networks than with legalese. Explanations of how Google used personal data were spread across multiple documents that were vague and difficult to access, sometimes requiring up to five or six actions to find them. This amounted to a violation of the GDPR obligation to provide information about the collection and use of personal data in a 'clear' and 'intelligible' manner,[82] rather than challenging the use of an opaque AI system as such. Nonetheless, the decision is still noteworthy for the fact that it was initiated by two not-for-profit organizations representing a class of just under ten thousand users. Though no specific harm was alleged, this was deemed sufficient for the CNIL to commence an investigation, which took place only online. It is possible that future class actions will go after the use of opaque algorithms, though it is far simpler to show the inadequacy of language governing consent

---

[79] Ibid, art 36.
[80] Deliberation of the Restricted Committee Pronouncing a Financial Sanction Against Google LLC (CNIL, SAN-2019-001, 21 January 2019), para 111.
[81] RGPD: le Conseil d'État rejette le recours dirigé contre la sanction de 50 millions d'euros infligée à Google par la CNIL [GDPR: The Council of State Rejects the Appeal against the Sanction of 50 Million Euros Imposed on Google by the CNIL] (Conseil d'État, 19 June 2020).
[82] GDPR, art 12(1).

than to demonstrate opacity in how personal data so collected is being used.

6.3.2   Council of Europe Convention 108

The Council of Europe's Convention for the Protection of Individuals with regard to Automatic Processing of Personal Data was first adopted in 1981 and entered into force in 1985. Aside from 1999 measures opening it up to the EU, the most important amendments were adopted in 2018 – a week before the GDPR entered into force – and sought to address the 'new challenges' posed by AI systems.[83]

Among other changes, these introduced new obligations of transparency in the sense of both the identity of data controllers as well as the legal basis and purpose of any processing. This was to be enforced by users having the right 'to obtain, on request, knowledge of the reasoning underlying data processing where the results of such processing are applied to him or her'.[84] As the explanatory report makes clear, however, this amendment presumes that data controllers have this information at their disposal and should make it available to data subjects.[85] It is therefore of limited application here.

6.3.3   France

In 2016, France passed its own *République numérique* [Digital Republic] law. Limited to administrative bodies, this creates a right to request information about algorithmic decisions, including the rules and main characteristics of the algorithm.[86] A subsequent decree elaborated that the information was to include the parameters of the algorithm as well as their weighting, and that it should be in 'intelligible form'.[87] This last

---

[83] Protocol amending the Convention for the Protection of Individuals with regard to Automatic Processing of Personal Data (ETS No 108), done at Elsinore, Denmark, 17–18 May 2018.

[84] Convention for the Protection of Individuals with regard to Automatic Processing of Personal Data (Convention 108), done at Strasbourg, 29 January 1981, ETS No 108, in force 1 October 1985, art 9(1)(c).

[85] Explanatory Report to the Protocol amending the Convention for the Protection of Individuals with regard to Automatic Processing of Personal Data (Council of Europe, 10 October 2018), para 77.

[86] Loi no 2016-1321 du 7 octobre 2016 pour une République numérique 2016 (France), art 4.

[87] Décret n° 2017-330 du 14 mars 2017 relatif aux droits des personnes faisant l'objet de décisions individuelles prises sur le fondement d'un traitement algorithmique 2017

provision points to one of the key limitations of 'explanation' or 'transparency' as the remedy to opacity. Providing information in a manner that is intelligible to the average person, yet complete enough to give a full explanation of an algorithmic process, while not unreasonably compromising trade secrets or allowing users to game the system, is exceedingly difficult.[88]

6.3.4   United States

In April 2019, bills proposing a new Algorithmic Accountability Act were introduced in the US Senate and House. Driven by revelations of bias – the press release cited accusations that Facebook violated the Fair Housing Act by allowing advertisers to discriminate based on race, religion, and disability status – the proposed law would require impact assessments for 'high risk' automated decision-making systems concerning their 'accuracy, fairness, bias, discrimination, privacy, and security'. Limited to entities with revenue in excess of $50m or holding data of more than a million customers, it would not create a private right of action or operate extraterritorially. Enforcement would be through the US Federal Trade Commission (FTC) or state attorneys-general.[89]

Though unlikely to become law, the draft legislation is of interest for at least two reasons. First, it would address regulation of AI generally, rather than being sector-specific – something that has undermined the coherence of US privacy and data protection laws over the decades.[90] Consideration of discrimination would shift from enforcement based on a patchwork of existing laws to prevention or mitigation based on a single law. Secondly, its scope more properly covers how algorithms are developed and used. The proposed impact assessment encompasses the system itself as well as its development process, including its design and training data, though there is no requirement that the findings be made public. Unlike the GDPR, automated decision-making is defined as a computational process that makes a decision 'or facilitates human

---

(France), art 1. See also Lilian Edwards and Michael Veale, 'Enslaving the Algorithm: From a "Right to an Explanation" to a "Right to Better Decisions"?' (2018) 16(3) IEEE Security & Privacy 46, 48–49.

[88] Sandra Wachter, Brent Mittelstadt, and Chris Russell, 'Counterfactual Explanations without Opening the Black Box: Automated Decisions and the GDPR' (2018) 31 Harvard Journal of Law & Technology 841, 842–43.

[89] Algorithmic Accountability Act of 2019, S 1108, HR 2231, 116th Congress 2019 (US).

[90] Simon Chesterman, *One Nation under Surveillance: A New Social Contract to Defend Freedom without Sacrificing Liberty* (Oxford University Press 2011) 244.

decision making', avoiding the problem of confining protections to decisions based 'solely on automated processing'.[91]

The press release included the soundbite 'Algorithms shouldn't have an exemption from our anti-discrimination laws.' This oversimplified the regulatory challenge of addressing algorithmic bias – algorithms are not 'exempt' from the law. But it is true that their opacity makes it more difficult to discover or remedy discriminatory behaviour. If the legislation or something like it is passed, it would make it easier to do both.

6.3.5   Canada

In April 2020, Canada's Directive on Automated Decision-Making came into force. Covering most Federal administrative decisions, it requires that an algorithmic impact assessment be carried out prior to deploying 'any technology that either assists or replaces the judgment of human decision-makers'.[92] The impact assessment follows a standard form and must be completed prior to production.

The breadth of coverage is important, but of particular interest is the sliding scale of transparency requirements, based on the level of potential harm. Where decisions will likely have 'little to no impact' on individuals or communities, no notice is required. For decisions with 'moderate' impact, a plain language notice must be published on the programme or service's website. Where 'high' or 'very high' impact is anticipated, the website must also include a description of how the components work, how it supports the decision, the results of any reviews or audits, and a description of the training data (or a link to the anonymized data itself, if publicly available). A separate provision covers explanations of decisions. Those with minimal impact need provide only a 'frequently asked questions' section on a website. Moderate impact decisions should offer 'meaningful explanation' on request, while high and very high impact decisions that deny a benefit or service should include the explanation with the decision itself.[93]

Though limited to the public sector, the Canadian directive is one of the most progressive yet adopted. Government agencies had earlier been urged to use open source software; the directive adds a presumption that the custom source code of a system owned by the Canadian government

---

[91] GDPR, art 22(1).
[92] Directive on Automated Decision-Making 2019 (Canada), Appendix A.
[93] Ibid, s 6.2.

should also be released, subject to prescribed exceptions for classified and other data. It is too early to evaluate implementation of the directive, but some concerns have already been expressed about using it in immigration decisions in place of more formal, enforced standards.[94]

6.3.6 Other Jurisdictions

Other jurisdictions have considered ways to preserve or encourage transparency while taking advantage of AI, though most have remained in the realm of voluntary principles comparable to Singapore's Model Framework, discussed earlier.[95] In Australia, for example, the Federal government published a set of AI Ethics Principles in November 2019, among other things stating that people should be able to 'know when they are being significantly impacted by an AI system, and can find out when an AI system is engaging with them'.[96] Some governments have followed the Canadian lead in exploring tighter restrictions for public sector processes. In July 2020, New Zealand published its 'Algorithm Charter', under which government agencies promise to 'clearly [explain] how significant decisions are informed by algorithms'. A draft had included that agencies would also state 'who is responsible for automated decisions', but this was dropped from the final text.[97]

For its part, China's Ministry of Science and Technology also adopted principles for AI governance in 2019 with the aim of ensuring that AI systems are safe, controllable, and reliable. The eight principles overlap somewhat with comparable frameworks elsewhere,[98] but transparency is not high among them. Fairness is to be promoted and discrimination 'eliminated', but transparency and interpretability are targeted for 'continuous improvement', while 'gradually achieving' auditability.[99]

---

[94] Fenwick McKelvey and Margaret MacDonald, 'Artificial Intelligence Policy Innovations at the Canadian Federal Government' (2019) 44(2) Canadian Journal of Communication 43, 46.

[95] See above n 63.

[96] AI Ethics Principles (Department of Industry, Science, Energy and Resources, November 2019). Cf the Commonwealth Scientific and Industrial Research Organisation (CSIRO) discussion paper earlier in 2019, which called for a broad interpretation of transparency. People should be informed 'when an algorithm is being used that impacts them and they should be provided with information about what information the algorithm uses to make decisions'. D Dawson et al, Artificial Intelligence: Australia's Ethics Framework (Data61 CSIRO, 2019) 6–7.

[97] Algorithm Charter for Aotearoa New Zealand (Department of Internal Affairs, July 2020).

[98] See chapter seven, introduction.

[99] 新一代人工智能治理原则——发展负责任的人工智能 [The New Generation of Artificial Intelligence Governance Principles – the Development of Responsible Artificial

6.4   The Limits of Transparency

Transparency is a means, not an end. Its purpose is, in part, to avoid or limit the risks of opacity discussed in chapter three: inferior, impermissible, and illegitimate decisions. But transparency also builds trust. That is routinely acknowledged to be one of the major barriers to adoption and acceptance of new technologies in general and AI in particular.[100] The shift in focus that this chapter describes – from transparency to explainability – acknowledges individualized concerns about the use of AI and the practical challenges posed by natural opacity. While individual explanations may help correct some inferior decisions or reveal impermissible ones, however, this depends on affected users knowing that they have been harmed and being in a position to complain about it. Such explanations do not address the illegitimacy of a decision where reasons should precede rather than follow the making of it.

Even with the best of intentions and resources, it is important to be realistic about the limitations of transparency – indeed, openness about those limitations may be the most important form of transparency.[101] Clearly, transparency is not a panacea. But sometimes it is a distraction and sometimes it is undesirable.

As a distraction, illusory transparency can be worse than opacity. This illusion, sometimes termed the transparency fallacy, takes two forms. First, much as some governments demonstrate their commitment to 'openness' by burying constituents in unstructured records, the provision of vast amounts of data or source code may be transparency in form only. Secondly, a theoretical individual right to explanation that cannot in practice be exercised deflects criticism without providing a genuine remedy. Even if it is understood, in the absence of the possibility to use information to bring about systemic change, it will not help achieve meaningful accountability. Much as the theoretical consent of users has long provided the fig leaf for data protection law, the illusion of transparency could give false comfort to those seeking to hold AI systems to account.

Intelligence] (Ministry of Science and Technology, 17 June 2019), paras 2 ('消除 … 歧视'), 5 ('人工智能系统应不断提升透明性, 可解释性 … 逐步实现可审核').
[100] See, eg, Robin C Feldman, Ehrik Aldana, and Kara Stein, 'Artificial Intelligence in the Health Care Space: How We Can Trust What We Cannot Know' (2019) 30 Stanford Law & Policy Review 399.
[101] Cf Karl de Fine Licht and Jenny de Fine Licht, 'Artificial Intelligence, Transparency, and Public Decision-Making: Why Explanations Are Key When Trying to Produce Perceived Legitimacy' (2020) 35 AI & Society 917.

In some cases, though, transparency may be undesirable. Systems intended to maintain security or prevent fraud or other wrongdoing should preserve sufficient opacity to carry out their functions.[102] Disclosing details of algorithms – whom to screen more thoroughly at checkpoints, for example – might uncover bias but also enable manipulation.[103] If datasets are made public, the personal data that forms the basis for some decisions will be exposed. Even without the dataset, some model explanations can be exploited to reveal the underlying training data.[104] It is no coincidence that many legislative efforts at requiring transparency are found in data protection law.

A different critique of transparency and explainability is that we sometimes ask them to do too much. Calls for transparency on the part of AI systems often start from questionable assumptions about human decision-making – contrasting algorithmic processing, for example, with 'traditional decision-making, where human decision-makers can *in principle* articulate their rationale when queried, limited only by their desire and capacity to give an explanation, and the questioner's capacity to understand it'.[105] The 'in principle' is doing a lot of work here, as the process by which humans actually make decisions is known to be inextricably tied to intuition, hunches, personal impressions – with a layer of after-the-fact ratiocination.[106] When we require a human decision-maker to give reasons, we do not ask them to undergo functional magnetic resonance imaging in order to understand the cognitive process by which a decision was actually reached.

Language does not always help here. When considering explanations of different phenomena, we think of volitional human behaviour in terms of reasons rather than causes. When explaining a human decision, it would be odd to present the *cause* of a particular choice. Though we might say that new shoes cause us to walk in a particular way, we would not say that their discounted price 'caused' us to buy them. In the physical world, the reverse is true: we would not normally speak of the *reason* a fire

---

[102] Jenna Burrell, 'How the Machine "Thinks": Understanding Opacity in Machine Learning Algorithms' (2016) 3(1) Big Data & Society 4.

[103] Anupam Chander, 'The Racist Algorithm?' (2017) 115 Michigan Law Review 1023, 1034.

[104] Reza Shokri, Martin Strobel, and Yair Zick, 'On the Privacy Risks of Model Explanations' (2020) arXiv 1907.00164v5.

[105] Brent Daniel Mittelstadt et al, 'The Ethics of Algorithms: Mapping the Debate' (2016) 3 (2) Big Data & Society 7 (emphasis added).

[106] John Zerilli et al, 'Transparency in Algorithmic and Human Decision-Making: Is There a Double Standard?' (2019) 32 Philosophy & Technology 661, 665–68.

started, except perhaps as the prelude to an explanation about a cause.[107] The language of 'reasons' presumes a degree of subjectivity and rationality on the part of an actor: they belong to that actor in a way that causes do not.[108] In the case of computers, then, the demand for reasons suggests another form of anthropomorphism. From what *caused* the computer to do *x* (shut down, say, or catch fire), we slide into what were the computer's *reasons* for doing *y* (deny me a loan, suggest that I watch a particular movie, and so on).

Transparency in AI systems is sought not for its own sake but for purposes similar to why it is sought in human decisions. The methods of achieving it are distinct, however. Sometimes that is beneficial – such as when we can test for bias by running multiple simulations without worrying that an AI system will become defensive and dissemble. Sometimes it is challenging. Useful explanations offer contrasts – not merely why *x* happened but why *x* rather than *y* – and they are selective in the sense that they prioritize relevance and context over completeness. Human explanations emphasize factors influencing a decision rather than raw probabilities and are expressed in a manner that is tailored to the world views of the parties concerned. None of this is easy for an AI system. And sometimes the difference between AI and human explanations can be misleading. Where there is discretion to be exercised, for example, it can be artificial to ascribe reasons.

This is particularly the case for certain public decisions, where the legitimacy of the outcome is tied to the identity of the decision-maker.[109] Many arguments warning of opaque AI systems determining the fate of humans conjure a dystopian world without explanations, epitomized by Franz Kafka's *The Trial*.[110] A man, known only as Josef K, is arrested and prosecuted by unknown agents for an unknown crime; attempts to understand or escape his absurd ordeal are fruitless. The metaphor is a compelling one. But it is flawed. For the power of *The Trial* is not that there are hidden explanations being withheld from the hapless Josef K but that there is no logic to his predicament at all.

---

[107] For example: 'The reason that the fire started was because . . .' in which the opening of the sentence is redundant.
[108] Tim Miller, 'Explanation in Artificial Intelligence: Insights from the Social Sciences' (2019) 267 Artificial Intelligence 1, 16.
[109] See chapter three, section 3.3.
[110] See, eg, Andrew Selbst and Solon Barocas, 'The Intuitive Appeal of Explainable Machines' (2018) 87 Fordham Law Review 1085, 1118; Daniel J Solove, 'Privacy and Power: Computer Databases and Metaphors for Information Privacy' (2001) 53 Stanford Law Review 1393, 1419–23.

The increased role of AI systems in making or assisting decisions will, in a great many cases, optimize outcomes; individuals who are denied a service or adversely affected by such decisions are entitled to an explanation. But avoiding inferior, impermissible, or illegitimate decisions requires more than this. Impact assessments before, audits during, and an independent advocate after those decisions will lead to better decisions as well as increasing trust in those decisions.

The starting point is transparency as to the involvement of AI systems in the first place. At present this is, for the most part, a simple yes or no question. Increasingly, however, AI-assisted decision-making will blend human and machine. Some chatbots start on automatic (human-out-of-the-loop) for basic queries, moving through suggested responses that are vetted by a human (over-the-loop), escalating up to direct contact with a person (in-the-loop) for unusual or more complex interactions.[111] Though decisions based 'solely on automated processing' are going to increase, 'machine-assisted' decisions will skyrocket. Much as passengers in autonomous vehicles need clarity as to who is meant to be holding the wheel, humans interacting with AI systems should be aware of with whom – or with what – they are dealing.

This goes both ways. To guard against overuse or malicious attacks, many websites now utilize challenge tests such as CAPTCHA. These function as a kind of reverse Turing Test, with computers requiring proof that a user is not another computer.[112]

A year after the Ashley Madison scandal, the parent company had a new name and chief executive, while the company itself adopted a new slogan: 'Find your moment.' In place of a wedding ring and a woman putting a finger to her lips, a ruby logo was deemed more 'multi-faceted' and relevant to a wider user-base. In addition to the class action lawsuit, it was reported that the US FTC was investigating the company's use of bots to chat with paying male customers.

Within another twelve months, however, the 'have an affair' language returned, as did the company's focus on connecting adulterous couples.

---

[111] See, eg, Pavel Kucherbaev, Alessandro Bozzon, and Geert-Jan Houben, 'Human-Aided Bots' (2018) 22(6) IEEE Internet Computing 36.

[112] CAPTCHA is a contrived acronym standing for Completely Automated Public Turing test to tell Computers and Humans Apart. See Luis von Ahn et al, 'CAPTCHA: Using Hard AI Problems for Security' in Eli Biham (ed), *Advances in Cryptology – EUROCRYPT 2003* (Springer 2003) 294; Henry S Baird, Allison L Coates, and Richard J Fateman, 'PessimalPrint: A Reverse Turing Test' (2003) 5 International Journal on Document Analysis and Recognition 158.

In an interview with the *New York Post*, its Vice President for Communications said that the summer of 2015 had led to 'unprecedented media coverage of our business'. Despite the nature of that coverage, the number of users had increased by more than half to over 50 million. He also insisted that the company no longer used bots – indeed, that it was unnecessary since the new sign-ups were almost equal numbers of men and women. 'Our monthly new member account additions have not been verified by a third party,' he conceded, 'but we stand behind them.'[113] The company later went one step further and retained the accounting firm EY for what must have been one of its more unusual audits. In addition to verifying new user registrations, it confirmed that the 'Bot programs' had been decommissioned.[114]

The lawsuits and the FTC investigation against Ashley Madison were eventually settled.[115] The FTC imposed a $1.6m fine and a requirement for a comprehensive data security programme. For the class action, a final amount of $11.2m was put into a dedicated account. Because many users had signed up using fake email addresses, targeted banner advertisements were purchased to expand the class of potential claimants. Forty-two unnamed plaintiffs sought leave to take part in the action and settlement under pseudonyms – 'to reduce the risk of potentially catastrophic personal and professional consequences that could befall them and their families' should they be publicly identified. The court was sympathetic but denied this request, holding that their concerns about embarrassment did not outweigh the public's interest in transparency.[116]

---

[113] Richard Morgan, 'Ashley Madison Is Back – and Claims Surprising User Numbers', *New York Post* (21 May 2017).

[114] Ruby Life, Inc: Report on Customer Statistics for the Calendar Year 2017 (Ernst & Young LLP, 2018) 1.

[115] 'Operators of AshleyMadison.com Settle FTC, State Data Breach Charges' (2017) 34(3) Computer and Internet Lawyer 27.

[116] *In re Ashley Madison Customer Data Security Breach Litigation* MDL No 2669 (Eastern District of Missouri, Eastern Division, 6 April 2016).

PART III

Possibilities

New Rules

Three-quarters of a century ago, the science fiction author Isaac Asimov imagined a future in which robots have become an integral part of daily life. At the time, he later recalled, most robot stories fell into either of two classes. One was robots-as-menace: technological innovations that rise up against their creators in the tradition of *Frankenstein* but with echoes at least as far back as the Greek myth of Prometheus, the subtitle of Mary Shelley's 1818 novel. Less commonly, another group of tales considered robots-as-pathos – lovable creations that are treated as slaves by their cruel human masters; morality tales about the danger posed not by humanity's creations but by humanity itself.[1]

Asimov's contribution was to create a third category: robots as industrial products built by engineers. In this speculative world, a safety device is built into these morally neutral robots in the form of three laws of robotics. The first is that a robot may not injure a human or, through inaction, allow a human to come to harm. Secondly, orders given by humans must be obeyed, unless that would conflict with the first law. Thirdly, robots must protect their own existence, unless that conflicts with the first or second laws.[2]

The three laws are a staple of the literature on regulating new technology, though, like the Turing Test, they are more of a cultural touchstone than serious scientific proposal.[3] Among other things, the laws presume the need to address physically embodied robots only with human-level intelligence – an example of the android fallacy discussed in chapter five.[4] They have also been criticized for putting obligations on the technology

---

[1] Isaac Asimov, *The Complete Robot* (Doubleday 1982) 9–10. On the robot apocalypse in literature, see chapter five, section 5.3. See also the discussion of *R.U.R.* in the conclusion to this book.

[2] Isaac Asimov, 'Runaround', *Astounding Science Fiction* (March 1942).

[3] See, eg, Susan Leigh Anderson, 'Asimov's "Three Laws of Robotics" and Machine Metaethics' (2008) 22 AI & Society 477. On the Turing Test, see chapter five, introduction.

[4] See chapter five, section 5.2.

itself, rather than the people creating it.[5] Here it is worth noting that Asimov's laws were not 'law' in the sense of a command to be enforced by the state. They were, rather, encoded into the positronic brains of his fictional creations: constraining what robots *could* do, rather than specifying what they *should*.[6]

More importantly, for present purposes, the idea that relevant ethical principles can be reduced to a few dozen words, or that those words might be encoded in a manner interpretable by an AI system, misconceives the nature of ethics and of law.[7] Nonetheless, it was reported in 2007 that Korea had considered using them as the basis for a proposed Robot Ethics Charter.[8] This was one of many attempts to codify norms governing robots or AI since the turn of the century, accelerating in the wake of the First International Symposium on Roboethics in Sanremo, Italy, in 2004. The European Robotics Research Network produced its 'Roboethics Roadmap' in 2006, while the first multidisciplinary set of principles for robotics was adopted at a 'Robotics Retreat' held by two British Research Councils in 2010.[9]

The years since 2016 in particular saw a proliferation of guides, frameworks, and principles focused on AI. Some were the product of conferences or industry associations, notably the Partnership on AI's Tenets (2016),[10] the Future of Life Institute's Asilomar AI Principles (2017),[11] the Beijing Academy of Artificial Intelligence's Beijing AI Principles (2019),[12] and the IEEE's Ethically Aligned Design (2019).[13] Others were drafted by individual companies, including Microsoft's Responsible AI Principles,[14] IBM's Principles for Trust and

---

[5] Jack M Balkin, 'The Three Laws of Robotics in the Age of Big Data' (2017) 78 Ohio State Law Journal 1217.

[6] For a discussion of the limitations to constraining a hypothetical superintelligence (eg through a 'kill switch'), see chapter five, section 5.3.

[7] See chapter nine, section 9.1.

[8] 'South Korea Creates Ethical Code for Righteous Robots', *New Scientist* (8 March 2007). See Intelligent Robots Development and Distribution Promotion Act 2008 (Republic of Korea).

[9] Principles of Robotics (Engineering and Physical Sciences Research Council and Arts and Humanities Research Council, 2010).

[10] Tenets (Partnership on AI, 28 September 2016).

[11] Asilomar AI Principles (Future of Life Institute, 6 January 2017).

[12] Beijing AI Principles (北京智源人工智能研究院 [Beijing Academy of Artificial Intelligence], 28 May 2019).

[13] Ethically Aligned Design: A Vision for Prioritizing Human Well-Being with Autonomous and Intelligent Systems (IEEE, 2019).

[14] The Future Computed: Artificial Intelligence and Its Role in Society (Microsoft, 17 January 2018) 57.

Transparency,[15] and Google's AI Principles[16] – all published in the first half of 2018.

Governments have been slow to pass laws governing AI.[17] Several have developed softer norms, however, including Singapore's Model AI Governance Framework (2019),[18] Australia's AI Ethics Principles (2019),[19] China's AI Governance Principles (2019),[20] and New Zealand's Algorithm Charter (2020).[21] At the intergovernmental level, the G7 adopted the Charlevoix Common Vision for the Future of Artificial Intelligence (2018)[22] and the EU has published Ethics Guidelines for Trustworthy AI (2019),[23] in addition to the OECD's Recommendation of the Council on Artificial Intelligence (2019).[24] Even the Pope has endorsed a set of principles in the Rome Call for AI Ethics (2020).[25]

What is striking about these documents is the overlapping consensus that has emerged as to the norms that should govern AI.[26] Though the language and the emphasis may change, virtually all those written since 2018 include variations on the following six themes:

1. *Human control* – AI should augment rather than reduce human potential, and remain under human control.

[15] IBM's Principles for Trust and Transparency (IBM, 30 May 2018).
[16] Artificial Intelligence at Google: Our Principles (Google, 7 June 2018).
[17] Sector-specific responses include the measures to address high-frequency trading (see chapter one, section 1.2), autonomous vehicles (see chapter two, section 2.1), and algorithmic transparency (see chapter six, section 6.3).
[18] A Proposed Model Artificial Intelligence Governance Framework (Personal Data Protection Commission, 2019).
[19] AI Ethics Principles (Department of Industry, Science, Energy and Resources, November 2019).
[20] 新一代人工智能治理原则——发展负责任的人工智能 [The New Generation of Artificial Intelligence Governance Principles – the Development of Responsible Artificial Intelligence] (Ministry of Science and Technology, 17 June 2019).
[21] Algorithm Charter for Aotearoa New Zealand (Department of Internal Affairs, July 2020).
[22] Charlevoix Common Vision for the Future of Artificial Intelligence (G7, 9 June 2018).
[23] Ethics Guidelines for Trustworthy AI (European Commission High-Level Expert Group on Artificial Intelligence, 8 April 2019).
[24] OECD, Recommendation of the Council on Artificial Intelligence (OECD/LEGAL/0449, 22 May 2019).
[25] Rome Call for AI Ethics (Pontificia Accademia per la Vita, 28 February 2020).
[26] Cf Anna Jobin, Marcello Ienca, and Effy Vayena, 'The Global Landscape of AI Ethics Guidelines' (2019) 1 Nature Machine Intelligence 389; Jessica Fjeld et al, Principled Artificial Intelligence: Mapping Consensus in Ethical and Rights-Based Approaches to Principles for AI (Berkman Klein Center for Internet & Society, 2020); Thilo Hagendorff, 'The Ethics of AI Ethics: An Evaluation of Guidelines' (2020) 30 Minds & Machines 99.

2. *Transparency* – AI systems should be capable of being understood and their decisions capable of being explained.
3. *Safety* – AI systems should perform as intended and be resistant to hacking.
4. *Accountability* – Though often left undefined, calls for accountable or responsible AI assume or imply that remedies should be available when harm results.
5. *Non-discrimination* – AI systems should be inclusive and 'fair', avoiding impermissible bias.
6. *Privacy* – Given the extent to which AI relies on access to data, including personal data, privacy or personal data protection is often highlighted as a specific right to be safeguarded.

Additional concepts include the need for professional responsibility on the part of those developing and deploying AI systems, and for AI to promote human values or to be 'beneficent'.[27] At this level of generality, these amount to calls for upholding ethics generally or the human control principle in particular. Some documents call for AI to be developed sustainably and for its benefits to be distributed equitably,[28] though these more properly address how AI is deployed rather than what it should or should not be able to do.

None of the six principles listed above seems controversial. Yet, for all the time and effort that has gone into convening workshops and retreats to draft the various documents, curiously little has been applied to what they mean in practice or how they would be implemented. This is sometimes explicitly acknowledged and addressed, with the justification that a document is intended to be applicable to technologies as yet unknown and to address problems not yet foreseen.[29]

A different question yields a more revealing answer, which is whether any of these principles are, in fact, necessary. Calls for accountability, non-discrimination, and privacy essentially amount to demands that those making or using AI systems comply with laws already in place in most jurisdictions. As discussed in Part I, these laws will be able to cover most instances of harm. Safety requirements recall issues of product

[27] See, eg, Floridi. Luciano et al, 'AI4People—An Ethical Framework for a Good AI Society: Opportunities, Risks, Principles, and Recommendations' (2018) 28 Minds and Machines 689, 696–97.
[28] See, eg, Ethics Guidelines for Trustworthy AI (n 23).
[29] See, eg, Model Artificial Intelligence Governance Framework (2nd edn) (Personal Data Protection Commission, 2020) 10. See also the compendium of use cases developed under the framework.

liability from chapter four,[30] with the additional aspect of taking reasonable cybersecurity precautions.[31] Transparency is not an ethical principle as such but a condition precedent to understanding and evaluating conduct.[32] Together with human control, however, it could be a potential restriction on the development of AI systems above and beyond existing laws.

Rather than add to the proliferation of principles, this chapter shifts focus away from the question of *what* new rules are required for regulating AI.[33] Instead, the three questions that it will attempt to answer are *why* regulation is necessary, *when* changes to regulatory structures (including rules) should be adopted, and *how* they might be implemented. The hope is that this will reveal both the actual new rules that are required as well as a process for keeping them up to date. Chapter eight then turns to *who* should be doing the regulating.

7.1 Why (Not) Regulate?

In theory, governments regulate activities to address market failures, or in support of social or other policies. In practice, relationships with industry and political interests may cause politicians to act – or refrain from acting – in less principled ways.[34] Though the troubled relationship between big tech and government is well documented,[35] this section will assume good faith on the part of regulators and outline considerations relevant to the choices to be made. (Questions of regulatory capture and related matters will be discussed in chapter eight.[36])

---

[30] See chapter four, section 4.1.3.

[31] See, eg, Draft Report with Recommendations to the Commission on a Civil liability regime for Artificial Intelligence (EU Parliament Committee on Legal Affairs, 2020/2014 (INL), 27 April 2020), art 8(2)(b).

[32] Matteo Turilli and Luciano Floridi, 'The Ethics of Information Transparency' (2009) 11 Ethics and Information Technology 105. See also chapter six.

[33] Cf Jacob Turner, *Robot Rules: Regulating Artificial Intelligence* (Palgrave Macmillan 2019).

[34] Robert Baldwin, Martin Cave, and Martin Lodge, *Understanding Regulation: Theory, Strategy, and Practice* (2nd edn, Oxford University Press 2011) 15–24.

[35] See, eg, Carlotta Alfonsi, 'Taming Tech Giants Requires Fixing the Revolving Door' (2019) 19 Kennedy School Review 166; Tony Romm, 'Tech Giants Led by Amazon, Facebook, and Google Spent Nearly Half a Billion on Lobbying over the Past Decade, New Data Shows', *Washington Post* (22 January 2020).

[36] See chapter eight, section 8.1.2.

In the context of AI systems, market justifications for regulation include addressing information inadequacies as between producers and consumers of technology, as well as protecting third parties from externalities – harms that may arise from deploying AI. This broadly corresponds to the practical reasons for regulating AI discussed in previous chapters, with regulation ensuring the proper allocation of risk and attribution of responsibility. In the case of autonomous vehicles, for example, we are already seeing a shift of liability from driver to manufacturer, with a likely obligation to maintain adequate levels of insurance.[37] This provides a model for civil liability for harm caused by some other AI systems – notably transportation more generally (including drones) and medical devices – under product liability laws.[38]

Regulation is not simply intended to facilitate markets, however. It can also defend rights or promote social policies, in some cases imposing additional costs.[39] Such justifications reflect the moral arguments for limiting AI. In the case of bias, for example, discrimination on the basis of race or gender is prohibited even if it is on some other measure 'efficient'.[40] Similarly, the prohibition on AI systems making kill decisions in armed conflict is not easily defended on the utilitarian basis that this will lead to better outcomes; these systems may eventually be more compliant with the law of armed conflict than humans. The prohibition stems, instead, from a determination that morality requires that a human being take responsibility for such choices. As chapter four argued, nondelegable duties could also apply to situations where the protection of vulnerable individuals outweighs the potential benefits of optimization – the relationship between hospitals and patients, for example, or between schools and their students.[41]

Different considerations may restrict the outsourcing of certain functions to AI – notably certain public decisions, the legitimacy of which depends on the process by which they are made as much as the efficiency of the outcome. Even if an AI system were believed to make superior determinations than politicians and judges, inherently governmental functions that affect the rights and obligations of individuals should

---

[37] See chapter two, section 2.1.1.
[38] See chapter four, sections 4.1.3 and 4.1.4.
[39] See Tony Prosser, 'Regulation and Social Solidarity' (2006) 33 Journal of Law and Society 364.
[40] See chapter three, section 3.2.
[41] See chapter four, section 4.2.

nonetheless be undertaken by office-holders who can be held accountable through political or constitutional mechanisms.[42]

A further reason for regulating AI is more procedural in nature. As discussed in chapter six, transparency is a necessary precursor to effective regulation. Though not a panacea and bringing additional costs, requirements for minimum levels of transparency and the ability to explain decisions can make oversight and accountability possible.

Against all this, governments may also have good reasons *not* to regulate a particular sector if it would constrain innovation, impose unnecessary burdens, or otherwise distort the market.[43] Different political communities will weigh these considerations differently, though it is interesting that regulation of AI appears to track the adoption of data protection laws in many jurisdictions. The United States, for example, has largely followed a market-based approach, with relatively light touch sectoral regulation and experimentation across its 50 states. That is true of data protection, where a general Federal law is lacking but particular interests and sectors, such as children's privacy or financial institutions, are governed by statute. In the case of AI, towards the end of the Obama Administration in 2016, the US National Science and Technology Council argued against broad regulation of AI research or practice. Where regulatory responses threatened to increase the cost of compliance or slow innovation, the Council called for softening them, if that could be done without adversely impacting safety or market fairness.[44]

That document was finalized six months after the EU enacted the GDPR, with sweeping new powers covering both data protection and, as we have seen, automated processing of that data.[45] The EU approach has long been characterized by a privileging of human rights, with privacy enshrined as a right after the Second World War,[46] laying the foundation for the 1995 Data Protection Directive and now the GDPR.

---

[42] See chapter four, section 4.3.
[43] See generally Mehmet Ugur (ed), *Governance, Regulation, and Innovation: Theory and Evidence from Firms and Nations* (Edward Elgar 2013).
[44] Preparing for the Future of Artificial Intelligence (National Science and Technology Council, October 2016) 17. Cf Remarks of FCC Chairman Ajit Pai at FCC Forum on Artificial Intelligence and Machine Learning (Federal Communications Commission, 30 November 2018) (describing the need for 'regulatory humility').
[45] See chapter two, section 2.3.2.
[46] [European] Convention for the Protection of Human Rights and Fundamental Freedoms, done at Rome, 4 November 1950, 213 UNTS 222, in force 3 September 1953, art 8.

Human rights is also a dominant theme in EU considerations of AI,[47] though there are occasional murmurings that this makes the continent less competitive.[48]

China offers a different model again, embracing a strong role for the state and less concern about the market or human rights. As with data protection, a driving motivation has been sovereignty. In the context of data protection, this is expressed through calls for data localization – ensuring that personal data is accessible by Chinese state authorities.[49] As for AI, Beijing identified it as an important developmental goal in 2006[50] and a national priority in 2016.[51] The State Council's New Generation AI Development Plan, released the following year, nods at the role of markets but sets a target of 2025 for China to achieve major breakthroughs in AI research with 'world-leading' applications – the same year forecast for 'the *preliminary* establishment of AI laws and regulations'.[52]

Though it is easy to be cynical about China's lack of regulation – its relaxed approach to personal data is credited as giving the AI sector a tremendous advantage[53] – projections about future regulation show that, for emerging technologies, the true underlying question is not whether to regulate but when.

7.2   When to Regulate

Writing in 1980 at Aston University in Birmingham, England, David Collingridge observed that any effort to control new technology faces a double bind. During the early stages, when control would be possible,

---

[47] White Paper on Artificial Intelligence (European Commission, COM(2020) 65 final, 19 February 2020) 10. See also the draft regulation published on 21 April 2021.

[48] See, eg, Ulf Pehrsson, 'Europe's Obsession with Privacy Rights Hinders Growth', *Politico* (17 June 2016).

[49] Anupam Chander and Uyên P Lê, 'Data Nationalism' (2015) 64 Emory Law Journal 677; John Selby, 'Data Localization Laws: Trade Barriers or Legitimate Responses to Cybersecurity Risks, or Both?' (2017) 25 International Journal of Law and Information Technology 213. For a nuanced but quasi-official defence of China's position, see Jinhe Liu, 'China's Data Localization' (2020) 13 Chinese Journal of Communication 84.

[50] The National Medium- and Long-Term Program for Science and Technology Development (2006–2020) (State Council, 2006).

[51] The 13th Five-Year Plan for Economic and Social Development of the People's Republic of China (2016–2020) (Central Compilation & Translation Press, 17 March 2016).

[52] 国务院关于印发新一代人工智能发展规划的通知 [State Council Issued Notice of the New Generation Artificial Intelligence Development Plan] (State Council, Guofa [2017] No 35, 20 July 2017) (author's translation, emphasis added).

[53] Huw Roberts et al, 'The Chinese Approach to Artificial Intelligence: An Analysis of Policy, Ethics, and Regulation' (2021) 36 AI & Society 59.

not enough is known about the technology's harmful social consequences to warrant slowing its development. By the time those consequences are apparent, however, control has become costly and slow.[54]

The climate emergency offers an example of what is now termed the Collingridge dilemma. Before automobiles entered into widespread usage, a 1906 Royal Commission studied the potential risks of the new machines plying Britain's roads; chief among these was thought to be the dust that the vehicles threw up behind them.[55] Today, transportation produces about a quarter of all energy-related CO_2 emissions and its continued growth could outweigh all other mitigation measures.[56] Though the 2020 Covid-19 pandemic had a discernible effect on emissions, regulatory efforts to reduce those emissions face economic and political hurdles.[57]

Many efforts to address technological innovation focus on the first horn of the dilemma – predicting and averting harms. That has been the approach of most of the principles discussed at the start of this chapter. In addition to conferences and workshops, research institutes have been established to evaluate the risks of AI, with some warning apocalyptically about the threat of general AI.[58] If general AI truly poses an existential threat to humanity, it could justify a ban on research, comparable to restrictions on biological and chemical weapons.[59] No major jurisdiction has imposed a ban, however, either because the threat does not seem immediate or due to concerns that it would merely drive that research elsewhere. When the United States imposed limits on stem cell research in 2001, for example, one of the main consequences was that US

---

[54] David Collingridge, *The Social Control of Technology* (Frances Pinter 1980) 19.

[55] Royal Commission on Motor Cars (Cd 3080-1, 1906).

[56] CO2 Emissions from Fuel Combustion: Overview (International Energy Agency, 2020); Ralph Sims et al, 'Transport' in O Edenhofer et al (eds), *Mitigation of Climate Change. Contribution of Working Group III to the Fifth Assessment Report of the Intergovernmental Panel on Climate Change* (Cambridge University Press 2014) at 403.

[57] See, eg, Yong-Hong Liu et al, 'Reduction Measures for Air Pollutants and Greenhouse Gas in the Transportation Sector: A Cost-Benefit Analysis' (2019) 207 Journal of Cleaner Production 1023.

[58] See chapter five, section 5.3.

[59] Convention on the Prohibition of the Development, Production and Stockpiling of Bacteriological (Biological) and Toxin Weapons and on Their Destruction, done at Washington, London, and Moscow, 10 April 1972, in force 26 March 1975; Convention on the Prohibition of the Development, Production, Stockpiling, and Use of Chemical Weapons and on Their Destruction, done at Paris, 13 January 1993, in force 29 April 1997. But see the self-imposed limits on recombinant DNA, discussed in chapter eight, section 8.1.1.

researchers in the field fell behind their international counterparts.[60] A different challenge is that if regulation targets near-term threats, the pace of technological innovation can result in regulators playing an endless game of catch-up. Technology can change exponentially, while social, economic, and legal systems tend to change incrementally.[61] For these reasons, the principles discussed at the start of this chapter aim to be future-proof and technology-neutral. This has the advantage of being broad enough to adapt to changing circumstances, albeit at the risk of being so vague as to not offer meaningful guidance in specific cases.

Collingridge himself argued that instead of trying to anticipate the risks, more promise lies in laying the groundwork to address the second aspect of the dilemma: ensuring that decisions about technology are flexible or reversible.[62] This is also not easy, presenting what some wags describe as the 'barn door' problem of attempting to shut it after the horse has bolted. As described in the introduction to this book, social media and the gig economy are examples of how the failure to put in place regulatory controls enabled the rise of surveillance capitalism.[63]

This section considers two approaches to the timing of regulation that may offer some promise in addressing or mitigating the Collingridge dilemma: the precautionary principle and masterly inactivity.

7.2.1   The Precautionary Principle

A natural response to uncertainty is caution. The precautionary principle holds that if the consequences of an activity could be serious but are subject to scientific uncertainties, then precautionary measures should be taken or the activity should not be carried out at all.[64] The principle features in many domestic laws concerning the environment and has played a key role in most international instruments on the topic. The 1992 Rio Declaration, for example, states that '[w]here there are threats of serious or irreversible damage, lack of full scientific certainty shall not be used as a reason for postponing cost-effective measures to prevent

---

[60] Varnee Murugan, 'Embryonic Stem Cell Research: A Decade of Debate from Bush to Obama' (2009) 82 Yale Journal of Biology and Medicine 101.

[61] Larry Downes, *The Laws of Disruption: Harnessing the New Forces That Govern Life and Business in the Digital Age* (Basic Books 2009) 2.

[62] Collingridge (n 54) 23–43.

[63] See the introduction to this book at nn 30–32.

[64] Terje Aven, 'On Different Types of Uncertainties in the Context of the Precautionary Principle' (2011) 31 Risk Analysis 1515.

environmental degradation'.[65] In some implementations, the principle amounts to a reversal of the burden of proof: those who claim an activity is safe must prove it to be so.[66]

Critics argue that the principle is vague, incoherent, or both. A weak interpretation amounts to a truism, as few would argue that scientific certainty is required for precautions to be taken; a strong interpretation is self-defeating, since precautionary measures can themselves have harmful effects.[67] In a book-length treatment denouncing it as 'European', Cass Sunstein outlines the predictably irrational ways in which fears play out in deliberative democracies, notably the overvaluation of loss and the reactive nature of public opinion with regard to risk. That said, the notion that there are at least *some* risks against which precautionary steps should be taken before they materialize or can be quantified is widely accepted.[68]

In the context of AI, the precautionary principle is routinely invoked with regard to autonomous vehicles,[69] lethal autonomous weapons,[70] the use of algorithms processing personal data in judicial systems,[71] and the possibility of general AI turning on its human creators.[72] Only the last is a proper application of the principle, however, in that there is genuine uncertainty about the nature and the probability of the risk. The precise failure rate of autonomous vehicles may be unknown, for example, but the harm itself is well understood and capable of being balanced as

---

[65] Rio Declaration on Environment and Development, 12 August 1992, UN Doc A/CONF.151/26 (Vol. I), Annex I, Principle 15.

[66] Ginevra Le Moli, Parthan S Vishvanathan, and Anjali Aeri, 'Whither the Proof? The Progressive Reversal of the Burden of Proof in Environmental Cases before International Courts and Tribunals' (2017) 8 Journal of International Dispute Settlement 644.

[67] Thomas Boyer-Kassem, 'Is the Precautionary Principle Really Incoherent?' (2017) 37 Risk Analysis 2026.

[68] Sunstein himself accepts the idea of an anti-catastrophe principle. Cass Sunstein, *Laws of Fear: Beyond the Precautionary Principle* (Cambridge University Press 2005) 109–15.

[69] Bryant Walker Smith, 'Regulation and the Risk of Inaction' in Markus Maurer et al (eds), *Autonomous Driving: Technical, Legal and Social Aspects* (Springer 2016) 571 at 572.

[70] Nehal Bhuta and Stavros-Evdokimos Pantazopoulos, 'Autonomy and Uncertainty: Increasingly Autonomous Weapons Systems and the International Legal Regulation of Risk' in Nehal Bhuta et al (eds), *Autonomous Weapons Systems: Law, Ethics, Policy* (Cambridge University Press 2016) 284 at 290–94.

[71] European Ethical Charter on the Use of Artificial Intelligence in Judicial Systems and Their Environment (European Commission for the Efficiency of Justice (CEPEJ), 4 December 2018) 56.

[72] Matthijs M Maas, 'Regulating for "Normal AI Accidents": Operational Lessons for the Responsible Governance of Artificial Intelligence Deployment' (2018) Proceedings of 2018 AAAI/ACM Conference on AI, Ethics, and Society (AIES '18) 223.

against the existing threat posed by human drivers.[73] As for lethal autonomous weapons, opponents explicitly reject a cost–benefit analysis in favour of a bright moral line with regard to decisions concerning human life; though there are ongoing debates about the appropriate degree of human control, the 'risk' itself is not in question.[74] Similarly, wariness of outsourcing public sector decisions to machines is not founded – or, at least, not *only* founded – on uncertainty as to the consequences that might follow. Rather, it is tied to the view that such decisions should be made by humans within a system of political accountability.[75]

Nevertheless, as indicated earlier, it is telling that, despite the risks of general AI, there has thus far been no concerted effort to restrict pure or applied research in the area. More promising are calls that implicitly focus on the second horn of Collingridge's dilemma: requirements to incorporate measures such as a kill switch, or attempts to align the values of any future superintelligence with our own. These can be seen as applications of the principle that human control should be prioritized. If a path to general AI becomes clearer, they should become mandatory.[76]

7.2.2   Masterly Inactivity

Another response to uncertainty is to do nothing. Refraining from action may be appropriate to avoid distorting the market through pre-emptive rule-making or delaying its evolution through adjudication. The term sometimes used to describe this is 'masterly inactivity'.[77] With origins in nineteenth-century British policy on Afghanistan, it suggests a watchful restraint in the face of undesirable alternatives.[78] (Britain's involvement in Afghanistan, it should be noted, ended in humiliating defeat.)

In the context of AI, for many governments this amounts to a 'wait and see' approach. Yet there is a difference between passively allowing events to play out and actively monitoring and engaging with an emerging

---

[73] See chapter two, section 2.1.
[74] See chapter two, section 2.2.
[75] See chapter four, section 4.3.
[76] See chapter five, section 5.3.
[77] Dominika Nestarcova, Report on Tech.Law Fest 2018 (Centre for Banking & Finance Law, National University of Singapore Faculty of Law, CBFL-Rep-1804, February 2018) 5 (quoting Singaporean Minister Vivian Balakrishnan).
[78] Major-General John Adye, 'England, Russia, and Afghanistan', *The Times* (18 October 1878); Kaushik Roy, *War and Society in Afghanistan: From the Mughals to the Americans, 1500–2013* (Oxford University Press 2015) 69.

market and its actors. Government engagement in the processes that led to the principles described at the start of this chapter is an example, as is the encouragement of industry associations to develop standards and research into governance possibilities.

Inactivity may also amount to a buck-passing exercise. Even if governments choose not to regulate, decisions with legal consequences will be made – most prominently by judges within the common law tradition, who exercise a law-making function. As we have seen, such decisions are already influencing norms in areas from contracts between computer programs[79] and the use of algorithms in sentencing[80] to the ownership of intellectual property created by AI.[81] This can be problematic if the law is nudged in an unhelpful direction because of the vagaries of how specific cases make it to court. It is also limited to applying legal principles after the event – 'when something untoward has already happened', as the British House of Commons Science and Technology Committee warned.[82]

Masterly inactivity, then, is not a strategy. Properly used, however, it may buy time to develop one.

7.3   How to Regulate

As highlighted in the introduction to this book, regulation is a contested concept and embraces more than mere 'rules'.[83] A leading text distinguishes three distinct modalities of regulation that are useful in considering the options available. First, regulation can mean a specific set of commands – binding obligations applied by a body devoted to this purpose. Secondly, it can refer to state influence more broadly, including financial and other incentives. Broader still, regulation is sometimes used to denote all forms of social or economic suasion, including market forces.[84] The theory of 'smart regulation' has shown that regulatory functions can be carried out not only by institutions of the state but also by professional associations, standard-setting bodies, and advocacy groups. In most circumstances, multiple instruments and a range of

---

[79] See chapter two, section 2.3.1.
[80] See chapter three, section 3.3.2.
[81] See chapter five, section 5.2.2.
[82] Robotics and Artificial Intelligence, Fifth Report of Session 2016–17 (House of Commons Science and Technology Committee, HC 145, 2016), para 54 (quoting a submission from the Law Society).
[83] See the introduction to this book at nn 12–16.
[84] Baldwin, Cave, and Lodge (n 34) 3.

regulatory actors will produce better outcomes than a narrow focus on a single regulator.[85] These modalities of regulation can interact. An industry may invest in self-regulation, for example, due to concerns that failure to do so will lead to more coercive regulation at the hands of the state.

Regulation is not limited to restricting or prohibiting undesirable conduct; it may also enable or facilitate positive activities – 'green light' as opposed to 'red light' regulation.[86] 'Responsive regulation' argues in favour of a more co-operative relationship, encouraging regulated parties to comply with the goals of the law rather than merely strict rule compliance.[87] Other approaches emphasize efficiency: risk-based and problem-centred regulatory techniques seek to prioritize the most important issues – though identification, selection, and prioritization of future risks and current problems involve uncertainty as well as normative and political choices.[88]

The tools available to regulatory bodies may be thought of in three categories also: traditional rule-making, adjudication by courts or tribunals, and informal guidance – the last comprising standards, interpretive guides, and public and private communications concerning the regulated activity. Tim Wu has provocatively suggested that regulators of industries undergoing rapid change should consider linking the third with the first two by issuing 'threats' – informally requesting compliance but under the shadow of possible formalization and enforcement.[89]

Many discussions of AI regulation recount the options available – a sliding scale, a pyramid, a toolbox, and so on – but the application is either too general or too specific. It is, self-evidently, inappropriate to apply one regulatory approach to all of the activities impacted by AI. Yet it is also impractical to adopt specific laws for every one of those activities. A degree of clarity may, however, be achieved by using the lenses

---

[85] Neil Gunningham and Peter Grabosky, *Smart Regulation: Designing Environmental Policy* (Clarendon Press 1998). Cf Michael Guihot, Anne F Matthew, and Nicolas P Suzor, 'Nudging Robots: Innovative Solutions to Regulate Artificial Intelligence' (2017) 20 Vanderbilt Journal of Entertainment & Technology Law 385.

[86] Carol Harlow and Richard Rawlings, *Law and Administration* (3rd edn, Cambridge University Press 2009) 1–48.

[87] Ian Ayres and John Braithwaite, *Responsive Regulation: Transcending the Deregulation Debate* (Oxford University Press 1992).

[88] Robert Baldwin and Julia Black, 'Driving Priorities in Risk-Based Regulation: What's the Problem?' (2016) 43 Journal of Law and Society 565. See generally Malcolm K Sparrow, *The Regulatory Craft: Controlling Risks, Solving Problems, and Managing Compliance* (Brookings Institution 2000).

[89] Tim Wu, 'Agency Threats' (2011) 60 Duke Law Journal 1841. Cf Nathan Cortez, 'Regulating Disruptive Innovation' (2014) 29 Berkeley Technology Law Journal 175.

developed earlier to distinguish among three classes of problems associated with AI: managing some risks, proscribing others, while in a third set of cases ensuring that proper processes are followed.

7.3.1 Managed Risks

As discussed in chapter four, civil liability provides a basis for allocating responsibility for risk – particularly in areas that can be examined on a cost–benefit basis. This will cover the majority, perhaps the vast majority, of AI activities in the private sector: from transportation to medical devices, from smart home application to cognitive enhancements and implants. The issue here is not new rules but how to apply or adapt existing rules to technology that operates at speed, autonomously, and with varying degrees of opacity. Minimum transparency requirements may be needed to ensure that AI systems are identified as such[90] and that harmful conduct can be attributed to the appropriate owner, operator, or manufacturer.[91] Mandatory insurance will spread those risks more efficiently.[92] But the fundamental principles remain sound.

For situations in which cost–benefit analysis is appropriate but the potential risks are difficult to determine, regulatory 'sandboxes' allow new technologies to be tested in controlled environments. Though some jurisdictions have applied this to embodied technology, such as designated areas for autonomous vehicles,[93] the approach is particularly suited to AI systems that operate online. Originating in computer science, a virtual sandbox lets software run in a manner that limits the potential damage if there are errors or vulnerabilities. Though not amounting to the immunity that Ryan Calo once argued was essential to research into robotics,[94] sandboxes offer 'safe spaces' to trial innovative products without immediately incurring all the normal regulatory consequences.[95] The technique has been most commonly used with respect to finance technology (or 'fintech'), enabling entrepreneurs to test their products with real customers, fewer regulatory constraints, reduced risk of enforcement action, and ongoing guidance from

---

[90] See chapter eight, section 8.2.2(b).
[91] See chapter four, section 4.1.1.
[92] See chapter four, section 4.1.4.
[93] See, eg, Road Traffic (Autonomous Motor Vehicles) Rules 2017 (Singapore), rule 9; Unmanned Vehicles Technology Innovative Experimental Act 2018 (Taiwan).
[94] See chapter four, section 4.1.3.
[95] Regulatory Sandbox (Financial Conduct Authority (UK), November 2015) 1.

regulators.[96] Pioneered by Britain in 2016, it is credited with giving London a first-mover advantage in fintech and has since been copied in other jurisdictions around the world.[97]

7.3.2 Red Lines

In some cases, however, lines will need to be drawn as to what is permissible and what is not. These red lines will, in some cases, go beyond merely applying existing rules to AI. Linked with the ethical principle of maintaining human control, an obvious candidate is prohibiting AI from making decisions to use lethal force.[98]

Yet even that apparently clear prohibition becomes blurred under closer analysis. If machines are able to make every choice up to that point – scanning an environment, identifying and selecting a target, proposing an angle of attack – the final decision may be an artificial one. As discussed in chapter three, automation bias makes the default choice significantly more likely to be accepted in such circumstances.[99] That is an argument not against the prohibition but in favour of ensuring not only that a human is at least 'in' or 'over' the loop but also that he or she knows that accountability for it will follow him or her.[100] This is the link between the principles of human control and accountability – not that humans will remain in control and machines will be kept accountable but that humans (and other legal persons) will continue to be accountable for their conduct, even if perpetrated by or through a machine.

A discrete area in which new rules will be needed concerns human interaction with AI systems. The lacuna here, however, is not laws to protect us from them but laws to protect them from us. Anodyne examples include those adopted in Singapore in early 2017, making it an offence to interfere with autonomous vehicle trials.[101] These are more

---

[96] Dirk A Zetzsche et al, 'Regulating a Revolution: From Regulatory Sandboxes to Smart Regulation' (2017) 23 Fordham Journal of Corporate & Financial Law 31, 45; Mark Fenwick, Wulf A Kaal, and Erik PM Vermeulen, 'Regulation Tomorrow: What Happens When Technology Is Faster than the Law?' (2017) 6 American University Business Law Review 561, 591–93.

[97] Hillary J Allen, 'Regulatory Sandboxes' (2019) 87 George Washington Law Review 579, 580. See, eg, Federal Law No 123-FZ 2020 (Russia).

[98] See chapter two, section 2.2.

[99] See chapter three, section 3.1.

[100] See chapter four, section 4.2.2.

[101] Road Traffic (Amendment) Act 2017 (Singapore). Beginning in 2018, the basic guide for driving published by the Singapore Traffic Police added a page describing interactions

properly considered an extension of the management of risk associated with such technologies.[102] More problematic will be laws preserving human morality from offences perpetrated against machines. As discussed in chapter five, it is presently a crime to torture a chimpanzee but not a computer. As 'social robots' become more prevalent – in industries from eldercare to prostitution – it may be necessary to regulate what can be created and how those creations may be used.

In 2014, for example, Ronald Arkin ignited controversy by proposing that child sex robots be used to 'treat' paedophiles in the same way that methadone is used by heroin addicts.[103] Though simulated pornography is treated differently across jurisdictions,[104] many have now prohibited the manufacture and use of these devices through creative interpretations of existing laws or passing new ones such as the CREEPER Act in the United States.[105]

As lifelike embodied robots become more common, and as they play more active roles in society, it will be necessary to protect them not merely to reduce the risk of malfunction but because the act of harming them will be regarded as a wrong in itself. The closest analogy will, initially, be animal cruelty laws.[106] This is, arguably, another manifestation of the android fallacy – purchasing a lifelike robot and setting it on fire will cause more distress than deleting its operating system. Moving forward, however, the ability of AI systems to perceive pain and comprehend the prospect of non-existence may change that calculation.[107]

---

with autonomous vehicles on trial. Basic Theory of Driving (10th Edition) (Singapore Traffic Police, 2018) 76.

[102] The same can be said of laws requiring that users update safety-critical software. See, eg, Automated and Electric Vehicles Act 2018 (UK), s 4(1)(b).

[103] Kashmir Hill, 'Are Child Sex-Robots Inevitable?', Forbes (14 July 2014) (quoting Georgia Institute of Technology Professor Ronald Arkin).

[104] See, eg, Nicola Henry and Anastasia Powell, 'Sexual Violence in the Digital Age: The Scope and Limits of Criminal Law' (2016) 25 Social & Legal Studies 397. Images of a wrong (abuse of children or acts of violence) are generally prohibited. The question is whether a simulation itself is a wrong. The US Supreme Court, for example, has struck down provisions of the Child Pornography Prevention Act of 1996 that would have criminalized such 'speech' that 'records no crime and creates no victims by its production'. Ashcroft v Free Speech Coalition, 535 US 234 (2002).

[105] Curbing Realistic Exploitative Electronic Pedophilic Robots (CREEPER) Act 2017 (US). See generally John Danaher, 'Regulating Child Sex Robots: Restriction or Experimentation?' (2019) 27 Medical Law Review 553.

[106] See chapter five, section 5.2.1.

[107] See, eg, Hutan Ashrafian, 'Can Artificial Intelligences Suffer from Mental Illness? A Philosophical Matter to Consider' (2017) 23 Science and Engineering Ethics 403; Muh Anshar and Mary-Anne Williams, 'Simplified Pain Matrix Method for Artificial

This raises the question of whether red lines should be established for AI research that might bring about self-awareness – or the kind of superintelligence discussed in chapter five.[108] Though many experts have advocated caution about the prospect of general AI, few have called for a halt to research in the area and no government has done so.[109] As indicated earlier, there is a non-trivial risk that attempts to contain or hobble general AI may bring about the threat that they are intended to avert. A 'precautionary principle' approach might be, therefore, to stop well short of such capabilities. Yet general AI seems far enough beyond our present capacities that this would be an excessive response if implemented today.

In any case, a ban in one jurisdiction may not bind another. Short of an international treaty, with a body competent to administer it, a ban would be ineffective. The prospects for a treaty of this kind and an implementing agency will be discussed in chapter eight.[110]

7.3.3   Process Legitimacy

Limiting the decisions that can be outsourced to AI is an area in which new rules are both necessary and possible.

One approach is to restrict the use of AI for inherently governmental functions, as discussed in chapter four. There have been occasional calls for a ban on government use of algorithms, typically in response to actual or perceived failures in public sector decision-making. These include scandals over automated programs that purported to identify benefit fraud in Australia[111] and the Netherlands,[112] and the Covid-19 university admissions debacle in Britain.[113]

Pain Activation Embedded into Robot Framework' (2021) 13 International Journal of Social Robotics 187–95.

[108] See chapter five, section 5.3.

[109] See, eg, Research Priorities for Robust and Beneficial Artificial Intelligence: An Open Letter (Future of Life Institute, 2015).

[110] See chapter eight, section 8.2.2.

[111] Matthew Doran, 'Robodebt Legal Warning Came on Same Day Scheme Was Suspended by Federal Government', *ABC News (Australia)* (6 February 2020) (discussing the Australian government's Online Compliance Intervention, colloquially known as 'Robodebt').

[112] 'Government's Fraud Algorithm SyRI Breaks Human Rights, Privacy Law', *DutchNews. nl* (5 February 2020) (discussing the Dutch government's algorithm-based fraud detection system SyRI).

[113] Adam Satariano, 'British Grading Debacle Shows Pitfalls of Automating Government', *New York Times* (20 August 2020). See also chapter two, section 2.3.2, and chapter three, section 3.3.

Other jurisdictions have banned specific applications, such as facial recognition. San Francisco made headlines by prohibiting its use by police and other agencies in 2019, a move that was replicated in various US cities and the state of California but not at the Federal level. As in the case of data protection, Washington has thus far resisted broad legislation while Europe approached the same question as an application of the GDPR and mooted a continent-wide ban or moratorium.[114] China, for its part, has far fewer restrictions on facial recognition – though the government has acknowledged the need for greater guidance and there has been at least one (unsuccessful) lawsuit.[115]

Banning algorithms completely is unnecessary, not least because any definition might include arithmetic and other basic functions that exercise no discretion. More importantly, it misidentifies the problem. Returning to the discussion of autonomy and opacity in chapters two and three, the problem is not that machines are making decisions but that humans are abdicating responsibility for them. Public sector decisions exercising inherently governmental functions are legitimate not because they are correct but because they are capable of being held to account through a political or other process.

Such concerns activate the first two principles discussed at the start of this chapter: human control and transparency. A more realistic and generalizable approach to the regulation of AI in the public sector is escalating provisions for both in public sector decision-making. We have seen this already in the Canadian provisions on transparency of administrative decisions.[116] A similar approach is taken in New Zealand's Algorithm Charter. Signed by two dozen government agencies, the Charter includes a matrix that moves from optional to mandatory based on the probability and the severity of the impact on the 'wellbeing of people'. Among other provisions, mandatory application of the Charter requires 'human oversight', comprising a point of contact for public inquiries, an avenue for appeals against a decision, and 'clearly explaining the role of humans in decisions informed by algorithms'. It also includes provisions on transparency that go beyond notions of explainability and include

---

[114] 'US and Europe Clash over Facial Recognition Law', *Biometric Technology Today* (February 2020) 1. See also the draft regulation published by the European Commission on 21 April 2021.
[115] Seungha Lee, Coming into Focus: China's Facial Recognition Regulations (Center for Strategic and International Studies, 4 May 2020).
[116] See chapter six, section 6.3.5.

requirements for plain English documentation of algorithms and publishing information about how data is collected, secured, and stored.[117]

These are important steps, but they are insufficient. For such public sector decisions, it is not simply a question of striking 'the right balance', as the Charter states, between accessing the power of algorithms and maintaining the trust and confidence of citizens. A more basic commitment would guarantee the means of challenging those decisions – not just legally, in the case of decisions that violate the law, but also politically, by identifying human decision-makers in positions of public trust who can be held to account through democratic processes for their actions or inaction.

7.4   The Prospects for Rules

If Asimov's three laws had avoided or resolved all the ethical dilemmas of machine intelligence, his literary career would have been brief. In fact, the very story in which they were introduced focuses on a robot that is paralysed by a contradiction between the second and third laws, resolved only by a human putting himself in harm's way to invoke the first.[118]

A blanket rule not to harm humans is obviously inadequate when forced to choose between the lesser of two evils. Asimov himself later added a 'zeroth' law, which provided that a robot's highest duty was to humanity as a whole. In one of his last novels, a robot is asked how it could ever determine what was injurious to humanity as a whole. 'Precisely, sir,' the robot replies. 'In theory, the Zeroth Law was the answer to our problems. In practice, we could never decide.'[119]

The demand for new rules to deal with AI is often overstated. Ryan Abbott, for example, argues in a recent book that the guiding principle for regulatory change should be AI legal neutrality, meaning that the law should not discriminate at all between human and AI behaviour.[120] Though provocatively simple, the full import of such a 'rule' is quickly abandoned: personality is not sought for AI systems, nor are the

---

[117] Algorithm Charter (NZ) (n 21).

[118] The robot initially tries to comply with a weakly phrased order that would entail its own certain destruction and ends up stuck in an 'equilibrium' – quoting Gilbert and Sullivan, for reasons that are never explained – until the need to save a human life breaks it free. Asimov (n 2).

[119] Isaac Asimov, *Foundation and Earth* (Doubleday 1986), ch 21.

[120] Ryan Abbott, *The Reasonable Robot: Artificial Intelligence and the Law* (Cambridge University Press 2020) 2–4.

standards of AI (the 'reasonable robots' of the title) to be applied to human conduct. Rather, Abbott's thesis boils down to a case-by-case examination of different areas of AI activity to determine whether specific sectors warrant change or not.[121]

This is a sensible enough approach, but some new rules of general application are required, primarily to ensure that the first two 'principles' quoted at the start of this chapter – human control and transparency – can be achieved. Human control requires limits on the kinds of AI system that can be developed. The precautionary principle offers a means of thinking about such risks, though the clearest decisions can be made in bright line moral cases like lethal autonomous weapons. More nuanced limitations are required in the public sector, not constraining the behaviour of AI systems but limiting the ability of public officials to outsource decisions to them. On the question of transparency, accountability of government officials also requires a limit on the use of opaque processes. Above and beyond that, the measures discussed in chapter six – impact assessments, audits, an AI ombudsperson – should mitigate some harms and assist in ensuring that others can be attributed back to legal persons capable of being held to account.[122]

As AI becomes more sophisticated and pervasive, a key question will be whether users should be made aware that they are interacting with an AI system or a human. As indicated in chapter six, this is coming to be seen as a basic right. Oren Etzioni and Frank Pasquale, among others, have argued that a requirement for AI systems to disclose that they are not human should be one of an updated Azimovian set of laws;[123] Toby Walsh agrees, but contends that this should be framed as a positive obligation for autonomous systems to identify themselves as such – drawing an analogy with nineteenth-century red flag laws that required a person to walk in front of any motorized vehicle, warning of the oncoming danger.[124]

---

[121] Ibid 136–43.

[122] Other rules may include requirements to slow down some functions, such as high-frequency trading, discussed in chapter one. Still others may draw upon advantages of AI, such as the ability to keep detailed records that can assist in understanding the reason for a harm. Autonomous vehicles, for example, may be required to retain information about their functioning comparable to the flight data recorders used in modern aircraft. See also chapter eight, section 8.2.2(b), and chapter nine, section 9.3.2.

[123] Oren Etzioni, 'How to Regulate Artificial Intelligence', *New York Times* (1 September 2017); Frank Pasquale, *New Laws of Robotics: Defending Human Expertise in the Age of AI* (Belknap Press 2020).

[124] Toby Walsh, *Android Dreams: The Past, Present, and Future of Artificial Intelligence* (Hurst 2017) 111. See also Turner (n 33) 320–24.

Commercial pressures already militate against disclosure, as AI systems are more effective in their interactions with humans when their nature is not known or at least not disclosed openly.[125] Even bigger challenges may be practical ones, however, as many consumer-facing AI systems – chatbots, for example – operate with varying levels of human involvement. While a human call centre may distinguish clearly between levels of authorization, transferring a telephone inquiry from an agent to a manager, chatbots may blur these lines by referring complex or unusual aspects of a query to a human supervisor while carrying on the 'conversation' without interruption.[126]

This again highlights the central challenge of regulating AI, which is not so much a lack of rules as it is uncertainty as to their applicability and application in specific cases. The problem will not be Asimov's industrial products seeking to find their moral path in the universe but distributed systems operating with humans in, out of, and over the 'loop' across jurisdictional boundaries. That will require new ways of thinking about regulation and, in particular, new institutions to implement it.

---

[125] Alex Engler, The Case for AI Transparency Requirements (Brookings Institution, 22 January 2020).

[126] Natalie Petouhoff, 'What Is a Chatbot and How Is It Changing Customer Experience?', *Salesforce Blog* (3 March 2020). Cf chapter six, section 6.4.

8

New Institutions

Around the same time that Asimov published his short story introducing the laws of robotics, the world's first nuclear reactor was being built under the viewing stands of a football field at the University of Chicago. There had been some misgivings about initiating a chain reaction in the middle of a densely populated city, but Enrico Fermi, the Italian physicist leading the experiment, calculated that it was safe to do so. On its initial successful run, the Chicago Pile-1 reactor ran for four minutes, generating less than a watt of power – about enough to illuminate one small Christmas tree ornament. The reaction was a major step in the development of nuclear energy, but it was also one of the earliest technical achievements of the Manhattan Project, the US-led initiative during the Second World War culminating in the atomic bombs that incinerated Hiroshima and Nagasaki two and a half years later.[1]

The scientists involved knew that their work had the potential for creation as well as destruction. Though the awesome power of the bomb and the exigencies of war meant that secrecy was an 'unwelcome necessity', Fermi himself believed that preventing the basic knowledge from spreading was akin to hoping the Earth would stop revolving around the Sun.[2] The question was how to ensure that its beneficial use in power generation and medicine did not also lead to proliferation of weapons threatening the existence of humanity.

After the conclusion of the war, that was the subject of the very first resolution passed by the General Assembly of the United Nations (UN) in January 1946. It created a commission tasked with recommending how to eliminate such weapons, while enabling all nations to benefit from

---

[1] Richard Rhodes, *The Making of the Atomic Bomb* (Simon & Schuster 1986).
[2] Enrico Fermi, 'Atomic Energy for Power' in AV Hill (ed), *Science and Civilization: The Future of Atomic Energy* (McGraw-Hill 1946) 93 at 103; Enrico Fermi, 'Fermi's Own Story', *Chicago Sun-Times* (23 November 1952).

peaceful uses of nuclear energy.[3] Five months later, the United States, Britain, and Canada proposed that a new international organization be given exclusive control of all aspects of atomic power, from ownership of raw materials to the operation of nuclear power plants. The Soviet Union, wary of Western motives, rejected the plan – creating a rift that came to be seen as both a cause and a consequence of the Cold War.[4]

It was another seven years before US President Dwight Eisenhower presented an alternative idea to the UN. If the earlier plan had been utopian, his 'Atoms for Peace' address was idealistic in a different way: instead of concentrating materials and expertise in a supranational body, they would be disseminated widely – encouraging states to use them for peaceful purposes, in exchange for commitments to renounce the search for the bomb.[5]

The history of efforts to safeguard nuclear power is relevant for three reasons. The first is as an example of a technology with enormous potential for good and ill that has, for the most part, been used positively. Nuclear power, though currently out of favour, is one of few realistic energy alternatives to hydrocarbons; its use in medicine and agriculture is more accepted and widespread. Observers from the dark days of the Cold War anticipated this, but would have been surprised to learn that nuclear weapons were not used in conflict after 1945 and that only a handful of states possess them the better part of a century later.[6]

Secondly, the international regime offers a possible model for regulation of AI at the global level. The grand bargain at the heart of the International Atomic Energy Agency (IAEA), created four years after Eisenhower's speech, was that the beneficial purposes of technology could be distributed in tandem with a mechanism to ensure that those were the only purposes to which it was applied. That trade-off raised the level of trust between the then-superpowers, as well as between the nuclear haves and have-nots. The equivalent weaponization of AI – either

---

[3] Establishment of a Commission to Deal with the Problems Raised by the Discovery of Atomic Energy, UN Doc A/RES/1(I) (1946).

[4] Larry G Gerber, 'The Baruch Plan and the Origins of the Cold War' (1982) 6(4) Diplomatic History 69, 70.

[5] Address by Mr Dwight D Eisenhower, President of the United States of America, to the 470th Plenary Meeting of the United Nations General Assembly (Atoms for Peace) (United Nations, 8 December 1953); Robert L Brown, *Nuclear Authority: The IAEA and the Absolute Weapon* (Georgetown University Press 2015) 41–50. By 1953, both Russia and Britain had also conducted successful tests of their own weapons.

[6] For an extreme view, see Kenneth Waltz, The Spread of Nuclear Weapons: More May Be Better (International Institute for Strategic Studies, Adelphi Papers, Number 171, 1981).

narrowly, through the development of autonomous weapon systems, or broadly, in the form of a general AI or superintelligence that might threaten humanity – is today beyond the capacity of most states. For weapon systems, at least, that technical gap will not last long.[7] Much as the small number of nuclear armed states is due to the decision of states not to develop such weapons and a non-proliferation regime to verify this, limits on the dangerous application of AI will need to rely on the choices of states as well as enforcement.

A third reason for the comparison is that, much like Fermi and his colleagues, the scientists deeply involved in AI research have been the most vocal in calling for international regulation. The various guides, frameworks, and principles discussed in chapter seven were largely driven by scientists, with states tending to follow rather than lead. As the nuclear non-proliferation regime shows, however, good norms are necessary but not sufficient for effective regulation.

This chapter considers the institutional possibilities for regulation, with options ranging from a completely free market to global control by an international organization. In between lie more or less formal industry and sectoral associations, as well as public agencies at the national and international levels. Rather than laying these out as a menu, a more helpful approach is to use once again the lenses developed in chapter two – focusing on the demand for regulation, rather than sources of supply. The management of risks associated with AI can and should, for example, rely heavily on standards that are developed by industry. Best practices, interoperability protocols, and so on will continue to evolve faster than laws can be written. Section one discusses institutional structures that would support rather than hinder that evolution.

Not all risks should be managed, however. It will be necessary to establish red lines to prohibit certain activities. Weaponized or uncontainable AI are the most obvious candidates but not the only ones.[8] Mere reliance on industry self-restraint will not preserve such prohibitions. Moreover, if those red lines are to be enforced consistently and effectively then some measure of global co-ordination and co-operation is required. Here the analogy with nuclear weapons is most pertinent. Section two

---

[7] See, eg, Elsa B Kania, 'AI Weapons' in China's Military Innovation (Brookings Institution, April 2020).

[8] See, eg, the need to protect 'social robots' against victimization, discussed in chapter seven, section 7.3.2.

posits a hypothetical IAIA, modelled on the IAEA, as a means of achieving this.

The third section returns to the legitimate actions of states. Though the EU has gone furthest in establishing supranational norms, restrictions on outsourcing of public authority will rely on states themselves for enforcement. Indeed, this will be true of most norms regulating AI. Though industry standards will shape practices and international treaties may limit them, states will remain essential players – able to use command and control methods and wielding the 'regulatory hammer' when necessary.[9]

Much as complete internationalization of the nuclear life cycle in the 1950s was unrealistic and letting the sector develop unchecked was unthinkable, the aim here is to build on existing institutions – most importantly, states – while structuring incentives and co-ordinating responses. In this way, it should be possible to address these problems of practicality, morality, and legitimacy – ideally, without any bombs going off at all.

8.1   Industry Standards

The libertarian streak among technology entrepreneurs runs deep. For many years, Bill Gates bragged that Microsoft did not even have an office in Washington, DC – he wanted nothing from the government except to be left alone. Gates was representative of the wider culture in Silicon Valley: most saw their work as undeserving of regulation while a good many deemed themselves morally superior to the governments that might presume to impose it.[10]

In the 2010s this began to change. Three factors appear to have been operating. The first was a growing realization on the part of experts that the potential damage from unchecked innovation did pose a non-trivial risk of catastrophic harm. Much as Fermi and his colleagues saw the

---

[9] Margot E Kaminski, 'Binary Governance: Lessons from the GDPR's Approach to Algorithmic Accountability' (2019) 92 Southern California Law Review 1529, 1564. In public international law this is known as the principle of subsidiarity. See Andreas Follesdal, 'The Principle of Subsidiarity as a Constitutional Principle in International Law' (2013) 2 Global Constitutionalism 37.

[10] See, eg, Emanuel Moss and Jacob Metcalf, 'The Ethical Dilemma at the Heart of Big Tech Companies', *Harvard Business Review* (14 November 2019). Cf David Broockman, Greg F Ferenstein, and Neil Malhotra, 'Predispositions and the Political Behavior of American Economic Elites: Evidence from Technology Entrepreneurs' (2019) 63 American Journal of Political Science 212.

dangers of nuclear power, some of the world's leading exponents of technology began to warn of its potential dangers. In addition to public warnings and signing an open letter on the need to ensure that AI remains beneficial, Elon Musk among others donated tens of millions of dollars to the cause.[11]

Secondly, the Cambridge Analytica scandal was a tipping point after which consumer trust in technology companies eroded. The harvesting of data began in 2014 and was used, most prominently, to influence the 2016 US presidential election, but reports had been anonymously sourced until a whistle-blower went on the record in March 2018.[12] Facebook's share price fell by almost a quarter over the following week, losing more than $130bn in market value. Early 2018 was the period in which Microsoft, Google, and IBM all published their AI principles.[13]

A third reason, related to the second, was that companies and researchers correctly anticipated that consumer mistrust would be followed by government action. Though the EU GDPR had been in development for some time, this was also the point at which it came into force – even as other jurisdictions were contemplating additional regulation of personal data in particular or technology more generally.[14]

Debates over the obligations of organizations beyond compliance with the law are hardly unique to the technology sector. Linked with larger concerns about the impact of climate change and economic inequality, there is a growing recognition that corporations have responsibilities other than making money.[15] In August 2019, for example, the US Business Roundtable published an open letter on the purpose of a corporation. It stated that its members were committed to delivering value to all their stakeholders: shareholders, employees, suppliers, customers, and communities.[16] The text was unremarkable – such pabulum

---

[11] Research Priorities for Robust and Beneficial Artificial Intelligence: An Open Letter (Future of Life Institute, 2015). See also the warnings cited in the introduction to this book.

[12] Matthew Rosenberg, Nicholas Confessore, and Carole Cadwalladr, 'How Trump Consultants Exploited the Facebook Data of Millions', *New York Times* (17 March 2018).

[13] See chapter seven, introduction. Facebook announced its own AI ethics team in May of the same year.

[14] These moves were also linked to criticisms concerning the tax strategies and anti-competitive conduct of technology companies.

[15] Cf Simon Chesterman, 'The Turn to Ethics: Disinvestment from Multinational Corporations for Human Rights Violations – The Case of Norway's Sovereign Wealth Fund' (2008) 23 American University International Law Review 577.

[16] Business Roundtable Redefines the Purpose of a Corporation to Promote 'An Economy That Serves All Americans' (Business Roundtable, 19 August 2019).

can be found in annual reports and prospectuses of companies large and small. But to be adopted as policy, signed by 181 chief executive officers of companies from Apple to Walmart, caused a minor stir in economic circles. In particular, it was a public repudiation of the view, championed by Milton Friedman, that the primary responsibility of CEOs is to maximize profits for their shareholders: the business of business, Friedman had argued, is business.[17]

It is not possible in these pages to do justice to the debates over corporate social responsibility or global business activities and human rights.[18] The focus will be on two questions: what is the role of industry in establishing its own standards for safety and what are the limitations of that approach?

8.1.1 Common Language, Best Practice

One of the most commonly invoked examples of self-governance by researchers is the 1975 Asilomar Conference on recombinant DNA. Given the uncertain dangers associated with the new technique, also known as gene-splicing, US scientists had initially called for a moratorium. The conference brought together more than a hundred biologists from around the world, who developed guidelines for future research. These emphasized the importance of containment as an essential consideration in experiment design, with the level of containment matching, as far as possible, the estimated risk. Certain classes of high-risk experiment for which containment could not be guaranteed were to be 'deferred' – in essence, prohibited.[19] The guidelines were soon endorsed as laws or funding requirements in many countries, with experiments restarting soon afterwards.

It is no coincidence that the Future of Life Institute held its own event at the same conference centre some 42 years later to draft the Asilomar AI

---

[17] Milton Friedman, 'The Social Responsibility of Business Is to Increase Its Profits', *New York Times* (13 September 1970). See Claudine Gartenberg and George Serafeim, '181 Top CEOs Have Realized Companies Need a Purpose Beyond Profit', *Harvard Business Review* (20 August 2019).

[18] See generally Abagail McWilliams et al (eds), *The Oxford Handbook of Corporate Social Responsibility: Psychological and Organizational Perspectives* (Oxford University Press 2019); John Gerard Ruggie, Guiding Principles on Business and Human Rights: Implementing the United Nations 'Protect, Respect and Remedy' Framework, UN Doc A/HRC/17/31 (2011).

[19] Paul Berg et al, 'Summary Statement of the Asilomar Conference on Recombinant DNA Molecules' (1975) 72 Proceedings of the National Academy of Sciences 1981.

Principles. Among those principles are an approach to risk that increases control measures commensurate with the expected impact, and an effective prohibition on the development of undirected or uncontainable AI.[20] Yet nostalgia for the 1975 event overestimates the ability of such a gathering to have the same impact today. The biologists involved in the earlier meeting almost all worked at public institutions and were confident that a moratorium would be respected; it was also possible to bring most of the world's leading researchers together at a single event.[21] The disparate and competitive world of AI makes any norms difficult to monitor, let alone police.[22] The Asilomar AI Principles are now merely one of dozens of documents – noticed, to be sure, but hardly authoritative.[23]

Nonetheless, bodies like the Future of Life Institute clearly have a role to play. Apart from anything else, agreeing on terminology can ensure that developers and regulators are not talking past each other. As we saw in chapter two, for example, the industry standard to describe 'autonomous' vehicles follows levels established by the SAE.[24] Similarly, the IEEE has elaborated principles for ethically aligned design, intended to offer standards and benchmarks for autonomous and intelligent systems.[25]

Indeed, private ordering has governed many aspects of the Internet for decades. Though its origins lie in the US military, since 1998 it has been administered by the Internet Corporation for Assigned Names and Numbers (ICANN), a multi-stakeholder entity with global representation that is incorporated as a non-profit organization in the state of California.[26] This arrangement is desirable because it avoids the problems of either being bound too closely to one state's interests or being held hostage by the lowest common denominator of a group of states.[27]

---

[20] Asilomar AI Principles (Future of Life Institute, 6 January 2017).
[21] Paul Berg, 'Asilomar 1975: DNA Modification Secured' (2008) 455 Nature 290.
[22] 'After Asilomar' (2015) 526 Nature 293. US restrictions on stem cell research in 2001, for example, merely drove research elsewhere. See chapter seven, section 7.2.
[23] See chapter seven, introduction.
[24] See chapter two, section 2.1.
[25] Ethically Aligned Design: A Vision for Prioritizing Human Well-Being with Autonomous and Intelligent Systems (IEEE, 2019).
[26] Jeanette Hofmann, Christian Katzenbach, and Kirsten Gollatz, 'Between Coordination and Regulation: Finding the Governance in Internet Governance' (2017) 19 New Media & Society 1406.
[27] Hans Klein, 'ICANN and Internet Governance: Leveraging Technical Coordination to Realize Global Public Policy' (2002) 18 The Information Society 193; Manuel Becker, 'When Public Principals Give Up Control over Private Agents: The New Independence of ICANN in Internet Governance' (2019) 13 Regulation & Governance 561. Cf Jonathan

More generally, bodies like the International Organization for Standardization (ISO) establish technical and organizational standards that become de facto norms, despite operating outside traditional structures of domestic or international law.[28] Such standards may be appropriate for emerging industries or practices – among other things, helping to establish what amounts to 'reasonable' conduct for the purposes of determining liability in a claim under tort.[29]

8.1.2   Perverse Incentives, Regulatory Capture

Standards may be necessary, but they are not sufficient. When working properly, encouraging structured and unstructured conversations among scientists can help build consensus on norms and identify dangerous behaviour, along the lines of the Asilomar recombinant DNA limits. Informal interactions may reveal deviant behaviour, as they did in the case of Russian and South African biological weapons programmes; academic 'gossip' was also instrumental to tracking the Nazi atomic bomb effort during the Second World War.[30] Even if the norms applicable to AI can be agreed on, however, the actors involved in research and development of AI today are too numerous and too diverse to put much hope in industry-wide collective action. A more likely scenario, already apparent in many areas, is fragmentation into regulated and unregulated segments.[31] That is what we see today on the Internet in the form of the dark web.[32]

Alternatively, reliance on self-policing of conduct may lead to organizations seeing regulation as more a matter of communications than compliance. Much as 'greenwashing' emerged as a method for companies to signal their environmental values without necessarily committing to specific standards,[33] ethics boards at technology companies have at times

---

GS Koppell, 'Pathologies of Accountability: ICANN and the Challenge of "Multiple Accountabilities Disorder"' (2005) 65 Public Administration Review 94.

[28] See Nico Krisch and Benedict Kingsbury, 'Global Governance and Global Administrative Law in the International Legal Order' (2006) 17 European Journal of International Law 1.

[29] See chapter four, section 4.1.1.

[30] Jeffery T Richelson, *Spying on the Bomb: American Nuclear Intelligence from Nazi Germany to Iran and North Korea* (Norton 2006) 35.

[31] Stephen M Maurer, *Self-Governance in Science: Community-Based Strategies for Managing Dangerous Knowledge* (Cambridge University Press 2017) 215–17.

[32] Robert W Gehl, *Weaving the Dark Web: Legitimacy on Freenet, Tor, and I2P* (MIT Press 2018).

[33] Ho Cheung Brian Lee, Jose M Cruz, and Ramesh Shankar, 'Corporate Social Responsibility (CSR) Issues in Supply Chain Competition: Should Greenwashing Be Regulated?' (2018) 49 Decision Sciences 1088.

been tools of marketing rather than management. Google, for example, launched an Advanced Technology External Advisory Council in March 2019 – then shut it down less than two weeks later due to internal criticism and negative publicity.

Even if standards were universally agreed upon and taken seriously, proximity to industry increases the risk of regulatory capture. This is the phenomenon when those charged with oversight identify more closely with the objectives and problems of the group being regulated, thereby becoming incapable of carrying out their functions independently or effectively.[34] Regulatory capture is not unique to industry regulators – it may apply to government officials, judges, and other actors. Guarding against it is helped by institutionalizing the independence of regulators and reducing the ability to limit the flow of information.[35] Governance at multiple levels can also mitigate the difficulties posed by complexity and the Collingridge dilemma of when to regulate an emerging technology.[36] In the case of AI in particular, connectivity across sectors and borders means that one of those levels needs to be global.

8.2 Global Red Lines

As discussed in chapter one, the effacement of distance is a key structural challenge for regulation of AI.[37] Laws in one jurisdiction may not be enforced in another; efforts to prevent or contain deviant behaviour of global reach are only as strong as their weakest link. This is not new and affects various forms of transboundary harm. Willingness to address those deficiencies at the global level has been inconsistent, limited by barriers to agreement due to the nature of international law and impediments to meaningful enforcement for want of powerful institutions. Though international organizations can facilitate the development of standards, comprehensive global regulation of AI generally is unrealistic and probably undesirable. The focus should therefore be on establishing common red lines for activities that violate fundamental norms or pose

---

[34] Michael E Levine and Jennifer L Forrence, 'Regulatory Capture, Public Interest, and the Public Agenda: Toward a Synthesis' (1990) 6(Special Issue) Journal of Law, Economics, and Organization 167; Jean-Jacques Laffont and Jean Tirole, 'The Politics of Government Decision-Making: A Theory of Regulatory Capture' (1991) 106 Quarterly Journal of Economics 1089.

[35] Ernesto Dal Bó, 'Regulatory Capture: A Review' (2006) 22 Oxford Review of Economic Policy 203.

[36] See chapter seven, section 7.2.

[37] See chapter one, section 1.1.

significant transboundary threats, with institutional arrangements limited to these purposes.

8.2.1   Structural Challenges

AI systems are not merely a problem for international organizations to manage; they may undermine such organizations themselves. In part, this is because some AI systems represent a shift of power away from the state. That is true indirectly, through enabling citizens to access information and engage in transactions without the intermediation of traditional public institutions. Yet they may also pose a direct threat to the state, through undermining faith in institutions or processes – spreading 'fake news' and manipulating elections, to pick an extreme but hardly fantastical example.[38]

Historically, international organizations have been ineffective at responding to technological innovation. If regulation lags at the domestic level, it trails internationally.[39] Sovereign equality and the need to reach consensus encourage a lowest common denominator approach to norms, taking years or decades to negotiate. Moreover, the universal membership of forums like the UN makes states understandably wary of sharing sensitive information.[40]

Two relevant areas of modest success on the part of international law are banning particular weapons and facilitating global connectivity. From the 1868 St Petersburg Declaration on exploding bullets to more recent attempts to ban landmines and nuclear weapons, IHL has sought to mitigate human suffering in conflict. As discussed in chapter two, this has extended to concerns raised by lethal autonomous weapon systems.[41] International organizations have also supported globalization. One of the oldest such bodies is the International Telecommunication Union (ITU), formed in 1865 as the International Telegraph Union before adopting its current name in 1934. Though incorporated as a specialized agency of the UN, proposals that it should play a greater role in regulating content on

---

[38] Eyal Benvenisti, 'Upholding Democracy amid the Challenges of New Technology: What Role for the Law of Global Governance?' (2018) 29 European Journal of International Law 9.

[39] Rosemary Rayfuse, 'Public International Law and the Regulation of Emerging Technologies' in Roger Brownsword, Eloise Scotford, and Karen Yeung (eds), The Oxford Handbook of Law, Regulation, and Technology (Oxford University Press 2017) 500.

[40] Simon Chesterman, 'Does the UN Have Intelligence?' (2006) 48(3) Survival 149.

[41] See chapter two, section 2.2.

the Internet were met with alarm by many stakeholders – wary that it would restrict the free flow of information online.[42]

The international record is patchier still on providing other public goods. The eradication of smallpox was one of the great achievements of the World Health Organization (WHO), but it took almost two hundred years. A vaccine had been developed in the late eighteenth century, yet it was only after more than a decade of joint global action that the disease was declared eradicated in 1980.[43] As the 2020 Covid-19 pandemic demonstrated, co-ordinating a global response to a crisis remains extremely difficult when national interests clash.[44] Global action is easiest when the goal is both narrow and shared.[45] In relation to the environment, for example, success in preserving the ozone layer from the damage caused by chlorofluorocarbons may be contrasted with the far greater barriers to addressing global climate change.[46]

Even if there is political will and relative clarity about the activity to be regulated, international law will be ineffective if there is no agreement on the applicable norms, if conduct cannot be attributed to states or other actors at the international level, or if the consequences for breaches are inadequate.

(a)   Norms

On the question of norms, international law generally does not prohibit activities by states unless they have specifically consented to the prohibition.[47] This may take the form of a treaty obligation or customary international law, the latter demonstrated through general practice accepted as law by states.[48] As we saw in chapter two, for example, the

---

[42] Cf Ramses A Wessel, 'Regulating Technological Innovation through Informal International Law: The Exercise of International Public Authority by Transnational Actors' in Michiel A Heldeweg and Evisa Kica (eds), *Regulating Technological Innovation* (Palgrave Macmillan 2011) 77; Ingo Take, 'Regulating the Internet Infrastructure: A Comparative Appraisal of the Legitimacy of ICANN, ITU, and the WSIS' (2012) 6 Regulation & Governance 499.

[43] DA Henderson, *Smallpox: The Death of a Disease* (Prometheus 2009).

[44] Peter G Danchin et al, 'The Pandemic Paradox in International Law' (2020) 114 American Journal of International Law 598.

[45] Eyal Benvenisti, 'The WHO – Destined to Fail? Political Cooperation and the Covid-19 Pandemic' (2020) 114 American Journal of International Law 588, 592.

[46] Chris Peloso, 'Crafting an International Climate Change Protocol: Applying the Lessons Learned from the Success of the Montreal Protocol and the Ozone Depletion Problem' (2010) 25 Journal of Land Use & Environmental Law 305.

[47] *Case of the SS 'Lotus' (France v Turkey) (Merits)* (1927 1927) PCIJ Series A, No 10 (Permanent Court of International Justice).

[48] Statute of the International Court of Justice, 1945, art 38(1).

regime applicable to lethal autonomous weapons largely draws upon treaties.[49] Treaties are also relevant in establishing human rights norms that prohibit discrimination of the form discussed in chapter three.[50]

Customary international law does regulate certain transboundary harms: states are obliged to ensure that activities within their jurisdiction and control do not cause harm to other states or areas beyond national control.[51] In limited circumstances, this has been expanded by treaty into strict liability.[52] The 1972 Space Liability Convention provides an interesting model whereby a state is 'absolutely liable' to pay compensation for damage caused on the surface of the Earth by space objects launched from its territory.[53] For the most part, however, due diligence is all that is required – based on the nature of the activity, scientific knowledge at the time, and the capabilities of the state in question.[54] As long as this is satisfied, a state will not be responsible for unintentional or accidental acts, including malicious acts by rogue actors.[55] In such cases, the state's obligation is limited to notification of potentially affected states – though, in the case of catastrophic risks, that may be insufficient to avert the threat.[56]

---

[49] See chapter two, section 2.2.1.

[50] See chapter three, section 3.2.

[51] *Legality of the Threat or Use of Nuclear Weapons (Advisory Opinion)* [1996] ICJ Rep 226 (International Court of Justice), para 29. Cf *Corfu Channel (United Kingdom v Albania) (Merits)* [1949] ICJ Rep 4, 22 (every state has an obligation 'not to allow knowingly its territory to be used for acts contrary to the rights of other States').

[52] Cf chapter four, section 4.1.2.

[53] Convention on International Liability for Damage Caused by Space Objects, done at London, Moscow, and Washington, 29 March 1972, in force 1 September 1972, art II. This may be contrasted with the more limited regime on the high seas where piracy or other hostile activity may serve to absolve a state of its responsibilities. See Joel A Dennerley, 'State Liability for Space Object Collisions: The Proper Interpretation of "Fault" for the Purposes of International Space Law' (2018) 29 European Journal of International Law 281; Trevor Kehrer, 'Closing the Liability Loophole: The Liability Convention and the Future of Conflict in Space' (2019) 20 Chicago Journal of International Law 178. Cf Vienna Convention on Civil Liability for Nuclear Damage, done at Vienna, 21 May 1963, in force 12 November 1977.

[54] *Pulp Mills on the River Uruguay (Argentina v Uruguay) (Judgment)* [2010] ICJ Rep 14, para 197; *Responsibilities and Obligations of States with Respect to Activities in the Area (Advisory Opinion)* [2011] ITLOS Reports 10, paras 117–20.

[55] Patricia Birnie, Alan Boyle, and Catherine Redgwell, *International Law and the Environment* (3rd edn, Oxford University Press 2009) 147–50.

[56] International Law Commission, Prevention of Transboundary Harm from Hazardous Activities (Articles), UN Doc A/RES/62/68, Annex (2007), art 17; Grant Wilson, 'Minimizing Global Catastrophic and Existential Risks from Emerging Technologies through International Law' (2013) 31 Virginia Environmental Law Journal 307, 342.

In the absence of a treaty, then, the obligations with respect to an AI system that poses transboundary threats – from polluting a river, say, to a general AI capable of seizing military assets – would be due diligence in attempting to prevent the harm and notification were that harm to materialize.

It is important to stress that these obligations fall on states. In areas like human rights, the obligation may be to respect rights and ensure that they are protected, sometimes requiring the passage of legislation and administrative action as well as refraining from direct violation of the rights in question.[57] Some international legal obligations do fall directly on individuals – notably the international criminal law regime, discussed in chapter four[58] – but international law first and foremost manages relations between states, only rarely reaching inside them without consent.[59] A key question, then, is whether wrongdoing, or a failure to prevent it, can be attributed to a state.

(b) Attribution

The International Law Commission (ILC) grappled with this topic for half a century, finally producing 'draft' articles on the responsibility of states for internationally wrongful acts that are now accepted as reflecting custom.[60] Completion of the articles was possible only because the ILC deftly set aside the matter of what primary norms might constitute international wrongs to focus on the more technical – and less political – secondary questions of attribution and consequences of liability.

In general, a state is responsible for the acts of 'persons or entities' exercising governmental authority.[61] The term 'governmental authority' is not defined, as it depends on 'the particular society, its history and traditions', but there is a clear overlap with the discussion of 'inherently governmental' functions in chapter four.[62] Responsibility of the state encompasses situations that involve 'an independent discretion or

---

[57] This would encompass, for example, some of the prohibited discrimination discussed in chapter three. Cf Paolo G Carozza, 'Subsidiarity as a Structural Principle of International Human Rights Law' (2003) 97 American Journal of International Law 38.

[58] See chapter four, section 4.2.2.

[59] The most prominent example is enforcement action against a threat to the peace under Chapter VII of the UN Charter. See generally Simon Chesterman, *Just War or Just Peace? Humanitarian Intervention and International Law* (Oxford University Press 2001).

[60] James Crawford, *The International Law Commission's Articles on State Responsibility: Introduction, Text and Commentaries* (Cambridge University Press 2002).

[61] International Law Commission, Responsibility of States for Internationally Wrongful Acts (Articles on State Responsibility), UN Doc A/56/83, Annex (2001), art 5. The ILC commentary makes clear that 'entity' is not limited to legal persons.

[62] See chapter four, section 4.3.

power to act' on the part of a person or entity – even if the entity 'exceeds its authority or contravenes instructions' while acting in that capacity.[63]

This would cover AI systems used by government agencies and sub-contractors, even if the AI system subsequently went beyond intended protocols. The acts of private individuals or corporations would not be covered directly, though the state may have specific treaty commitments or customary obligations to guard against transboundary harm.[64] Failure to satisfy those, at least, is attributable to the state.

Situations may arise where it is difficult to attribute conduct to a particular state or, indeed, to any actor. That is a practical rather than a normative challenge, already well known in the context of cybercrime.[65] It points, however, to a potential 'red line' that could be demanded globally: a requirement to ensure that the conduct of AI systems remains traceable back to an entity with a presence in at least one state.[66]

(c) Consequences

The biggest hurdle for international law, however, is the difficulty of enforcing compliance. This is a standard critique of the regime, which suffers from invidious comparisons with domestic legal regimes and periodic accusations that it is not really 'law' at all.[67] The debates are largely sterile due to the dearth of strong theories of international law and the abundance of practice accepting its legality nonetheless.[68] Those debates fail to take account of structural differences in the normative regimes: international law presumes the horizontal organization of notionally equal sovereign and quasi-sovereign entities, whereas domestic law posits a vertical hierarchy of subjects under a sovereign.[69]

---

[63] International Law Commission (n 61), art 7; International Law Commission, Draft Articles on Responsibility of States for Internationally Wrongful Acts, with Commentaries, UN Doc A/56/10 (2001) 43. Article 8 separately provides that a state is also responsible for the conduct of a 'person or group of persons' if they are in fact acting under the direction or control of that state. The requisite level of 'control' is unclear, but, in any case, this seems less applicable to truly autonomous AI systems.

[64] See above section 8.2.1(a).

[65] See, eg, Peter Margulies, 'Sovereignty and Cyber Attacks: Technology's Challenge to the Law of State Responsibility' (2013) 14 Melbourne Journal of International Law 496; Florian J Egloff, 'Public Attribution of Cyber Intrusions' (2021) 6 Journal of Cybersecurity 1.

[66] See below section 8.2.2(b).

[67] See, eg, HLA Hart, *The Concept of Law* (3rd edn, Clarendon Press 2012) 213–37.

[68] Louis Henkin, *How Nations Behave: Law and Foreign Policy* (2nd edn, Columbia University Press 1979).

[69] See Simon Chesterman, 'An International Rule of Law?' (2008) 56 American Journal of Comparative Law 331.

This weakness of international law is a feature, not a bug. Stricter laws would have fewer adherents; more robust institutions fewer members. Nonetheless, mismanaged expectations lead to frustration when collective action problems manifest – as in the case of climate change or pandemics, for example, where international co-ordination and co-operation are entrusted to institutions lacking the power to impose either.[70]

8.2.2   An International Artificial Intelligence Agency?

Despite all these caveats, it remains the case that effective regulation of AI requires norms and institutions that operate at the global level. Various scholars and policymakers have recognized this, with the most common prescription being a multi-stakeholder model. Jacob Turner, for example, proposes an analogy with ICANN, the entity that maintains key infrastructure supporting the global Internet.[71] Its elaborate governance model includes representation from the public sector, the private sector, and technical experts. The intuitive appeal is understandable, given the overlap of subject matter and personnel with the AI industry. The actual functions of ICANN are confined to co-ordinating the Domain Name System and resolving disputes, however.[72] This is important, but the need for a global body to regulate AI goes beyond technical co-ordination.

In December 2018, Canada and France announced plans to establish an International Panel on AI, modelled on the Intergovernmental Panel on Climate Change (IPCC) established some 30 years earlier.[73] It was later renamed the Global Partnership on AI (GPAI) with a secretariat at the OECD in Paris.[74] The analogy with climate change acknowledges that AI poses a similar collective action problem for the global system. Yet the link with the OECD and the emphasis on human rights point less to concerns about efficient management than to a desire to exclude China –

---

[70] Sam Johnston, 'The Practice of UN Treaty-Making Concerning Science' in Simon Chesterman, David M Malone, and Santiago Villalpando (eds), *The Oxford Handbook of United Nations Treaties* (Oxford University Press 2019) 321 at 328–31.

[71] Jacob Turner, *Robot Rules: Regulating Artificial Intelligence* (Palgrave Macmillan 2019) 240–42. See also above n 26.

[72] Bylaws for Internet Corporation for Assigned Names and Numbers (ICANN, 1 October 2016) s 1.1.

[73] France and Canada Create New Expert International Panel on Artificial Intelligence (Gouvernement, 7 December 2018).

[74] Joint Statement from Founding Members of the Global Partnership on Artificial Intelligence (US State Department, 15 June 2020).

indeed, the United States had refused to join due to the potential impact on business but reversed course, citing the need to check China's approach to AI.[75] Experts will take part in working groups on themes including responsible AI, data governance, the future of work, and innovation and commercialization – worthy goals, but increasing the risk of a bifurcated Internet and an approach to AI that is the antithesis of a global response.

These and other examples recognize the need for action but also wariness about the practicality and desirability of seeking consensus among states. In theory, for example, the UN or the ITU could be entrusted with such a role. They might be helpful forums for norm-setting, but an operational role would inspire reactions comparable to when the ITU was proposed as a successor to ICANN to administer the Internet.[76]

International institution-building is an architecture of compromise.[77] Proposals to start with a less formal organization, laying foundations for more elaborate possibilities, reflect the practical challenges of finding common ground.[78] Yet these less ambitious or more political proposals lack both the normative teeth and the aspiration to universalism – the depth and breadth necessary to address the global challenge.

Here the IAEA offers a better model as an example of a regime that confronted a regulatory deficit directly – how to limit the proliferation of nuclear weapons – and embraced the politics of the situation openly: seeking buy-in from non-nuclear states by allowing access to technology while giving nuclear states assurances that their military advantage would not be lost (at least not until some unspecified point in the future).

As indicated earlier, the IAEA was created at a time of high – perhaps excessive – optimism concerning the potential for nuclear energy,

---

[75] Max Chafkin, 'US Will Join G-7 AI Pact, Citing Threat from China', *Bloomberg* (28 May 2020).

[76] See above n 42. In May 2020, the UN Secretary-General produced a report on digital co-operation, identifying key gaps as being a lack of inclusiveness, co-ordination, and capacity-building. Report of the Secretary-General on the Road Map for Digital Cooperation, UN Doc A/74/821 (2020), para 56.

[77] Timothy LH McCormack and Gerry J Simpson, 'A New International Criminal Law Regime?' (1995) 42 Netherlands International Law Review 177.

[78] See, eg, Olivia J Erdélyi and Judy Goldsmith, 'Regulating Artificial Intelligence: Proposal for a Global Solution' (2018) AAAI/ACM Conference on AI, Ethics, and Society (AIES'18) 95; Jiabao Wang et al, 'Artificial Intelligence and International Norms' in Donghan Jin (ed), *Reconstructing Our Orders: Artificial Intelligence and Human Society* (Springer 2018) 195.

tempered by fears of its weaponization. The Agency's stated objectives are to 'accelerate and enlarge the contribution of atomic energy to peace, health and prosperity throughout the world', while ensuring that this does not further any military purpose.[79] The first of these objectives was pursued through technology transfer, although dreams of electricity 'too cheap to meter' never materialized and more was achieved in medicine and agriculture than power generation.[80] The second objective eventually saw the signing of the Nuclear Non-Proliferation Treaty (NPT). That formalized the two-tier system of nuclear haves and have-nots, with the IAEA tasked with verifying that non-nuclear powers do not divert nuclear material to weapons programmes.[81] The nuclear powers, for their part, committed to 'pursue negotiations in good faith'[82] towards disarmament, but even its own history acknowledges that the IAEA was 'essentially irrelevant' to the nuclear arms race in the course of the Cold War.[83]

Broader standard-setting was, initially at least, an incidental role for the IAEA. Its Statute provides that it can establish 'standards of safety for protection of health and minimization of danger to life and property'.[84] Though the standards are not binding, in practice they are relied upon by states developing and implementing national legislation and standards for nuclear energy.[85] The 1986 Chernobyl disaster revealed major deficiencies in this arrangement. A review group recommended better exchanges of information, additional safety standards and guidelines, and enhancing the capacity to perform evaluations. Additional treaties were also concluded, hardening soft law into rules.[86]

---

[79] Statute of the International Atomic Energy Agency, done at New York, 23 October 1956, in force 29 July 1957, art II.

[80] Brown (n 5) 55–61.

[81] Treaty on the Non-Proliferation of Nuclear Weapons, done at Washington, London, and Moscow, 1 July 1968, in force 5 March 1970, art III.

[82] Ibid, art VI.

[83] David Fischer, *History of the International Atomic Energy Agency: The First Forty Years* (IAEA 1997) 10.

[84] IAEA Statute, art III(A)(6); Paul C Szasz, *The Law and Practices of the International Atomic Energy Agency* (International Atomic Energy Agency 1970).

[85] Philippe Sands and Jacqueline Peel, *Principles of Environmental Law* (4th edn, Cambridge University Press 2018) 595.

[86] Convention on Early Notification of a Nuclear Accident, done at Vienna, 26 September 1986, in force 27 October 1986; Convention on Assistance in the Case of a Nuclear Accident or Radiological Emergency, done at Vienna, 26 September 1986, in force 26 February 1987; Convention on Nuclear Safety, 17 June 1994, in force 24 October 1996; Joint Convention on the Safety of Spent Fuel Management and on the

A hypothetical IAIA could draw upon the experience of its nuclear counterpart in three ways: the bargain to encourage buy-in, the scope of its authority, and the structure of the organization itself.

(a) Bargain

First, an explicit bargain could bridge the medium-term interests of the most technologically advanced states – the United States and China, for example – and the shorter-term needs of others. The IAEA and the non-proliferation regime were negotiated at a time when the nuclear powers enjoyed a monopoly over nuclear energy's destructive power that they knew could not last. Those states with the most advanced lethal autonomous weapon systems today may come to see that a world in which such weapons are widely distributed would be deeply unstable; if or when advances towards general AI indicate the dangers of a superintelligence, hopes that the technology could be kept secret recall Fermi's warning that the Earth will not cease its motion around the Sun.

Though the link does not appear to have been made before now, the rhetoric of 'AI for Good', used by the ITU at its global AI conferences since 2017, has echoes of Eisenhower's 'Atoms for Peace' from 64 years earlier.[87] Where Eisenhower spoke of nuclear energy's potential to be a 'great boon, for the benefit of all mankind', the AI for Good summits emphasize that AI innovation will be central to the achievement of the UN Sustainable Development Goals.[88] Eisenhower's proposal, it should be noted, took time to be accepted by the Soviet Union and was denounced as 'insane' by US Senator Douglas McCarthy.[89] The creation and relative success of the IAEA were tied to the demand for international co-operation on peaceful nuclear technology and non-proliferation, as well as the clear and delimited role for the new organization.[90]

It is, of course, far from clear that similar conditions obtain today, at a time when the legitimacy of global public institutions has been called into question and the United States and China are, for distinct reasons, especially wary of constraint by external bodies.[91] How to manage the

---

Safety of Radioactive Waste Management, done at Vienna, 5 September 1997, in force 18 June 2001.

[87] See above n 5.

[88] See, eg, AI for Good Global Summit 2017 (ITU, 7–9 June 2017).

[89] 'McCarthy Scorches Plan of Giving Atom Materials', *The News-Review* (Roseburg, OR, 9 February 1957).

[90] Brown (n 5) 64–65.

[91] See Simon Chesterman, 'Can International Law Survive a Rising China?' (2021) 31 *European Journal of International Law* 1507.

privileges of the powerful without compromising the legitimacy of the
organization is one of the trickiest aspects of international institution-
building. Acceptance as a nuclear power stands alongside the veto power
in the UN Security Council as the most blatant concessions of special
privileges based on military might. There is no direct comparison in the
field of AI at this point, but an alternative analogy can be drawn with
pandemics. After the eventual eradication of smallpox in 1980, all known
stocks of the virus were destroyed – with two exceptions. The United
States and Russia kept small quantities of the virus: officially because
these were the two WHO reference laboratories with the highest security
storage facilities; unofficially in deference to the political realities of the
Cold War.[92]

(b) Authority

A second lesson from the IAEA is to have a clear and limited normative
agenda, with a graduated approach to enforcement. The main 'red line'
proposed here would be the weaponization of AI – understood narrowly
as the development of lethal autonomous weapon systems lacking 'meaningful human control' and more broadly as the development of AI
systems posing a real risk of being uncontrollable or uncontainable.[93]

On the narrower interpretation, it may be asked whether states would
ever willingly give up weapons that might provide a military advantage.
Yet, in addition to the limits on nuclear weapons, that is precisely what
states have done in respect of chemical and biological weapons, as well as
more recent limitations on blinding weapons.[94] Provided that it could be
imposed in a reciprocal manner, there is no reason why a ban on lethal
autonomous weapon systems should be unattainable. Indeed, much of
IHL consists of rules that constrain the methods that a state may use in

---

[92] Resolution WHA33.4 (World Health Assembly, 1980), recommendations 9 and 10;
Smallpox Eradication: Destruction of Variola Virus Stocks (World Health
Organization, A52/5, 15 April 1999).
[93] See chapter five, section 5.3. Cf Draft Report with Recommendations to the Commission
on a Civil liability regime for Artificial Intelligence (EU Parliament Committee on Legal
Affairs, 2020/2014(INL), 27 April 2020) (distinguishing between 'high-risk' and other
applications of AI).
[94] Convention on the Prohibition of the Development, Production and Stockpiling of
Bacteriological (Biological) and Toxin Weapons and on Their Destruction, done at
Washington, London, and Moscow, 10 April 1972, in force 26 March 1975; Convention
on the Prohibition of the Development, Production, Stockpiling, and Use of Chemical
Weapons and on Their Destruction, done at Paris, 13 January 1993, in force
29 April 1997. See chapter two, section 2.2.2.

armed conflict – accepted because it is known that similar constraints apply to one's potential opponents. Though it is a relatively recent addition, a central justification today is that such laws 'maintain some humanity in warfare'.[95]

The broader interpretation – linked with the question of superintelligence discussed in chapter five – is more open to debate. From chapter seven, there is widespread agreement that AI systems should remain under human control.[96] At present there does not appear to be an immediate danger that an uncontrollable AI in the sense of a sentient being will be created anytime soon.[97] There are, however, many examples of computer viruses that have gotten out of control.[98] The most realistic prospect here would be that states agree to the principle of control, with periodic reviews on progress towards general AI and an accompanying reconsideration of whether limitations on further research are required.[99]

Much as the IAEA developed safety standards over time, these could be an additional function of the proposed IAIA. Standards might draw upon the various principles discussed in chapter seven, but the priority should be human control and transparency. The control aspect applies to autonomous weapons and general AI discussed above. Transparency raises questions that distinct political systems will answer in their own way.[100] In terms of a red line at the international level, however, it would be to require that states prevent AI systems being deployed in a manner that cannot be traced back to a legal person identifiable as the owner, operator, or manufacturer.[101] The IEEE, for example, stresses the importance of traceability of errors, comparing it to the role of flight data recorders in the field of aviation.[102] The analogy is important with respect

---

[95] Robert Kolb, 'The Protection of the Individual in Times of War and Peace' in Bardo Fassbender and Anne Peters (eds), *The Oxford Handbook of the History of International Law* (Oxford University Press 2012) 317 at 321.

[96] See chapter seven, section 7.3.2.

[97] See chapter five, section 5.3.

[98] See, eg, Danny Palmer, 'MyDoom: The 15-Year-Old Malware That's Still Being Used in Phishing Attacks in 2019', *Wired* (26 July 2019).

[99] Cf Stephan Guttinger, 'Trust in Science: CRISPR-Cas9 and the Ban on Human Germline Editing' (2018) 24 Science Engineering Ethics 1077.

[100] See generally chapter six.

[101] This would include ships at sea (such as those mooted by Google more than a decade ago), which remain under the jurisdiction of a territorially bounded state. See Steven R Swanson, 'Google Sets Sail: Ocean-Based Server Farms and International Law' (2011) 43 Connecticut Law Review 709.

[102] Ethically Aligned Design (n 25) 137.

to analysing failures, but an even more important equivalent technology is the use of transponders to track aircraft and identify them in the first place.

Such a requirement would not be new to AI. As we saw in chapter one, the EU requires that high-frequency trading algorithms identify themselves;[103] there is also a growing recognition that AI systems should not pretend that they are human – or should be required to make clear that they are not.[104] Proposals to maintain a register of autonomous agents have been floated in the past, drawing upon existing practices such as maintaining a national register of companies.[105] Indeed, in September 2020, Helsinki and Amsterdam launched AI registers as 'a window' to the systems that the cities use.[106] This was laudable as a form of disclosure by public bodies, but, given the likely proliferation and pervasiveness of AI systems, registers are unworkable at scale as they would potentially require every computer program to be 'registered'. It might be possible to automate aspects of this, for example mediating transactions through a distributed-ledger regime.[107] AI systems could be required to identify themselves either actively, through notification, or passively, through including a digital signature in their code with a prohibition against removal.

No regime will be perfect or immune to gaming by sophisticated actors. It would need to be supplemented by a forensic capability to identify those responsible for 'rogue' AI systems. This would be a challenging – perhaps impossible – task.[108] But the IAIA could serve as a clearinghouse to gather and share information about such systems.

---

[103] See chapter one, section 1.2.

[104] See chapter seven, section 7.4.

[105] See, eg, Curtis EA Karnow, 'Liability for Distributed Artificial Intelligences' (1996) 11 Berkeley Technology Law Journal 147, 193–96; European Parliament Resolution with Recommendations to the Commission on Civil Law Rules on Robotics (2015/2103 (INL)) (European Parliament, 16 February 2017), paras 2, 59. Cf chapter five, section 5.1. Proposals to establish an IAEA database of nuclear materials were resisted by states due to concerns about compromising commercial information – or the possibility that they might be held responsible in the event that their materials were used in a terrorist incident. Brown (n 5) 162. Instead, states are encouraged to maintain their own national register of sources. Fischer (n 83) 204.

[106] Sarah Wray, 'Helsinki and Amsterdam Launch AI Registers to Detail City Systems', *ITU News Magazine* (30 September 2020).

[107] Cf Turner (n 71) 197–201; Kelvin Low and Eliza Mik, 'Pause the Blockchain Legal Revolution' (2020) 69 International and Comparative Law Quarterly 135.

[108] Cf Edwin Dauber et al, 'Git Blame Who? Stylistic Authorship Attribution of Small, Incomplete Source Code Fragments' (2017) 1701.05681v3 arXiv.

Again, a parallel can be found in the IAEA, which established an illicit
trafficking database in 1995 to facilitate tracing of nuclear material 'out of
regulatory control'.[109]

A final role of the IAIA could be in response to emergencies. Though
states would remain the primary actors, it could serve as a focal point for
notification of emergencies threatening transboundary harm and for co-
ordination of a response. There should be no illusion that a state will be
forthcoming in raising the alarm about an uncontrollable or uncontainable AI, particularly if there is a chance that it will not be identified as the
source. Indeed, this was Russia's initial response to the Chernobyl
nuclear disaster in 1986. States subsequently adopted a treaty obliging
parties to notify the IAEA or affected states of any accident within their
jurisdiction or control in which release of radioactive material is likely
and may be of 'radiological safety significance'.[110] If similar obligations
are not accepted by states before the first true AI emergency, they would
likely be adopted soon after it.

(c)   Structure

A third learning point from the IAEA is the mundane yet important
question of structure. Most international organizations are weak by
design, with governance powers held closely by member states while
management is carried out by a secretariat. The UN is the clearest
example of this, headed by a Secretary-General whose position in the
organization's founding document is styled as its 'Chief Administrative
Officer'.[111] The UN Security Council, for its part, is an outlier – a body
with real teeth in the form of enforcement powers ranging from economic sanctions to the use of military force. The Council's remit is
limited to threats to international peace and security, however, and its
powers are firmly under the control of member states. An AI emergency
could rise to the level that it justifies Security Council action. Even then,
the Council has in the past relied on expert agencies. In the context of

---

[109] IAEA Incident and Trafficking Database (ITDB) (IAEA, 2020); Klaus Mayer,
Maria Wallenius, and Ian Ray, 'Tracing the Origin of Diverted or Stolen Nuclear
Material through Nuclear Forensic Investigations' in Rudolf Avenhaus et al (eds),
*Verifying Treaty Compliance: Limiting Weapons of Mass Destruction and Monitoring
Kyoto Protocol Provisions* (Springer 2006) 389 at 402.

[110] Convention on Early Notification of a Nuclear Accident, arts 1, 2. See also IAEA
Response and Assistance Network (IAEA, 2018).

[111] Charter of the United Nations, done at San Francisco, 26 June 1945, in force
24 October 1945, art 97. See Simon Chesterman (ed), *Secretary or General? The UN
Secretary-General in World Politics* (Cambridge University Press 2007).

counter-proliferation, for example, the Council has drawn on IAEA expertise and resources in relation to North Korea, Iraq, and Iran.

Unusually among intergovernmental organizations, it is the Board of Governors of the IAEA, a subset of member states that meets five times a year – not the General Conference of all members that gathers annually – that has ongoing oversight of its operations, appoints its executive head, and evaluates compliance with its Statute.[112] This has allowed the IAEA to function more effectively, but it demands more of the men and women sent as national representatives. Indeed, its history reflects a shift from heads of nuclear agencies in the early years, evangelizing nuclear power, to diplomats more concerned with non-proliferation and budgets.[113]

In the case of a notional IAIA, positioning it as an expert body with additional mechanisms to involve industry, academia, and activists would enhance its legitimacy and relevance. Yet, to have 'teeth', it would need to be grounded in the public authority of states.

8.3   State Responsibility

Tasked with promoting the safe, secure, and peaceful use of nuclear technology, the IAEA is, in the scheme of things, small. With a budget of US$700m and around 2,500 staff, it is comparable in size to the local government of a small town and less than a quarter of the size of Tokyo's Fire Department. Lacking its own enforcement powers, it has relied *in extremis* on the UN Security Council. But compliance – as with most of international law – depends on the behaviour and attitudes of its member states.

This book has argued that existing state institutions and norms are capable of regulating most applications of AI. Legislatures, executives, and judiciaries within virtually all states can adapt to fast, autonomous, and opaque AI systems. The effectiveness of those adaptations is tied to the unique legitimacy of public institutions at the state level, which requires that these powers be exercised by officials that are publicly accountable – and not themselves outsourced to machines.[114] This section will briefly discuss the roles and the limits of the different branches

---

[112] Brown (n 5) 55. Cf Simon Chesterman, 'Executive Heads' in Jacob Katz Cogan, Ian Hurd, and Ian Johnstone (eds), *The Oxford Handbook of International Organizations* (Oxford University Press 2016) 822 at 824.

[113] Fischer (n 83) 425.

[114] See chapter four, section 4.3.

of government. To identify and fill gaps in the regulatory ecosystem, an independent agency or official with a wide mandate would be an important addition. The example proffered here is an AI ombudsperson.

8.3.1 Legislature

Though legislatures around the world have been wary of over-regulating AI systems, they are being forced to enact or amend laws to address anachronisms like presuming that all vehicles have a 'driver'.[115] In addition to ensuring that laws are not skirted because of the speed, autonomy, and opacity of AI systems, additional new laws may be required to ensure human control and transparency.[116]

Legislatures have the advantage of democratic legitimacy, with many jurisdictions favouring them as the body to take decisions on fundamental social policies or involving choices between contested values. Decisions are made by men and women chosen as political representatives rather than subject matter experts, but they have the force of law and are of general application. Because of this, legislatures may be slow to deliberate and their edicts hard to undo. As discussed in chapter seven, this poses a dilemma for states uncertain about the risks associated with new technology, but also wary of unnecessarily constraining innovation. When there is consensus on the need for clear rules and strong enforcement, legislation is the most legitimate and effective path. Until that time, states may prefer 'masterly inactivity'.[117]

8.3.2 Executive

Implementation of laws falls to the executive. Agencies tasked with this may develop subject matter expertise and be more flexible in their approach to regulation. In terms of expertise, however, the public sector struggles to keep up with the private sector. As we saw in chapter one, this is true in both securities regulation and competition or antitrust law, as well as technology regulation more generally.[118] Flexibility and the ability to react quickly raise accountability questions the further that agencies

---

[115] See chapter two, section 2.1.
[116] See chapter six, section 6.3, and chapter seven, section 7.3. It may also be necessary to legislate for the protection of 'social robots' against abuse. See chapter seven, section 7.3.2.
[117] See chapter seven, section 7.2.
[118] See chapter one, sections 1.2 and 1.3.

get from democratic legitimacy. The problem may manifest in over- or under-zealous regulation, along with the possibility of capture. These concerns can be mitigated through monitoring and review strategies.[119]

Around the world, licensing bodies, product safety regulators, securities regulators, transportation authorities, police forces, national security agencies, and data protection authorities will be at the front line of whether and how to regulate AI systems. Where laws are framed widely or vaguely, significant discretion devolves to these entities. Their ability to act in advance of problems, to publish guidance material, to engage proactively with developers and manufacturers as well as consumers, distinguishes them from other arms of government. When they fail to act, uncertainty may impose its own costs if companies shy away from risky behaviour or if those risks are pushed onto consumers.[120]

8.3.3 Judiciary

Where harm results or disputes arise, courts may be asked to step in.[121] The strength and the weakness of judicial law-making is its responsiveness to changing circumstances. This enables judges to exercise a modicum of creativity in interpreting the law or applying precedent, but it also means that they are beholden to the cases that come before them. In most jurisdictions, courts are unable to opine on hypothetical situations; when they do so in the common law tradition, their observations are *obiter dicta* – things said in passing that do not bind other tribunals. The *ex post* role of courts may also be a long time *post*: appellate proceedings can take years, meaning that a final determination is made only after the technology in question is obsolete.[122]

'Hard cases make bad law', as Oliver Wendell Holmes, Jr, famously warned a century ago. Yet the context from which the cliché is typically lifted adds nuance to this observation. Because hard cases are frequently great ones:

> Great cases like hard cases make bad law. For great cases are called great, not by reason of their real importance in shaping the law of the future, but because of some accident of immediate overwhelming interest which

[119] Robert Baldwin, Martin Cave, and Martin Lodge, *Understanding Regulation: Theory, Strategy, and Practice* (2nd edn, Oxford University Press 2011) 343–44. See also section 8.1.2.
[120] Nathan Cortez, 'Regulating Disruptive Innovation' (2014) 29 Berkeley Technology Law Journal 175, 203–4. See also chapter seven, section 7.2.
[121] See chapter seven, section 7.2.2.
[122] Mark R Patterson, *Antitrust Law in the New Economy* (Harvard University Press 2017).

appeals to the feelings and distorts the judgment. These immediate interests exercise a kind of hydraulic pressure which makes what previously
was clear seem doubtful, and before which even well settled principles of
law will bend.[123]

Will AI exert 'hydraulic pressure' on settled norms? Again, courts have –
for the most part – been able to adapt. In the absence of new forms of
legal personality,[124] and presuming that conduct by AI systems can be
attributed to traditional legal persons[125] and that evidentiary burdens can
be met,[126] the problems of speed, autonomy, and opacity pose difficult
but not insurmountable challenges.

For the most part. On the margins, as we have also seen, AI systems
create risks or enable conduct that does not fall neatly into existing
categories. Though enterprising judges will endeavour to apply laws
sensibly, even as agencies and legislatures strive to ensure the relevance
of those laws and their implementation, it would be prudent to add an
entity tasked precisely with the function of identifying and addressing
those gaps as they arise.

8.3.4 An AI Ombudsperson?

Though various jurisdictions have long had comparable officials, the
term ombudsperson (or ombudsman) has Scandinavian roots. In general, it refers to an individual appointed by the state to represent the
interests of the public. He or she typically enjoys some measure of
independence and flexibility in his or her mandate, which is sometimes
cast as upholding administrative justice, human rights, or the rule of law
itself. In addition to responding to complaints, that mandate may extend
to representing the public interest with respect to systemic issues.[127]

Powers of enforcement may be limited – classically, an ombudsperson
was limited to 'soft' powers of investigation, recommendation, and
reporting. Despite these limitations, ombudsperson institutions were

---

[123] *Northern Securities Company v United States*, 193 US 197, 400–1 (1904).
[124] See chapter five.
[125] See chapter four.
[126] See chapter six.
[127] See Varda Bondy and Margaret Doyle, 'What's in a Name? A Discussion Paper on
Ombud Terminology' in Marc Hertogh and Richard Kirkham (eds), *Research Handbook
on the Ombudsman* (Edward Elgar 2018) 485; Richard Kirkham and Chris Gill (eds),
A Manifesto for Ombudsman Reform (Palgrave Macmillan 2020). Cf Lord Sales,
'Algorithms, Artificial Intelligence, and the Law' (2020) 25 Judicial Review 46, 54–57
(proposing an expert algorithm commission).

embraced as a tool to address diverse accountability problems in the latter half of the twentieth century as 'ombudsmania' took hold. In the 1980s this overlapped with human rights discourses; from the mid-1990s it was linked to global governance. Today, the International Ombudsman Institute boasts member institutions in more than 120 countries.[128]

Though many such offices have mandates that cut across the public sector or beyond, dedicated ombudsperson institutions have proven useful in other areas where traditional regulation is inadequate. In relation to national security concerns, for example, the ability to address complaints with a degree of informality has on occasion been more effective than judicial processes.[129]

In some countries the term commissioner, inspector-general, or people's advocate may be preferred. The precise name is less important than the office's independence, mandate, powers, and resources. Independence from government and industry is essential if it is to be taken seriously. In addition to avoiding regulatory capture, this should assist in being able to cut across administrative silos. The mandate should be framed broadly as identifying and addressing harms and injustice caused by AI that cannot be prevented or resolved through existing norms and institutions. This should include the ability to initiate inquiries as well as to respond to complaints. As highlighted in chapter six, limiting transparency to explainability puts an undue onus on individuals to *know* that they have been harmed and initiate an inquiry themselves.[130]

To be effective, the ombudsperson needs to be able to require cooperation and have access to relevant documents, including those that would otherwise be privileged. Though proceedings can be confidential, it is vital that there be an option to make the outcome public. Reports should not be limited to resolving disputes but should include the ability to make wider recommendations to change practices, policies, and legislation. Those recommendations need not be binding, but best practice is

---

[128] Charles S Ascher, 'The Grievance Man or Ombudsmania' (1967) 27 Public Administration Review 174; Chris Gill, 'The Evolving Role of the Ombudsman: A Conceptual and Constitutional Analysis of the "Scottish Solution" to Administrative Justice' [2014] Public Law 662; Tero Erkkilä, *Ombudsman as a Global Institution: Transnational Governance and Accountability* (Palgrave Macmillan 2020).

[129] Simon Chesterman, *One Nation under Surveillance: A New Social Contract to Defend Freedom without Sacrificing Liberty* (Oxford University Press 2011) 218.

[130] Cf Lilian Edwards and Michael Veale, 'Slave to the Algorithm? Why a "Right to an Explanation" Is Probably Not the Remedy You Are Looking For' (2017) 16 Duke Law & Technology Review 18, 83–84.

for the legislature or other receiving body to be required to give reasons for not accepting them.[131]

Much of the work of an AI ombudsperson might be redirecting cases to appropriate government agencies or the relevant part of the legal system. Yet the role should go beyond ensuring legality and compliance: the value of an ombudsperson is in promoting human rights and good administration.[132] In the EU, data protection authorities fulfil some of these functions.[133] They might also be taken on by existing ombudsperson institutions. Indeed, in March 2020 the International Ombudsman Institute organized a workshop with Catalan's Ombudsman on the role of ombudsperson institutions in protecting and upholding human rights in a world of AI.[134] Given the steep learning curve and the likely expansion of the impact of AI, however, a dedicated office – either stand-alone or as part of a larger entity – would give the issue the proper attention and prevent wheels being constantly reinvented.

8.4   The Prospects for Institutions

One consequence of Eisenhower's 'Atoms for Peace' speech was the biggest scientific conference the world had ever seen. Proposed by the United States and convened by the General Assembly in 1955, the First International Conference on the Peaceful Uses of Atomic Energy, later known as the First Geneva Conference, brought together some 1,500 delegates from 38 countries, with over 1,000 papers presented. The Second Geneva Conference, held in 1958, was nearly twice as large. It was a period of euphoria and optimism, with many states establishing nuclear research and development programmes even as the IAEA Statute was being drafted and ratified.[135]

The limitations of an analogy between nuclear energy and AI are obvious. Nuclear energy refers to a well-defined set of processes related to specific materials that are unevenly distributed; AI is an amorphous

[131] Developing and Reforming Ombudsman Institutions (International Ombudsman Institute, June 2017).
[132] P Nikiforos Diamandouros, 'From Maladministration to Good Administration: Retrospective Reflections on a Ten-Year Journey' in Herwig CH Hofmann and Jacques Ziller (eds), Accountability in the EU: The Role of the European Ombudsman (Edward Elgar 2017) 217.
[133] General Data Protection Regulation 2016/679 (GDPR) 2016 (EU), art 57.
[134] Ombudsmen Alert about Artificial Intelligence and Human Rights (International Ombudsman Institute, 11 March 2020).
[135] Robert A Charpie, 'The Geneva Conference' (1955) 193(4) Scientific American 27; Fischer (n 83) 31.

term and its applications are extremely wide. The IAEA's grand bargain focused on weapons that are expensive to build and difficult to hide; weaponization of AI promises to be neither.

Nonetheless, some kind of mechanism at the global level is essential if regulation of AI is going to be effective. This chapter has argued that industry standards will be important for managing risk and that states will be a vital part of enforcement, with gaps to be plugged by an AI ombudsperson or equivalent institution at the national level. In an interconnected world, however, regulation premised on the sovereignty of territorially bound states is not fit for purpose. The hypothetical IAIA offered here is one way of addressing that structural problem.

Yet the biggest difference between attempts to control nuclear power in the 1950s and AI today is that when Eisenhower addressed the UN, the effects of the nuclear blasts on Hiroshima and Nagasaki were still being felt.[136] The 'dread secret' of those weapons, he warned, was no longer confined to the United States. The Soviet Union had tested its own devices and the knowledge was likely to be shared by others – perhaps all others. Doing nothing was to accept the hopeless finality that 'two atomic colossi are doomed malevolently to eye each other indefinitely across a trembling world'.[137]

There is no such threat from AI at present and certainly no comparably visceral evidence of its destructive power. Absent that threat, getting agreement on meaningful regulation of AI at the global level will be difficult. One reason why the UN Security Council enjoys powers that its predecessor in the League of Nations lacked is that the member states negotiated the UN Charter while the bombs of the Second World War were still falling. The final document was crafted in aspirational but knowing language, promising to save succeeding generations from 'the scourge of war, which twice in our lifetime has brought untold sorrow to mankind'.[138]

It is possible, as the next chapter discusses, that AI itself will help solve the problems raised here. If it does not, global institutions that might have prevented the first true AI emergency will need to be created in a hurry if they are to prevent the second.

---

[136] Lesley MM Blume, *Fallout: The Hiroshima Cover-Up and the Reporter Who Revealed It to the World* (Scribe 2020).
[137] Atoms for Peace (n 5).
[138] UN Charter, preamble.

9

Regulation *by* AI?

The judge's robes are a deep black, though subtle touches of colour complement the national emblem dominating the courtroom wall. Red symbolizes revolution; golden stars rising over the Tiananmen Gate signify the unity of the people under the Party's leadership. Until the turn of the century, judicial officers wore military uniforms – the Supreme People's Court sits at the apex of the legal system but below the Communist Party. By appearance, this judge would not have even been in law school back then. Appearances can be deceiving, of course, since her generic face and simple hairstyle were designed by computer scientists. The avatar's lips move as the synthesized voice asks in Mandarin, 'Does the defendant have any objection to the nature of the judicial blockchain evidence submitted by the plaintiff?'

'No objection,' the human defendant responds.

The video of the pre-trial meeting at Hangzhou's Internet Court, released in late 2019, is part propaganda, part evangelism. Courts were identified as one of the areas ripe for improvement in China's New Generation Artificial Intelligence Development Plan. In a section on social governance [社会治理], it called for the creation of 'smart courts' [智慧法庭].[1] This builds on moves to digitize and standardize litigation across the country, with experiments like those in Hangzhou paving the way for further advances. The avatar can handle online trade disputes, copyright cases, and e-commerce product liability claims.[2] Hangzhou was chosen because it is the home of Alibaba, enabling integration with

---

[1] 国务院关于印发新一代人工智能发展规划的通知 [State Council Issued Notice of the New Generation Artificial Intelligence Development Plan] (State Council, Guofa [2017] No 35, 20 July 2017).

[2] 最高人民法院关于互联网法院审理案件若干问题的规定 [The Provisions of the Supreme People's Court on Several Issues Concerning the Trial of Cases by Internet Courts] (Supreme People's Court, Fasi [2018] No 16, 6 September 2018); Chuanman You, 'Law and Policy of Platform Economy in China' (2020) 39 Computer Law & Security Review 1.

trading platforms like Taobao for the purpose of evidence gathering as well as 'technical support'.[3]

Online dispute resolution is not new; eBay has long used it to help parties settle tens of millions of disputes annually.[4] What is interesting in the Chinese context is the extent to which technology is permeating the court hierarchy not just in mediating small claims but all the way up to the Supreme People's Court itself.

The Judicial Accountability System [司法责任制] began as a campaign to promote consistency in judgments.[5] Past efforts had relied on reviews by superiors, but this was deemed impractical and undermined the authority of the judge who heard the case.[6] AI systems now push similar cases up to a judge prior to a decision, flagging an 'abnormal judgment warning' if a proposed outcome departs significantly from past data.[7] This is part of a suite of technologies that have been adopted, influenced by both the supply of technology companies in China and the demands of a complex and developing legal system. The Wujiang District of Suzhou has trialled a 'one-click' summary judgment process, automatically generating proposed grounds of decision complete with sentence.[8] Other courts are following suit.[9]

Singapore's Chief Justice has said that developments in China are making 'machine-assisted court adjudication a reality'. At the same time, he noted, the use of AI within the justice system gives rise to

---

[3] Du Guodong and Yu Meng, 'A Close Look at Hangzhou Internet Court', *China Justice Observer* (3 November 2019).

[4] Pablo Cortés, *The Law of Consumer Redress in an Evolving Digital Market: Upgrading from Alternative to Online Dispute Resolution* (Cambridge University Press 2017) 8; Ethan Katsh and Orna Rabinovich-Einy, Digital Justice: *Technology and the Internet of Disputes* (Oxford University Press 2017).

[5] 最高人民法院关于统一法律适用加强类案检索的指导意见（试行）[Guiding Opinions of the Supreme People's Court on Unifying the Application of Laws to Strengthen the Retrieval of Similar Cases (for Trial Implementation)] (Supreme People's Court, Fafa [2020] No 24, 27 July 2020).

[6] Cf Margaret YK Woo, 'Court Reform with Chinese Characteristics' (2017) 27 Washington International Law Journal 241; Junfeng Li et al, 'Artificial Intelligence Governed by Laws and Regulations' in Donghan Jin (ed), *Reconstructing Our Orders: Artificial Intelligence and Human Society* (Springer 2018) 61 at 67–71.

[7] Yu Meng and Du Guodong, 'Why Are Chinese Courts Turning to AI?', *The Diplomat* (19 January 2019).

[8] '苏州法院刑案简易判决一键生成 [One-click Generation of the Summary Judgment of the Criminal Case in Suzhou Court]', 法制日报 [*Legal Daily*] (19 June 2017).

[9] 中国法院的互联网司法 [Chinese Courts and Internet Justice] (Supreme People's Court of the People's Republic of China, 2019) 63–65; Yadong Cui, *Artificial Intelligence and Judicial Modernization* (Springer 2020).

a 'unique set of ethical concerns, including those relating to credibility, transparency and accountability'.[10] To this one might add considerations of equity, since the drive towards greater automation is dominated by deep-pocketed clients and ever-closer ties to technology companies, with uncertain consequences for the future administration of justice.[11]

The impact of AI on the practice of law goes well beyond the scope of this book.[12] This chapter considers the narrower question of whether and how AI systems themselves could support regulation of AI. Insofar as gaps are revealed by the rise of fast, autonomous, and opaque systems, do new rules and new institutions need to be supplemented by new actors in the form of AI regulators and judges?

The first section briefly sketches out past efforts to automate the law. Though AI judges are the most provocative example,[13] many areas of legal practice and regulation have long been seen as ripe for automation. Despite successes in simple and repetitive tasks, these efforts tended to founder because they were premised on a misconception of law as the mere application of clear rules to agreed facts. In practice, the rules are rarely so clear, and disagreement over facts explains a significant portion of legal disputes.

A more promising approach has been to abandon the goal of thinking 'like a lawyer' and approach legal analysis not as the application of rules to facts but as data. The second section discusses this bottom-up approach to legal analytics, which reveals distinct limitations that are not technical so much as social and political. Even though AI systems are getting ever better at forecasting regulatory outcomes, embracing this across the legal system would represent a fundamental shift from making decisions to predicting them.

Even if regulation by AI generally were possible, then, it is not desirable. Can a special case be made, however, for the regulation of AI systems themselves? If the objection to AI regulators and judges is their inability to appreciate the social context within which legal determinations take place, or legitimacy questions about humans having their fate

---

[10] Sundaresh Menon, 'Opening of the Legal Year' (Supreme Court, Singapore, 7 January 2019).

[11] Seth Katsuya Endo, 'Technological Opacity & Procedural Injustice' (2018) 59 Boston College Law Review 821.

[12] See references cited in the introduction to this book at n 7.

[13] See, eg, Tania Sourdin, 'Judge v Robot? Artificial Intelligence and Judicial Decision-Making' (2018) 41 UNSW Law Journal 1114; Eugene Volokh, 'Chief Justice Robots' (2019) 68 Duke Law Journal 1135.

determined by statistics, one response is that this need not apply to regulation of AI. The third section discusses how systems could be made to be self-policing. As we have seen, for example, one of the virtues of AI is relative transparency in that simulations can be run with slight variations to look for bias. And, unlike humans, a machine is far more likely to admit to its errors.[14]

To the extent that they increase the transparency and human control of AI systems, these developments may be useful. But self-regulation by AI ultimately confronts similar limitations to self-regulation by industry. Though helpful in establishing standards and best practices, red lines will need to be drawn and ultimate oversight conducted by politically legitimate and accountable actors. And, if it is impermissible to outsource inherently governmental functions to fast, autonomous, and opaque machines, enforcement of that prohibition cannot itself be left to those same machines.

9.1   Automating the Law

In the literature on AI and the law, an early theme was that legal practice – viewed essentially as the logical application of rules to established facts – was a strong candidate for automation. Though initially confined to theory,[15] in the 1980s researchers developed prototype systems based on manually created representations of rules in machine-readable form.[16] The enthusiasm was characteristic of the time, preceding as it did one of the 'AI winters' that has periodically seen inflated expectations crash against reality.[17]

Subsequent decades did see transformations in legal research and document management. These increased lawyers' access to information and their efficiency in using and sharing it, but did not fundamentally alter their role. Even those encouraging the adoption of technology believed that the inability of AI to emulate human qualities limited its scope for taking on the higher functions of lawyers – the role of judges in particular.[18] As we have

---

[14] See chapter three, section 3.2.2.
[15] See, eg, L Thorne McCarty, 'Reflections on TAXMAN: An Experiment in Artificial Intelligence and Legal Reasoning' (1977) 90 Harvard Law Review 837.
[16] See, eg, MJ Sergot et al, 'The British Nationality Act as a Logic Program' (1986) 29 Communications of the ACM 370.
[17] Anja Oskamp and Marc Lauritsen, 'AI in Law Practice? So Far, Not Much' (2002) 10 Artificial Intelligence and Law 227.
[18] Richard Susskind, 'Detmold's Refutation of Positivism and the Computer Judge' (1986) 49 Modern Law Review 125.

seen in other areas, however, emulating human methods may not be the right or the best approach for reaping the benefits of AI. Autonomous vehicles, to pick an obvious case, are not driven by humanoid robots controlling speed and direction with mechanical hands and feet in substitution of their absent 'drivers'.

The DoNotPay chatbot, launched in 2015, offered an indication of what might be possible. Written by a seventeen-year-old Stanford student, it followed a series of rules to appeal against parking fines. Similar technology now facilitates other simple tasks from the making of wills to reporting suspected discrimination, yielding efficiencies as well as offering greater access to basic legal services for the wider public.[19] It is also leading to a re-evaluation of what the practice of law means, in the sense of a regulated profession. If a practising certificate or membership of a bar is required to offer legal advice, at what point does an automated system cross that line? Rules-based chatbots do not seem problematic, analogous to a textbook with a flowchart indicating how the law may handle various hypothetical situations. But if an AI system takes in new information, analyses it, and recommends a course of action in a manner that goes beyond the expertise of the programmer, does that become legal advice? Should it be regulated in the same manner as a lawyer?[20]

These are some of the questions raised by legal tech, a growing area of legal practice.[21] Having a lawyer sign off on advice is the current solution, much as a partner in a firm might approve a memo drafted in significant part by an intern.[22] That was the approach accompanying another high-profile example

---

[19] Paul Gowder, 'Transformative Legal Technology and the Rule of Law' (2018) 68 \(Supplement 1) University of Toronto Law Journal 82; Frank Pasquale, 'A Rule of Persons, Not Machines: The Limits of Legal Automation' (2019) 87 George Washington Law Review 1, 7–17. It is a stretch, however, to call this automation of certain legal processes 'AI' in any meaningful sense.

[20] In October 2019, for example, the Hanseatic Bar Association Hamburg successfully challenged Smartlaw, a bot operated by Wolters Kluwer, in the district court of Cologne for operating inconsistently with Germany's Legal Services Act [*Rechtsdienstleistungsgesetz*]. See further Michael Stockdale and Rebecca Mitchell, 'Legal Advice Privilege and Artificial Legal Intelligence: Can Robots Give Privileged Legal Advice?' (2019) 23 International Journal of Evidence & Proof 422; Polly Botsford, Future of Law: Courts Debate Legality of Legal 'Bots' (International Bar Association, 11 March 2020).

[21] Sanda Erdelez and Sheila O'Hare, 'Legal Informatics: Application of Information Technology in Law' (1997) 32 Annual Review of Information Science and Technology 367; Jens Frankenreiter and Michael A Livermore, 'Computational Methods in Legal Analysis' (2020) 16 Annual Review of Law and Social Science 39.

[22] See, eg, Model Rules of Professional Conduct (American Bar Association, 2020), rule 5.3 (responsibilities regarding non-lawyer assistance – though the language of the rule clearly

of technology making inroads into the legal profession, when white-shoe law firm Baker & Hostetler announced that IBM's Ross was joining its bankruptcy practice.[23] Though routinely referred to as a 'robot lawyer', Ross was neither: it was a subscription service lacking any physical form (certainly not a humanoid one), and it did not provide legal advice as such. It was, however, adept at sifting through vast numbers of documents for relevant information in support of the firm's cases.[24]

Many lawyers long assumed that litigation would be the last part of legal practice to be automated, though the example of China from the introduction to this chapter points to inroads being made there, also. Online dispute settlement has a long history and, for smaller claims in particular, has been embraced not only by online traders like eBay and PayPal but also in the legal systems of Canada and Britain.[25]

And yet the tsunami of change long forecast by Richard Susskind and others has not (yet) occurred.[26]

In part this is due to institutional resistance. Lawyers have defended their domain against encroachment by accounting firms and other actors; some view computers as just the next horde to be repelled.[27] As a profession, lawyers are also notoriously conservative. Though transactional lawyering must accommodate the needs of business, courtroom procedures retain elements both byzantine and archaic. The Covid-19

assumes that such assistance comes from a 'person'). Cf Ed Walters, 'The Model Rules of Autonomous Conduct: Ethical Responsibilities of Lawyers and Artificial Intelligence' (2019) 35 Georgia State University Law Review 1073; Anthony E Davis, 'The Future of Law Firms (and Lawyers) in the Age of Artificial Intelligence' (2020) 27(1) The Professional Lawyer 3.

[23] Michal Addady, 'Meet Ross, the World's First Robot Lawyer', *Forbes* (12 May 2016).

[24] See, eg, Dena Dervanović, 'I, Inhuman Lawyer: Developing Artificial Intelligence in the Legal Profession' in Marcelo Corrales, Mark Fenwick, and Nikolaus Forgó (eds), *Robotics, AI and the Future of Law* (Springer 2018) 209 at 226–27; Sergio Alberto Gramitto Ricci, 'Artificial Agents in Corporate Boardrooms' (2020) 105 Cornell Law Review 869, 876. Ross Intelligence announced in December 2020 that it was shutting down operations – defeated not by the limitations of its programming or the open-textured nature of law but by a lawsuit from competitors. Rhys Dipshan, 'ROSS Shuts Down Operations, Citing Financial Burden from Thomson Reuters Lawsuit', *Law.com* (11 December 2020).

[25] Richard Susskind, *Online Courts and the Future of Justice* (Oxford University Press 2019).

[26] See, eg, Richard Susskind, *The Future of Law: Facing the Challenges of Information Technology* (Oxford University Press 1996); Richard Susskind, *The End of Lawyers? Rethinking the Nature of Legal Services* (Oxford University Press 2008).

[27] Chay Brooks, Cristian Gherhes, and Tim Vorley, 'Artificial Intelligence in the Legal Sector: Pressures and Challenges of Transformation' (2020) 13 Cambridge Journal of Regions, Economy, and Society 135, 148.

pandemic of 2020 forced a reassessment of information technology in law firms and the courtroom.[28] Much as classes at schools and universities utilized video-conferencing services like Zoom, however, this was a change of medium rather than a transformation of the way in which law is practised.

A second reason why the legal profession has resisted radical change, and may continue to do so, is less self-serving. For it turns out that neither of the assumptions underpinning the hopes for widespread automation – that law is a contained logical system and that facts can be unambiguously established – withstands scrutiny.

9.1.1   The Inner Illogic of the Law

A preliminary problem is that legal rules are typically expressed in natural language that may be difficult for a computer to parse. This is a familiar issue in linguistics: humans often interpret language consistently but not logically. Imagine an instruction to go shopping, for example, with the following request: 'Please buy me a newspaper; and if the store has bananas, buy six.' A naïve and literal interpretation could lead an autonomous agent to return with six copies of the newspaper. Similarly, the difference between saying that 'I hunted the bear with my wife' and 'I hunted the bear with my knife' is immediately clear to a human but requires additional information outside the text to make sense.[29] Sometimes language may be inherently ambiguous. The statement that 'I saw the girl with the telescope' might mean either that the speaker looked through a telescope or that the girl was carrying one.

Advances in natural language processing have overcome many of these difficulties, though statutes and case law may be more challenging than the average text.[30] Indeed, the profession of law depends on the ability to

---

[28] Julie Marie Baldwin, John M Eassey, and Erika J Brooke, 'Court Operations During the COVID-19 Pandemic' (2020) 45 American Journal of Criminal Justice 743. Cf Daphne Yong, 'The Courtroom Performance' (1985) 10(3) The Cambridge Journal of Anthropology 74.

[29] Ian McEwan, *Machines Like Me* (Vintage 2019) 178.

[30] See, eg, Livio Robaldo et al, 'Introduction for Artificial Intelligence and Law: Special Issue "Natural Language Processing for Legal Texts"' (2019) 27 Artificial Intelligence and Law 113; Loïc Vial, Benjamin Lecouteux, and Didier Schwab, 'Sense Vocabulary Compression through the Semantic Knowledge of WordNet for Neural Word Sense Disambiguation' (2019) arXiv 1905.05677v3; Boon Peng Yap, Andrew Koh, and Eng Siong Chng, 'Adapting BERT for Word Sense Disambiguation with Gloss Selection Objective and Example Sentences' (2020) arXiv 2009.11795v2; Zakaria Kaddari et al, 'Natural Language Processing: Challenges and Future

charge clients for advice as to how to structure their activities to comply with the law, and advocating on their behalf to enforce it in support of their interests. There may be multiple plausible constructions of a given text – even a carefully drafted one. And until statutes and judgments are written in a manner that can be represented using formal logic, the authoritative text is the original one.[31]

This points to a more fundamental problem, which is that many laws are not reducible to logical representation.[32] To be sure, some may be. Road traffic laws, for example, state that exceeding a given speed limit constitutes an offence. Many jurisdictions use speed cameras that automatically record infringements and issue fines. Yet it is telling that these laws – among the most commonly experienced, for much of the population – rarely feature in law school curricula, precisely because they are so clear.[33]

Others are not. The tort of negligence, considered in chapter four, is not representable as duty of care plus breach plus causation minus defences equals liability. It explicitly incorporates judgments based on human experience – the famous 'man on the Clapham omnibus'[34] – and notions of reasonableness. In other areas of law, terms such as 'good faith' or 'unconscionability' are notoriously difficult to define in terms that would be useful to a machine.[35] Pretending otherwise is to delegate the interpretive task from the judge not to the machine but to the program-mer who establishes its parameters.[36] More formally, it is sometimes argued that efforts to treat the law as a logical system susceptible to automation will fail due to the necessary incompleteness of that system – and all such systems.[37]

Directions' in Tawfik Masrour, Ibtissam El Hassani, and Anass Cherrafi (eds), *Artificial Intelligence and Industrial Applications* (Springer 2021) 236.

[31] L Karl Branting, 'Artificial Intelligence and the Law from a Research Perspective' (2018) 14(3) Scitech Lawyer 32.

[32] Cf H Patrick Glenn and Lionel D Smith (eds), *Law and the New Logics* (Cambridge University Press 2017).

[33] Note that many jurisdictions allow 'reasonable excuse' as a defence, so perhaps even this example is not so simple.

[34] *McQuire v Western Morning News* [1903] 2 KB 100, 109 (Collins MR).

[35] See, eg, Mindy Chen-Wishart and Victoria Dixon, 'Humble Good Faith: 3 x 4' in Paul Miller and John Oberdiek (eds), *Oxford Studies in Private Law Theory* (Oxford University Press 2020) 187.

[36] Francesco Contini, 'Artificial Intelligence and the Transformation of Humans, Law and Technology Interactions in Judicial Proceedings' (2020) 2(1) Law, Technology, and Humans 4, 7.

[37] CF Huws and JC Finnis, 'On Computable Numbers with an Application to the AlanTuringproblem' (2017) 25 Artificial Intelligence and Law 181, 183.

In any case, few legal theorists today would adhere to a strictly formal-ist position that law can or should be interpreted mechanically. Ronald Dworkin, for example, did hold that there is one correct answer to legal questions – even the difficult ones – but he explicitly rejected the notion that this implied that the answer was reachable by a computer designed by an 'electronic magician'.[38] On the contrary, the difficulty in applying the law is that it is always an exercise in political morality, interpreting the law in its best light on behalf of a community in search of a justification for state coercion.[39] Joseph Raz rejected Dworkin's view of uniquely correct solutions, arguing that judges in such cases are analogous to subordinate legislators, with legal duties to enact particular rules.[40] The positivist tradition is often seen as the most sympathetic to automation of legal processes, but even HLA Hart held that judges must make choices where existing law fails to dictate that any decision is the 'correct' one.[41] Legal realists and critical legal studies scholars, who emphasize the role of judges and the influence of power on the social order, would regard the question of automating the law as so ridiculous to not be worth taking seriously.[42]

9.1.2   In Fact

In his confirmation hearings before the US Senate, Chief Justice John Roberts deflected criticisms of partisanship by quipping that his job was merely 'to call balls and strikes'. The answer was disingenuous regarding the politicized nature of the court, but Roberts also underestimated the moves to automation in major league sport. In baseball in particular, there have been many calls for umpires to be assisted by a computerized strike zone or replaced entirely. If the role of judges was as simple as determining whether a leather-encased ball passed within a three square

---

[38] Ronald Dworkin, *Law's Empire* (Harvard University Press 1986) 412.
[39] Brian Sheppard, 'Warming Up to Inscrutability: How Technology Could Challenge Our Concept of Law' (2018) 68(Supplement 1) University of Toronto Law Journal 36, 60.
[40] Joseph Raz, *Ethics in the Public Domain: Essays in the Morality of Law and Politics* (Clarendon Press 1995) 249–50.
[41] HLA Hart, *The Concept of Law* (3rd edn, Clarendon Press 2012) 273. Cf Abdul Paliwala, 'Rediscovering Artificial Intelligence and Law: An Inadequate Jurisprudence?' (2016) 30 International Review of Law, Computers & Technology 107.
[42] Cf Sangchul Park and Haksoo Ko, 'Machine Learning and Law and Economics: A Preliminary Overview' (202) 11(2) Asian Journal of Law and Economics 15 (adopting a law and economics analysis and concluding that such systems might be treated as expert witnesses but not as substituting for the human judge).

foot zone or not, then they probably should be replaced by machines – it would be both more efficient and more consistent.[43]

Even if a law appears on its face to be expressed clearly, however – 'no vehicles in the park', to pick a well-known example first offered by Hart – how it is to be applied in practice may be less so. We might agree that it covers automobiles, but what about bicycles, roller skates, toy cars?[44] How about a stroller? Or the statue of a Second World War tank?[45]

The underlying problem is that the strength and the weakness of language is that it is open textured, an idea traceable back to Wittgenstein.[46] Even when there may be near-universal agreement on many applications of the law, marginal cases will arise. The open-textured nature of language and law has an important connection to time, since future cases may arise that were unknowable by the drafter of a rule. Twentieth-century legislators, for example, could be forgiven for failing to contemplate whether the vehicles prohibited from entering the park include drones.[47]

The need for flexibility in applying the law to particular facts is not merely hypothetical. In the late nineteenth century, the New York State Court of Appeals heard a case in which the plain language of a will and the relevant legislation made clear that the grandson of Francis B Palmer should inherit his estate. Yet the fact that the younger Mr Palmer had poisoned his late grandfather gave them pause. Dworkin uses this example to argue that nearly universal principles of justice may require a departure even from clear textual rules. (The murderer did not get his inheritance.)[48]

Perhaps the strongest illustration of the difficulty of applying law to facts is the market for legal services, in particular litigation. If laws were clearly drafted and easily applied, few disputes would go to court because

---

[43] Jennifer Walker Elrod, 'Trial by Siri: AI Comes to the Courtroom' (2020) 57 Houston Law Review 1085.

[44] HLA Hart, 'Positivism and the Separation of Law and Morals' (1958) 71 Harvard Law Review 593, 607.

[45] Pierre Schlag, 'No Vehicles in the Park' (1999) 23 Seattle University Law Review 381; Frederick Schauer, 'A Critical Guide to Vehicles in the Park' (2008) 83 New York University Law Review 1109.

[46] Hart (n 41) 124; Ralf Poscher, 'Ambiguity and Vagueness in Legal Interpretation' in Lawrence M Solan and Peter M Tiersma (eds), *The Oxford Handbook of Language and Law* (Oxford University Press 2012) 128.

[47] Michael A Livermore, 'Rules by Rules' in Ryan Whalen (ed), *Computational Legal Studies: The Promise and Challenge of Data-Driven Research* (Edward Elgar 2020) 238 at 246–47.

[48] Ronald Dworkin, *Taking Rights Seriously* (Harvard University Press 1977) 23, citing *Riggs v Palmer*, 115 NY 506 (1889).

rational, well-informed actors would reach the correct conclusion on their own. There would be no need for appellate courts. The reason that cases end up in court is only rarely because one side is objectively and obviously 'wrong'. This is borne out in practice. Assuming that potential litigants in civil suits make rational estimates of the likely outcome at trial, for example, the individual maximizing decisions of parties should mean that their success rate approaches 50 per cent, regardless of the substantive area of law.[49] That figure is a limit case only – approached as the standard of decision is clearer, parties' estimate of the quality of their own cases is more accurate, and the stakes on either side are of similar value. But it finds empirical support.[50]

9.2   Law as Data

Inherent in many of the debates over AI and legal regulation are fundamental differences in the understanding not of AI but of law. If law is understood in a narrowly formalistic way – the blind application of rules to uncontested facts – then processing it through algorithms makes sense, in the same way that it would be inefficient to have regulators or judges doing long division by hand instead of using a calculator.[51] But, to state the obvious, law is not long division. The simplest of cases aside, regulation of behaviour and the resolution of disputes is an inherently agonistic enterprise that involves values and meaning that are necessarily contested.[52] As Oliver Wendell Holmes famously said, 'The life of the law has not been logic: it has been experience.'[53]

Ah yes, the computer scientist might respond. But experience is precisely what machine learning can replicate now.

Indeed, more recent innovations reflect a shift in the approach to the law analogous to the move in AI research towards machine learning. Rather than trying to encode legal rules in fixed systems that can then be applied to sanitized facts – top down, as it were – key achievements have

---

[49] George L Priest and Benjamin Klein, 'The Selection of Disputes for Litigation' (1984) 13 Journal of Legal Studies 1.

[50] Simon Chesterman, 'Do Better Lawyers Win More Often? Measures of Advocate Quality and Their Impact in Singapore's Supreme Court' (2020) 15 Asian Journal of Comparative Law 250.

[51] Mireille Hildebrandt, 'Law as Information in the Era of Data-Driven Agency' (2016) 79 Modern Law Review 1. For an example of using AI to rethink the notion of legal logic, see Douglas Walton, *Argumentation Methods for Artificial Intelligence in Law* (Springer 2005).

[52] Jeremy Waldron, 'The Rule of Law and the Importance of Procedure' in James E Fleming (ed), *Nomos L: Getting to the Rule of Law* (New York University Press 2011) 3 at 22.

[53] Oliver Wendell Holmes, Jr, *The Common Law* (Little, Brown 1881) 1.

been made in analysing large amounts of data from the bottom up. This approach does not seek to answer an individual case, but it does offer a prediction as to the outcome based on past experience.[54] It represents, as Mireille Hildebrandt observes, a shift 'from reason to statistics and from argumentation to simulation'.[55]

The turn to AI in this context has proven useful in identifying relevance for the purposes of legal research, contract review, and discovery.[56] But if extended to regulation and adjudication, it would fundamentally change the task from making a decision to predicting it.[57] Rather than being part of an ongoing social process in the development of the law, such determinations are more akin to forecasting the weather.[58] Analytics may provide more information to disputing parties and encourage efficient resolution of disputes while reducing bias and error,[59] but they could not be a replacement of the judicial function itself.[60]

Indeed, in some jurisdictions the approach has been met with outright hostility. Recall France's 2019 law prohibiting the publication of data analytics that reveal or predict how particular judges will decide on cases, with a maximum punishment of five years in prison.[61] Though France will likely remain an outlier, AI systems will not replace lawyers or judges in the near term. A more probable scenario is increasing use of AI systems as part of legal services, a partnership sometimes compared to the pairing of humans and machines to play advanced chess, also known as centaur or cyborg chess.[62]

---

[54] Maxi Scherer, 'Artificial Intelligence and Legal Decision-Making: The Wide Open?' (2019) 36 Journal of International Arbitration 539, 569–71. See, eg, Nikolaos Aletras et al, 'Predicting Judicial Decisions of the European Court of Human Rights: A Natural Language Processing Perspective' (2016) 2:e93 PeerJ Computer Science.

[55] Mireille Hildebrandt, 'Law as Computation in the Era of Artificial Legal Intelligence: Speaking Law to the Power of Statistics' (2018) 68(Supplement 1) University of Toronto Law Journal 12, 29.

[56] See Robert Dale, 'Law and Word Order: NLP in Legal Tech' (2019) 25 Natural Language Engineering 211.

[57] Cf Oliver Wendell Holmes, Jr, 'The Path of the Law' (1897) 10 Harvard Law Review 457, 461 ('The prophecies of what the courts will do in fact, and nothing more pretentious, are what I mean by law').

[58] Frank Pasquale and Glyn Cashwell, 'Prediction, Persuasion, and the Jurisprudence of Behaviourism' (2018) 68(Supplement 1) University of Toronto Law Journal 63, 64–65.

[59] Daniel L Chen, 'Judicial Analytics and the Great Transformation of American Law' (2019) 27 Artificial Intelligence and Law 15.

[60] See also the discussion of medical as opposed to legal research in chapter three, introduction.

[61] See chapter three, section 3.3.2.

[62] See, eg, Rebecca Crootof, '"Cyborg Justice" and the Risk of Technological–Legal Lock-In' (2019) 119 Columbia Law Review Forum 233, 243; John Morison and Adam Harkens,

In this context, it is common to draw a distinction between technology assisting in the retrieval of information and that helping in the exercise of judgment.[63] The former is analogous to use of a calculator and deemed unproblematic; the latter raises troubling questions about who is exercising discretion. But when the 'information' being retrieved goes to the heart of a decision, that distinction may be artificial. As we saw in chapter three, reliance on opaque systems to make recommendations on matters like sentencing is an abdication of the judicial function not because those recommendations may be incorrect but because they are illegitimate. More generally, automation bias raises concerns that human agency may diminish in favour of reliance on the machine.[64] Even for sophisticated decision-makers, it can be difficult to tell where an algorithm's 'nudge' ends and the accountable individual's choice begins.[65]

For present purposes, it is sufficient to conclude that AI will continue to transform the legal profession and the role of lawyers – but not to replace them completely. The limits are not so much technical as inherent in the nature of law and the legitimacy accorded to it through political structures in most well-ordered societies.

9.3   Law as Code

Is there, however, a special case to be made for AI playing a larger role in regulating AI itself?

The speed, autonomy, and opacity of AI systems do occasionally give rise to practical and conceptual difficulties for human regulators. In some cases, the response has been to slow them down, as in the case of high-frequency trading.[66] In others, it has been to ensure the possibility of accountability through requiring that actions be attributable to traditional legal persons – typically the owner, operator, or manufacturer.[67]

'Re-engineering Justice? Robot Judges, Computerised Courts and (Semi) Automated Legal Decision-Making' (2019) 39 Legal Studies 618, 634–35.

[63] Zihuan Xu et al, 'Case Facts Analysis Method Based on Deep Learning' in Weiwei Ni et al (eds), *Web Information Systems and Applications* (Springer 2020) 92.

[64] See chapter three, section 3.1.

[65] Mariano-Florentino Cuéllar, 'Cyberdelegation and the Administrative State' in Nicholas R Parrillo (ed), *Administrative Law from the Inside Out: Essays on Themes in the Work of Jerry L Mashaw* (Cambridge University Press 2017) 134 at 159.

[66] See chapter one, section 1.2.

[67] See chapter four, section 4.1.1.

In still others, it has been to call for prohibiting certain activities entirely – most prominently the use of lethal force.[68]

AI does offer means of supporting regulation of AI, although, as discussed in chapter five, the traditional justifications for regulation do not translate easily onto AI systems themselves. In particular, in the absence of AI with legal personality, the targets of regulation are not the AI systems themselves but those who own, operate, and make those systems. That said, the unique features of AI suggest two avenues for a form of self-regulation. First, regulatory objectives can be built into the software itself. Analogous to requirements that privacy values be incorporated into software harvesting personal data, this may be termed regulation by design. Secondly, AI systems allow for interrogation of mistakes and adverse outcomes in a manner not possible with traditional legal actors. This should enable greater transparency concerning errors, but the consequences should also be different than for traditional legal persons. It will be described here as regulation by debugging.

9.3.1   Regulation by Design

The idea of incorporating law-compliant behaviour into an AI system may seem self-evident. Autonomous vehicles should comply with traffic laws; algorithms allocating social benefits or recommending loans should not discriminate on the basis of gender or race. But it is possible to go far beyond this.

The notion that regulation can be achieved through design is not new. Though legal scholars often focus on 'command and control' approaches, design standards can gather information, set standards, and shape behaviour for regulatory ends.[69] The usual tools of regulation – commands, incentives, influence – presume the need to compel or persuade human actors (or their corporate proxies) to do or refrain from doing certain actions.[70] Programmable devices and systems, which include most applications of AI considered in this book, offer the possibility of incorporating regulatory standards directly into their code.

---

[68] See chapter two, section 2.2.

[69] Karen Yeung, "'Hypernudge': Big Data as a Mode of Regulation by Design' (2017) 20 Information, Communication & Society 118, 120. See generally Lawrence Lessig, *Code: Version 2.0* (Basic Books 2006); Mireille Hildebrandt, 'Saved by Design? The Case of Legal Protection by Design' (2017) 11 Nanoethics 307; Nynke Tromp and Paul Hekkert, *Designing for Society: Products and Services for a Better World* (Bloomsbury Visual Arts 2019).

[70] See chapter seven, section 7.3.

There are limits. As chapter seven argued, proposals analogous to Asimov's laws of robotics misconceive the nature of law and will never be a complete solution to the regulatory challenges posed by AI systems. But as a restriction on what such systems can do, they point to a promising path forward. As stressed in chapter eight, effective standard-setting will, in some cases, require global rules. Implementing those rules should not rely upon state enforcement alone – to the extent possible, they should be encoded into AI systems themselves. As for the content of those rules, most will be the same that would apply to any product or service. Rather than requiring robots not to murder humans, for example, the prohibition would be against producers making devices that could do so.

Of more interest is how regulation by design might support the two areas identified in chapter seven as potential gaps: human control and transparency.

On human control, building in capability restrictions and a 'kill switch' may sound like obvious design solutions. For the time being, that is true – chapter eight proposed a global agency to support a ban on the creation of uncontrollable or uncontainable AI. As discussed in chapter five, however, in the event that the emergence of a superintelligence becomes more realistic, such constraints could bring about the evil that they are intended to prevent; it may be more prudent to seek to instil alignment with human values instead.[71]

In terms of transparency, different degrees are appropriate depending on the type of decision or activity in question. Generally, however, AI systems should be designed to identify themselves as such and in a manner that enables identification of a legal person who is the owner, operator, or manufacturer.[72] In addition, systems should at a minimum maintain a basic audit trail of how decisions are made.[73] This points to the second way in which AI could assist in its own regulation, which is through enabling interrogation of its failures.

9.3.2   Regulation by Debugging

When one human kills another, it may give rise to criminal prosecution and lawsuits – these raise legal questions to be resolved. When a machine kills someone, there may be investigation of its owner, operator, or

---

[71] See chapter five, section 5.3.
[72] See chapter eight, section 8.2.2(b).
[73] See chapter six, section 6.2.2(b).

manufacturer. But with regard to the machine itself, the problem is more likely to be seen as an engineering one. Much as airplane crashes are studied using information from flight data recorders, audit trails in AI systems offer the chance to review how and why errors occurred. If these disclose culpability on the part of the owner, operator, or manufacturer, legal remedies may follow. As for the AI system itself, however, punishment for an error would make no more sense than punishing a plane for its engine failure.[74]

If a system is deemed unsafe, it may be removed from the market; a more likely scenario is that it would be improved. Much as software is now continuously updated with patches as bugs and vulnerabilities are discovered, AI systems operating in the world should be expected to evolve in response to their environment. Market pressure will encourage such updates, but they could also be the subject of regulations or a court order.[75]

Debugging in this way satisfies the aims of regulation at far less cost. Assuming that the improvements do not introduce other errors, it may also be more reliable than traditional regulatory tools if an AI system cannot be tempted once more into deviance. It presumes, of course, a degree of transparency that is unavailable in traditional regulatory settings. If one asks a human driver whether she ran a red light, or a human manager if he discriminated on the basis of race, the answer may be unreliable. Proper audit logs should avoid this problem with respect to AI systems.

This ability to get straight answers also points to another potential strength of such systems, which is that they could be tasked with monitoring themselves. As described in chapter six, two broad theories of oversight are known as 'police patrol' and 'fire alarm', depending on whether it is conducted through periodic surveys or waiting for problems to be escalated.[76] AI systems offer a third possibility of self-investigation. This would be more than a regime of self-regulation, as it would not rely on the good faith of actors with incentives to defect.[77] Provided that the

---

[74] See chapter five, section 5.1.2(b).

[75] Mark A Lemley and Bryan Casey, 'Remedies for Robots' (2019) 86 University of Chicago Law Review 1311, 1386–89.

[76] See chapter six, section 6.1.2.

[77] See chapter eight, section 8.1. But see Casey Chu, Andrey Zhmoginov, and Mark Sandler, 'CycleGAN, a Master of Steganography' (2017) 1712.02950v2 arXiv; Joel Lehman et al, 'The Surprising Creativity of Digital Evolution: A Collection of Anecdotes from the Evolutionary Computation and Artificial Life Research Communities' (2018) arXiv

instructions were clear, a system could report on its compliance with rules and policies, among other things examining its conduct for bias with a degree of candour not possible with humans.[78] Problems disclosed in this way would also point to a need to rethink the remedies available – not as sins to be punished but as errors to be corrected.

9.4 The Prospects for Regulation

After the avatar's brief interaction with the parties concludes, the video celebrating Hangzhou's Internet Court shows an interview with its very human vice president, Ni Defeng. 'What we are doing now,' he enthuses, 'you can't understand it as merely improving efficiency. It also speaks to the issue of legal justice. The faster speed – is kind of justice on its own, because justice delayed is justice denied.'

The desire for efficiency and consistency is driving China's push to digitize its court system, with strong endorsement by government as well as the judiciary, and strong support from industry. Though judges themselves remain, for the most part, human, Shanghai's courts are replacing law clerks with AI systems to perform basic legal research – another step in the push to modernize the judicial system through the use of technology.[79] These developments have been matched by the embrace of computational legal studies in Chinese legal academia. The past decade has seen a more widespread turn to empirical legal studies than in the United States; computational methods are now routinely used in articles published in the top generalist Chinese law journals.[80]

A partial explanation of the greater traction of computational approaches in theory as well as in practice is that China's embrace of the rule of law is more instrumental than its Western counterparts'.[81]

1803.03453v1; Tom Simonite, 'When Bots Teach Themselves to Cheat', *Wired* (8 August 2018) (describing AI systems that learned to 'cheat').

[78] See chapter three, section 3.2.2.

[79] Sarah Dai, 'Shanghai Judicial Courts Start to Replace Clerks with AI Assistants', *South China Morning Post* (1 April 2020).

[80] Yingmao Tang and John Zhuang Liu, 'Computational Legal Studies in China: Progress, Challenges, and Future' in Ryan Whalen (ed), *Computational Legal Studies: The Promise and Challenge of Data-Driven Research* (Edward Elgar 2020) 124.

[81] Randall Peerenboom, *China's Long March Toward Rule of Law* (Cambridge University Press 2002) 280–330; Cong-rui Qiao, 'Jurisprudent Shift in China: A Functional Interpretation' (2017) 8(1) Asian Journal of Law and Economics; Simon Chesterman, 'Can International Law Survive a Rising China?' (2020) 31 European Journal of International Law 1507.

Chinese judges refer to interpretation and the exercise of discretion in the context of 'judicial measurement' [裁判尺度], a term without a precise equivalent in the Western tradition but routinely invoked in China with a view to unifying judicial standards.[82] Judgments at the district and intermediate level tend to be short – a couple of paragraphs stating the facts, an outline of the applicable law and responses to the parties' arguments, and a decision.

Nevertheless, Chinese judges also express wariness about 'black box' decision-making.[83] In part this is due to concerns about the accuracy of the outcomes. Initial efforts to train computers on murder cases had to be shelved, for example, because there was an insufficient number of cases and the facts in each varied so greatly.[84] But it also goes to the trust that underpins the legal system and the rule of law itself.

It remains to be seen whether China represents the future of regulation by AI or its limit case. This chapter has argued that some of the qualities of AI systems that make them hard to regulate through traditional processes may also offer tools to regulate them through new ones. Regulation by design and regulation by debugging suggest ways in which AI systems can be built to comply with the law and tasked with investigating their own biases and failings in a way that most humans would find uncomfortable or impossible.

Yet there are limits to this role. Even if AI systems are more efficient and more consistent than human regulators and judges, that would not justify the handover of their powers more generally.

For the authority of law depends on its processes not only in a formal sense but in a substantive sense also. Regulation, legal decisions, are not mere Turing Tests in which we speculate whether the public can guess if the regulator or judge is a person or a robot. Legitimacy lies in the process itself, the ability to tie the exercise of discretion to a being capable of

[82] 统一裁判尺度 规范法律适用 [Uniform Judgment Standards and Standardize the Application of Law] (Supreme People's Court of the People's Republic of China, 12 January 2018). Cf Jiang Na, 'Old Wine in New Bottles? New Strategies for Judicial Accountability in China' (2018) 52 International Journal of Law, Crime and Justice 74.
[83] 郭富民 [Guo Fumin], '人工智能无法取代法官的审慎艺术 [Artificial Intelligence Cannot Replace the Prudential Art of Judges]', 中国法院网 [China Court Network] (5 July 2017); Jie-jing Yao and Peng Hui, 'Research on the Application of Artificial Intelligence in Judicial Trial: Experience from China' (2020) 1487 Journal of Physics: Conference Series 012013, 4.
[84] Jinting Deng, 'Should the Common Law System Welcome Artificial Intelligence: A Case Study of China's Same-Type Case Reference System' (2019) 3 Georgetown Law Technology Review 223, 275.

weighing uncertain values and standing behind that exercise of discretion. Accepting otherwise would be to accept that legal reasoning is not a mix of doctrinal, normative, and interdisciplinary scholarship. Rather, it would come to be seen as a kind of history – the emphasis on appropriate categorization of past practice rather than participation in a forward-looking social project.[85]

As Robert H Jackson, another US Supreme Court judge, once observed: 'We are not final because we are infallible, but we are infallible only because we are final.'[86] Many decisions might therefore properly be handed over to the machines. But the final exercise of discretion, public control over the legal processes that regulate our interactions with the world around us, should be transferred only when we are also prepared to transfer political control – when we give up the ballot box for the Xbox.

---

[85] Cf Michael A Livermore (ed), *Law as Data: Computation, Text, and the Future of Legal Analysis* (Santa Fe Institute Press 2019).

[86] *Brown v Allen*, 344 US 443, 540 (1953) (Jackson, J concurring).

Conclusion

We, the Robots?

The word 'robot' entered the modern lexicon a hundred years ago with the première of Karel Čapek's play *R.U.R.* at Prague's National Theatre. Set on an island 'somewhere on our planet', *Rossum's Universal Robots* recounts the creation of *roboti*. Not so much mechanical creatures as stripped-down versions of humans, they are biological entities created to be strong and intelligent, but without souls.

Though dated in many ways – the limited humour derives from six men on the island vying for the hand of the only woman – the play was prescient in its vision of a world in which automatons are entrusted with serving ever more of humanity's needs and, eventually, fighting its wars. To its Czech audience, the political undertones were evident in the title: *robota* is a term meaning forced labour, of the kind serfs once performed on their masters' lands. In case this was missed, the opening scene has the company's general manager extol the primary virtues of his new work-force: their cheapness and expendability. A review of the 1922 New York production called it a 'brilliant satire on our mechanized civilization; the grimmest yet subtlest arraignment of this strange, mad thing we call the industrial society of today'.[1]

A century later, debates over AI's place in society still echo themes in the play: how to take advantage of the benefits of technology without unacceptable risk; what entitlements are owed to entities that at least mimic and perhaps embody human qualities; what place is left for humanity if and when we are surpassed by our creations.

This book has explored the regulatory issues posed by the emergence of fast, autonomous, and opaque AI systems. In this, Čapek's vision of an eventual robot revolution is no more helpful than Asimov's introspective androids, agonizing over the three laws intended to keep them in check. Much of the more serious subsequent writing on this topic similarly

---

[1] Karel Čapek, *R.U.R. (Rossum's Universal Robots)* (Paul Selver tr, Doubleday 1923) 10 (quoting Maida Castellum in *The Call*).

focuses on the speculative future of general AI at one extreme or the development of specific technologies at the other. The emphasis here, by contrast, has been on regulation itself – the challenges posed, the tools available, and the possibilities that are emerging – adding a public law and international law perspective that has been lacking.

Part I set the stage with illustrations of the speed, autonomy, and opacity of modern AI. It also offered three discrete ways to view the regulatory dilemma through the lenses of practicality, morality, and legitimacy. Some risks, such as economic losses due to high-frequency trading or the physical danger posed by autonomous vehicles, can be managed. Others, such as autonomous weapons making battlefield decisions over life and death, or the emergence of uncontrollable or uncontainable AI, should be forbidden. Still others, in particular the exercise of discretion by judges and other public officers, should not be outsourced to machines or anyone else.

For the most part, existing laws and institutions can deal with these challenges. Part II brought out the available props in the form of responsibility, personality, and transparency. A near-term problem is ensuring that harmful activity conducted by AI can be attributed to traditional legal persons, with mandatory insurance used to avoid inefficiencies or injustices that arise. The alternative is that AI could be granted some form of legal status in its own right. As such systems approach human intelligence, take on ever more responsibilities, create things of beauty and value, should we recognize them as persons before the law? No – or, at least, not yet. Though there may be instrumental reasons for inculcating sensitivity to human laws and mores, for the foreseeable future this does not require a fundamental change in how we think of moral or legal obligations. Central to maintaining this position, however, will be transparency in our creations, which must mean more than a limited right to have adverse decisions explained.

Part III then outlined plot developments: rules, institutions, and the role that AI might play in regulating itself. The amount of creativity and energy that has gone into developing ethical guides, frameworks, and principles is prodigious. Rather than add to this proliferation, the aim here was to pare down to what is actually missing. That was shown to be a procedural guarantee of transparency and a substantive norm of maintaining human control – in the sense of both constraining AI activities and continuing to take responsibility for them. For regulation, for public control of AI to continue to be possible, active involvement of states will therefore be vital. Though self-regulation and international co-ordination will be important in developing standards and policing red lines, the dominant politically accountable institutions of governance remain states. The authority entrusted to state institutions should not be outsourced to AI, any more than it should be outsourced to private or other actors. Given the globalization of information technology, however, a global approach is needed. A hypothetical IAIA was therefore proposed, to encourage positive applications of AI as well as to help maintain red lines against humanity's creations being either weaponized or victimized.

In *R.U.R.* they are both. The play opens with the daughter of the company president sneaking into the factory to advocate on behalf of robots as a representative of the idealistic League of Humanity; it ends with them rising up and killing all but one of their makers. The man spared is Mr Alquist, chief of construction, because they saw that he worked with his hands 'like a robot'. When he asks what prompted their genocide, the robots are incredulous. It had to be, they explain; they had learnt everything that humans had to offer. 'You have to kill and rule if you want to be like people. Read history! Read people's books! You have to conquer and murder if you want to be human!' In a line dropped from the first English translation, Alquist replies, helplessly: 'Nothing is more alien to a man than his own image.'[2]

This is, in fact, the greatest failing in Čapek's play: that it abandons the conceit of robots as being distinct from their creators. Through dramatic sleight of hand, the differences are effaced – the *roboti* develop souls and the ability to reproduce. There is, in the end, no revolt of robots: one group of humans is simply dethroned by another.[3] The curtain falls on a new Adam and Eve walking off into the sunset.

The rule of law is the epitome of anthropocentrism: humans are the primary subject and object of norms that are created, interpreted, and enforced by humans – made manifest in government of the people, by the people, for the people. Though legal constructs such as corporations may have rights and obligations, these are in turn traceable back to human agency in their acts of creation, their daily conduct overseen to varying degrees by human agents. Even

---

[2] Karel Čapek, *R.U.R. Rossum's Universal Robots; Kolektivní Drama v Vstupní Komedii a Tech Aktech* (Aventinum 1920) 85. Cf Karel Čapek, 'R.U.R. (Rossum's Universal Robots)' in Peter Kussi (ed), *Toward the Radical Center: A Karel Čapek Reader* (Claudia Novack-Jones tr, Catbird 1990) at 99. See further Merritt Abrash, 'R.U.R. Restored and Reconsidered' (1991) 32 Extrapolation 184.

[3] René Wellek, 'Karel Čapek' (1936) 15 Slavonic and East European Review 191, 196.

international law, which governs relations between states, begins its foundational text with the words 'We the peoples ...'[4] The emergence of fast, autonomous, and opaque AI systems forces us to question this assumption of our own centrality, though it is not yet time to relinquish it.

---

[4] Charter of the United Nations, done at San Francisco, 26 June 1945, in force 24 October 1945, preamble.

BIBLIOGRAPHY

Abate RS, *Climate Change and the Voiceless: Protecting Future Generations, Wildlife, and Natural Resources* (Cambridge University Press 2019).

Abbott R, 'I Think, Therefore I Invent: Creative Computers and the Future of Patent Law' (2016) 57 Boston College Law Review 1079.

—— 'The Reasonable Computer: Disrupting the Paradigm of Tort Liability' (2018) 86 George Washington Law Review 1.

—— *The Reasonable Robot: Artificial Intelligence and the Law* (Cambridge University Press 2020).

Abraham KS and Rabin RL, 'Automated Vehicles and Manufacturer Responsibility for Accidents: A New Legal Regime for a New Era' (2019) 105 Virginia Law Review 127.

Abrash M, 'R.U.R. Restored and Reconsidered' (1991) 32 Extrapolation 184.

Aguiar L, Claussen J, and Peukert C, 'Catch Me If You Can: Effectiveness and Consequences of Online Copyright Enforcement' (2018) 29 Information Systems Research 656.

Ajunwa I, 'The Paradox of Automation as Anti-bias Intervention' (2020) 41 Cardozo Law Review 1671.

Aldridge I and Krawciw S, *Real-Time Risk: What Investors Should Know about FinTech, High-Frequency Trading, and Flash Crashes* (Wiley 2017).

Aletras N et al, 'Predicting Judicial Decisions of the European Court of Human Rights: A Natural Language Processing Perspective' (2016) 2:e93 PeerJ Computer Science.

Alfonsi C, 'Taming Tech Giants Requires Fixing the Revolving Door' (2019) 19 Kennedy School Review 166.

Allain J (ed), *The Legal Understanding of Slavery: From the Historical to the Contemporary* (Oxford University Press 2013).

Allen HJ, 'Regulatory Sandboxes' (2019) 87 George Washington Law Review 579.

Alschuler AW, 'The Changing Purposes of Criminal Punishment: A Retrospective on the Past Century and Some Thoughts about the Next' (2003) 70 University of Chicago Law Review 1.

Amirthalingam K, 'The Non-delegable Duty: Some Clarifications, Some Questions' (2017) 29 Singapore Academy of Law Journal 500.

Amsler CE, Bartlett RL, and Bolton CJ, 'Thoughts of Some British Economists on Early Limited Liability and Corporate Legislation' (1981) 13 History of Political Economy 774.

Ananny M, 'Toward an Ethics of Algorithms: Convening, Observation, Probability, and Timeliness' (2016) 41 Science, Technology, & Human Values 93.

Ananny M and Crawford K, 'Seeing without Knowing: Limitations of the Transparency Ideal and Its Application to Algorithmic Accountability' (2018) 20 New Media & Society 973.

Anderson JM et al, *Autonomous Vehicle Technology: A Guide for Policymakers* (RAND 2014).

Anderson K, Reisner D, and Waxman M, 'Adapting the Law of Armed Conflict to Autonomous Weapon Systems' (2014) 90 International Law Studies 386.

Anderson SL, 'Asimov's "Three Laws of Robotics" and Machine Metaethics' (2008) 22 AI & Society 477.

Angel JJ and McCabe DM, 'Insider Trading 2.0? The Ethics of Information Sales' (2018) 147 Journal of Business Ethics 747.

Anshar M and Williams M-A, 'Simplified Pain Matrix Method for Artificial Pain Activation Embedded into Robot Framework' (2021) 13 International Journal of Social Robotics 187.

Aquinas T, *Summa Theologica* (Fathers of the English Dominican Province trs, first published 1265–74, Benziger Brothers 1911).

Arkin RC, 'The Case for Ethical Autonomy in Unmanned Systems' (2010) 9 Journal of Military Ethics 332.

Armstrong MJ, 'Modeling Short-Range Ballistic Missile Defense and Israel's Iron Dome System' (2014) 62 Operations Research 1028.

Ascher CS, 'The Grievance Man or Ombudsmania' (1967) 27 Public Administration Review 174.

Ashley KD, *Artificial Intelligence and Legal Analytics: New Tools for Law Practice in the Digital Age* (Cambridge University Press 2017).

Ashrafian H, 'Artificial Intelligence and Robot Responsibilities: Innovating Beyond Rights' (2015) 21 Science and Engineering Ethics 317.

'Can Artificial Intelligences Suffer from Mental Illness? A Philosophical Matter to Consider' (2017) 23 Science and Engineering Ethics 403.

Asimov I, 'Runaround', *Astounding Science Fiction* (March 1942).

The Complete Robot (Doubleday 1982).

Foundation and Earth (Doubleday 1986).

Auletta K, *Googled: The End of the World as We Know It* (Penguin 2009).

Austin J, *The Province of Jurisprudence Determined* (first published 1832, Cambridge University Press 1995).

Avant D, 'From Mercenary to Citizen Armies: Explaining Change in the Practice of War' (2000) 54 International Organization 41.

The Market for Force: The Consequences of Privatizing Security (Cambridge University Press 2005).

Aven T, 'On Different Types of Uncertainties in the Context of the Precautionary Principle' (2011) 31 Risk Analysis 1515.

Awad E et al, 'The Moral Machine Experiment' (2018) 563 Nature 59.

Ayres I and Braithwaite J, *Responsive Regulation: Transcending the Deregulation Debate* (Oxford University Press 1992).

Babbage C, *Passages from the Life of a Philosopher* (Longman 1864).

Baird HS, Coates AL, and Fateman RJ, 'PessimalPrint: A Reverse Turing Test' (2003) 5 International Journal on Document Analysis and Recognition 158.

Baldwin JM, Eassey JM, and Brooke EJ, 'Court Operations during the COVID-19 Pandemic' (2020) 45 American Journal of Criminal Justice 743.

Baldwin R and Black J, 'Driving Priorities in Risk-Based Regulation: What's the Problem?' (2016) 43 Journal of Law and Society 565.

Baldwin R, Cave M, and Lodge M, *Understanding Regulation: Theory, Strategy, and Practice* (2nd edn, Oxford University Press 2011).

(eds), *The Oxford Handbook of Regulation* (Oxford University Press 2010).

Balkin JM, 'The Three Laws of Robotics in the Age of Big Data' (2017) 78 Ohio State Law Journal 1217.

Balp G and Strampelli G, 'Preserving Capital Markets Efficiency in the High-Frequency Trading Era' [2018] University of Illinois Journal of Law, Technology & Policy 349.

Banteka N, 'Artificially Intelligent Persons' (2021) 58 Houston Law Review 537.

Barabas C et al, 'Interventions over Predictions: Reframing the Ethical Debate for Actuarial Risk Assessment' (2018) 81 Proceedings of Machine Learning Research 1.

Barfield W and Pagallo U (eds), *Research Handbook on the Law of Artificial Intelligence* (Edward Elgar 2018).

Barocas S and Selbst AD, 'Big Data's Disparate Impact' (2016) 104 California Law Review 671.

Barocas S, Selbst AD, and Raghavan M, 'The Hidden Assumptions Behind Counterfactual Explanations and Principal Reasons' (ACM Conference on Fairness, Accountability, and Transparency (FAT*), 2020) 80.

Barredo Arrieta A et al, 'Explainable Artificial Intelligence (XAI): Concepts, Taxonomies, Opportunities, and Challenges Toward Responsible AI' (2020) 58 Information Fusion 82.

Baudrillard J, *The Gulf War Never Happened* (Polity Press 1995).

Bayern S, 'Of Bitcoins, Independently Wealthy Software, and the Zero-Member LLC' (2014) 108 Northwestern University Law Review 1485.

'The Implications of Modern Business-Entity Law for the Regulation of Autonomous Systems' (2015) 19 Stanford Technology Law Review 93.

Beard JM, 'Autonomous Weapons and Human Responsibilities' (2014) 45 Georgetown Journal of International Law 617.

Becker M, 'When Public Principals Give Up Control over Private Agents: The New Independence of ICANN in Internet Governance' (2019) 13 Regulation & Governance 561.

Benvenisti E, 'Upholding Democracy amid the Challenges of New Technology: What Role for the Law of Global Governance?' (2018) 29 European Journal of International Law 9.

'The WHO – Destined to Fail? Political Cooperation and the Covid-19 Pandemic' (2020) 114 American Journal of International Law 588.

Berg P, 'Asilomar 1975: DNA Modification Secured' (2008) 455 Nature 290.

Berg P et al, 'Summary Statement of the Asilomar Conference on Recombinant DNA Molecules' (1975) 72 Proceedings of the National Academy of Sciences 1981.

Berk R, *Machine Learning Risk Assessments in Criminal Justice Settings* (Springer 2019).

Bethel EW et al, 'Federal Market Information Technology in the Post Flash Crash Era: Roles for Supercomputing' (2012) 7(2) The Journal of Trading 9.

Bhatt U et al, 'Explainable Machine Learning in Deployment' (2020) 1909.06342v4 arXiv.

Bhuta N et al (eds), *Autonomous Weapons Systems: Law, Ethics, Policy* (Cambridge University Press 2016).

Birnie P, A Boyle, and C Redgwell, *International Law and the Environment* (3rd edn, Oxford 2009).

Blanco-Justicia A et al, 'Machine Learning Explainability via Microaggregation and Shallow Decision Trees' (2020) 194 Knowledge-Based Systems 105532.

Blume LMM, *Fallout: The Hiroshima Cover-Up and the Reporter Who Revealed It to the World* (Scribe 2020).

Bonnefon J-F, A Shariff, and I Rahwan, 'The Social Dilemma of Autonomous Vehicles' (2016) 352(6293) Science 1573.

Bostrom N, 'Ethical Issues in Advanced Artificial Intelligence' in I Smit and GE Lasker (eds), *Cognitive, Emotive and Ethical Aspects of Decision Making in Humans and in Artificial Intelligence* (International Institute for Advanced Studies in Systems Research 2003) vol 2, 12.

Superintelligence: Paths, Dangers, Strategies (Oxford University Press 2014).

Bovis CH, *EU Public Procurement Law* (Edward Elgar 2007).

Box GEP and NR Draper, *Empirical Model-Building and Response Surfaces* (Wiley 1987).

Boyer-Kassem T, 'Is the Precautionary Principle Really Incoherent?' (2017) 37 Risk Analysis 2026.

Bradley P, 'Risk Management Standards and the Active Management of Malicious Intent in Artificial Superintelligence' (2019) 35 AI & Society 319.

Branting LK, 'Artificial Intelligence and the Law from a Research Perspective' (2018) 14(3) Scitech Lawyer 32.

Brauneis R and EP Goodman, 'Algorithmic Transparency for the Smart City' (2018) 20 Yale Journal of Law & Technology 103.

Brin D, *The Transparent Society: Will Technology Force Us to Choose between Privacy and Freedom?* (Addison-Wesley 1998).

Brogaarda J et al, 'High Frequency Trading and Extreme Price Movements' (2018) 128 Journal of Financial Economics 253.

Broockman D, GF Ferenstein, and N Malhotra, 'Predispositions and the Political Behavior of American Economic Elites: Evidence from Technology Entrepreneurs' (2019) 63 American Journal of Political Science 212.

Brooks C, C Gherhes, and T Vorley, 'Artificial Intelligence in the Legal Sector: Pressures and Challenges of Transformation' (2020) 13 Cambridge Journal of Regions, Economy, and Society 135.

Brown A et al, *Contemporary Intellectual Property: Law and Policy* (5th edn, Oxford University Press 2019).

Brown RL, *Nuclear Authority: The IAEA and the Absolute Weapon* (Georgetown University Press 2015).

Brownsword R, E Scotford, and K Yeung (eds), *The Oxford Handbook of Law, Regulation, and Technology* (Oxford University Press 2017).

Bryson JJ, ME Diamantis, and TD Grant, 'Of, for, and by the People: The Legal Lacuna of Synthetic Persons' (2017) 25 Artificial Intelligence and Law 273.

Budish E, P Cramton, and J Shim, 'The High-Frequency Trading Arms Race: Frequent Batch Auctions as a Market Design Response' (2015) 130 Quarterly Journal of Economics 1547.

Burrell J, 'How the Machine "Thinks": Understanding Opacity in Machine Learning Algorithms' (2016) 3(1) Big Data & Society.

Buyers J, *Artificial Intelligence: The Practical Legal Issues* (Law Brief 2018).

Bygrave LA, 'Automated Profiling: Minding the Machine – Article 15 of the EC Data Protection Directive and Automated Profiling' (2001) 17 Computer Law & Security Review 17.

Calo MR, 'Open Robotics' (2011) 70 Maryland Law Review 571.

Calo R, AM Froomkin, and I Kerr (eds), *Robot Law* (Edward Elgar 2016).

Čapek K, *RU.R. Rossum's Universal Robots; Kolektivní Drama v Vstupní Komedii a Tech Aktech* (Aventinum 1920).

 R.U.R. (Rossum's Universal Robots) (Paul Selver tr, Doubleday 1923).

 'R.U.R. (Rossum's Universal Robots)' in P Kussi (ed), *Toward the Radical Center: A Karel Čapek Reader* (C Novack-Jones tr, Catbird 1990).

Carozza PG, 'Subsidiarity as a Structural Principle of International Human Rights Law' (2003) 97 American Journal of International Law 38.

Carson HL, 'The Trial of Animals and Insects: A Little Known Chapter of Mediæval Jurisprudence' (1917) 56 Proceedings of the American Philosophical Society 410.

Cartwright J, 'Unilateral Mistake in the English Courts: Reasserting the Traditional Approach' [2009] Singapore Journal of Legal Studies 226.

Casey-Maslen S et al, *Drones and Other Unmanned Weapons Systems under International Law* (Brill 2018).

Casey B, 'Robot Ipsa Loquitur' (2019) 108 Georgetown Law Journal 225.

Casey B, A Farhangi, and R Vogl, 'Rethinking Explainable Machines: The GDPR's "Right to Explanation" Debate and the Rise of Algorithmic Audits in Enterprise' (2019) 34 Berkeley Technology Law Journal 145.

Cassese A, 'The Martens Clause: Half a Loaf or Simply Pie in the Sky?' (2000) 11 European Journal of International Law 187.

  Cassese's International Criminal Law (3rd edn, Oxford University Press 2013).

Cathcart T, *The Trolley Problem; or, Would You Throw the Fat Guy Off the Bridge? A Philosophical Conundrum* (Workman 2013).

Chagal-Feferkorn KA, 'Am I an Algorithm or a Product? When Products Liability Should Apply to Algorithmic Decision-Makers' (2019) 30 Stanford Law & Policy Review 61.

Chalmers D, G Davies, and G Monti, *European Union Law: Text and Materials* (4th edn, Cambridge University Press 2019).

Chalmers DJ, 'The Singularity: A Philosophical Analysis' (2010) 17(9–10) Journal of Consciousness Studies 7.

Chander A, 'The Racist Algorithm?' (2017) 115 Michigan Law Review 1023.

Chander A and UP Lê, 'Data Nationalism' (2015) 64 Emory Law Journal 677.

Charpie RA, 'The Geneva Conference' (1955) 193(4) Scientific American 27.

Chen DL, 'Judicial Analytics and the Great Transformation of American Law' (2019) 27 Artificial Intelligence and Law 15.

Chen JH and SM Asch, 'Machine Learning and Prediction in Medicine – Beyond the Peak of Inflated Expectations' (2017) 376(26) New England Journal of Medicine 2507.

Chen M, 'Beijing Internet Court Denies Copyright to Works Created Solely by Artificial Intelligence' (2019) 14 Journal of Intellectual Property Law & Practice 593.

Chesterman S, *Just War or Just Peace? Humanitarian Intervention and International Law* (Oxford University Press 2001).

  You, the People: The United Nations, Transitional Administration, and State-Building (Oxford University Press 2004).

  'An International Rule of Law?' (2008) 56 American Journal of Comparative Law 331.

'The Turn to Ethics: Disinvestment from Multinational Corporations for Human Rights Violations – The Case of Norway's Sovereign Wealth Fund' (2008) 23 American University International Law Review 577.

One Nation under Surveillance: A New Social Contract to Defend Freedom without Sacrificing Liberty (Oxford University Press 2011).

(ed), *Data Protection Law in Singapore: Privacy and Sovereignty in an Interconnected World* (2nd edn, Academy 2018).

'Can International Law Survive a Rising China?' (2021) European Journal of International Law 1507.

Chesterman S and A Fisher (eds), *Private Security, Public Order: The Outsourcing of Public Services and Its Limits* (Oxford University Press 2009).

Chesterman S and C Lehnardt (eds), *From Mercenaries to Market: The Rise and Regulation of Private Military Companies* (Oxford University Press 2007).

Chinen M, *Law and Autonomous Machines: The Co-evolution of Legal Responsibility and Technology* (Edward Elgar 2019).

Chopra S and LF White, *A Legal Theory for Autonomous Artificial Agents* (University of Michigan Press 2011).

Chouldechova A, 'Fair Prediction with Disparate Impact: A Study of Bias in Recidivism Prediction Instruments' (2017) 5 Big Data 153.

Chu C, A Zhmoginov, and M Sandler, 'CycleGAN, a Master of Steganography' (2017) 1712.02950v2 arXiv.

Citron DK, 'Technological Due Process' (2008) 85 Washington University Law Review 1249.

Clarke AC, *2001: A Space Odyssey* (Hutchinson 1968).

Coase R, 'The Nature of the Firm' (1937) 4 Economica 386.

Cobbe J, 'Administrative Law and the Machines of Government: Judicial Review of Automated Public-Sector Decision-Making' (2019) 39 Legal Studies 636.

Coca-Vila I, 'Self-Driving Cars in Dilemmatic Situations: An Approach Based on the Theory of Justification in Criminal Law' (2018) 12 Criminal Law and Philosophy 59.

Coffee JC, Jr, '"No Soul to Damn: No Body to Kick": An Unscandalized Inquiry into the Problem of Corporate Punishment' (1981) 79 Michigan Law Review 386.

Cofone IN, 'Algorithmic Discrimination Is an Information Problem' (2019) 70 Hastings Law Journal 1389.

Cohen E, 'Law, Folklore, and Animal Lore' (1986) 110 Past & Present 6.

Cohen JE, *Between Truth and Power: The Legal Constructions of Informational Capitalism* (Oxford University Press 2019).

Cohen M, 'When Judges Have Reasons Not to Give Reasons: A Comparative Law Approach' (2015) 72 Washington & Lee Law Review 483.

Collingridge D, *The Social Control of Technology* (Frances Pinter 1980).

Contini F, 'Artificial Intelligence and the Transformation of Humans, Law and Technology Interactions in Judicial Proceedings' (2020) 2(1) Law, Technology, and Humans 4.

Coombs N, 'What Is an Algorithm? Financial Regulation in the Era of High-Frequency Trading' (2016) 45 Economy and Society 278.

Corrales M, M Fenwick, and N Forgó (eds), *Robotics, AI and the Future of Law* (Springer 2018).

Cortés P, *The Law of Consumer Redress in an Evolving Digital Market: Upgrading from Alternative to Online Dispute Resolution* (Cambridge University Press 2017).

Cortez N, 'Regulating Disruptive Innovation' (2014) 29 Berkeley Technology Law Journal 175.

Craik N, *The International Law of Environmental Impact Assessment: Process, Substance and Integration* (Cambridge University Press 2008).

Crane DA, KD Logue, and BC Pilz, 'A Survey of Legal Issues Arising from the Deployment of Autonomous and Connected Vehicles' (2017) 23 Michigan Telecommunications and Technology Law Review 191.

Crawford J, *The International Law Commission's Articles on State Responsibility: Introduction, Text and Commentaries* (Cambridge University Press 2002).

Crootof R, 'War Torts: Accountability for Autonomous Weapons' (2016) 164 University of Pennsylvania Law Review 1347.

    '"Cyborg Justice" and the Risk of Technological–Legal Lock-In' (2019) 119 Columbia Law Review Forum 233.

Cuéllar M-F, 'Cyberdelegation and the Administrative State' in NR Parrillo (ed), *Administrative Law from the Inside Out: Essays on Themes in the Work of Jerry L Mashaw* (Cambridge University Press 2017) 134.

Cui Y, *Artificial Intelligence and Judicial Modernization* (Springer 2020).

Čuk T and A van Waeyenberge, 'European Legal Framework for Algorithmic and High Frequency Trading (Mifid 2 and MAR): A Global Approach to Managing the Risks of the Modern Trading Paradigm' (2018) 9 European Journal of Risk Regulation 146.

Cullen FT and KE Gilbert, *Reaffirming Rehabilitation* (2nd edn, Anderson 2013).

Cunningham S, *Driving Offences: Law, Policy and Practice* (Routledge 2008).

Dal Bó E, 'Regulatory Capture: A Review' (2006) 22 Oxford Review of Economic Policy 203.

Dale R, 'Law and Word Order: NLP in Legal Tech' (2019) 25 Natural Language Engineering 211.

Damiano L and P Dumouchel, 'Anthropomorphism in Human–Robot Co-evolution' (2018) 9 Frontiers in Psychology 468.

Danaher J, 'Why AI Doomsayers Are Like Sceptical Theists and Why It Matters' (2015) 25 Mind and Machines 231.

'Regulating Child Sex Robots: Restriction or Experimentation?' (2019) 27 Medical Law Review 553.

Danchin PG et al, 'The Pandemic Paradox in International Law' (2020) 114 American Journal of International Law 598.

Dari-Mattiacci G et al, 'The Emergence of the Corporate Form' (2017) 33 Journal of Law, Economics and Organization 193.

Datta A, MC Tschantz, and A Datta, 'Automated Experiments on Ad Privacy Settings: A Tale of Opacity, Choice, and Discrimination' [2015] 1 Proceedings on Privacy Enhancing Technologies 92.

Datta A, S Sen, and Y Zick, 'Algorithmic Transparency via Quantitative Input Influence: Theory and Experiments with Learning Systems' (2016) IEEE Symposium on Security and Privacy (SP) 598.

Dauber E et al, 'Git Blame Who? Stylistic Authorship Attribution of Small, Incomplete Source Code Fragments' (2017) 1701.05681v3 arXiv.

Davis AE, 'The Future of Law Firms (and Lawyers) in the Age of Artificial Intelligence' (2020) 27(1) The Professional Lawyer 3.

Dawes J, 'Speculative Human Rights: Artificial Intelligence and the Future of the Human' (2020) 42 Human Rights Quarterly 573.

de Fine Licht K and J de Fine Licht, 'Artificial Intelligence, Transparency, and Public Decision-Making: Why Explanations Are Key When Trying to Produce Perceived Legitimacy' (2020) 35 AI & Society 917.

de Laat PB, 'Algorithmic Decision-Making Based on Machine Learning from Big Data: Can Transparency Restore Accountability?' (2018) 31 Philosophy & Technology 525.

Deakin S, 'Organisational Torts: Vicarious Liability versus Non-delegable Duty' [2018] Cambridge Law Journal 15.

Deakin S and Z Adams, *Markesinis and Deakin's Tort Law* (8th edn, Oxford University Press 2019).

Deakin S and C Markou (eds), *Is Law Computable? Critical Perspectives on Law and Artificial Intelligence* (Hart 2020).

Deeks A, 'The Judicial Demand for Explainable Artificial Intelligence' (2019) 119 Columbia Law Review 1829.

Deng J, 'Should the Common Law System Welcome Artificial Intelligence: A Case Study of China's Same-Type Case Reference System' (2019) 3 Georgetown Law Technology Review 223.

Dennerley JA, 'State Liability for Space Object Collisions: The Proper Interpretation of "Fault" for the Purposes of International Space Law' (2018) 29 European Journal of International Law 281.

Dewey J, 'The Historic Background of Corporate Legal Personality' (1926) 35 Yale Law Journal 655.

Diamantis ME, 'Clockwork Corporations: A Character Theory of Corporate Punishment' (2018) 103 Iowa Law Review 507.

Dick PK, *Do Androids Dream of Electric Sheep?* (Doubleday 1968).

Domingos P, *The Master Algorithm: How the Quest for the Ultimate Learning Machine Will Remake Our World* (Basic Books 2015).

Downes L, *The Laws of Disruption: Harnessing the New Forces that Govern Life and Business in the Digital Age* (Basic Books 2009).

du Sautoy M, *The Creativity Code: Art and Innovation in the Age of AI* (Harvard University Press 2019).

Dubber MD, F Pasquale, and S Das (eds), *The Oxford Handbook of Ethics of AI* (Oxford University Press 2020).

Duffy SH and JP Hopkins, 'Sit, Stay, Drive: The Future of Autonomous Car Liability' (2013) 16 SMU Science and Technology Law Review 453.

Dunlap CJ, Jr, 'Accountability and Autonomous Weapons: Much Ado about Nothing' (2016) 30 Temple International & Comparative Law Journal 63.

Duwe G and KD Kim, 'Sacrificing Accuracy for Transparency in Recidivism Risk Assessment: The Impact of Classification Method on Predictive Performance' (2016) 1 Corrections 155.

Dworkin R, *Taking Rights Seriously* (Harvard University Press 1977).

    Law's Empire (Harvard University Press 1986).

Dyson M, *Comparing Tort and Crime: Learning from across and within Legal Systems* (Cambridge University Press 2015).

Easterbrook FH and DR Fischel, 'Limited Liability and the Corporation' (1985) 52 University of Chicago Law Review 89.

Ebers M and S Navas (eds), *Algorithms and Law* (Cambridge University Press 2020).

Edmonds D, *Would You Kill the Fat Man? The Trolley Problem and What Your Answer Tells Us about Right and Wrong* (Princeton University Press 2013).

Edwards L (ed), *Law, Policy, and the Internet* (Hart 2019).

Edwards L and M Veale, 'Slave to the Algorithm? Why a "Right to an Explanation" Is Probably Not the Remedy You Are Looking For' (2017) 16 Duke Law & Technology Review 18.

    'Enslaving the Algorithm: From a "Right to an Explanation" to a "Right to Better Decisions"?' (2018) 16(3) IEEE Security & Privacy 46.

Egloff FJ, 'Public Attribution of Cyber Intrusions' (2021) 6 Journal of Cybersecurity 1.

Elrod JW, 'Trial by Siri: AI Comes to the Courtroom' (2020) 57 Houston Law Review 1085.

Endo SK, 'Technological Opacity & Procedural Injustice' (2018) 59 Boston College Law Review 821.

Engstrom NF, 'When Cars Crash: The Automobile's Tort Law Legacy' (2018) 53 Wake Forest Law Review 293.

Enough B and T Mussweiler, 'Sentencing under Uncertainty: Anchoring Effects in the Courtroom' (2001) 31 Journal of Applied Social Psychology 1535.

Epstein R, G Roberts, and G Beber (eds), *Parsing the Turing Test: Philosophical and Methodological Issues in the Quest for the Thinking Computer* (Springer 2009).

Erdelez S and S O'Hare, 'Legal Informatics: Application of Information Technology in Law' (1997) 32 Annual Review of Information Science and Technology 367.

Erdélyi OJ and J Goldsmith, 'Regulating Artificial Intelligence: Proposal for a Global Solution' (2018) AAAI/ACM Conference on AI, Ethics, and Society (AIES '18) 95.

Erkkilä T, *Ombudsman as a Global Institution: Transnational Governance and Accountability* (Palgrave Macmillan 2020).

Etzioni A and O Etzioni, 'Pros and Cons of Autonomous Weapons Systems', *Military Review* (May–June 2017) 71.

Eubanks V, *Automating Inequality: How High-Tech Tools Profile, Police, and Punish the Poor* (St Martin's 2017).

Evans EP, *The Criminal Prosecution and Capital Punishment of Animals* (EP Dutton 1906).

Ezrachi A and ME Stucke, *Virtual Competition: The Promise and Perils of the Algorithm-Driven Economy* (Harvard University Press 2016).

'Artificial Intelligence & Collusion: When Computers Inhibit Competition' [2017] University of Illinois Law Review 1775.

Fairgrieve D, *Product Liability in Comparative Perspective* (Cambridge University Press 2005).

Farjama M and O Kirchkampb, 'Bubbles in Hybrid Markets: How Expectations about Algorithmic Trading Affect Human Trading' (2018) 146 Journal of Economic Behavior & Organization 248.

Feeley MM and J Simon, 'The New Penology: Notes on the Emerging Strategy of Corrections and Its Implications' (1992) 30 Criminology 449.

Feldman RC, E Aldana, and K Stein, 'Artificial Intelligence in the Health Care Space: How We Can Trust What We Cannot Know' (2019) 30 Stanford Law & Policy Review 399.

Fellous J-M and MA Arbib, *Who Needs Emotions? The Brain Meets the Robot* (Oxford University Press 2005).

Fenwick M, WA Kaal, and EPM Vermeulen, 'Regulation Tomorrow: What Happens When Technology Is Faster than the Law?' (2017) 6 American University Business Law Review 561.

Fermi E, 'Atomic Energy for Power' in AV Hill (ed), *Science and Civilization: The Future of Atomic Energy* (McGraw-Hill 1946) 93.

Fifield W, 'Pablo Picasso: A Composite Interview' (1964) 32 Paris Review 37.

Finch J, S Geiger, and E Reid, 'Captured by Technology? How Material Agency Sustains Interaction between Regulators and Industry Actors' (2017) 46 Research Policy 160.

Firth-Butterfield K, 'Artificial Intelligence and the Law: More Questions than Answers?' (2017) 14(1) Scitech Lawyer 28.

Fischer D, *History of the International Atomic Energy Agency: The First Forty Years* (IAEA 1997).

Flores AW, K Bechtel, and CT Lowenkamp, 'False Positives, False Negatives, and False Analyses: A Rejoinder to "Machine Bias: There's Software Used across the Country to Predict Future Criminals. And It's Biased against Blacks"' (2016) 80(2) Federal Probation 38.

Floridi L, 'Robots, Jobs, Taxes, and Responsibilities' (2017) 30 Philosophy & Technology 1.

Follesdal A, 'The Principle of Subsidiarity as a Constitutional Principle in International Law' (2013) 2 Global Constitutionalism 37.

Fosch-Villaronga E, *Robots, Healthcare, and the Law: Regulating Automation in Personal Care* (Routledge 2019).

Frank X, 'Is Watson for Oncology per se Unreasonably Dangerous? Making a Case for How to Prove Products Liability Based on a Flawed Artificial Intelligence Design' (2019) 45 American Journal of Law & Medicine 273.

Frankenreiter J and MA Livermore, 'Computational Methods in Legal Analysis' (2020) 16 Annual Review of Law and Social Science 39.

Franklin S and AC Graesser, 'Is It an Agent, or Just a Program?: A Taxonomy for Autonomous Agents' in JP Müller, MJ Wooldridge, and NR Jennings (eds), *Intelligent Agents III: Agent Theories, Architectures, and Languages* (Springer 1997) 21.

French P, 'The Corporation as a Moral Person' (1979) 16 American Philosophical Quarterly 207.

Gandy OH, Jr, 'Engaging Rational Discrimination: Exploring Reasons for Placing Regulatory Constraints on Decision Support Systems' (2010) 12 Ethics and Information Technology 29.

Gebru T et al, 'Datasheets for Datasets' (2020) arXiv 1803.09010v7.

Gehl RW, *Weaving the Dark Web: Legitimacy on Freenet, Tor, and I2P* (MIT Press 2018).

Geistfeld MA, 'A Roadmap for Autonomous Vehicles: State Tort Liability, Automobile Insurance, and Federal Safety Regulation' (2017) 105 California Law Review 1611.

    'The Regulatory Sweet Spot for Autonomous Vehicles' (2018) 53 Wake Forest Law Review 101.

Gelman A and J Hill, *Data Analysis Using Regression and Multilevel/Hierarchical Models* (Cambridge University Press 2007).

Gerber LG, 'The Baruch Plan and the Origins of the Cold War' (1982) 6(4) Diplomatic History 69.

Gervais DJ, 'The Machine as Author' (2020) 105 Iowa Law Review 2053.

Gill C, 'The Evolving Role of the Ombudsman: A Conceptual and Constitutional Analysis of the "Scottish Solution" to Administrative Justice' [2014] Public Law 662.

Gilligan B, *Practical Horse Law: A Guide for Owners and Riders* (Blackwell Science 2002).

Glenn HP and LD Smith (eds), *Law and the New Logics* (Cambridge University Press 2017).

Goel S et al, 'Combatting Police Discrimination in the Age of Big Data' (2017) 20 New Criminal Law Review 181.

Good IJ, 'Speculations Concerning the First Ultraintelligent Machine' in FL Alt and M Rubinoff (eds), *Advances in Computers* (Academic 1965) vol 6, 31.

Goodman B and S Flaxman, 'European Union Regulations on Algorithmic Decision Making and a "Right to Explanation"' (2017) 38(3) AI Magazine 50.

Gottesman O et al, 'Guidelines for Reinforcement Learning in Healthcare' (2019) 25 Nature Medicine 16.

Goudkamp J and D Nolan, 'Contributory Negligence in the Twenty-First Century: An Empirical Study of First Instance Decisions' (2016) 79 Modern Law Review 575.

Gowder P, 'Transformative Legal Technology and the Rule of Law' (2018) 68 (Supplement1) University of Toronto Law Journal 82.

Grabiner Lord A, 'Sex, Scandal and Super-Injunctions – The Controversies Surrounding the Protection of Privacy' (2012) 45 Israel Law Review 537.

Gramitto Ricci SA, 'Artificial Agents in Corporate Boardrooms' (2020) 105 Cornell Law Review 869.

Gravanis G et al, 'Behind the Cues: A Benchmarking Study for Fake News Detection' (2019) 128 Expert Systems with Applications 201.

Griffiths J, *The Great Firewall of China: How to Build and Control an Alternative Version of the Internet* (Zed Books 2019).

Grimmelmann J, 'There's No Such Thing as a Computer-Authored Work – and It's a Good Thing, Too' (2016) 39 Columbia Journal of Law & the Arts 403.

Guidotti R et al, 'A Survey of Methods for Explaining Black Box Models' (2018) arXiv 1802.01933v3.

Guihot M, AF Matthew, and NP Suzor, 'Nudging Robots: Innovative Solutions to Regulate Artificial Intelligence' (2017) 20 Vanderbilt Journal of Entertainment & Technology Law 385.

Guihot M and LB Moses, *Artificial Intelligence, Robots and the Law* (LexisNexis 2020).

Guiora AN, 'Accountability and Decision Making in Autonomous Warfare: Who Is Responsible?' [2017] Utah Law Review 393.

Gunningham N and P Grabosky, *Smart Regulation: Designing Environmental Policy* (Clarendon Press 1998).

Gunkel DJ, *Robot Rights* (MIT Press 2018).

郭富民 [Guo Fumin], '人工智能无法取代法官的审慎艺术 [Artificial Intelligence Cannot Replace the Prudential Art of Judges]', 中国法院网 *[China Court Network]* (5 July 2017).

Guo L, 'Regulating Investment Robo-Advisors in China: Problems and Prospects' (2020) 21 European Business Organization Law Review 69.

Guttinger S, 'Trust in Science: CRISPR-Cas9 and the Ban on Human Germline Editing' (2018) 24 Science Engineering Ethics 1077.

Hacker P and B Petkova, 'Reining in the Big Promise of Big Data: Transparency, Inequality, and New Regulatory Frontiers' (2017) 15 Northwestern Journal of Technology and Intellectual Property 1.

Hagendorff T, 'The Ethics of AI Ethics: An Evaluation of Guidelines' (2020) 30 Minds & Machines 99.

Häggström O, 'Challenges to the Omohundro–Bostrom Framework for AI Motivations' (2019) 21 Foresight 153.

Hallevy G, *When Robots Kill: Artificial Intelligence under Criminal Law* (Northeastern University Press 2013).

Liability for Crimes Involving Artificial Intelligence Systems (Springer 2015).

Hamdani A and A Klement, 'Corporate Crime and Deterrence' (2008) 61 Stanford Law Review 271.

Hancox-Li L, 'Robustness in Machine Learning Explanations: Does It Matter?' (2020) ACM Conference on Fairness, Accountability, and Transparency (FAT*) 640.

Hannah-Moffat K, 'Sacrosanct or Flawed: Risk, Accountability and Gender-Responsive Penal Politics' (2011) 22 Current Issues in Criminal Justice 193.

'The Uncertainties of Risk Assessment: Partiality, Transparency, and Just Decisions' (2015) 27 Federal Sentencing Reporter 244.

Hansmann H and R Kraakman, 'The Essential Role of Organizational Law' (2000) 110 Yale Law Journal 387.

Harasimiuk DE and T Braun, *Regulating Artificial Intelligence: Binary Ethics and the Law* (Routledge 2021).

Harlow C and R Rawlings, *Law and Administration* (3rd edn, Cambridge University Press 2009).

Harrington A, *Mind Fixers: Psychiatry's Troubled Search for the Biology of Mental Illness* (Norton 2019).

Harrison H, *War with the Robots* (Grafton 1962).

Hart HLA, 'Positivism and the Separation of Law and Morals' (1958) 71 Harvard Law Review 593.

The Concept of Law (3rd edn, Clarendon Press 2012).

He J et al, 'The Practical Implementation of Artificial Intelligence Technologies in Medicine' (2019) 25 Nature Medicine 30.

Heald D, 'Varieties of Transparency' in C Hood and D Heald (eds), *Transparency: The Key to Better Governance?* (Oxford University Press 2006) 25.

Henderson DA, *Smallpox: The Death of a Disease* (Prometheus 2009).

Henkin L, *How Nations Behave: Law and Foreign Policy* (2nd edn, Columbia University Press 1979).

Henrich J, SJ Heine, and A Norenzayan, 'The Weirdest People in the World?' (2010) 33 Behavioral and Brain Sciences 61.

Henry N and A Powell, 'Sexual Violence in the Digital Age: The Scope and Limits of Criminal Law' (2016) 25 Social & Legal Studies 397.

Herings PJ-J, R Peeters, and MS Yang, 'Piracy on the Internet: Accommodate It or Fight It? A Dynamic Approach' (2018) 266 European Journal of Operational Research 328.

Hertogh M and R Kirkham (eds), *Research Handbook on the Ombudsman* (Edward Elgar 2018).

Hildebrandt M, 'Law as Information in the Era of Data-Driven Agency' (2016) 79 Modern Law Review 1.

   'Saved by Design? The Case of Legal Protection by Design' (2017) 11 Nanoethics 307.

   'Law as Computation in the Era of Artificial Legal Intelligence: Speaking Law to the Power of Statistics' (2018) 68(Supplement1) University of Toronto Law Journal 12.

Hildt E, 'Artificial Intelligence: Does Consciousness Matter?' (2019) 10(1535) Frontiers in Psychology.

Hoffman RR et al, 'Metrics for Explainable AI: Challenges and Prospects' (2019) arXiv 1812.04608v2.

Hofmann J, C Katzenbach, and K Gollatz, 'Between Coordination and Regulation: Finding the Governance in Internet Governance' (2017) 19 New Media & Society 1406.

Hofstadter DR, *Gödel, Escher, Bach: An Eternal Golden Braid* (Basic Books 1979).

Holcombe L, *Wives and Property: Reform of the Married Women's Property Law in Nineteenth-Century England* (Martin Robertson 1983).

Holmes OW, Jr, *The Common Law* (Little, Brown 1881).

   'The Path of the Law' (1897) 10 Harvard Law Review 457.

Hu Y, 'Robot Criminals' (2019) 52 University of Michigan Journal of Law Reform 487.

Huang R and X Sun, 'Weibo Network, Information Diffusion and Implications for Collective Action in China' (2014) 17 Information, Communication & Society 86.

Hughes J, 'The Law of Armed Conflict Issues Created by Programming Automatic Target Recognition Systems Using Deep Learning Methods' [2019] Yearbook of International Humanitarian Law 99.

Humphreys P, 'The Philosophical Novelty of Computer Simulation Methods' (2009) 169 Synthese 615.

Huws CF and JC Finnis, 'On Computable Numbers with an Application to the AlanTuringproblem' (2017) 25 Artificial Intelligence and Law 181.

Imbens GW and DB Rubin, *Causal Inference for Statistics, Social, and Biomedical Sciences: An Introduction* (Cambridge University Press 2015).

Iuliano J, 'Jury Voting Paradoxes' (2014) 113 Michigan Law Review 405.

Iwai K, 'Persons, Things and Corporations: The Corporate Personality Controversy and Comparative Corporate Governance' (1999) 47 American Journal of Comparative Law 583.

Jiang N, 'Old Wine in New Bottles? New Strategies for Judicial Accountability in China' (2018) 52 International Journal of Law, Crime and Justice 74.

Jin D (ed), *Reconstructing Our Orders: Artificial Intelligence and Human Society* (Springer 2018).

Jobin A, M Ienca, and E Vayena, 'The Global Landscape of AI Ethics Guidelines' (2019) 1 Nature Machine Intelligence 389.

Johnston S, 'The Practice of UN Treaty-Making Concerning Science' in S Chesterman, DM Malone, and S Villalpando (eds), *The Oxford Handbook of United Nations Treaties* (Oxford University Press 2019) 321.

Jones CAG, *Expert Witnesses: Science, Medicine, and the Practice of Law* (Clarendon Press 1994).

Jordan P et al, 'Exploring the Referral and Usage of Science Fiction in HCI Literature' (2018) arXiv 1803.08395v2.

Kaddari Z et al, 'Natural Language Processing: Challenges and Future Directions' in T Masrour, I El Hassani, and A Cherrafi (eds), *Artificial Intelligence and Industrial Applications* (Springer 2021) 236.

Kaminski ME, 'Binary Governance: Lessons from the GDPR's Approach to Algorithmic Accountability' (2019) 92 Southern California Law Review 1529.

Kaminski ME and G Malgieri, 'Multi-layered Explanations from Algorithmic Impact Assessments in the GDPR' (2020) ACM Conference on Fairness, Accountability, and Transparency (FAT*) 68.

Karnow CEA, 'Liability for Distributed Artificial Intelligences' (1996) 11 Berkeley Technology Law Journal 147.

Katsh E and O Rabinovich-Einy, *Digital Justice: Technology and the Internet of Disputes* (Oxford University Press 2017).

Katz A, 'Intelligent Agents and Internet Commerce in Ancient Rome' (2008) 20 Society for Computers and Law 35.

Kazis NM, 'Tort Concepts in Traffic Crimes' (2016) 125 Yale Law Journal 1131.

Keating GC, 'Products Liability as Enterprise Liability' (2017) 10 Tort Law Journal 41.

Kehrer T, 'Closing the Liability Loophole: The Liability Convention and the Future of Conflict in Space' (2019) 20 Chicago Journal of International Law 178.

Kerr I and K Szilagyi, 'Evitable Conflicts, Inevitable Technologies? The Science and Fiction of Robotic Warfare and IHL' (2018) 14 Law, Culture and the Humanities 45.

Khaitan T, *A Theory of Discrimination Law* (Oxford University Press 2015).

Khanna VS, 'Corporate Criminal Liability: What Purpose Does It Serve?' (1996) 109 Harvard Law Review 1477.

Khoo K and J Soh, 'The Inefficiency of Quasi–Per Se Rules: Regulating Information Exchange in EU and US Antitrust Law' (2020) 57 American Business Law Journal 45.

Kim YH and JJ Yang, 'What Makes Circuit Breakers Attractive to Financial Markets? A Survey' (2004) 13 Financial Markets, Institutions & Instruments 109.

King BA, T Hammond, and J Harrington, 'Disruptive Technology: Economic Consequences of Artificial Intelligence and the Robotics Revolution' (2017) 12(2) Journal of Strategic Innovation and Sustainability 53.

King MA, *Public Policy and the Corporation* (Chapman and Hall 1977).

Kirilenko A et al, 'The Flash Crash: High-Frequency Trading in an Electronic Market' (2017) 72 Journal of Finance 967.

Kirkham R and C Gill (eds), *A Manifesto for Ombudsman Reform* (Palgrave Macmillan 2020).

Kirkwood WT, 'Inherently Governmental Functions, Organizational Conflicts of Interest, and the Outsourcing of the United Kingdom's MOD Defense Acquisition Function: Lessons Learned from the US Experience' (2015) 44 Public Contract Law Journal 443.

Klein H, 'ICANN and Internet Governance: Leveraging Technical Coordination to Realize Global Public Policy' (2002) 18 The Information Society 193.

Kleinberg J et al, 'Discrimination in the Age of Algorithms' (2018) 10 Journal of Legal Analysis 113.

Ko H et al, 'Human-Machine Interaction: A Case Study on Fake News Detection Using a Backtracking Based on a Cognitive System' (2019) 55 Cognitive Systems Research 77.

Koppell JGS, 'Pathologies of Accountability: ICANN and the Challenge of "Multiple Accountabilities Disorder"' (2005) 65 Public Administration Review 94.

Krisch N and B Kingsbury, 'Global Governance and Global Administrative Law in the International Legal Order' (2006) 17 European Journal of International Law 1.

Kroll JA et al, 'Accountable Algorithms' (2017) 165 University of Pennsylvania Law Review 633.

Krupiy T, 'Regulating a Game Changer: Using a Distributed Approach to Develop an Accountability Framework for Lethal Autonomous Weapon Systems' (2018) 50 Georgetown Journal of International Law 45.

Kucherbaev P, A Bozzon, and G-J Houben, 'Human-Aided Bots' (2018) 22(6) IEEE Internet Computing 36.

Kurki VAJ, *A Theory of Legal Personhood* (Oxford University Press 2019).

Kurki VAJ and T Pietrzykowski (eds), *Legal Personhood: Animals, Artificial Intelligence and the Unborn* (Springer 2017).

Kurzweil R, *The Singularity Is Near: When Humans Transcend Biology* (Viking 2005).

Laffont J-J and J Tirole, 'The Politics of Government Decision-Making: A Theory of Regulatory Capture' (1991) 106 Quarterly Journal of Economics 1089.

Lalive R et al, 'Parental Leave and Mothers' Careers: The Relative Importance of Job Protection and Cash Benefits' (2014) 81 Review of Economic Studies 219.

Lambert P, *Gringras: The Laws of the Internet* (5th edn, Bloomsbury 2018).

Lang RD and LE Benessere, 'Alexa, Siri, Bixby, Google's Assistant, and Cortana Testifying in Court: Novel Use of Emerging Technology in Litigation' (2018) 35(7) Computer and Internet Lawyer 16.

Lange A-C, M Lenglet, and R Seyfert, 'Cultures of High-Frequency Trading: Mapping the Landscape of Algorithmic Developments in Contemporary Financial Markets' (2016) 45 Economy and Society 149.

Lannetti DW, 'Toward a Revised Definition of "Product" under the Restatement (Third) of Torts: Products Liability' (2000) 35 Tort & Insurance Law Journal 845.

Lastowka FG, *Virtual Justice: The New Laws of Online Worlds* (Yale University Press 2010).

Laubacher TJ, 'Simplifying Inherently Governmental Functions: Creating a Principled Approach from Its ad hoc Beginnings' (2017) 46 Public Contract Law Journal 791.

Lavy M and M Hervey, *The Law of Artificial Intelligence* (Sweet & Maxwell 2020).

Le Moli G, PS Vishvanathan, and A Aeri, 'Whither the Proof? The Progressive Reversal of the Burden of Proof in Environmental Cases before International Courts and Tribunals' (2017) 8 Journal of International Dispute Settlement 644.

Lee HCB, JM Cruz, and R Shankar, 'Corporate Social Responsibility (CSR) Issues in Supply Chain Competition: Should Greenwashing Be Regulated?' (2018) 49 Decision Sciences 1088.

Lee KF, *AI Superpowers: China, Silicon Valley, and the New World Order* (Houghton Mifflin Harcourt 2018).

Legge D and S Brooman, *Law Relating to Animals* (Cavendish 2000).

Lehman-Wilzig SN, 'Frankenstein Unbound: Towards a Legal Definition of Artificial Intelligence' (1981) 13 Futures 442.

Lehman J et al, 'The Surprising Creativity of Digital Evolution: A Collection of Anecdotes from the Evolutionary Computation and Artificial Life Research Communities' (2018) arXiv 1803.03453v1.

Lemley MA and B Casey, 'Remedies for Robots' (2019) 86 University of Chicago Law Review 1311.

Lenglet M and J Mol, 'Squaring the Speed of Light? Regulating Market Access in Algorithmic Finance' (2016) 45 Economy and Society 201.

Lessig L, *Code: Version 2.0* (Basic Books 2006).

Levendowski A, 'How Copyright Law Can Fix Artificial Intelligence's Implicit Bias Problem' (2018) 93 Washington Law Review 579.

Leveringhaus A, *Ethics and Autonomous Weapons* (Palgrave Macmillan 2016).

Levine ME and JL Forrence, 'Regulatory Capture, Public Interest, and the Public Agenda: Toward a Synthesis' (1990) 6(Special Issue) Journal of Law, Economics, and Organization 167.

Levine SS and MJ Prietula, 'Open Collaboration for Innovation: Principles and Performance' (2014) 25 Organization Science 1287.

Levy D and AT Young, '"The Real Thing": Nominal Price Rigidity of the Nickel Coke, 1886-1959' (2004) 36 Journal of Money, Credit, and Banking 765.

Levy S, *In the Plex: How Google Thinks, Works, and Shapes Our Lives* (New York 2011).

Lewis M, *Flash Boys: A Wall Street Revolt* (WW Norton 2014).

Lim D, 'AI & IP: Innovation & Creativity in an Age of Accelerated Change' (2018) 52 Akron Law Review 813.

Lim HYF, *Autonomous Vehicles and the Law: Technology, Algorithms, and Ethics* (Edward Elgar 2018).

Lin P, K Abney, and R Jenkins (eds), *Robot Ethics 2.0: From Autonomous Cars to Artificial Intelligence* (Oxford University Press 2017).

Lipton J, *Rethinking Cyberlaw: A New Vision for Internet Law* (Edward Elgar 2015).

Liu J, 'China's Data Localization' (2020) 13 Chinese Journal of Communication 84.

Liu Y-H et al, 'Reduction Measures for Air Pollutants and Greenhouse Gas in the Transportation Sector: A Cost-Benefit Analysis' (2019) 207 Journal of Cleaner Production 1023.

(ed), *Law as Data: Computation, Text, and the Future of Legal Analysis* (Santa Fe Institute Press 2019).

Livingston S and M Risse, 'The Future Impact of Artificial Intelligence on Humans and Human Rights' (2019) 33 Ethics and International Affairs 141.

London AJ and J Kimmelman, 'Why Clinical Translation Cannot Succeed without Failure' (2015) 4 eLife e12844.

Loughnan A, *Manifest Madness: Mental Incapacity in the Criminal Law* (Oxford University Press 2012).

Low K and E Mik, 'Pause the Blockchain Legal Revolution' (2020) 69 International and Comparative Law Quarterly 135.

Luciano F et al, 'AI4People—An Ethical Framework for a Good AI Society: Opportunities, Risks, Principles, and Recommendations' (2018) 28 Minds and Machines 689.

Ludsin H, *Preventive Detention and the Democratic State* (Cambridge University Press 2016).

Luetge C, 'The German Ethics Code for Automated and Connected Driving' (2017) 30 Philosophy & Technology 547.

Maas MM, 'Regulating for "Normal AI Accidents": Operational Lessons for the Responsible Governance of Artificial Intelligence Deployment' (2018) Proceedings of 2018 AAAI/ACM Conference on AI, Ethics, and Society (AIES '18) 223.

Mac Síthigh D and M Siems, 'The Chinese Social Credit System: A Model for Other Countries?' (2019) 82 Modern Law Review 1034.

MacKenzie D, '"Making", "Taking", and the Material Political Economy of Algorithmic Trading' (2018) 47 Economy and Society 501.

Magnuson WJ, *Blockchain Democracy: Technology, Law, and the Rule of the Crowd* (Cambridge University Press 2020).

Manheim K and L Kaplan, 'Artificial Intelligence: Risks to Privacy and Democracy' (2019) 21 Yale Journal of Law & Technology 106.

Mantelero A, 'AI and Big Data: A Blueprint for a Human Rights, Social, and Ethical Impact Assessment' (2018) 34 Computer Law & Security Review 754.

Mantrov V, 'A Victim of a Road Traffic Accident Not Fastened by a Seat Belt and Contributory Negligence in the EU Motor Insurance Law' (2014) 5 European Journal of Risk Regulation 115.

Margulies P, 'Sovereignty and Cyber Attacks: Technology's Challenge to the Law of State Responsibility' (2013) 14 Melbourne Journal of International Law 496.

Marmura SME, *The WikiLeaks Paradigm: Paradoxes and Revelations* (Palgrave 2018).

Mattli W, *Darkness by Design: The Hidden Power in Global Capital Markets* (Princeton University Press 2019).

Maurer M et al (eds), *Autonomous Driving: Technical, Legal and Social Aspects* (Springer 2016).

Maurer SM, *Self-Governance in Science: Community-Based Strategies for Managing Dangerous Knowledge* (Cambridge University Press 2017).

Maurutto P and K Hannah-Moffat, 'Assembling Risk and the Restructuring of Penal Control' (2006) 46 British Journal of Criminology 438.

McBride NJ and R Bagshaw, *Tort Law* (6th edn, Pearson 2018).

McCarty LT, 'Reflections on TAXMAN: An Experiment in Artificial Intelligence and Legal Reasoning' (1977) 90 Harvard Law Review 837.

McCormack TLH and GJ Simpson, 'A New International Criminal Law Regime?' (1995) 42 Netherlands International Law Review 177.

McCubbins MD and T Schwartz, 'Congressional Oversight Overlooked: Police Patrols versus Fire Alarms' (1984) 28 American Journal of Political Science 165.

McDougall C, 'Autonomous Weapon Systems and Accountability: Putting the Cart before the Horse' (2019) 20 Melbourne Journal of International Law 58.

McEwan I, *Machines Like Me* (Vintage 2019).

McFarland T and T McCormack, 'Mind the Gap: Can Developers of Autonomous Weapons Systems Be Liable for War Crimes?' (2014) 90 International Studies 361.

McKelvey F and M MacDonald, 'Artificial Intelligence Policy Innovations at the Canadian Federal Government' (2019) 44(2) Canadian Journal of Communication 43.

McNair B, *Fake News: Falsehood, Fabrication and Fantasy in Journalism* (Routledge 2018).

McNamara SR, 'The Law and Ethics of High-Frequency Trading' (2016) 17 Minnesota Journal of Law, Science & Technology 71.

McWilliams A et al (eds), *The Oxford Handbook of Corporate Social Responsibility: Psychological and Organizational Perspectives* (Oxford University Press 2019).

Meissner G, 'Artificial Intelligence: Consciousness and Conscience' (2020) 35 AI & Society 225.

Meloni C, 'Command Responsibility: Mode of Liability for the Crimes of Subordinates or Separate Offence of the Superior?' (2007) 5 Journal of International Criminal Justice 618.

Menn J, *All the Rave: The Rise and Fall of Shawn Fanning's Napster* (Crown 2003).

Merat N et al, 'The "Out-of-the-Loop" Concept in Automated Driving: Proposed Definition, Measures and Implications' (2019) 21 Cognition, Technology & Work 87.

Merkin R and J Steele, *Insurance and the Law of Obligations* (Oxford University Press 2013).

Merkin RM and J Stuart-Smith, *The Law of Motor Insurance* (Sweet & Maxwell 2004).

Mettraux G, *The Law of Command Responsibility* (Oxford University Press 2009).

Meyer DR and G Guernsey, 'Hong Kong and Singapore Exchanges Confront High Frequency Trading' (2017) 23 Asia Pacific Business Review 63.

Miller T, 'Explanation in Artificial Intelligence: Insights from the Social Sciences' (2019) 267 Artificial Intelligence 1.

Millon D, 'Piercing the Corporate Veil, Financial Responsibility, and the Limits of Limited Liability' (2007) 56 Emory Law Journal 1305.

Mitchell M et al, 'Model Cards for Model Reporting' (2019) ACM Conference on Fairness, Accountability, and Transparency (FAT*) 220.

Mitnick BM, *The Political Economy of Regulation: Creating, Designing, and Removing Regulatory Forms* (Columbia University Press 1980).

Mittelstadt BD et al, 'The Ethics of Algorithms: Mapping the Debate' (2016) 3(2) Big Data & Society.

Mittelstadt B, C Russell, and S Wachter, 'Explaining Explanations in AI' (2018) arXiv 1811.01439v1.

Mohseni S, N Zarei, and ED Ragan, 'A Multidisciplinary Survey and Framework for Design and Evaluation of Explainable AI Systems' (2020) arXiv 1811.11839v4.

Molnar C, *Interpretable Machine Learning* (Lulu 2019).

Montavon G et al, 'Explaining Nonlinear Classification Decisions with Deep Taylor Decomposition' (2017) 65 Pattern Recognition 211.

Morawetz V, *A Treatise on the Law of Private Corporations* (Little, Brown 1886).

Morison J and A Harkens, 'Re-engineering Justice? Robot Judges, Computerised Courts and (Semi) Automated Legal Decision-Making' (2019) 39 Legal Studies 618.

Mothilal RK, A Sharma, and C Tan, 'Explaining Machine Learning Classifiers Through Diverse Counterfactual Explanations' (2020) ACM Conference on Fairness, Accountability, and Transparency (FAT*) 607.

Mulligan C, 'Revenge Against Robots' (2018) 69 South Carolina Law Review 579.

Munday R, *Agency: Law and Principles* (3rd edn, Oxford University Press 2016).

Murphy J, 'The Liability Bases of Common Law Non-delegable Duties: A Reply to Christian Witting' (2007) 30 UNSW Law Journal 86.

Murphy KP, *Machine Learning: A Probabilistic Perspective* (MIT Press 2012).

Murray A, *Information Technology Law: The Law and Society* (3rd edn, Oxford University Press 2016).

Murugan V, 'Embryonic Stem Cell Research: A Decade of Debate from Bush to Obama' (2009) 82 Yale Journal of Biology and Medicine 101.

Naffine N, 'Who Are Law's Persons? From Cheshire Cats to Responsible Subjects' (2003) 66 Modern Law Review 346.

Nasarre-Aznar S, 'Ownership at Stake (Once Again): Housing, Digital Contents, Animals, and Robots' (2018) 10 Journal of Property, Planning, and Environmental Law 69.

Nissenbaum H, 'Protecting Privacy in an Information Age: The Problem of Privacy in Public' (1998) 17 Law and Philosophy 559.

Nwana HS, 'Software Agents: An Overview' (1996) 21 Knowledge Engineering Review 205.

O'Carroll F, 'Inherently Governmental: A Legal Argument for Ending Private Federal Prisons and Detention Centers' (2017) 67 Emory Law Journal 293.

O'Connell M, *To Be a Machine: Adventures among Cyborgs, Utopians, Hackers, and the Futurists Solving the Modest Problem of Death* (Granta 2017).

O'Neil C, *Weapons of Math Destruction: How Big Data Increases Inequality and Threatens Democracy* (Broadway Books 2016).

O'Sullivan T and K Tokeley, 'Consumer Product Failure Causing Personal Injury under the No-Fault Accident Compensation Scheme in New Zealand – A Let-Off for Manufacturers?' (2018) 41 Journal of Consumer Policy 211.

Ogus A, *Regulation: Legal Form and Economic Theory* (Hart 2004).

Ohlin JD, 'The Combatant's Stance: Autonomous Weapons on the Battlefield' (2016) 92 International Law Studies 1.

Ohlin JD (ed), *Research Handbook on Remote Warfare* (Edward Elgar 2017).

Omohundro S, 'Autonomous Technology and the Greater Human Good' (2014) 26 Journal of Experimental & Theoretical Artificial Intelligence 303.

Oskamp A and M Lauritsen, 'AI in Law Practice? So Far, Not Much' (2002) 10 Artificial Intelligence and Law 227.

Pagallo U, *The Laws of Robots: Crimes, Contracts, and Torts* (Springer 2013).

Page LL, 'Write This Down: A Model Market-Share Liability Statute' (2019) 68 Duke Law Journal 1469.

Page WH, 'The Gary Dinners and the Meaning of Concerted Action' (2009) 62 Southern Methodist University Law Review 597.

Paliwala A, 'Rediscovering Artificial Intelligence and Law: An Inadequate Jurisprudence?' (2016) 30 International Review of Law, Computers & Technology 107.

Parasuraman R and D Manzey, 'Complacency and Bias in Human Use of Automation: An Attentional Integration' (2010) 52 Human Factors 381.

Park S and Haksoo Ko, 'Machine Learning and Law and Economics: A Preliminary Overview' (2020) 11(2) Asian Journal of Law and Economics.

Parkin J, 'Adaptable Due Process' (2012) 160 University of Pennsylvania Law Review 1309.

Pasquale F, *The Black Box Society: The Secret Algorithms That Control Money and Information* (Harvard University Press 2015).

'A Rule of Persons, Not Machines: The Limits of Legal Automation' (2019) 87 George Washington Law Review 1.

New Laws of Robotics: Defending Human Expertise in the Age of AI (Belknap Press 2020).

Pasquale F and G Cashwell, 'Prediction, Persuasion, and the Jurisprudence of Behaviourism' (2018) 68(Supplement1) University of Toronto Law Journal 63.

Patterson FD and K Neailey, 'A Risk Register Database System to Aid the Management of Project Risk' (2002) 20 International Journal of Project Management 365.

Patterson MR, *Antitrust Law in the New Economy* (Harvard University Press 2017).

Pearl TH, 'Fast & Furious: The Misregulation of Driverless Cars' (2017) 73 New York University Annual Survey of American Law 24.

Peerenboom R, *China's Long March Toward Rule of Law* (Cambridge University Press 2002).

Peloso C, 'Crafting an International Climate Change Protocol: Applying the Lessons Learned from the Success of the Montreal Protocol and the Ozone Depletion Problem' (2010) 25 Journal of Land Use & Environmental Law 305.

Percy S, *Mercenaries: The History of a Norm in International Relations* (Oxford University Press 2007).

Peters B (ed), *Digital Keywords: A Vocabulary of Information Society and Culture* (Princeton University Press 2016) 18.

Petit N, 'Antitrust and Artificial Intelligence: A Research Agenda' (2017) 8 Journal of European Competition Law & Practice 361.

Poitras R, 'Article 36 Weapons Reviews & Autonomous Weapons Systems: Supporting an International Review Standard' (2018) 34 American University International Law Review 465.

Poscher R, 'Ambiguity and Vagueness in Legal Interpretation' in LM Solan and PM Tiersma (eds), *The Oxford Handbook of Language and Law* (Oxford University Press 2012) 128.

Powell TW, 'Command Responsibility: How the International Criminal Court's Jean-Pierre Bemba Gombo Conviction Exposes the Uniform Code of Military Justice' (2017) 225 Military Law Review 837.

Prassl J, *Humans as a Service: The Promise and Perils of Work in the Gig Economy* (Oxford University Press 2018).

Press M, 'Of Robots and Rules: Autonomous Weapon Systems in the Law of Armed Conflict' (2017) 48 Georgetown Journal of International Law 1337.

Priest GL and B Klein, 'The Selection of Disputes for Litigation' (1984) 13 Journal of Legal Studies 1.

Prins SJ and A Reich, 'Can We Avoid Reductionism in Risk Reduction?' (2018) 22 Theoretical Criminology 258.

Prosser T, 'Regulation and Social Solidarity' (2006) 33 Journal of Law and Society 364.

   The Regulatory Enterprise: Government, Regulation, and Legitimacy (Oxford University Press 2010).

Qiao C-r, 'Jurisprudent Shift in China: A Functional Interpretation' (2017) 8(1) Asian Journal of Law and Economics.

Radu R, *Negotiating Internet Governance* (Oxford University Press 2019).

Raji ID et al, 'Closing the AI Accountability Gap: Defining an End-to-End Framework for Internal Algorithmic Auditing' (2020) 2001.00973v1 arXiv.

Raustiala K and CJ Sprigman, 'The Second Digital Disruption: Streaming and the Dawn of Datadriven Creativity' (2019) 94 New York University Law Review 1555.

Rawls J, *Political Liberalism* (Columbia University Press 1996).

Raz J, *Ethics in the Public Domain: Essays in the Morality of Law and Politics* (Clarendon Press 1995).

Reiling D, *Technology for Justice: How Information Technology Can Support Judicial Reform* (Leiden University Press 2010).

Rhodes R, *The Making of the Atomic Bomb* (Simon & Schuster 1986).

Richardson R, JM Schultz, and K Crawford, 'Dirty Data, Bad Predictions: How Civil Rights Violations Impact Police Data, Predictive Policing Systems, and Justice' (2019) 94 New York University Law Review 192.

Richelson JT, *Spying on the Bomb: American Nuclear Intelligence from Nazi Germany to Iran and North Korea* (Norton 2006).

Rifkin J, *The Zero Marginal Cost Society: The Internet of Things, the Collaborative Commons, and the Eclipse of Capitalism* (St Martin's Press 2014).

Robaldo L et al, 'Introduction for Artificial Intelligence and Law: Special Issue "Natural Language Processing for Legal Texts"' (2019) 27 Artificial Intelligence and Law 113.

Roberts H et al, 'The Chinese Approach to Artificial Intelligence: An Analysis of Policy, Ethics, and Regulation' (2021) 36 AI & Society 59.

Rodgers C, 'A New Approach to Protecting Ecosystems' (2017) 19 Environmental Law Review 266.

Roig A, 'Safeguards for the Right Not to Be Subject to a Decision Based Solely on Automated Processing (Article 22 GDPR)' (2017) 8(3) European Journal of Law and Technology.

Rose SPR and H Rose, '"Do Not Adjust Your Mind, There Is a Fault in Reality" – Ideology in Neurobiology' (1973) 2 Cognition 479.

Rosenberg A, 'Strict Liability: Imagining a Legal Framework for Autonomous Vehicles' (2017) 20 Tulane Journal of Technology and Intellectual Property 205.

Rousseau J-J, *The Social Contract* (GDH Cole tr, first published 1762, JM Dent 1923).

Roy K, *War and Society in Afghanistan: From the Mughals to the Americans, 1500–2013* (Oxford University Press 2015).

Rudin C, 'Stop Explaining Black Box Machine Learning Models for High Stakes Decisions and Use Interpretable Models Instead' (2019) 1 Nature Machine Intelligence 206.

Ruggie JG, Guiding Principles on Business and Human Rights: Implementing the United Nations 'Protect, Respect and Remedy' Framework, UN Doc A/HRC/17/31 (2011).

Russell SJ, *Human Compatible: Artificial Intelligence and the Problem of Control* (Viking 2019).

Russell SJ and P Norvig, *Artificial Intelligence: A Modern Approach* (3rd edn, Prentice Hall 2010).

Sadat LN, 'Prosecutor v Jean-Pierre Bemba Gombo' (2019) 113 American Journal of International Law 353.

Sales Lord, 'Algorithms, Artificial Intelligence, and the Law' (2020) 25 Judicial Review 46.

Samek W et al, 'Evaluating the Visualization of What a Deep Neural Network Has Learned' (2017) 28(11) IEEE Transactions on Neural Networks and Learning Systems 2660.

Samuelson P, 'Allocating Ownership Rights in Computer-Generated Works' (1986) 47 University of Pittsburgh Law Review 1185.

Sands P and J Peel, *Principles of Environmental Law* (4th edn, Cambridge University Press 2018).

Santoni de Sio, F, 'Killing by Autonomous Vehicles and the Legal Doctrine of Necessity' (2017) 20 Ethical Theory and Moral Practice 411.

Schär F and A Berentsen, *Bitcoin, Blockchain, and Cryptoassets* (MIT Press 2020).

Schauer F, 'A Critical Guide to Vehicles in the Park' (2008) 83 New York University Law Review 1109.

Schellekens M, 'No-Fault Compensation Schemes for Self-Driving Vehicles' (2018) 10 Law, Innovation and Technology 314.

Scherer MU, 'Regulating Artificial Intelligence Systems: Risks, Challenges, Competencies, and Strategies' (2016) 29 Harvard Journal of Law & Technology 353.

Scherer M, 'Artificial Intelligence and Legal Decision-Making: The Wide Open?' (2019) 36 Journal of International Arbitration 539.

Schlag P, 'No Vehicles in the Park' (1999) 23 Seattle University Law Review 381.

Schneewind JB, *The Invention of Autonomy: A History of Modern Moral Philosophy* (Cambridge University Press 1997).

Schwab K, *The Fourth Industrial Revolution* (Crown 2017).

Searle JR, 'Minds, Brains, and Programs' (1980) 3 Behavioral and Brain Sciences 417.

Selbst A and S Barocas, 'The Intuitive Appeal of Explainable Machines' (2018) 87 Fordham Law Review 1085.

Selbst AD, 'Disparate Impact in Big Data Policing' (2017) 52 Georgia Law Review 109.

Selbst AD et al, 'Fairness and Abstraction in Sociotechnical Systems' (2019) ACM Conference on Fairness, Accountability, and Transparency (FAT*) 59.

Selby J, 'Data Localization Laws: Trade Barriers or Legitimate Responses to Cybersecurity Risks, or Both?' (2017) 25 International Journal of Law and Information Technology 213.

Selznick P, 'Focusing Organizational Research on Regulation' in R Noll (ed), *Regulatory Policy and the Social Sciences* (University of California Press 1985) 363.

Seng D, 'The State of the Discordant Union: An Empirical Analysis of DMCA Takedown Notices' (2014) 18 Virginia Journal of Law & Technology 369.

Sergot MJ et al, 'The British Nationality Act as a Logic Program' (1986) 29 Communications of the ACM 370.

Service RF, 'Chipmakers Look Past Moore's Law, and Silicon' (2018) 361(6400) Science 321.

Shearer D, *Private Armies and Military Intervention* (Oxford University Press 1998).

Sheiner N, 'DES and a Proposed Theory of Enterprise Liability' (1978) 46 Fordham Law Review 963.

Sheppard B, 'Warming Up to Inscrutability: How Technology Could Challenge Our Concept of Law' (2018) 68(Supplement1) University of Toronto Law Journal 36.

Shils EA, *The Torment of Secrecy: The Background and Consequences of American Security Policies* (Heinemann 1956).

Shokri R, M Strobel, and Y Zick, 'On the Privacy Risks of Model Explanations' (2020) arXiv 1907.00164v5.

Siciliani P, 'Tackling Algorithmic-Facilitated Tacit Collusion in a Proportionate Way' (2019) 10 Journal of European Competition Law & Practice 31.

Silver D et al, 'Mastering the Game of Go without Human Knowledge' (2017) 550 Nature 354.

Silver N, *The Signal and the Noise: Why So Many Predictions Fail – But Some Don't* (Penguin 2012).

Singer P, 'Speciesism and Moral Status' (2009) 40 Metaphilosophy 567.

Soares N and B Fallenstein, 'Agent Foundations for Aligning Machine Intelligence with Human Interests: A Technical Research Agenda' in V Callaghan et al (eds), *The Technological Singularity: Managing the Journey* (Springer 2017) 103.

Solaiman SM, 'Legal Personality of Robots, Corporations, Idols and Chimpanzees: A Quest for Legitimacy' (2017) 25 Artificial Intelligence and Law 155.

Solove DJ, 'Privacy and Power: Computer Databases and Metaphors for Information Privacy' (2001) 53 Stanford Law Review 1393.

Solum LB, 'Legal Personhood for Artificial Intelligences' (1992) 70 North Carolina Law Review 1231.

Sourdin T, 'Judge v Robot? Artificial Intelligence and Judicial Decision-Making' (2018) 41 UNSW Law Journal 1114.

Sparrow A, *The Law of Virtual Worlds and Internet Social Networks* (Gower 2010).

Sparrow MK, *The Regulatory Craft: Controlling Risks, Solving Problems, and Managing Compliance* (Brookings Institution 2000).

Stapleton J, *Product Liability* (Butterworths 1994).

Steiner C, *Automate This: How Algorithms Came to Rule Our World* (Penguin 2012).

Stockdale M and R Mitchell, 'Legal Advice Privilege and Artificial Legal Intelligence: Can Robots Give Privileged Legal Advice?' (2019) 23 International Journal of Evidence & Proof 422.

Stone CD, 'Should Trees Have Standing? Towards Legal Rights for Natural Objects' (1972) 45 Southern California Law Review 450.

Strandburg KJ, 'Rulemaking and Inscrutable Automated Decision Tools' (2019) 119 Columbia Law Review 1851.

Stucki S, 'Towards a Theory of Legal Animal Rights: Simple and Fundamental Rights' (2020) 40 Oxford Journal of Legal Studies 533.

Sullivan LA, WS Grimes, and CL Sagers, *The Law of Antitrust, An Integrated Handbook* (3rd edn, West 2014).

Sunstein C, *Laws of Fear: Beyond the Precautionary Principle* (Cambridge University Press 2005).

Susskind R, 'Detmold's Refutation of Positivism and the Computer Judge' (1986) 49 Modern Law Review 125.

   The Future of Law: Facing the Challenges of Information Technology (Oxford University Press 1996).

   Transforming the Law: Essays on Technology, Justice, and the Legal Marketplace (Oxford University Press 2000).

   The End of Lawyers? Rethinking the Nature of Legal Services (Oxford University Press 2008).

   Tomorrow's Lawyers: An Introduction to Your Future (Oxford University Press 2013).

   Online Courts and the Future of Justice (Oxford University Press 2019).

Susskind R and D Susskind, *The Future of the Professions: How Technology Will Transform the Work of Human Experts* (Oxford University Press 2015).

Swanson SR, 'Google Sets Sail: Ocean-Based Server Farms and International Law' (2011) 43 Connecticut Law Review 709.

Sykes K, 'Human Drama, Animal Trials: What the Medieval Animal Trials Can Teach Us about Justice for Animals' (2011) 17 Animal Law 273.

Szasz PC, *The Law and Practices of the International Atomic Energy Agency* (International Atomic Energy Agency 1970).

Taeihagh A and HSM Lim, 'Governing Autonomous Vehicles: Emerging Responses for Safety, Liability, Privacy, Cybersecurity, and Industry Risks' (2019) 39 Transport Reviews 103.

Take I, 'Regulating the Internet Infrastructure: A Comparative Appraisal of the Legitimacy of ICANN, ITU, and the WSIS' (2012) 6 Regulation & Governance 499.

Tan D, 'Fair Use and Transformative Play in the Digital Age' in M Richardson and S Ricketson (eds), *Research Handbook on Intellectual Property in Media and Entertainment* (Edward Elgar 2017) 102.

Taplin J, *Move Fast and Break Things: How Facebook, Google, and Amazon Cornered Culture and Undermined Democracy* (Little, Brown 2017).

Taylor PM, *A Commentary on the International Covenant on Civil and Political Rights* (Cambridge University Press 2020).

腾讯研究院 [Tencent Research Institute] and 中国信通院互联网法律研究中心 [China ICT Internet Law Research Center], 人工智能：国家人工智能战略行动抓手 *[Artificial Intelligence: National Artificial Intelligence Strategy]* (Renmin University Press 2017).

Thomas WR, 'Incapacitating Criminal Corporations' (2019) 72 Vanderbilt Law Review 905.

Tjio H, 'Lifting the Veil on Piercing the Veil' [2014] Lloyd's Maritime and Commercial Law Quarterly 19.

Tomsett R et al, 'Interpretable to Whom? A Role-Based Model for Analyzing Interpretable Machine Learning Systems' (2018) arXiv 1806.07552.

Totschnig W, 'The Problem of Superintelligence: Political, Not Technological' (2019) 34 AI & Society 907.

Trainor SA, 'A Comparative Analysis of a Corporation's Right Against Self-Incrimination' (1994) 18 Fordham International Law Journal 2139.

Tromp N and P Hekkert, *Designing for Society: Products and Services for a Better World* (Bloomsbury Visual Arts 2019).

Turchin A and D Denkenberger, 'Classification of Global Catastrophic Risks Connected with Artificial Intelligence' (2020) 35 AI & Society 147.

Turilli M and L Floridi, 'The Ethics of Information Transparency' (2009) 11 Ethics and Information Technology 105.

Turing AM, 'Computing Machinery and Intelligence' (1950) 59 Mind 433.

Intelligent Machinery, a Heretical Theory (lecture given to the '51 Society' at Manchester) (Turing Digital Archive, AMT/B/4, 1951).

'Intelligent Machinery, A Heretical Theory' (1996) 4 Philosophia Mathematica 256.

Turing D, *Prof Alan Turing Decoded: A Biography* (History Press 2015).

Turner J, *Robot Rules: Regulating Artificial Intelligence* (Palgrave Macmillan 2019).

Ugur M (ed), *Governance, Regulation, and Innovation: Theory and Evidence from Firms and Nations* (Edward Elgar 2013).

Upson J and RA Van Ness, 'Multiple Markets, Algorithmic Trading, and Market Liquidity' (2017) 32 Journal of Financial Markets 49.

Valentine S, 'Impoverished Algorithms: Misguided Governments, Flawed Technologies, and Social Control' (2019) 46 Fordham Urban Law Journal 364.

Veal R and M Tsimplis, 'The Integration of Unmanned Ships into the Lex Maritima' [2017] Lloyd's Maritime and Commercial Law Quarterly 303.

Veale M and L Edwards, 'Clarity, Surprises, and Further Questions in the Article 29 Working Party Draft Guidance on Automated Decision-Making and Profiling' (2018) 34 Computer Law & Security Review 398.

Vial L, B Lecouteux, and D Schwab, 'Sense Vocabulary Compression through the Semantic Knowledge of WordNet for Neural Word Sense Disambiguation' (2019) arXiv 1905.05677v3.

Vladeck DC, 'Machines without Principals: Liability Rules and Artificial Intelligence' (2014) 89 Washington Law Review 117.

Volokh E, 'Chief Justice Robots' (2019) 68 Duke Law Journal 1135.

Von Ahn L et al, 'CAPTCHA: Using Hard AI Problems for Security' in E Biham (ed), *Advances in Cryptology – EUROCRYPT 2003* (Springer 2003) 294.

von Heinegg WH, R Frau, and T Singer (eds), *Dehumanization of Warfare: Legal Implications of New Weapon Technologies* (Springer 2018).

Vosoughi S, D Roy, and S Aral, 'The Spread of True and False News Online' (2018) 359(6380) Science 1146.

Wachter S and B Mittelstadt, 'A Right to Reasonable Inferences: Re-thinking Data Protection Law in the Age of Big Data and AI' [2019] Columbia Business Law Review 494.

Wachter S, B Mittelstadt, and L Floridi, 'Why a Right to Explanation of Automated Decision-Making Does Not Exist in the General Data Protection Regulation' (2017) 7 International Data Privacy Law 76.

Wachter S, B Mittelstadt, and C Russell, 'Counterfactual Explanations without Opening the Black Box: Automated Decisions and the GDPR' (2018) 31 Harvard Journal of Law & Technology 841.

Wagner B, 'Liable, but Not in Control? Ensuring Meaningful Human Agency in Automated Decision-Making Systems' (2019) 11 Policy & Internet 104.

Waldron J, 'Theoretical Foundations of Liberalism' (1987) 37(147) The Philosophical Quarterly 127.

'The Rule of Law and the Importance of Procedure' in JE Fleming (ed), *Nomos L: Getting to the Rule of Law* (New York University Press 2011) 3.

Wallach W, *A Dangerous Master: How to Keep Technology from Slipping Beyond Our Control* (Basic Books 2015).

Wallach W and C Allen, *Moral Machines: Teaching Robots Right from Wrong* (Oxford University Press 2009).

Walsh T, *Android Dreams: The Past, Present, and Future of Artificial Intelligence* (Hurst 2017).

Walters E, 'The Model Rules of Autonomous Conduct: Ethical Responsibilities of Lawyers and Artificial Intelligence' (2019) 35 Georgia State University Law Review 1073.

Walton D, *Argumentation Methods for Artificial Intelligence in Law* (Springer 2005).

Waltz K, The Spread of Nuclear Weapons: More May Better (International Institute for Strategic Studies, Adelphi Papers, Number 171, 1981).

Walzer M, *Just and Unjust Wars: A Moral Argument with Historical Illustrations* (3rd edn, Basic Books 2000).

Wang D et al, 'Designing Theory-Driven User-Centric Explainable AI' (2019) CHI '19: Proceedings of the 2019 CHI Conference on Human Factors in Computing Systems Paper No 601.

Wang FF, *Law of Electronic Commercial Transactions: Contemporary Issues in the EU, US and China* (2nd edn, Routledge 2014).

Ward T and S Maruna, *Rehabilitation* (Routledge 2007).

Watson SM, 'The Corporate Legal Person' (2019) 19 Journal of Corporate Law Studies 137.

Watts P and FMB Reynolds, *Bowstead and Reynolds on Agency* (21st edn, Sweet & Maxwell 2018).

Weaver JF, *Robots Are People Too: How Siri, Google Car, and Artificial Intelligence Will Force Us to Change Our Laws* (Praeger 2014).

Wechsler H, 'Toward Neutral Principles of Constitutional Law' (1959) 73 Harvard Law Review 1.

Weinrib EJ, 'Causal Uncertainty' (2016) 36 Oxford Journal of Legal Studies 135.

Wellek R, 'Karel Čapek' (1936) 15 Slavonic and East European Review 191.

Weller BM, 'Does Algorithmic Trading Reduce Information Acquisition?' (2018) 31 Review of Financial Studies 2184.

Wessel RA, 'Regulating Technological Innovation through Informal International Law: The Exercise of International Public Authority by Transnational Actors', in MA Heldeweg and E Kica (eds), *Regulating Technological Innovation* (Palgrave Macmillan 2011) 77.

Wexler R, 'Life, Liberty, and Trade Secrets: Intellectual Property in the Criminal Justice System' (2018) 70 Stanford Law Review 1343.

Whalen R (ed), *Computational Legal Studies: The Promise and Challenge of Data-Driven Research* (Edward Elgar 2020).

Wilson G, 'Minimizing Global Catastrophic and Existential Risks from Emerging Technologies through International Law' (2013) 31 Virginia Environmental Law Journal 307.

Wischmeyer T and T Rademacher (eds), *Regulating Artificial Intelligence* (Springer 2020).

Witting C, 'Breach of the Non-delegable Duty: Defending Limited Strict Liability in Tort' (2006) 29 UNSW Law Journal 33.

Street on Torts (15th edn, Oxford University Press 2018).

Wong P-H, 'Democratizing Algorithmic Fairness' (2020) 33 Philosophy & Technology 225.

Woo MYK, 'Court Reform with Chinese Characteristics' (2017) 27 Washington International Law Journal 241.

Woodward M, 'The Need for Speed: Regulatory Approaches to High Frequency Trading in the United States and the European Union' (2011) 50 Vanderbilt Journal of Transnational Law 1359.

Wright P, *Spycatcher: The Candid Autobiography of a Senior Intelligence Officer* (Viking 1987).

Wringe B, *An Expressive Theory of Punishment* (Palgrave Macmillan 2016).

Wu T, 'Agency Threats' (2011) 60 Duke Law Journal 1841.

Xu X and F Chiang-Ku, 'Autonomous Vehicles, Risk Perceptions and Insurance Demand: An Individual Survey in China' (2019) 124(C) Transportation Research Part A: Policy and Practice 549.

Xu Z et al, 'Case Facts Analysis Method Based on Deep Learning' in Weiwei Ni et al (eds), *Web Information Systems and Applications* (Springer 2020) 92.

Yao J-j and P Hui, 'Research on the Application of Artificial Intelligence in Judicial Trial: Experience from China' (2020) 1487 Journal of Physics: Conference Series 012013.

Yap BP, A Koh, and ES Chng, 'Adapting BERT for Word Sense Disambiguation with Gloss Selection Objective and Example Sentences' (2020) arXiv 2009.11795v2.

Yeo TM, 'Unilateral Mistake in Contract: Five Degrees of Fusion of Common Law and Equity' [2004] Singapore Journal of Legal Studies 227.

Yeung K, '"Hypernudge": Big Data as a Mode of Regulation by Design' (2017) 20 Information, Communication & Society 118.

'Algorithmic Regulation: A Critical Interrogation' (2018) 12 Regulation & Governance 505.

Yong D, 'The Courtroom Performance' (1985) 10(3) The Cambridge Journal of Anthropology 74.

You C, 'Law and Policy of Platform Economy in China' (2020) 39 Computer Law & Security Review 1.

Yudkowsky E, 'Complex Value Systems in Friendly AI' in J Schmidhuber, KR Thórisson, and M Looks (eds), *Artificial General Intelligence* (Springer 2011) 388.

Zalnieriute M, LB Moses, and G Williams, 'The Rule of Law and Automation of Government Decision-Making' (2019) 82 Modern Law Review 425.

Zarsky TZ, 'Transparent Predictions' [2013] University of Illinois Law Review 1503.

Zerilli J et al, 'Transparency in Algorithmic and Human Decision-Making: Is There a Double Standard?' (2019) 32 Philosophy & Technology 661.

Zetzsche DA et al, 'Regulating a Revolution: From Regulatory Sandboxes to Smart Regulation' (2017) 23 Fordham Journal of Corporate & Financial Law 31.

Zhang M and S Jian, 'Outsourcing in Municipal Governments: Experiences from the United States and China' (2012) 35 Public Performance & Management Review 696.

Zhang X, *Legislation of Tort Liability Law in China* (Springer 2018).

Zhou H and PS Kalev, 'Algorithmic and High Frequency Trading in Asia-Pacific, Now and the Future' (2019) 53 Pacific-Basin Finance Journal 186.

Zhou H and Q Pan, 'Information, Community, and Action on Sina-Weibo: How Chinese Philanthropic NGOs Use Social Media Authors' (2016) 27 VOLUNTAS: International Journal of Voluntary and Nonprofit Organizations 2433.

Zuboff S, *The Age of Surveillance Capitalism: The Fight for a Human Future at the New Frontier of Power* (Public Affairs 2019).

INDEX

2010 Flash Crash, 15–17, 22–23, 29–30

Abbott, Ryan, 192
accessory liability, 106
accountability. *See also* human control;
    judicial function
  autonomous vehicles, 32, 36
  of humans, 104, 188
  for legal decisions, 64
  lethal force decisions and, 48–49,
    105–6
  oversight and, 66
actuarial risk assessment, 71–74. *See
  also* COMPAS recidivism
  assessment
administrative law, 78
Advanced Targeting and Lethality
  Automated System (ATLAS), 45
Advanced Technology External
  Advisory Council, 202
African Americans, risk assessment
  and, 71–72
agency, 88–90
aggregate theory of juridical
  personality, 118
AI Ethics Principles (Australia), 165
AI for Good summits, 212
AI winter, 11, 227
Algorithm Charter (New Zealand),
  165, 191
Algorithmic Accountability Act (USA,
  proposed), 163–64
algorithmic audits, 156–57
algorithmic impact assessments, 149,
  154–56, 160–61, 163–64
algorithmic transparency, 151
AlphaGo, 1, 65
android fallacy, 127–28, 141, 173, 189
animals

  personality and, 129–31
  strict liability for, 91–92
  trials of, 85–86, 113
anthropocentric predicament, 64
anthropocentrism, 245
anthropomorphic fallacy, 8
anthropomorphism, 86, 125–26, 127
antitrust (competition law), 17, 25–28
Aquinas, Thomas, 113
Article 29 Working Party (European
  Data Protection Board), 159
artificial intelligence (AI)
  concerns with, 1
  general versus narrow, 1–2
  superintelligence, 138–41, 190
  treatment by humans of, 188–89
  updating of, 239
artificial intelligence regulation. *See also*
  globalization issues; International
  Artificial Intelligence Agency
  (IAIA); international law;
  regulation by AI; self-governance
  overview, xv–xvi, 197–98
  approaches to, 185–92
  dangers of delay in, 10–11
  data protection, view of and, 179–80
  definition and scope, 3–6
  general AI and, 181
  industry standards for, 198–203
  innovation and, 10–12, 29
  justification for, 177–80
  laws of robotics and, 173–74
  modalities of, 185
  need for, 198–99
  nuclear power regulation compared,
    195–97
  principles for, 175–77
  prospects for, 192–94
  as public control, 4

responsibility for, 4
state responsibility for, 217–22
timing issues, 180–85
Ashley Madison data breach, 144–45,
169–70
Asilomar AI Principles, 200
Asilomar Conference on recombinant
DNA, 200
Asimov, Isaac, 173–74, 192
ATLAS (Advanced Targeting and
Lethality Automated System), 45
atomic power, 195–97. *See also*
International Atomic Energy
Agency (IAEA)
Atoms for Peace speech (Eisenhower),
196, 212, 222
audit trails, 238, 239
audits, 149, 156–57
Australia, 165
automated, autonomous compared, 31
Automated and Electric Vehicles Act
(Britain, 2018), 98
automation bias, 68, 188, 236
autonomous vehicles
overview, 32, 33–36
accidents caused by, 31, 32, 62
autonomous weapons compared, 44
civil liability issues, 36–38
criminal law issues, 38–41
ethical issues, 41–44
insurance and, 97, 98
levels of, 34–35
vehicle condition and, 90
autonomous weapons. *See also*
International Artificial
Intelligence Agency (IAIA)
overview, 33, 44–46
autonomous vehicles compared, 44
command responsibility and, 104–8
defined, 44
human-out-of-the-loop as sanitizing
military operations, 48–51
international humanitarian law and,
46–48
meaningful human control
requirement, 50–51
mercenaries and, 51–53
autonomy of AI

overview, 7, 31–33
automated compared, 31
autonomous vehicles, 32, 33–42
autonomous weapons, 33, 44–53
decision-making algorithms, 33,
53–60
problems with, 60–62
terminology issues, 61
aviation, strict liability and, 92

B2C2/Quoine case, 55–57
Babbage, Charles, 67
Baker & Hostetler, 228
ballistic missile defence systems, 45
Bemba, Jean-Pierre, 107–8
Bentham, Jeremy, 81
bias
algorithmic audits and, 156
algorithmic decision-making based
on, 70–74
automation bias, 68, 188, 236
opacity of AI and, 68–69, 70–75
reasons for, 68
remedies for, 81
in training data, 70–71, 156
transparency of AI and, 163–64
unlearning of, 74–75
The Black Box Society (Pasquale), 64
Board of Governors (IAEA), 217
boards of directors, members of, 122
bots, software agents as, 88
Box, George, 146
Britain
Automated and Electric Vehicles
Act, 98
copyright protection for AI-created
works, 134
patent protection for AI-created
works, 135, 137
privatization, 111
product liability, 95
burdens of proof, 66

Calo, Ryan, 96
Cambridge Analytica scandal, 20, 199
Canada, 164–65, 209
Capek, Karel, 243, 245
captchas, 169

causes versus reasons, 167
chatbots, 193
China
  autonomous vehicles, 39
  copyright protection for AI-created
    works, 133–34
  data protection and AI
    regulation, 180
  facial recognition technology,
    191
  Internet Court, 240–41
  judicial function and, 79, 224–26,
    240–41
  New Generation AI Development
    Plan, 180, 224
  New Generation of Artificial
    Intelligence Governance
    Principles, 165
  privatization, 111
  transparency of AI, 165
circuit breakers or speed bumps,
    22–23, 24
civil law. See also risk management
  autonomous vehicles, 36–38
  negligence, 36, 37, 88–91, 231
  opacity of AI and, 79
  regulation and, 187
  unilateral mistake, 55–57
close-in weapon systems (CIWS), 45
collective action, 9. See also
    globalization issues; International
    Artificial Intelligence Agency
    (IAIA)
Collingridge, David, 180–81, 182
Collingridge dilemma, 180–82
collusion, 26, 27–28
command responsibility, 103–8
COMPAS recidivism assessment
  African Americans versus whites, 71
  challenge to as unsuccessful, 80
  gender used by, 74
  as regression model, 72
  use of, 63–64, 82
competition law (antitrust), 17, 25–28
complacency, 68
concession theory of juridical
    personality, 118
conditional automation, 34

contractarian theory of juridical
    personality, 118
contracts, personality and, 121
contributory negligence, 37
Convention for the Protection of
    Individuals with regard to
    Automatic Processing of Personal
    Data, 162
copyright protection, 131–35
corporations
  legal personhood, 118–19, 120, 126
  responsibility of, 199
correlation versus causation, 72
Council of Europe, 162
counterfactuals, 153
creativity, rewarding of, 131–35
criminal law. See also COMPAS
    recidivism assessment
  autonomous vehicles, 38–41, 62
  decision-making algorithms, 57
  legal personality and, 123–25
  opacity of AI and, 79
criminal punishment, reasons for,
    123–25
customary international law, 206
cybersecurity issues, autonomous
    vehicles and, 37

dangerous species, 91–92
Data Protection Directive (EU, 1995),
    58, 77, 154
Data Protection Impact Assessment
    (DPIA), 160–61
data selection, 70–71, 156
data sharing, 26
datasheets, 157
debt, personality and, 121
debugging, regulation by, 238–40, 241
decision-making algorithms. See also
    COMPAS recidivism assessment;
    impermissible decisions from
    automated decision-making;
    transparency of AI
  overview, 33, 53–55
  automated processing and
    legitimacy, 57–60
  contracts and knowledge and, 55–57
  human control of, 191–92

judicial function and, 66
levels of, 53–54
protections against, 58–59
decomposability, 151
deep fakes, 19
design, regulation by, 237–38, 241
design defects. *See* product liability
deterrence, 124
Dewey, John, 116, 119
Digital Republic Law [*République
    numérique*] (France, 2016), 162
Directive on Automated Decision-
    Making (Canada, 2020), 164–65
disparate impact, 70
disparate treatment, 70
dissemination of prohibited
    material, 19
doctrine of unilateral mistake, 55–57
DoNotPay chatbot, 228
DPIA (Data Protection Impact
    Assessment), 160–61
driver assistance technologies, 34
driverless vehicles. *See* autonomous
    vehicles
drivers, automated driving system
    defined as, 40
drivers versus passengers, 34–36
drones (unmanned aerial vehicles), 45
duty of care violations, 36, 37, 88
Dworkin, Ronald, 232
dynamic pricing, 26–28

Ecuador, personality for environment
    in, 119
Eisenhower, Dwight, 196, 212,
    222, 223
Eliza program, 114
emergency response, 216
ends justifying means, 66
environmental impact assessments, 154
Equivant, 63. *See also* COMPAS
    recidivism assessment
ethics, 41–44, 165, 174
European Data Protection Board
    (Article 29 Working Party), 159
European Union (EU). *See also* General
    Data Protection Regulation
    (GDPR) (EU, 2016)

copyright protection for AI-created
    works, 134
data protection and AI
    regulation, 179
Data Protection Directive, 58, 77, 154
Markets in Financial Instruments
    Directive II, 23
patent protection for AI-created
    works, 135, 137
privatization, 111
Product Liability Directive, 95
executive, role of, 218–19
explainability. *See also* transparency
    of AI
    overview, 9
    cost of user complaints based on,
        150–51
    defined, 146
    problems with, 147
    timing of, 149
    transparency compared, 152

Facebook, 20, 28, 163, 199
facial recognition technology, 74, 191
fake news, 19–21
Falaise pig trial, 85–86
fear, role of, 183
fear index, 15
Fermi, Enrico, 195
fiction theory of juridical
    personality, 118
financial markets
    2010 Flash Crash, 15–17, 22–23, 29–30
    circuit breakers or speed bumps,
        22–23, 24
    high-frequency trading, 16, 17,
        21–25
    Markets in Financial Instruments
        Directive II and, 23
    timing of trades and, 24
    volatility index, 15
fines and penalties, 124
fire alarm oversight, 148
First Additional Protocol to the Geneva
    Convention, 46, 49
First International Conference on the
    Peaceful Uses of Atomic Energy
    (First Geneva Conference), 222

Flash Crash of 2010, 15–17, 22–23,
    29–30
France
    Digital Republic Law, 162
    Google fined by, 161–62
    International Panel on AI, 209
    judicial function and, 79, 235
Friedman, Milton, 199
friendly fire, 47
'frolics', 89
full automation, 34
Future of Life Institute, 200–1

garbage in, garbage out, 67
Gates, Bill, 198
general AI, 1–2, 181, 183–84
General Data Protection Regulation
    (GDPR) (EU, 2016)
    overview, 58–59
    Article 15, 159
    Article 22, 159
    Article 25, 160
    impact assessments, 154
    opacity of AI and, 69, 77–78
    Recital 71, 159
    transparency of AI and, 145, 154,
        158–62
gene-splicing, 200
Geneva Conventions, 46, 49, 111
Germany, 39
global interpretability, 147–48
Global Partnership on AI (GPAI), 209
globalization issues, 17, 18–21, 203–17.
    See also International Artificial
    Intelligence Agency (IAIA);
    international law
Go, AI and, 1, 65
Google, 48, 161–62, 202
government functions
    automated processing and
        legitimacy, 57–60, 236, 241
    opacity undermining legitimacy of,
        76–79
    regulation of AI and, 178, 190–92
    responsibility and outsourcing of,
        109–12
    transfer to mercenaries of, 52–53
GPAI (Global Partnership on AI), 209

Hart, HLA, 232
Herzberg, Elaine, death, 31, 32, 62
high automation, 34
high-frequency traders (HFTs), 16, 17,
    21–25
Hildebrandt, Mireille, 234
Holmes, Oliver Wendell, Jr,
    219–20, 234
human control. See also government
    functions
    accountability and, 104, 188
    of AI in general, 214
    automation bias and, 68, 188, 236
    of autonomous weapons, 50–51
    of decision-making algorithms,
        191–92
    as guiding principle, 175, 184,
        214–15
    precautionary principle and, 193
    regulation by design and, 238
    types of, 53
human-in-the-loop, 53
human-out-of-the-loop, 48–51, 53, 193
human-over-the-loop, 53
humans, centrality of, 245
humans, seen as less than human,
    126–27

IAEA. See International Atomic Energy
    Agency (IAEA)
IAIA (International Artificial
    Intelligence Agency), 209–17
ICANN (Internet Corporation for
    Assigned Names and Numbers),
    201, 209
ICRC (International Committee of the
    Red Cross), 49, 52
IEEE (Institute of Electrical and
    Electronics Engineers), 152,
    201, 214
ILC (International Law
    Commission), 207
illusory transparency, 166
immunity, 96
impact assessments, 149, 154–56,
    160–61, 163–64
Impact Team hack of Ashley Madison,
    144–45, 169–70

impermissible decisions from
   automated decision-making,
   69–74, 81–82
inaction as choice, 184–85
incapacitation as punishment, 124
information asymmetry, 23
inherently hazardous activities, 102–3
innovation, precaution and, 10–12, 29,
   120, 181
instance-based interpretability, 147–48
Institute of Electrical and Electronics
   Engineers (IEEE), 152, 201, 214
institutions for regulation, 195–203,
   222–23. *See also* International
   Artificial Intelligence Agency
   (IAIA); international law
insurance, 97–101, 112
intellectual property, 18, 131–38
intelligence, surpassing of human,
   138–41
International Artificial Intelligence
   Agency (IAIA), 209–17
International Atomic Energy Agency
   (IAEA)
   creation of, 196, 222
   as role model for IAIA, 210–12
   size of, 217
   structure of, 217
International Committee of the Red
   Cross (ICRC), 49, 52
international humanitarian law, 46–48,
   104, 111, 204
international law
   attribution of responsibility, 207–8
   consequences for non-compliance,
      208–9
   International Artificial Intelligence
   Agency creation, 209–17
   norms for, 205–7
   public good from, 204–5
   structural challenges for, 204–9
International Law Commission
   (ILC), 207
International Ombudsman
   Institute, 220
International Organization for
   Standardization (ISO), 201
International Panel on AI, 209

International Telecommunication
   Union (ITU), 204, 210
International Telegraph Union, 204
Internet, governance of, 201, 209
Internet Corporation for Assigned
   Names and Numbers (ICANN),
   201, 209
Internet Court, 224–26, 240–41
inventions, 135–38
ISO (International Organization for
   Standardization), 201
ITU (International
   Telecommunication Union),
   204, 210

Jackson, Robert H, 242
Judicial Accountability System, 225
judicial function. *See also* law
   algorithmic decision-making, 66
   burdens of proof, 66
   human control of, 58
   legal analytics replacing, 224–26,
      235–36, 240
   opacity of AI and, 79–80, 81
   trials of animals, 85–86
judicial measurement, 240
judiciary, role of, 219–20
juridical personhood. *See* legal
   personality
juries, 79
justice versus law, 233

Kafka, Franz, 168
Katz, Andrew, 129
Korea, 174
Kurki, Visa, 138

language, ambiguity of, 230–31
language, as open textured, 233
law. *See also* judicial function
   application of law to facts as difficult,
      232–34
   automation of, 226, 227–34
   as code, 236–40
   as data, 226, 234–36
   illogic of, 230–32
   online dispute resolution,
      224–26, 229

law reform, overview, 9, 10–11
legal advice, what constitutes, 228
legal personality
    overview, 116–17
    anthropomorphism and, 125–26
    facets of, 119–25
    superintelligence and, 139–40
    theories of, 117–19
legal profession, resistance to change
    by, 229–30
legislatures, role of, 218
legitimacy. See government functions
local interpretability, 147–48
long-range anti-ship missiles
    (LRASMs), 44
Loomis, Eric, 63–64, 74, 80, 82

machine learning
    about the law, 234
    defined, 1
    opacity and, 65, 73
    transparency and, 157
Machines Like Me (McEwan), 142–43
market justifications for regulation, 178
market share liability, 94–95
Markets in Financial Instruments
    Directive II (MiFID II) (EU,
    2014), 23
Martens Clause, 46–47
masterly inactivity, 184–85, 218
McCarthy, John, 11–12
McEwan, Ian, 142–43
meaningful information, 159
mercenaries, 51–53
MiFID II (Markets in Financial
    Instruments Directive II) (EU,
    2014), 23
Ministry of Science and Technology
    (China), 165
mistake (contract law), 55–57
model cards, 157
model-centric interpretability, 147–48
monkeys, ownership of photos taken
    by, 132
Montreux Document, 52
Moore's law, 16
Moral Machine, 42–43
morality, 41–44, 165, 174

narrow AI, general compared, 1–2
national registry, 215
natural language processing, 230
natural personality, 126–27, 128–31
natural versus juridical persons, 117
negligence, 36, 37, 88–91, 231
New Generation AI Development Plan
    (China), 180, 224
New Generation of Artificial
    Intelligence Governance
    Principles (China), 165
New Zealand, 99, 165, 191
Newitz, Annalee, 144
Ni Defeng, 240
no-fault insurance, 98
non-delegable duties. See also
    government functions
    overview, 101
    command responsibility and, 103–8
    common law and, 101–3
    omissions and failures to act, 109
    vicarious liability and, 102
Nuclear Non-Proliferation Treaty
    (NPT), 210
nuclear power regulation, 195–97. See
    also International Atomic Energy
    Agency (IAEA)

ombudspersons, 157–58, 220–22
online dispute resolution, 224–26, 229
opacity of AI. See also transparency
    of AI
    overview, 7, 63–67
    bias and, 68–69, 70–75
    Catch-22 of, 78
    defined, 65, 146
    forms of, 65
    General Data Protection Regulation
        and, 69, 77–78
    impermissible decisions from,
        69–75
    inferior decisions from, 67–69, 81
    judicial function and, 79–80, 81
    legitimacy undermined by, 75–80
    problems with, 81–82
    regulation of and remedies for,
        81–82
    secrecy compared, 76

transparency to address, 67
open source movement, 69

Pagallo, Ugo, 129
partial automation, 34
Pasquale, Frank, 64
passengers versus drivers, 34–36
passengers versus pedestrians, 42–43
patent law, 135–38
peculium, 129
pedestrians, passengers versus, 42–43
penalties and fines, 124
periodic audits, 149, 156–57
personality for AI
    overview, 8, 114–16
    agency and, 88–89
    entitlement to, 126–38
    legal personality, 116–26, 139–40
    limits of, 141–43
    reasons for, 115–16
    superintelligence and, 138–41
personally identifying data, 74
piercing the corporate veil, 120
PMSCs (private military and security
    companies), 51–53
police patrol oversight, 148
practical obscurity, 6
precautionary principle, 182–84, 193
preventive detention, 73
price-fixing, 27
pricing, dynamic, 26–28
privacy, 6, 76
privacy impact assessments, 154
private law, personality and,
    120–23
private military and security companies
    (PMSCs), 51–53
privatization, 110–11
product liability, 36–38, 93–97
Product Liability Directive (EU,
    1985), 95
Project Maven, 48
property management, personality
    and, 122
property ownership, personality
    and, 121
proportionality in weapons use, 104
ProPublica report, 71

public authority. *See* government
    functions
punishment, reasons for, 123–25

Quoine/B2C2 case, 55–57

Random Darknet Shopper, 57
Raz, Joseph, 232
realist theory of juridical
    personality, 119
reasons versus causes, 167
red line regulation, 188, 203–17
registry of companies for AI, 215
regression models, 72–73
regulation. *See* artificial intelligence
    regulation; institutions for
    regulation; International Artificial
    Intelligence Agency (IAIA);
    regulation by AI
regulation by AI
    overview, 10, 224–27
    automation of the law, 227–34
    by debugging, 238–40, 241
    by design, 237–38, 241
    law as code, 236–40
    law as data, 234–36
    prospects for, 240–42
regulatory capture, 203
regulatory sandboxes, 187
rehabilitation, 125
République numérique [Digital
    Republic Law] (France, 2016), 162
responsibility. *See also* personality
    for AI
    overview, 8, 85–87
    inherently governmental functions,
        109–12
    limits of, 112–13
    non-delegable duties and, 101–9
    risk management and, 87–101
responsive regulation, 186
retribution, 123
reverse Turing Test, 169
Richards, Neil, 127
right to explanation, 158–62. *See also*
    General Data Protection
    Regulation (GDPR) (EU, 2016);
    transparency of AI

Rio Declaration, 182
risk assessment, 71–74
risk management
    overview, 87
    insurance for, 97–101, 112
    negligence and, 88–91
    product liability, 36–38, 93–97
    regulation and, 187–88
    shifting away from people, 120
    strict liability, 91–93
    superintelligence and, 139–40
road traffic laws, goals of, 41
Roberts, John, 232
Robo-debt program, 54
robot, origin of term, 243
Robot Ethics Charter (proposed), 174
Ross system, 228
R.U.R. (Capek), 243, 245
Russell, Christopher, 144
Rylands v Fletcher, 91

SAE (Society of Automotive Engineers)
    report, 34, 201
Samuelson, Pamela, 133
sandboxes, 187
Sarao, Navinder Singh, 30
screening decisions, 70
secrecy, 76
Security Council (UN), 216, 223
self-driving cars. See autonomous
    vehicles
self-governance, 199, 200–3, 209. See
    also nuclear power regulation;
    regulation by AI
self-investigation, 239. See also
    regulation by AI
Shils, Edward, 76
Singapore, 10, 39, 158, 225
Slater, David, 132
slavery, 127, 129, 137
Smart, William, 127
smart regulation theory, 185
social media, fake news and, 20–21
Society of Automotive Engineers (SAE)
    report, 34, 201
software, as product or service, 95
software agents, 88
Space Liability Convention, 206

speed bumps or circuit breakers,
    22–23, 24
speed of AI
    overview, 6, 15–18
    competition law and, 25–28
    fake news and, 19–21
    globalization of information and, 17,
        18–21
    high-frequency trading, 16, 17,
        21–25
    Moore's law and, 16
    problems with, 28–30
spoofing, 30
standard of care, 90–91
standing, legal, 119, 149
state role. See government functions
stationary anti-personnel weapons, 45
stereotyping, 73
stock market. See financial markets
strict liability, 91–93
subject-centric interpretability, 147–48
sued, ability to be, 120
Summa Theologica (Aquinas), 113
Sunstein, Cass, 183
superintelligence, 138–41, 190
symbolist theory of juridical
    personality, 118

taxation, 121
Taxes Management Act (England,
    1970), 57
tort law. See negligence; non-delegable
    duties; product liability; strict
    liability
trading algorithms, high-frequency
    traders, 16, 17
training data, bias in, 70–71, 156
transboundary harms. See globalization
    issues
transparency fallacy, 166
transparency of AI
    overview, 9, 144–46
    benefits of, 67
    defined, 146
    explainability compared, 152
    high-frequency trading and, 24–25
    knowing who you are interacting
        with, importance of, 144–45

laws addressing, 158–65
limits of, 166–70
methods of, 151–54
opacity types and, 67
regulation by design and, 238
in theory, 146–51
timing of, 148–49
tools for, 154–58
types of, 147–48, 151
undesirability of, 167
treaties, 205
The Trial (Kafka), 168
trolley problem, 42
trust, 166, 169
Turing, Alan, 114, 142
Turing Test
defined, 114
imitation of humans and, 141
incentivizing innovation and, 133
legal personality and, 114, 116
reverse Turing Test, 169
Twitter, 20

UN Security Council, 216, 223
unilateral mistake, 55–57
United Nations, 210, 216
United States
autonomous vehicles, 38
copyright protection for AI-created
works, 132–33
data protection and AI
regulation, 209

patent protection for AI-created
works, 135–36, 137
privatization, 110
product liability, 95
transparency of AI, 163–64
Universal Declaration of Human
Rights, 129
unmanned aerial vehicles (drones), 45
unrepresentative data, 70–71
US Business Roundtable, 199
user-in-charge concept, 35

value of people, 42–43, 49
Vasquez, Rafaela, 32, 62
veil piercing, 120
vicarious liability, 89, 102
virtual sandboxes, 187
volatility index (VIX), 15

wait and see approach, 184–85
Walsh, Toby, 193
Walzer, Michael, 48–49
watchful restraint, 184–85
weapons. *See* autonomous weapons
weapons review, 49
WhatsApp, 20
works for hire, 133
World Intellectual Property
Organization (WIPO), 134
Wu, Tim, 186

zeroth law, 192

For EU product safety concerns, contact us at Calle de José Abascal, 56–1°, 28003 Madrid, Spain or eugpsr@cambridge.org.

www.ingramcontent.com/pod-product-compliance
Ingram Content Group UK Ltd.
Pitfield, Milton Keynes, MK11 3LW, UK
UKHW020358140625
459647UK00020B/2536